THE SHAPE OF
A SWISS-US
FREE TRADE
AGREEMENT

THE SHAPE OF A SWISS-US FREE TRADE AGREEMENT

Gary Clyde Hufbauer and Richard E. Baldwin

INSTITUTE FOR INTERNATIONAL ECONOMICS
Washington, DC
February 2006

Gary Clyde Hufbauer, Reginald Jones
Senior Fellow since 1992, was the Marcus
Wallenberg Professor of International
Finance Diplomacy at Georgetown University (1985–92), senior fellow at the Institute
(1981–85), deputy director of the International Law Institute at Georgetown University (1979–81), deputy assistant secretary for
international trade and investment policy of
the US Treasury (1977–79), and director of
the International Tax Staff at the US Treasury (1974–76). He has written extensively
on international trade, investment, and tax
issues, with a particular focus on economic
sanctions and NAFTA. He is coauthor or
coeditor of *NAFTA Revisited: Achievements
and Challenges* (2005), *Reforming the US Corporate Tax* (2005), and *World Capital Markets:
Challenge to the G-10* (2001), among others.

Richard E. Baldwin is a professor of international economics at the Graduate Institute of International Studies in Geneva and
comanaging editor of *Economic Policy*. He is
a research associate at the National Bureau
of Economic Research and the Centre for
Economic Policy Research (CEPR). He was
a senior staff economist in the Council of
Economic Advisers (1990–91); a professor at
Columbia University's Business School; and
a consultant to the European Union, Organization for Economic Cooperation and
Development, World Bank, US Agency for
International Development, UN Conference
on Trade and Development, and European
Free Trade Association. His publications
include *Towards an Integrated Europe* (CEPR,
London, 1994) and *Economics of European
Integration* (McGraw Hill, London, 2003).

Assisted by Agustin Cornejo, Victoria
Courmes, Dean DeRosa, John Gilbert, Claire
Owen, Maya Shivakumar, and Yee Wong.

**INSTITUTE FOR INTERNATIONAL
ECONOMICS**
1750 Massachusetts Avenue, NW
Washington, DC 20036-1903
(202) 328-9000 FAX: (202) 659-3225
www.iie.com

C. Fred Bergsten, *Director*
Valerie Norville, *Director of Publications
    and Web Development*
Edward Tureen, *Director of Marketing*

Typesetting by Circle Graphics
Printing by Automated Graphic Systems, Inc.

**Library of Congress Cataloging-in-
Publication Data**

Hufbauer, Gary Clyde.
    The shape of a free trade agreement
between Switzerland and the United
States / Gary Clyde Hufbauer and Richard
Baldwin ; assisted by Agustin Cornejo . . .
[et al.].
        p. cm.
    ISBN 0-88132-385-3 (paper)
        978-0-88132-385-6
    1. Switzerland—Foreign economic rela-
tions—United States. 2. United States—
Foreign economic relations—Switzerland.
I. Baldwin, Richard E. II. Institute for
International Economics (U.S.) III. Title.

HF1574.5.U6H843 2005
382'.9730494—dc22   2005027712

Contents

Tables

Boxes

Preface

Over the past two decades, trading nations have increasingly used bilateral and regional agreements both to liberalize commerce with their immediate partners and to spur systemic reform. The process has come to be called "competitive liberalization." Even as the Doha Development Round proceeds in the World Trade Organization (WTO), many WTO members are negotiating new trade and investment agreements on a bilateral or regional basis.

The first US bilateral free trade agreement (FTA) was concluded with Israel (1986) and the second with Canada (1989), but the North American Free Trade Agreement (NAFTA) was the watershed pact. Others followed as the United States contemporaneously pursued multilateral liberalization in the Uruguay Round (1986–94) and now the Doha Round (2001–07). In addition to NAFTA, the United States has 10 FTAs in force or awaiting ratification and is conducting negotiations or exploratory talks with 19 other countries or country groups (e.g., Southern African Customs Union).[1] Most prospective partners are developing countries, but three of them belong to the Organization for Economic Cooperation and Development

---

1. Current US FTA partners (in chronological order) include Israel, Canada, Mexico, Jordan, Chile, Singapore, Australia, Morocco, Central America and the Dominican Republic, and Bahrain. Awaiting ratification are pacts with Oman and Peru. Under negotiation are agreements with Colombia, Panama, South Africa and its customs union partners (the Southern African Customs Union), South Korea, Thailand, and the United Arab Emirates. Possible US FTA partners in the intermediate term include the Caribbean Community (Caricom), Ecuador, Egypt, Indonesia, Malaysia, New Zealand, Pakistan, Philippines, Qatar, Sri Lanka, Switzerland, and Taiwan. In addition, the Free Trade Area of the Americas, linking all countries in the Western Hemisphere, remains an aspiration.

(OECD): New Zealand, South Korea, and Switzerland. The Institute has published studies on the US agreements or possibilities with Canada, NAFTA, South Korea, Taiwan, and Egypt, and it is now analyzing the Sri Lanka, Pakistan, Indonesia, and overall Middle East cases.

After several months of exploratory talks, the United States and Switzerland decided in January 2006 not to launch negotiations for an FTA at this time. Agricultural issues proved too difficult. However, the countries established a Swiss-US Trade and Investment Cooperation Forum to strengthen their already close bilateral economic relationship. The forum is designed to build on the momentum created by the intensive exploration of a possible FTA, which began in July 2005. The forum will pursue initiatives in specific areas where the United States and Switzerland share mutual interests, with a view to concluding agreements. The details of the initial work program will be decided in the spring of 2006. Senior officials will review progress periodically, beginning in mid-2006.

Both countries remain interested in a possible comprehensive FTA and may resume discussions at a later stage, possibly after the Doha Development Round is concluded (hopefully in 2007). The preliminary findings of this study—authored by a team led by Gary Hufbauer and Richard Baldwin—were posted on the Institute's Web site and previewed at an Institute luncheon meeting in September 2005. The results were used extensively by US and Swiss officials as they conducted their exploratory talks during the fall and winter of 2005. The published volume should be helpful as a guide and reference for the working groups that will now be established under the auspices of the Swiss-US Trade and Investment Cooperation Forum. If the partners resume negotiations for a comprehensive FTA, this book should provide useful background for officials, companies, and the public interested in the issue.

The study notes that Switzerland has much longer experience with regional and bilateral FTAs than the United States has, beginning with Switzerland's role in 1960 as a founding member of the European Free Trade Association (EFTA). Switzerland signed its first trade agreement with the European Union in 1972, and many additional Swiss-EU agreements have been concluded in the intervening decades. Together with its EFTA partners, Switzerland has negotiated multiple FTAs with partners in Europe, the Middle East, Asia, and the Americas.[2]

Unlike current US trade initiatives in the Middle East, a US agreement with Switzerland would not be inspired by political or military strategy. Instead, the case for a Swiss-US FTA rests almost entirely on economic benefits. These take two forms: deeper economic trade and investment ties between the partners and the potential for a Swiss-US FTA to serve as a "gold standard" for other FTAs. The purpose of this book is to examine the economic case and to

---

2. EFTA has agreements with Bulgaria, Chile, Croatia, Israel, Jordan, Lebanon, Macedonia, Mexico, Morocco, the Palestinian Authority, Romania, Singapore, Tunisia, and Turkey. An agreement with Japan is under negotiation.

offer specific recommendations for drafting an FTA that would most benefit Switzerland, the United States, and (by example) the world community.

While agriculture has proved to be the most difficult negotiating subject, it is a sector where both countries would benefit from lower barriers. Switzerland ranks among the largest importers of agricultural products, and the United States among the biggest exporters, but their bilateral agricultural trade remains quite small. The authors offer suggestions for gradually opening sensitive markets in both countries. In chapters 2 and 3, they recommend the liberalization not only of border barriers but also of a range of sanitary and phytosanitary (SPS) standards; they also recommend the recognition of geographical indications (GIs) in bilateral talks.

Manufactured goods account for over 90 percent of bilateral merchandise trade, and for the most part this commerce faces low or zero tariffs. Yet, as discussed in chapter 4, a surprising number of high rates obstruct trade in specific tariff lines—not only textiles and clothing (as might be expected) but also watches, instruments, and specialty chemicals. According to econometric estimates, Swiss-US bilateral trade would significantly increase with the elimination of these remaining tariffs.

As countries with world-class services firms, both the United States and Switzerland have reduced most of their own barriers to services trade. However, in chapter 5, the authors point out that an FTA offers the possibility for reaching new frontiers, by eliminating licensing restrictions and monopoly practices and by facilitating "fly-in fly-out" professional exchanges.

On a global basis, government procurement remains largely insulated from international competition. Switzerland and the United States could open many of their procurement markets, as discussed in chapter 5, starting with those already opened to existing FTA partners and then going beyond, not only for federal but also for state and cantonal procurement.

The authors report (in chapter 7) rough calculations that the stock of foreign direct investment in Switzerland—from all sources, not just the United States—might leap as much as 40 percent under the long-term influence of an FTA. This estimate could be excessive but even half that increase would bring new foreign companies and fresh dynamism to the Swiss economy. The authors also report (in chapter 8) on econometric models that suggest a comprehensive FTA could increase bilateral trade by 20 to 100 percent and generate GDP gains as high as 0.5 percent annually for Switzerland.

While the European Union would look carefully at a Swiss-US FTA, the authors conclude (in chapter 9) that Brussels is likely to regard such a venture in the same benign light as the United States views the Mexico-EU FTA. In both cases, the effect of out-of-area FTAs is to dilute existing preferences, bringing conditions closer to the ideal "level playing field."

The Institute for International Economics is a private, nonprofit institution for the study and discussion of international economic policy. Its purpose is to analyze important issues in that area and to develop and communicate practical new approaches for dealing with them. The Institute is completely nonpartisan.

The Institute is funded by a highly diversified group of philanthropic foundations, private corporations, and interested individuals. Major institutional grants are now being received from the William M. Keck, Jr. Foundation and the Starr Foundation. About 33 percent of the Institute's resources in our latest fiscal year was provided by contributors outside the United States, including about 16 percent from Japan. The government of Switzerland, through the State Secretariat for Economic Affairs (SECO), provided partial support for this study. Financing was also provided by the Ford Foundation as part of its support for the Institute's extensive program of research on free trade agreements.

The Institute's Board of Directors bears overall responsibilities for the Institute and gives general guidance and approval to its research program, including the identification of topics that are likely to become important over the medium run (one to three years) and that should be addressed by the Institute. The director, working closely with the staff and outside Advisory Committee, is responsible for the development of particular projects and makes the final decision to publish an individual study.

The Institute hopes that its studies and other activities will contribute to building a stronger foundation for international economic policy around the world. We invite readers of these publications to let us know how they think we can best accomplish this objective.

C. FRED BERGSTEN
Director
February 2006

Acknowledgments

We thank Michael Finger and Robert Scollay for helpful comments on preliminary drafts. We especially thank Valerie Norville, Marla Banov, Madona Devasahayam, and Helen Hillebrand for preparing this long and technical manuscript for publication.

1

Introduction

At first sight, a free trade agreement (FTA) between Switzerland and the United States seems implausible. Despite centuries of friendship, the countries are not political or military allies, for the simple reason that Switzerland above all prizes its neutrality with the great powers. Switzerland and the United States do not share a common border or even the same continent. Nor do they share the same language: While English is widely spoken in Switzerland, it is not among its four official languages. Both countries are rich and mature, subscribe to market capitalism, and are relatively open to the world economy (as measured by the average height of tariff barriers), but these similarities can be read as reasons not to enter an FTA. After all, what is the purpose of an FTA between two rich countries that embrace similar economic constitutions and are already quite open to each other's exports? Could another FTA just add to the "spaghetti bowl" of confusion that threatens to undermine the world trading system?[1] Finally, in the closing months of the World Trade Organization (WTO) Doha Development Round,[2] does it make sense to divert diplomatic and legislative energy from the overarching goal of global trade liberalization?

---

1. The virtues and vices of bilateral FTAs have been widely debated. For a critical view, see WTO (2005a); for a sympathetic exposition, see Schott (2004b).

2. The Doha Development Round must conclude no later than early 2007, if Congress is to ratify its terms before the US trade promotion authority expires on June 30, 2007.

Answers to Skeptical Questions: The FTA Case

Some observers, in both Switzerland and the United States, will find in these queries their definitive answer: A bilateral FTA makes no sense. Others will be less critical, but question the timing: Why not wait until after the Doha Round is concluded, and until the EU-25 gets a better sense of its direction? Still others will argue that each skeptical question can be turned into an argument for a bilateral FTA. This study will be of most interest to those in the second and third camps—in other words, observers who do not foreclose the possibility or desirability of a Swiss-US FTA. Before launching into the chapters issue by issue, however, it is worth seeing how the broad skeptical questions can be turned.

Is the Geographic and Political Distance Too Great?

To start, given the certainty of economic hurdles, can support for an FTA gain traction if the partners are not political or military allies, are separated by thousands of miles, and do not even speak the same language? Prior to the mid-1990s, FTAs and customs unions were, to be sure, dominated by pacts between countries that were already, or in the process of becoming, political allies: the European Common Market and European Union, the Association of Southeast Asian Nations, the Australia–New Zealand Closer Economic Relations pact, the North American Free Trade Agreement (NAFTA), and the Southern Cone Common Market (Mercosur). The European Free Trade Association (EFTA), of which Switzerland was a founding member, was a purely economic venture without the overlay of a political alliance from its inception. But in a way, EFTA seemed the exception that proved the rule, as several members peeled off to join the European Union. In short, experience up to the mid-1990s led many commentators to forecast a three-bloc world, composed of contiguous customs unions and FTAs organized around the European Union, the United States, and the Asian powers—China, Japan, or both. The FTAs came to be seen as building blocks for the sort of economic and political integration that characterizes modern geographically contiguous nations. Hence, these blocs might fortify internal political alliances, exacerbating political tensions and erecting walls that divide the global economy.

Simply put, this dark vision proved wrong, even as FTAs flourished. By one count, some 176 new trade agreements have been ratified since the birth of the WTO in January 1995, and the total number threatens to exceed 300 (WTO 2005a). Yet many of the post-1995 FTAs are "out of area," drawing no inspiration from existing or anticipated political alliances. The United States has FTAs with Chile and Singapore; the European Union has FTAs with Mexico and Chile. Japan has an FTA with Singapore, and Switzerland, under EFTA auspices, has FTAs with Chile, Singapore, and

South Korea.[3] Even China's menu of prospective FTA partners seems devoid of political alliances (Hufbauer and Wong 2005). The partners are often separated by thousands of miles and may not speak a common language, as US FTAs with Jordan, Morocco, and Bahrain illustrate. Rather than forming tightly knit geographic units centered on a major power, FTAs are creating crisscross networks spanning the globe, with no clear separation between "hubs" and "spokes." Compared with recent experience, rather than dark visions of the past, a Swiss-US FTA is perfectly compatible with the general FTA movement.

Are There Real Benefits to an FTA?

What about the argument that, since both Switzerland and the United States are rich, subscribe to market capitalism, and practice open economic policies, there is no real point in an FTA? At bottom, this argument echoes the textbooks of an earlier day, which argued that additional trade and consequent economic gains are greatest when two highly dissimilar countries open commerce with one another. According to the classic textbook exposition, large national differences portend sharp comparative advantages and disadvantages, and hence, large static gains from free trade. In a world of fixed technological attributes, no economies of scale or scope, exchange limited to final goods and services, complete factor immobility, perfect competition, and only static gains from trade, the classic thesis is still a good thesis. But that hypothetical world economy never accurately described the real one.

Recent econometric research demonstrates how misleadingly small the projected volumes of new trade and sizes of economic gains are when models are confined to the classic assumptions.[4] When the realities of modern economic systems are given room to play—learning from new competition and new markets, significant economies of scale and scope, international investment, erosion of monopolistic margins, and huge trade in intermediate goods and services with an economic role similar to that of the basic factors of production—the models and experience reveal that similar countries can gain enormously from free trade and investment, even when they already practice open-economy policies.

In the context of Swiss-US relations, it is simply wrong to assert that little or nothing remains to be gained from bilateral free trade and investment. As described in the chapters that follow, even though both countries are relatively open, they both still have significant barriers. Many of these are behind-the-border, nontariff barriers (NTBs). Agriculture, selected

---

3. The EFTA–South Korea FTA should be signed by the end of 2005.

4. For a short survey of the econometric methods for sizing up the gains from freer trade and investment, see Bradford, Grieco, and Hufbauer (2005).

manufactures, some services, and government procurement are far from the ideal of free trade and investment. Moreover, even when overall barriers are small or insignificant, recent econometric research using a gravity model[5] reveals that an "announcement" or "lock-in" effect appears to augment commerce between FTA partners.[6]

To preview our own econometric research presented in chapters 7 and 8, elimination of all bilateral barriers between Switzerland and the United States might actually double two-way merchandise trade. US foreign direct investment (FDI) in Switzerland, which is already substantial, might increase by as much as 40 percent. Deeper trade and investment links would erode the power of oligopolies in both economies, spur the exchange of technology and skilled personnel, and enhance economic efficiency.

Is the Timing Wrong?

Perhaps the strongest argument against a Swiss-US FTA is the matter of timing. Why distract attention from the final push to complete the Doha Development Round? For both countries, the political and economic payoff from a successful WTO negotiation far exceeds whatever achievements can be realized on a bilateral basis. The Central American–Dominican Republic Free Trade Agreement (CAFTA-DR) won approval from the US House of Representatives on June 28, 2005 by a tight 217 to 215 vote, but the congressional battle was prolonged and bruising, and in the aftermath, there is a certain amount of "trade fatigue" among business and legislative proponents of greater liberalization. A case can be made that these stalwarts need time to rest up before they take on the big battle: congressional ratification of the WTO Doha Development Round package.[7] Similarly,

---

5. Chapter 8, authored by Dean DeRosa and John Gilbert, summarizes the gravity model technique. While the technique has been well known since Linnemann (1966), it has been applied to assess the effect of FTAs only since the work of Frankel (1997) and Rose (2000). Most gravity model estimates of the FTA trade-creation effect substantially exceed the forecasts of basic computable general equilibrium (CGE) models (DeRosa and Gilbert 2005). Various explanations can be adduced for the difference, but announcement and lock-in effects are commonly cited.

6. The announcement effect presumably reflects the wake-up call that an FTA conveys to potential investors, exporters, and importers. This could be important for US firms deciding on a headquarters location for their European operations. The lock-in effect reflects the greater certainty that firms can place in a country's trade and investment policies, once barriers are capped in an FTA. In NAFTA, the lock-in effect was an important driver of new investment in Mexico. However, in a Swiss-US FTA, the lock-in effect would probably be modest, since neither country is prone to abrupt protectionist or antiforeign policies that affect the other (US antidumping duties play little or no role in bilateral trade; see chapter 4).

7. To be sure, US ratification of CAFTA-DR has already freed up US negotiating expertise to focus more attention on the sluggish WTO negotiations. However, the scarcest resource in US trade negotiations is not bureaucratic talent, but congressional time and energy.

within Switzerland, a free trade agreement with the United States will inspire a wide-ranging debate over Swiss relations with the European Union and Switzerland's historic protection of agriculture. A Swiss-US FTA may in the end be voted up or down in a popular, and hotly contested, referendum. Clearly, one can argue that this debate should be put off until the WTO Doha Round has been ratified.

The timing arguments would be persuasive if the Swiss-US FTA and the WTO Doha Round were alternatives. But the two agreements are complements, not substitutes. Over the next year, the central focus of the Swiss-US FTA should be negotiation, not ratification, either by the US Congress or the Swiss confederation. The ratification process should either be merged with approval of the Doha package (possibly the best timing in the United States) or initiated after the Doha package is approved (possibly the best timing in Switzerland).

Moreover, as a negotiated text, the Swiss-US FTA can liberalize trade in goods and services to a far greater extent than the Doha Round can. At best, within the WTO, modest progress seems possible on agricultural market-access barriers, although cuts in farm subsidies may be agreed to (Josling and Hathaway 2004). Service negotiations have made so little headway that a crisis has been declared.[8] WTO members are dickering over tariff-cutting formulas to improve nonagricultural market access (the NAMA group), but the foreseeable outcome is far from zero tariffs on manufactured goods. By contrast, in all of these areas and others—such as government procurement, geographical indications (GIs), and sanitary and phytosanitary (SPS) barriers—the Swiss-US FTA should go far beyond what can be achieved in the WTO. In fact, the starting point for liberalization between the two countries should be well ahead of the ending point for the Doha Round. Seen in this light, the Swiss-US FTA can join the array of "gold standard" agreements that serve as templates for the next WTO round, post-Doha.

Will the Agreement Comport with GATT Article 24?

Both the United States and Switzerland have entered into numerous FTAs. Apart from NAFTA, the United States has FTAs with Israel, Jordan, Chile, Singapore, Australia, Morocco, Central America, the Dominican Republic, and Bahrain. Several more are in various stages of discussion and negotiation (see chapter appendix table 1A.1). In the past, apart from its special agreements with the European Union, Switzerland has negotiated all of its

---

8. The Global Services Coalition, a group of Australian, Chilean, European, NASSCOM, Japan, and US providers, met with WTO officials in Geneva on June 24, 2005, and circulated an alert entitled "WTO Services Negotiations in Crisis; Political Will Must be Mobilized Urgently." Available at the Web site of the European Services Forum at www.esf.be.

FTAs in conjunction with EFTA, which has agreements with Bulgaria, Chile, Croatia, Israel, Jordan, Lebanon, Macedonia, Mexico, Morocco, the Palestinian Authority, Romania, Singapore, Tunisia, and Turkey—and others are pending.[9] From a Swiss standpoint, the exceptional feature of a Swiss-US FTA, apart from the size of its prospective American partner, is that the pact would be the first FTA negotiated separate from EFTA, leaving aside Swiss agreements with the European Union.

None of the US or EFTA free trade pacts have been found in violation of the General Agreement on Tariffs and Trade (GATT) Article 24, perhaps for the simple reason that Article 24 reviews invariably either say nothing or convey only bland misgivings (Schott 2004b). Indeed, only one review group (for the Czech-Slovak pact) reached an affirmative consensus (Sutherland et al. 2004).[10] Nevertheless, it is fair to say that US FTAs generally come close to the Article 24 ideal, eliminating barriers on substantially all of the merchandise trade of the partners. Their major shortcoming is their near exclusion of agriculture, as in the Canada-US FTA signed in 1989, or very long phaseouts for sensitive agricultural products—a conspicuous fault of the US-Australia FTA, at US insistence. The free trade pacts negotiated by EFTA fall somewhat shorter of the Article 24 ideal, in that they achieve only a very limited degree of liberalization in agriculture. Set against their agricultural shortcomings, the FTAs agreed to both by the United States and EFTA liberalize services and investment, areas that the GATT barely touches.

If Switzerland and the United States reach an FTA, it should come as close to the Article 24 ideal as any prior agreements of either party. Long phaseouts and special safeguards will be necessary on both sides for sensitive agricultural products. Otherwise, the coverage should be comprehensive, with rapid elimination of barriers.

Switzerland's Place in the Queue

As mentioned, the United States is engaged in free trade talks with many potential partners, mostly developing countries, though three of the potential partners—Switzerland, New Zealand, and South Korea—belong to the Organization for Economic Cooperation and Development (OECD). Given the relatively long list of potential FTA partners, the US Trade Rep-

---

9. As a stepping stone toward the negotiation of additional FTAs, EFTA also has Joint Declarations of Cooperations (JDCs) with Albania, Algeria, the Gulf Cooperation Council, Mercosur, Serbia and Montenegro, and Ukraine (EFTA 2005).

10. An agreement can be fully consistent with Article 24, yet one or both parties may owe compensation to other WTO members for trade diversion. Usually, such claims are settled in larger trade negotiations, such as the Tokyo Round or the Uruguay Round.

resentative, Ambassador Rob Portman, will inevitably establish priorities depending on a variety of considerations, among them political alliances, prospective economic payoff, speed and ease of negotiation, and quality of results. Most of these considerations cannot be quantified, but available data does shed light on the strength of trade and investment ties between the United States and its prospective partners, the height of protective barriers, and the degree of social similarity, measured by corruption, economic freedom, and labor and environmental standards.

Before turning to quantitative comparisons, we must emphasize an important aspect of post–September 11 FTA diplomacy. The Bush administration places a very high priority on economic diplomacy that buttresses US national interests in Muslim countries generally and the Middle and Near East specifically. The administration believes that market-oriented economies that are growing and run on democratic principles are far less likely to breed terrorists and far more likely to contribute to world peace and prosperity. That vision stands at the apex of policy, and accordingly, the administration favors new FTAs with countries in the Middle and Near East. Morocco was first on the list, and Bahrain is second. Egypt, Pakistan, and Indonesia are all prospects. Among this cluster of countries, the United States values FTAs for their potential to promote broad economic reform. Obviously, from the perspective of national security, Switzerland ranks near the bottom of the FTA queue, both because Switzerland already ranks among the safest and most stable countries in the world, and because its diplomacy is founded on the principle of neutrality with the great powers.

That said, we turn to an array of quantitative and qualitative indicators that enable comparisons of Switzerland with present and prospective US FTA partners (see chapter appendix tables 1A.1 through 1A.7). Quantitative indicators consist of inward and outward FDI stocks, two-way US merchandise trade, two-way US services trade, and the average most favored nation (MFN) tariff rates for agricultural and nonagricultural products. Qualitative indicators include a corruption index, two economic freedom indexes, and indexes for labor and environmental standards. As mentioned above, current FTA partners include Israel (1986), Canada (1989), Mexico (1993), Jordan (2001), Chile (2003), Singapore (2004), Australia (2004), and Morocco (2004). Prospective US FTA partners are divided into three different groups:

- partners for whom an FTA has been negotiated but not yet ratified: Bahrain, Oman and CAFTA (the CAFTA-DR pact still awaits ratification in Costa Rica);

- partners in the process of negotiation: Colombia, Ecuador, Panama, Peru, Thailand, the Southern African Customs Union (SACU) countries, and the United Arab Emirates;

- partners under consideration: Bangladesh, Bolivia, the Caribbean Community (Caricom), Egypt, Indonesia, Malaysia, New Zealand, Pakistan, Philippines, Qatar, South Korea, Switzerland, and Taiwan.

Quantitative Indicators

Chapter appendix table 1A.1 shows that Switzerland's two-way FDI stocks with the United States exceed those of many other countries seeking FTAs with the United States. The logic for this indicator is that, when two countries have an important base of two-way FDI stocks, the prospect of an FTA will enlist considerable enthusiasm in the business community. Moreover, once an FTA is concluded, firms will take a more favorable view to expanding their stakes in the partner country, creating a follow-on push for trade.

As one would expect, the two NAFTA partners, Canada and Mexico, rank high in two-way FDI stocks. However, with a two-way FDI stock of $199 billion, Switzerland ranks second, behind only Canada ($298 billion) and well ahead of Mexico ($68 billion). Chapter appendix table 1A.1 also shows that outward FDI from the United States to its NAFTA partners accounts for most of the total two-way FDI stocks. By comparison, Switzerland is a net exporter of FDI to the United States. In fact, along with Bahrain, Switzerland is the only country in the list to invest more in the United States than vice versa. The high ranking of Switzerland suggests both business support for an FTA and the prospect of substantial additional investment in both directions if an FTA is concluded.

Chapter appendix table 1A.2 presents US two-way merchandise trade with its current and potential FTA partners. The logic for this indicator follows the logic of two-way FDI stocks. When two countries have an important base of merchandise trade, not only do firms have a tangible reason to support an FTA, but the prospects are also excellent for a substantial dollar increase in bilateral trade. With two-way merchandise trade of $21 billion, Switzerland ranks 11th among current and prospective US partners. This figure is obviously far behind the NAFTA partners—Mexico and Canada total $356 billion of two-way trade with the United States—but it is only moderately behind CAFTA, Israel, Australia, and most East Asian countries (Singapore, Malaysia, Taiwan, Thailand, and South Korea). Moreover, Switzerland's two-way trade with the United States easily exceeds the two-way trade of three current partners, Chile, Jordan, and Morocco, and twenty potential partners situated in South America, the Middle East, and South Africa. Based on its merchandise trade with the United States, Switzerland occupies a solid upper-middle position relative to other current and prospective partners.

Chapter appendix table 1A.3 presents US two-way trade in services with its current and potential FTA partners. The logic of this indicator parallels the previous two. While data on services trade often does not exist for many countries, and is missing for several current and prospective FTA partners, certain conclusions can be drawn from the available figures. Based on these data, Switzerland ranks third in two-way trade in services, just behind Canada and Mexico, and ahead of other current and prospective FTA partners. The high ranking of Switzerland reflects substantial flows of interest, dividends, and royalties, as well as business services in both directions: The two-way trade in services, around $16 billion annually, is almost as large as it is in manufactured goods, around $17 billion annually.

Chapter appendix table 1A.4 presents recent MFN tariff rates for current and prospective FTA partners. The MFN figures are applied-rate averages for agricultural and nonagricultural products respectively. The main rationale for this indicator is that it suggests how difficult commercial negotiations will be. An FTA, by definition, aims at eliminating tariffs and quotas, and this will be easier if the partner country already has low applied MFN tariff rates.

On this indicator, Switzerland's position is sharply split. With an MFN rate of 2.3 percent, Switzerland has one of the lowest average rates for nonagricultural products; it ranks second, just behind Singapore. However, Switzerland has one of the highest applied average MFN rates for agricultural products, ranking 29 out of 31 current and prospective partners. Switzerland's wall of agricultural protection implies difficult FTA negotiations in that area. Looking on the bright side, however, high agricultural tariffs and restrictive quotas mean that the potential benefit of an FTA to both countries is substantial (as discussed in chapter 2). By the same token, freer trade between the United States and Switzerland could divert Swiss agricultural purchases from the European Union, which already enjoys significant preferences in the Swiss market. The possibility of "preference erosion" is discussed more fully in chapters 8 and 9.

The United States has concluded FTAs with countries that had both high and low applied MFN tariffs. Canada, Singapore, Australia, and Chile had relatively low applied MFN tariff rates, on both agricultural and nonagricultural products.[11] By contrast, Mexico, Jordan, Morocco, and Israel have much higher MFN rates. From this spectrum, one might conclude that the United States is indifferent to the level of MFN barriers when it selects FTA partners. But that conclusion ignores the fact that US FTAs with Middle Eastern countries were primarily motivated by geopolitical alliances. A Swiss-US FTA needs to be inspired by economic as much as geopolitical forces.

---

11. While the figures in chapter appendix table 1A.4 refer to the situation in 2004, at the time that the FTAs were negotiated, all of these partners had comparatively low average MFN tariffs.

Qualitative Indicators

Chapter appendix table 1A.5 compares the degree of corruption among current and prospective FTA partners. The logic of this indicator is two-fold. First, less corruption probably means less political influence from vested interests that preserve the economic rents generated by trade and investment barriers. Second, less corruption means a more desirable environment for expanding trade and investment relations.

Switzerland ranks third-best on the corruption index scale, just behind New Zealand and Singapore. Apart from Morocco, Mexico, and Jordan, current US FTA partners have low levels of corruption. By contrast, several of the prospective partners have somewhat higher levels. Other things being equal, the United States prefers FTA partners that score well in terms of honest government.

Chapter appendix table 1A.5 also presents two different indexes of economic freedom, as measured by the Heritage Foundation and the World Economic Forum. These indexes cover trade policy, fiscal burdens, government intervention in the economy, monetary policies, capital flows and FDI, wages and prices, banking and finance, property rights, and overt and informal market regulation. They suggest that Switzerland and Singapore offer the most attractive business environments compared to other current and prospective partners. Switzerland's honest governance and moderate regulatory environment give the country a very favorable position in the US FTA queue.

Chapter appendix table 1A.6 presents the environmental sustainability index (ESI) for all current and prospective partners. This index reflects water and air pollution, the extent of protected areas, and environmental regulations and enforcement. Switzerland ranks second—behind Canada and ahead of Australia—and seems to hold an advantageous position compared with other prospective partners. Its environmental standards exceed those of the United States.[12] Hence, it is unlikely that a trade agreement between the United States and Switzerland would run into environmental objections in Congress. Switzerland clearly will not face the onerous criticism that Central American countries faced over CAFTA.

Chapter appendix table 1A.7 compares labor standards for current and prospective partners. A labor standard index is constructed based on five different indicators: the right of association—that is, the right to form unions—bargain, and strike; extent of forced labor; extent of child labor; working conditions; and the number of international labor treaties that have been ratified. The labor index for each country reflects whether labor standards are high, medium-high, medium, medium-low, or low for each

---

12. With an ESI score of 52.9, the United States would rank 10th in the ESI ranking of chapter appendix table 1A.6.

of these five categories.[13] The labor index shows that Switzerland's labor standards surpass those of all current and potential US FTA partners. They are high for each of the five indicators, and are aligned with US labor standards. Clearly, they would not be a negative dimension of a US-Swiss FTA and might instead be a positive feature.

Plan of the Book

Two-way trade in agricultural goods and foodstuffs represents only 2 percent of merchandise trade between Switzerland and the United States. Yet two chapters of the report are devoted to agriculture and the related subjects of SPS and GI issues. The reason is that attention in the report is roughly scaled to the magnitude of barriers rather than the volume of trade. Agriculture and foodstuffs are extremely highly protected in Switzerland, and highly protected in the United States. Chapter 2 depicts the barriers and outlines recommendations for their gradual phaseout in a bilateral FTA. Chapter 3 addresses SPS and GI issues, centered on agriculture and foodstuffs, and again offers recommendations for avoiding unintended SPS barriers and improving the protection of intellectual property inherent in GI rights. The recommendations in chapters 2 and 3 are strongly influenced by US and Swiss approaches in prior FTAs and other bilateral agreements.

Chapter 4 turns to commerce in manufactured goods. Manufactures dominate bilateral merchandise trade, amounting to about $17 billion annually. Fortunately, most of this commerce is free of tariffs and NTBs.[14] The Swiss MFN rate on manufactured imports is only 2.3 percent, while the US MFN rate is only 4.2 percent. Nestled within these low averages, however, are fairly high rates on specific tariff lines. These products attract most of our attention, and the chapter concludes with recommendations for eliminating low tariffs immediately and phasing-out high tariffs over a short period.

Chapter 5 takes up services. Two-way trade in private services, amounting to about $16 billion annually, puts this sector close to manufactured goods in magnitude. Tariffs and quotas usually do not obstruct two-way trade in services; instead, the most important barriers are behind the border, such as licensing requirements and public and private monopolies. Chapter 5 concentrates on four service sectors: financial services; network industries, such as electricity and telecommunications; audiovisual

---

13. For a review of the detailed methodology for constructing labor indicators, see appendix A.

14. The most important NTBs involve different technical standards and different systems to ensure that products conform to the announced standards. Chapter 4 offers recommendations for more closely aligning US and Swiss systems.

services; and professional services. After reviewing US and Swiss barriers, and solutions devised in prior FTAs, chapter 5 offers recommendations for the Swiss-US FTA.

Chapter 6 reviews government procurement, an area that has proven highly resistant to liberalization in the WTO, and that evokes political sensitivities in individual states and cantons. The United States and Switzerland have opened up their markets on a reciprocal basis for selected entities. That concluded a 1996 bilateral agreement that was later incorporated in the WTO General Provision Agreement (GPA). Both countries have extended concessions to other GPA partners, and to partners in their respective FTAs. Chapter 6 recommends that Switzerland and the United States extend each other the best government procurement terms offered to any other country, either through the GPA or in bilateral FTAs (an unconditional MFN approach).

Direct and portfolio investment links between Switzerland and the United States are substantial, as shown in chapter 7. Among current and prospective FTA partners, Swiss-US links are second only to US investment links with Canada. Bilateral investment frictions are scarce, but still, an FTA could eliminate minor barriers and provide a framework for resolving future disputes. The recommendations offered in chapter 7 are intended to expand already robust bilateral investment ties. Rough calculations suggest that additional investment could boost two-way trade in manufactured goods, perhaps by a quarter. It would also foster the movement of skilled personnel, synergies in science and technology, and the creation of intellectual property embodied in patents, copyrights, and trademarks.

Chapter 8 summarizes estimates based on computable general equilibrium (CGE) and gravity models. The models attempt to forecast the effect of a bilateral FTA on the volume of trade created between Switzerland and the United States, the volume of trade diverted from third countries, and economic gains for the two partners. They suggest that additional two-way trade in agricultural and manufactured goods would certainly be substantial, perhaps doubling the level that would otherwise be reached.[15] Economic gains would be significant, especially for Switzerland.

Chapter 9 explores the consequences of a Swiss-US FTA for Switzerland's relations with the European Union. Geographically, Switzerland sits in the center of the European Union; economically, the preponderance of Switzerland's commerce is with Europe. In fact, Switzerland has more than 100 commercial treaties with the European Union (Hewitt Associates 2002). Accordingly, it must anticipate the effects of a Swiss-US FTA on its rela-

---

15. Analysis done by Adams et al. (2003) at the Australian Productivity Commission (APC), using a variant of the gravity model, comes to strikingly different conclusions. The authors claim to find very little trade creation between FTA partners, and net trade diversion for 12 of 16 recent FTAs. For reasons explained in chapter 8, we do not subscribe to their analysis.

tions with the European Union. The Swiss-EU Bilateral Agricultural Agreement contains an "evolutionary clause" that commits the two parties to regularly review their agricultural trade.[16] While this is far from an unconditional MFN clause, Switzerland's geographic, political, and economic circumstances ensure that the European Union will carefully examine commercial concessions granted to the United States. However, chapter 9 concludes that a Swiss-US FTA would, at most, inflict a degree of "preference dilution" on the European Union, and might come to be regarded by Brussels as a benign "reverse hub-and-spoke arrangement." Ideally, the European Union will show the same tolerance for a Swiss-US FTA as the United States has shown for the Mexican-EU FTA.

In sum, as we see it, an FTA between Switzerland and the United States could create substantial economic gains for both partners, at only moderate political and economic risk. Moreover, because both countries are highly developed and stable, with robust labor and environmental standards, a Swiss-US FTA could set a new standard in harmonizing domestic policies and liberalizing trade for other countries to follow. Before this can be accomplished, however, both countries must lower their considerable barriers to trade in agriculture, as the next chapter shows.

---

16. The bilateral agreement is formally known as The Agreement between the European Community and the Swiss Confederation on Trade in Agricultural Products, signed in 1999. Article 13 is the evolutionary clause.

Appendix 1A

Table 1A.1 Foreign direct investment stocks, 2003[a]
(millions of dollars)

Partners	Rank[c]	From United States	To United States	Two-way FDI
NAFTA				
Canada	1	192,400	105,255	297,655
Mexico	3	61,526	6,680	68,206
Other current partners				
Australia	4	40,985	24,652	65,637
Chile	12	9,986	63	10,049
Israel	13	6,208	3,834	10,042
Jordan	32	47	−17	30
Morocco	30	309	−23	286
Singapore	5	57,589	−162	57,427
To be ratified				
Bahrain	26	196	288	484
CAFTA	18	3,435	−29	3,406
Dominican Republic	25	860	18	878
Oman	29	358	−1	357
Under negotiation				
Colombia	20	2,751	−150	2,601
Ecuador	22	1,446	34	1,480
Panama	9	6,497	8,383	14,880
Peru[b]	21	2,659	−137	2,522
SACU-5	26	795	75	870
Thailand	15	7,393	182	7,575
United Arab Emirates	23	1430	39	1,469
Under consideration				
Europe				
Switzerland	2	86,435	112,856	199,291
Middle East				
Egypt	7	18,960	−38	18,922
Qatar	19	3,113	33	3,146
East Asia and Pacific				
Indonesia	11	10,387	27	10,414
Malaysia	14	7,580	208	7,788
New Zealand	17	3,849	607	4,456
Philippines	16	4,700	33	4,733
South Korea	8	13,318	2,337	15,655
Taiwan	10	10,961	2,708	13,669

(table continues next page)

Table 1A.1 Foreign direct investment stocks, 2003[a] (*continued*)
(millions of dollars)

Partners	Rank[c]	From United States	To United States	Two-way FDI
Latin America				
Bolivia	28	375	–5	370
Caricom	6	16,972	9,968	26,940
South Asia				
Bangladesh	31	169	4	173
Pakistan	24	1,074	31	1,105

CAFTA = Central American Free Trade Agreement
Caricom = Caribbean Common Market
SACU = Southern African Customs Union

a. FDI stock computed as direct investment position on a historical-cost basis.
b. Data for 2001.
c. Based on two-way FDI.

Source: US BEA (2004a).

Table 1A.2 US merchandise trade, 2003 (millions of dollars)

Partners	Rank[a]	Two-way trade	US exports	US imports
NAFTA				
Canada	1	445,028	189,101	255,927
Mexico	2	266,618	110,775	155,843
Other current partners				
Australia	10	21,814	14,270	7,544
Chile	18	8,358	3,625	4,733
Israel	9	23,725	9,198	14,527
Jordan	27	1,645	552	1,093
Morocco	28	1,038	523	515
Singapore	6	34,905	19,600	15,305
To be ratified				
Bahrain	31	706	301	405
CAFTA	7	33,430	15,730	17,700
Dominican Republic	17	8,871	4,343	4,528
Oman	30	748	330	418
Under negotiation				
Colombia	15	11,794	4,504	7,290
Ecuador	19	5,951	1,666	4,285
Panama	26	2,136	1,820	316
Peru	20	5,795	2,095	3,700
SACU-5	16	10,237	3,317	6,920
Thailand	8	23,940	6,363	17,577
United Arab Emirates	21	5,205	4,064	1,142
Under consideration				
Europe				
Switzerland	11	20,911	9,268	11,643
Middle East				
Egypt	24	4,435	3,105	1,330
Qatar	29	842	455	387
East Asia and Pacific				
Indonesia	13	13,480	2,669	10,811
Malaysia	5	39,082	10,897	28,185
New Zealand	22	5,043	2,076	2,967
Philippines	12	16,216	7,072	9,144
South Korea	3	72,496	26,333	46,163
Taiwan	4	56,348	21,731	34,617
Latin America				
Bolivia	32	454	194	261
Caricom	14	13,407	5,744	7,663
South Asia				
Bangladesh	25	2,592	289	2,302
Pakistan	23	4,685	1,811	2,874

a. Ranking based on two-way trade.

Source: US Department of Commerce, TradeStats Express, retrieved from http://tse.export.gov/.

Table 1A.3 Trade in US services, 2004 (millions of dollars)

Partners	Rank[b]	Two-way trade	US exports	US imports
NAFTA				
Canada	1	45,869	26,723	19,146
Mexico	2	28,280	16,599	11,681
Other current partners				
Australia	6	8,991	5,833	3,158
Chile	13	1,682	1,032	650
Israel	7	4,136	2,303	1,833
Jordan	n.a.	n.a.	n.a.	n.a.
Morocco	n.a.	n.a.	n.a.	n.a.
Singapore	5	11,819	6,912	4,907
To be ratified				
Bahrain	n.a.	n.a.	n.a.	n.a.
CAFTA	n.a.	n.a.	n.a.	n.a.
Dominican Republic	n.a.	n.a.	n.a.	n.a.
Oman	n.a.	n.a.	n.a.	n.a.
Under negotiation				
Colombia	n.a.	n.a.	n.a.	n.a.
Ecuador	n.a.	n.a.	n.a.	n.a.
Panama	n.a.	n.a.	n.a.	n.a.
Peru	n.a.	n.a.	n.a.	n.a.
SACU-5[a]	9	2,165	1,188	977
Thailand	11	1,800	1,061	739
United Arab Emirates	n.a.	n.a.	n.a.	n.a.
Under consideration				
Europe				
Switzerland	3	16,362	8,014	8,348
Middle East				
Egypt	n.a.	n.a.	n.a.	n.a.
Qatar	n.a.	n.a.	n.a.	n.a.
East Asia and Pacific				
Indonesia	14	1,366	1,088	278
Malaysia	12	1,702	1,208	494
New Zealand	10	2,087	973	1,115
Philippines	8	2,751	1,357	1,394
South Korea	4	12,780	8,402	4,377
Taiwan	n.a.	n.a.	n.a.	n.a.
Latin America				
Bolivia	n.a.	n.a.	n.a.	n.a.
Caricom	n.a.	n.a.	n.a.	n.a.
South Asia				
Bangladesh	n.a.	n.a.	n.a.	n.a.
Pakistan	n.a.	n.a.	n.a.	n.a.

n.a. = not available

a. Using data for South Africa.
b. Based on two-way trade; rank positions exclude countries for which information is not available.

Source: US BEA (2005b).

Table 1A.4 Average MFN tariff rates, 2003–04
(simple average ad valorem rates)

Partners	Agricultural			Nonagricultural		
	Bound	Applied	Rank[f]	Bound	Applied	Rank
NAFTA						
Canada	3.5	3.1	5	5.3	4.2	6
Mexico	35.1	24.5	27	34.9	17.1	28
Other current partners						
Australia	3.2	1.1	2	11.0	4.6	8
Chile	26.0	6.0	7	25.0	5.9	13
Israel	73.0	15.9	19	9.2	4.0	4
Jordan	23.7	19.8	23	19.8	12.1	24
Morocco	54.5	48.6	30	39.2	27.5	31
Singapore	9.5	0.0	1	6.3	0.0	1
To be ratified						
Bahrain	37.5	9.0	10	35.1	7.6	17
CAFTA[a]	42.3	10.5	14	38.2	5.7	11
Dominican Republic	39.6	13.0	16	34.2	7.8	18
Oman[d]	28.0	10.2	13	11.6	5.0	9
Under negotiation						
Colombia	91.9	14.9	15	35.4	11.9	23
Ecuador	25.5	14.7	17	21.1	11.5	22
Panama	27.7	14.8	18	22.9	7.4	16
Peru	30.8	17.2	21	30.0	13.1	25
SACU-5[b]	39.2	9.1	11	15.8	5.3	10
Thailand	35.5	29.0	28	24.2	14.2	26
United Arab Emirates	25.4	n.a.	n.a.	13.1	n.a.	n.a.
Under consideration						
Europe						
Switzerland[c]	n.a.	36.2	29	n.a.	2.3	2
Middle East						
Egypt	95.3	22.8	26	28.3	19.4	30
Qatar	25.7	4.9	6	14.5	4.1	5
East Asia and Pacific						
Indonesia	47.0	8.2	9	35.6	6.7	14
Malaysia	12.2	2.1	4	14.9	8.1	19
New Zealand	5.7	1.7	3	11.0	3.5	3
Philippines	34.7	8.0	8	61.8	4.3	7
South Korea	52.9	52.1	31	10.2	7.0	15
Taiwan	15.3	16.3	20	4.8	5.5	12
Latin America						
Bolivia	40.0	10.0	12	40.0	9.3	20
Caricom[e]	98.0	18.4	22	51.2	11.1	21

(table continues next page)

Table 1A.4 Average MFN tariff rates, 2003–04

(simple average ad valorem rates) (*continued*)

Partners	Agricultural			Nonagricultural		
	Bound	**Applied**	**Rank[f]**	**Bound**	**Applied**	**Rank**
South Asia						
Bangladesh	188.5	21.7	25	35.7	19.2	29
Pakistan	97.1	20.4	24	35.3	16.6	27
US comparison	6.9	5.1	7	3.2	3.7	4

n.a. = not available

a. Simple average of observations for Costa Rica, El Salvador, Guatemala, Honduras, and Nicaragua.

b. Using South Africa average bound tariff. Tariff binding figures are based on simple averages of national averages reported by the WTO and exclude Lesotho.

c. Using ad valorem equivalent (AVE). Switzerland has a 99.8 percent binding coverage, but bindings are in the form of specific tariffs.

d. Data for 2001.

e. Simple averages of observations reported by the WTO for each Caricom member.

f. Ranks based on applied rates, ranks run from low to high rates.

Sources: WTO 2004 *World Report* and *Trade Profiles*.

Table 1A.5 Corruption and economic freedom, 2005
(index values)

Partners	Corruption[a]	Corruption rank	Freedom[b]	Freedom[c]	Average rank
NAFTA					
Canada	8.4	5	4.1	5.1	6
Mexico	3.5	20	3.1	3.9	17
Other current partners					
Australia	8.8	4	4.2	5.2	5
Chile	7.3	7	4.2	4.9	7
Israel	6.3	8	3.6	4.8	11
Jordan	5.7	14	3.2	4.3	14
Morocco	3.2	24	2.8	3.5	23
Singapore	9.4	2	4.4	5.5	1
To be ratified					
Bahrain	5.8	13	3.9	4.5	9
CAFTA	n.a.	n.a.	n.a.	n.a.	n.a.
Dominican Republic	3.0	25	2.5	3.1	26
Oman	6.3	8	3.2	n.a.	n.a.
Under negotiation					
Colombia	4.0	18	2.8	3.8	20
Ecuador	2.5	26	2.5	3.0	28
Panama	3.5	20	3.3	3.6	18
Peru	3.5	20	3.2	3.7	19
SACU-5[d]	4.5	17	3.2	4.3	15
Thailand	3.8	19	3.0	4.5	16
United Arab Emirates	6.2	10	3.3	5.0	12
Under consideration					
Europe					
Switzerland	9.1	3	4.1	5.5	3
East Asia and Pacific					
Indonesia	2.2	29	2.5	3.5	25
Malaysia	5.1	15	3.0	4.9	13
New Zealand	9.6	1	4.3	5.1	4
Philippines	2.5	26	2.7	3.5	24
South Korea	5.0	16	3.4	5.1	10
Taiwan	5.9	11	3.7	5.6	8
Middle East					
Egypt	3.4	23	2.6	4.0	22
Qatar	5.9	11	2.9	n.a.	n.a.
Latin America					
Bolivia	2.5	26	3.3	3.1	21
Caricom	n.a.	n.a.	n.a.	n.a.	n.a.

(table continues next page)

Table 1A.5 Corruption and economic freedom, 2005
(index values) (*continued*)

Partners	Corruption[a]	Corruption rank	Freedom[b]	Freedom[c]	Average rank
South Asia					
Bangladesh	1.7	31	2.0	2.9	29
Pakistan	2.1	30	2.3	3.3	27
US comparison	7.6	6	4.1	5.8	2

n.a. = not available

a. Countries with high score are the most transparent (i.e., high score is better)
b. High score = economically more free. Heritage Index scores have been rescaled so that 5 = "economically free" and 1 = "economically unfree".
c. High score = economically more free (World Economic Forum).
d. Using data for South Africa.

Sources: Transparency International Corruption Perceptions Index 2005; The Heritage Foundation 2005 Index for Economic Freedom; World Economic Forum, 2005 Growth Competitiveness Index.

Table 1A.6 Environmental standards

Partners	ESI rank	ESI index[a]	CO_2 emissions damage[b]	Protected areas[c]	Compliance with environmental[d] agreements	Number of treaties[e]
NAFTA						
Canada	1	64.4	High	Low	High	High
Mexico	19	46.2	High	Low	Medium	Med/high
Other current partners						
Australia	3	61.0	Medium	Medium	Medium	High
Chile	10	53.6	Medium	Medium	Med/high	High
Israel	12	50.9	High	Medium	Medium	Medium
Jordan	18	47.8	Low	Medium	Med/high	Medium
Morocco	20	44.8	Medium	Low	Med/low	High
Singapore	13	50.0	Medium	Low	High	Low
To be ratified						
Bahrain	n.a.	n.a.	Low	Low	n.a.	Low
CAFTA	15	49.0	High	Medium	Low	Medium
Dominican Republic	25	43.7	Medium	High	Med/low	Medium
Oman	17	47.9	Medium	Medium	Med/low	Med/low
Under negotiation						
Colombia	7	58.9	High	High	Medium	Med/high
Ecuador	12	52.4	Low	High	Low	Med/high
Panama	8	57.7	Medium	High	Med/low	Med/high
Peru	5	60.4	High	Medium	Low	Med/high
SACU-5	11	52.9	Medium	Medium	Medium	Med/low
Thailand	14	49.7	Low	Medium	Medium	Medium
United Arab Emirates	21	44.6	Low	Low	n.a.	Med/low

Under consideration

	ESI rank[a]	ESI score[a]	[b]	[c]	[d]	[e]
Europe						
Switzerland	2	63.7	High	High	High	High
Middle East						
Egypt	24	44.0	Low	Medium	Medium	High
Qatar	n.a.	n.a.	Low	Low	n.a.	Low
East Asia and Pacific						
Indonesia	16	48.8	Medium	Low	Med/low	Medium
Malaysia	9	54.0	Low	High	Med/high	Medium
New Zealand	4	60.9	High	Medium	High	Med/high
Philippines	22	44.3	Medium	Low	Low	Med/high
South Korea	26	43.0	Medium	Low	Med/high	Med/high
Taiwan	29	32.7	Medium	Low	Med/high	Low
Latin America						
Bolivia	6	59.5	Low	Medium	Low	Medium
Caricom	27	41.0	Medium	Low	Medium	Medium
South Asia						
Bangladesh	23	44.1	High	Low	Low	Med/low
Pakistan	28	39.9	Low	Low	Low	Medium
US comparison	11	52.9	High	High	Medium	High

a. Environmental sustainability index (ESI); countries with high scores have high environmental standards.

b. High = CO_2 damage < 0.5 percent, Medium = CO_2 damage > 0.5 percent and < 1 percent, Low = CO_2 damage > 1 percent.

c. Ratio of protected area to total area: High = ratio > 0.2, Medium = ratio > 0.1 and < 0.2, Low = ratio < 0.1.

d. High = compliance score > 5.8, Medium/high = compliance < 5.8 and > 4.6, Medium = compliance < 4.6 and > 4.0, Medium/low = compliance > 3.6 and < 4.0, Low = compliance < 3.6.

e. High = more than 120 treaties, Medium/high = between 80 and 120, Medium = 60 to 80, Medium/low = between 50 and 60, Low = less than 50.

Sources: Environment Sustainability Index (ESI), 2004 Global Competitiveness Report for Compliance with Environmental Agreements, Word Bank Development Indicators for Carbon Dioxide Emissions Damage, UN Environmental Statistics for Protected Areas, Globalis Human Impact 2002, Environmental Treaties and Resource Indicators (ENTRI) for Treaties Participation.

Table 1A.7 Labor standards, 2004

Partners	Rank[a]	Index[b]	Right of association	Forced labor	Child labor	Working conditions	Conventions ratified[c]
NAFTA							
Canada	4	1.60	High	Med/high	High	High	Medium
Mexico	8	2.40	High	Medium	Medium	Medium	High
Current partners							
Australia	2	1.20	High	High	High	Med/high	High
Chile	4	1.60	Med/high	High	Med/high	Med/high	High
Israel	6	2.00	Medium	High	High	Medium	Med/high
Jordan	13	3.00	Medium	Medium	Med/high	Med/low	Medium
Morocco	19	3.40	Med/low	Medium	Medium	Low	Med/high
Singapore	7	2.20	Medium	High	Med/high	Med/high	Medium
To be ratified							
Bahrain	19	3.40	Medium	Medium	Medium	Medium	Low
CAFTA	8	2.40	Medium	Med/high	Med/high	Medium	Med/high
Dominican Republic	24	4.00	Med/low	Medium	Low	Low	Medium
Oman	22	3.80	Medium	Medium	High	Medium	Low
Under negotiation							
Colombia	13	3.00	Med/low	Med/high	Med/low	Med/low	High
Ecuador	16	3.20	Med/low	Medium	Med/low	Med/low	High
Panama	12	2.80	Medium	Medium	Med/low	Medium	High
Peru	13	3.00	Medium	Medium	Med/low	Med/low	High
SACU-5	27	4.20	Low	Medium	Low	Low	Medium
Thailand	30	4.60	Med/low	Low	Low	Med/low	Low
United Arab Emirates	22	3.80	Medium	Medium	Med/high	Medium	Low

Under consideration

Region / Country							
Europe							
Switzerland	1	1.00	High	High	High	High	High
Middle East							
Egypt	16	3.20	Med/low	Medium	Low	Medium	High
Qatar	27	4.20	Low	Med/low	Med/high	Low	Low
East Asia and Pacific							
Indonesia	24	4.00	Medium	Med/low	Low	Medium	Low
Malaysia	19	3.40	Med/low	Med/low	Medium	Medium	Medium
New Zealand	2	1.20	Med/high	High	High	High	High
Philippines	29	4.40	Medium	Low	Low	Med/low	Medium
South Korea	11	2.60	Medium	Med/high	Med/high	Medium	Medium
Taiwan	16	3.20	Med/low	Medium	Med/high	Med/low	Medium
Latin America							
Bolivia	24	4.00	Med/low	Low	Low	Med/low	Med/high
Caricom	8	2.40	Med/high	High	Med/high	Med/high	Medium
South Asia							
Bangladesh	30	4.60	Med/low	Low	Low	Low	Medium
Pakistan	30	4.60	Med/low	Low	Low	Low	Medium
US comparison	5	1.8	High	High	High	High	Low

Note: Methodology for labor indicators

Collective Bargaining, Right of Association, and Labor Strikes

Low: Collective bargaining, strikes, and right of association are all prohibited.

Med/low: Some prohibited or government approval needed.

Medium: Not prohibited and no requirement to seek authorization prior to forming unions, but labor rights are not really enforced, or widespread antiunion discrimination exists.

Med/high: Not prohibited, and labor rights are enforced most of the time.

High: All allowed, and labor rights enforced.

(table continues next page)

Table 1A.7 Labor standards, 2004 (continued)

Forced Labor

Low: Pervasive forced labor.

Medium/low: Law prohibits forced labor, but certain foreigners and local groups are consistently subject to forced labor.

Medium: Forced labor is prohibited, but some cases are reported.

Medium/high: Rare cases of forced labor reported.

High: No cases of forced labor reported.

Child Labor

Low: Pervasive (child labor exceeds 8 percent of the age group).

Medium/low: Prohibited, but many cases reported in different sectors of the economy (child labor represents 2 to 8 percent of the age group).

Medium: Prohibited, but some cases are reported in the informal sector (child labor represents 0 to 2 percent of the age group).

Medium/high: Prohibited, but rare cases of child labor are reported.

High: No child labor reported.

Working Conditions

Low: Low or no negotiations possible with employer, low or no protection, working standards not enforced, substandard living conditions, lack of protections, abuse, and labor law violations.

Medium/low: Labor laws exist, but protection, safety and health standards, and working hours exist but not well enforced.

Medium: Working conditions acceptable, usually with acceptable safety and health standards, and premium for working longer hours.

Medium/high: Most working conditions are satisfied.

High: All working conditions are satisfied.

a. High rank (e. g., "1") = high index (e. g., "1") and good labor standards.

b. Index based on average of the five indicators: High = 1, Medium/high = 2, Medium = 3, Medium/low = 4, Low = 5.

c. International Labor Organization (ILO) conventions ratified: High = ratified conventions > 50, Medium/high = ratified conventions > 40 and < 50, Medium = ratified conventions > 20 and < 40, Low = ratified conventions < 20.

Sources: Based on WTO and US Department of State (Bureau of Democracy, Human Rights, and Labor) country reports; ILO database; World Bank (2005b).

2

Agricultural Market Access

Agricultural trade is important for both Switzerland and the United States. Switzerland relies heavily on foreign agricultural production for domestic consumption and agrarian inputs for its world-renowned exports. In 2003, the value of Swiss agricultural imports surpassed the value of domestic production, measured at consumer prices. On a per capita basis, Switzerland ranks among the highest importers of agricultural products.[1] Meanwhile, agricultural and food products make up almost 8 percent of US merchandise exports to world markets.[2]

Despite the prospects for specialization, agricultural trade between the United States and Switzerland remains well below potential. In 2004, the United States and Switzerland exchanged agricultural goods with a total value of less than $400 million—only 2 percent of total trade between the two countries. This figure is low compared with agricultural trade between either country and other partners, notably the European Union. It is also less than the volume of agricultural trade between the United States and Switzerland in the recent past (see table 2.1).

Drilling below the aggregate two-way trade data, Swiss agricultural exports to the United States expanded sharply in recent years. If current rates are sustained, Swiss agricultural exports might double between 1999 and 2006. An FTA would encourage this trend, by removing barriers and

---

1. The source of data on production is the OECD PSE/CSE database. Estimates of Swiss agricultural imports are based on WTO Statistics Database.

2. The USDA Foreign Agricultural Service is the source of estimates of US agricultural exports, while USITC Dataweb was consulted for estimates of US total exports.

Table 2.1 Agriculture in US-Swiss bilateral trade, 1999–2004
(millions of US dollars)

	1999	2000	2001	2002	2003	2004
Agricultural bilateral trade						
US exports	421	352	546	492	251	152
Swiss exports	138	149	145	167	199	229
Trade balance	283	203	400	325	52	−77
Total bilateral trade						
US exports	8,365	9,942	9,835	7,782	8,660	9,268
Swiss exports	9,596	10,174	9,574	9,382	10,668	11,643
Trade balance	−1,232	−231	261	−1,600	−2,008	−2,374
Share of agriculture in						
bilateral trade (percent)[a]	3	2	4	4	2	2

a. (US + Swiss agricultural exports) / (US + Swiss total exports).

Source: US Department of Commerce (2005) and FAS (2005).

placing Swiss farmers and food processing companies on a level playing field with agricultural producers that already enjoy preferences in the US market—for example, Australia and Canada. On the other hand, US agricultural exports to Switzerland declined steeply in recent years, dropping from $550 million in 1999 to just $150 million in 2004. Part of the reason for the decline is the disagreement over certification and labeling that involves genetically modified organisms (GMOs) and animal hormones. For reasons that go well beyond agricultural trade with Switzerland, the United States does not certify "GMO-free" soy meal or "hormone-free" beef exports.

Meanwhile, because of consumer preferences, Switzerland has increased its purchases of European agricultural products. Between 1998 and 2003, the share of EU produce in Swiss agricultural imports rose from 69 to 76 percent (table 2.2). Meanwhile, the US share dropped from 6 to 4 percent. The Swiss-EU Agreement on Trade in Agricultural Products and the Revision to Protocol 2 of the 1972 FTA between Switzerland and the European Community may amplify these trends.[3] From the US perspective, an FTA with Switzerland could level the playing field with respect to EU and other suppliers in the Swiss market.

Agriculture will be the most difficult negotiating area in bilateral talks. Both countries maintain high barriers, both at and behind the border, to protect "sensitive" products. That many Swiss and some US farm goods

---

3. The agreement was signed in June 1999 and entered into force in June 2002. Duties on many products were not eliminated immediately: Free trade in cheese will not come into effect until June 2007.

Table 2.2 Swiss agricultural imports (millions of euros)

Partner country/area	1998	2000	2002	2003
EU-15	3,311	3,800	4,270	4,337
United States	276	329	281	239
Brazil	117	145	149	155
Rest of world	1,085	1,055	1,008	994
Total	*4,789*	*5,329*	*5,708*	*5,725*
Share of Swiss agricultural imports (percent)				
EU-15	69	71	75	76
United States	6	6	5	4
Rest of world[a]	25	23	20	20

a. Includes Brazil.

Source: FAS (2005).

simply cannot be produced at today's prevailing world prices will com-
plicate agricultural negotiations.[4] Therefore, the stakes go beyond market
access, and raise the social question of externalities associated with agriculture. It is well known that Switzerland relies on border barriers more
heavily than most countries to ensure the preservation of rural areas.

This chapter is divided into five sections. The first two identify existing barriers to agricultural trade in each country. The third and fourth sections review the previous negotiating experiences of the United States and
Switzerland, focusing on agricultural market access. Finally, the fifth section recommends possible elements of an FTA regarding the agricultural
sector.

United States: Barriers to Agricultural Trade

The United States ranks among the world's largest producers, exporters,
and importers of agricultural products; correspondingly, US agricultural
policy reflects a variety of objectives and interests. While the United States
is a very open economy, certain agricultural sectors enjoy exceptional levels of protection. It is well known that tobacco, peanuts, dairy products,

---

4. Commenting on Swiss agricultural conditions, a paper issued by the Swiss Federal Office
for Agriculture states, "Produire aux prix du marché mondial ne serait donc guère possible
aujourd'hui en Suisse"—Nowadays, it would not be possible to produce at world prices in
Switzerland (Swiss Federal Office for Agriculture 2005). In the United States, producers of
rice, peanuts, sugar, wool, lamb, butter, and cheese would all have difficulty meeting world
market prices.

sugar-based products, and chocolates are shielded by high tariffs, tariff-rate quotas (TRQs), or both. Agricultural protection is also conferred through other instruments, such as antidumping (AD) measures and safeguards, as in the case of fruit juices and certain vegetables. In addition, foreign reports indicate that US sanitary and phytosanitary (SPS) measures are sometimes implemented for protectionist reasons (explored in chapter 3). Over the last decade, however, US bilateral FTAs have liberalized some protected sectors, especially now that the longer transition periods are beginning to expire.

Tariffs

According to the World Trade Organization (WTO 2004c), in 2002, the simple average applied most favored nation (MFN) tariff, including ad valorem equivalents, was 5.2 percent on all merchandise and 9.8 percent on agricultural products.[5] Chapter appendix tables 2A.1 and 2A.2 summarize tariffs and identify the highest tariff peaks in the US agricultural profile. The agricultural figure is strongly affected by extraordinarily high tariffs on tobacco products, peanuts, and sugars, as well as high tariffs on dried and fresh vegetables, beef, most dairy products, and beverages. About 12 percent of all merchandise tariffs are not ad valorem, but specific or compound duties. Many of these apply to agricultural imports, such as dairy products, fruits and vegetables, and meats (chapter appendix table 2A.1).[6]

Average US agricultural tariffs in unilateral preference schemes and bilateral FTAs are lower than MFN rates. In 2002, average US applied agricultural tariffs, by the WTO definition, were 9.8 percent for countries granted MFN status, 8.4 percent for countries in the Generalized System of Preferences (GSP), 6.2 percent for less developed countries (LDCs), 4.4 percent for Israel and Canada, and 2.7 percent for Mexico (table 2.3).

With the exception of bilateral trade with Mexico and Chile, US bilateral FTAs do not promise full elimination of agricultural barriers.[7] Under the US-Canada FTA, certain agricultural products remain indefinitely subject to reduced tariff rates. Likewise, in the US-Israel FTA, reduced tariffs remain on about 220 lines for dairy products and peanuts. Under the US-

---

5. The figure for agriculture is based on the WTO definition of that category. The analogous figure using the ISIC definition is lower, at 5.6 percent.

6. The United States International Trade Commission (USITC) publishes ad valorem equivalents on its website (USITC 2005c).

7. It should be mentioned as well that the US-Bahrain and the US-Singapore FTAs do not contemplate exceptions to free trade in agricultural products. However, these US partners are essentially city-states, with very little agricultural production.

Table 2.3 US MFN and preferential tariffs by partner country or group, 2002ª (percent)

Country or group	Average tariffs		
	All products	Agriculture	Nonagriculture[b]
Canada	0.7	4.4	0.0
Israel	0.7	4.4	0.0
Jordan	2.7	6.2	2.1
Mexico	0.6	2.7	0.2
AGOA[c]	2.4	6.0	1.8
ATPDEA	2.6	6.0	1.9
CBERA	2.4	5.9	1.8
CBTPA	2.3	5.9	1.6
Less developed countries	2.7	6.2	2.1
Generalized system of preferences	3.7	8.4	2.8
Most-favored nation	5.1	9.8	4.2

Groups: African Growth and Opportunity Act (AGOA), Andean Trade Promotion and Drug Eradication Act (ATPDEA), Caribbean Basin Economic Recovery Act (CBERA), and Caribbean Basin Trade Partnership Act of 2000 (CBTPA).

a. If a tariff line is not eligible for the preferential program, the rate used in the calculation of averages is the GSP or MFN rate.
b. Excludes petroleum products.
c. Calculations made for LDC AGOA beneficiaries, as they constitute the majority of beneficiaries.

Source: WTO (2004c).

Jordan FTA, new TRQs were created to give certain Jordanian agricultural exports additional access to the US market.[8]

Many of Switzerland's top agricultural exports to the United States face comparatively high tariffs. Existing exports of chocolates, cheeses, and certain food preparations are subject to tariffs ranging between 5 and 10 percent (chapter appendix table 2A.3). Moreover, US tariffs or TRQs may play a role in the negligible size of Swiss exports to the United States for seven of Switzerland's top 10 exports to the world (the seven items are listed in table 2.4). US tariffs are particularly high for concentrates of coffee (9.4 percent) and tobacco (11.4),[9] and the combination of high tariffs (8 percent) and quotas may impede Swiss exports of certain chocolate products (HTS 1806.32 and 1806.90). In addition, some US high tariffs identified in chapter appendix table 2A.2 (e.g., dairy items and sugars) may stifle potential Swiss exports.

---

8. Exceptions are discussed in more detail in the section on phaseouts in US bilateral FTAs.

9. Note that tariffs and quotas for HTS 2402 are significantly lower than they are for other tobacco products (e.g., HTS 2401 and 2403), where they sometimes reach 150 percent.

Table 2.4 Swiss agricultural exports that fare poorly in the US market[a]

HS code	Product	Rank in Swiss agricultural exports to world	Average US tariff (percent)	Tarrif rate quotas
2402.20	Cigarettes containing tobacco	3	11.4	No
1806.32	Chocolate in blocks/slabs/bars, weighing 2kg	4	8.1	Yes[b]
2309.10	Dog or cat food	5	0.0	No
1806.90	Chocolate not included in 1806.20–1806.32	6	8.2	Yes[b]
4403.20	Wood, in the rough	7	0.0	No
2101.11	Extracts, essences, and concentrates of coffee	8	9.4	No
4410.32	Particle board of wood	9	0.0	No

a. Swiss exports of the product are not in the top 30 Swiss agricultural exports to the United States.

b. TRQs on 1806.32.04, 1806.32.14, 1806.90.15, and 1806.90.25.

Source: UN Statistics Division, 2005.

Tariff-Rate Quotas

The United States applies two distinct TRQ regimes, namely the US Section 22 TRQ regime and the preferential TRQ regime. The US Section 22 TRQ regime applies to all US trade partners, unless a special quota has been negotiated on a bilateral basis or applied in a unilateral preference scheme. The preferential TRQ regime applies to FTA partners or countries benefiting from unilateral preferences, notably in the Caribbean and Africa. These two regimes may be applied concurrently on products originating in a single country, as was proposed for beef imports from countries under the Central American Free Trade Agreement (CAFTA) and dairy imports from Australia.[10] We first explain the Section 22 TRQ system and then the preferential system.

The highest US ad valorem equivalent (AVE) tariffs on agricultural imports are generally US Section 22 TRQs and usually take the form of specific rates (chapter appendix table 2A.4). Certain out-of-quota tariffs are prohibitive, such as those in tobacco (350 percent), peanuts (140 percent), and butter and oil substitutes (98 percent). High out-of-quota rates also apply to dairy products, cotton waste, infant formulas, and cane or beet sugars or syrups. According to a Congressional Budget Office report (CBO 2005),

---

10. How the two regimes interact is not always clear, and the question of interpretation of certain provisions has already come up in the context of US FTAs.

TRQs affect slightly fewer than 200 tariff lines, but the simple average for out-of-quota duties on them stands at nearly 50 percent. However, since over-quota imports are found in more than 70 percent of products subject to TRQs, the United States argues that the TRQ system does not generally act as a quantitative restriction. We do not find this argument convincing.[11]

In-quota imports are typically subject to lower duties in line with average duties for the whole agricultural sector.[12] They are administered by first-come-first-served and country-based historical license systems. Several trading partners have objected to "certain built-in rigidities in the import-licensing system" and other features of quota administration (European Commission 2004a, 18).[13]

Switzerland has been granted exclusive access under three US Section 22 TRQs on Swiss Emmental, Gruyere, and other varieties of cheese. Nevertheless, other Swiss exports of cheese and dairy products, chocolate, and sugar-based products are probably constrained by the TRQ system (see chapter appendix table 2A.4 and table 2.4).

US bilateral agreements maintain protective barriers on sensitive products through special TRQs. Often in bilateral FTAs, preferential TRQs replace US Section 22 import quotas for imports originating in the partner country. Preferential TRQs typically allow duty-free access to in-quota imports, while in most cases, over-quota tariffs are gradually eliminated over a specified transition period. However, barriers are retained in many US bilateral FTAs.[14]

In both Section 22 and preferential regimes, the United States reserves the right to apply price- or volume-based safeguards, which take the form of additional tariffs on over-quota imports. These have been invoked in recent years.

Safeguard Measures

The United States applies two distinct safeguard regimes, namely those pursuant to Article 5 of the WTO Agreement on Agriculture (which enables safeguards under Section 22 of the Agricultural Adjustment Act) and

---

11. TRQs partly explain the low share of imports of dairy products (less than 3 percent) in domestic consumption (WTO 2004c).

12. The CBO (2005) report estimates the simple average in-quota tariff for TRQ lines at around 10 percent.

13. For example, foreign governments have requested clarification of the role of the Commodity Credit Corporation (CCC) in administering tariff quotas. It seems that in the past, the CCC has exchanged commodities already held in stock for certificates for quota eligibility. Canada has complained about "un-authorized" imports of refined sugar entering the United States against Canada's portion of the refined sugar in-quota level (USDA 2005a).

14. For more information, see the sections on phaseouts in US bilateral FTAs.

special bilateral safeguard regimes.[15] Article 5 safeguards are invoked on imports from WTO partners, while special safeguards are applied to imports from bilateral FTA partners. The two regimes cannot be applied concurrently on a product originating in a single country.

Article 5 safeguard measures may be applied for an initial period of four years, and then extended. In practice, however, the United States applies safeguards for a maximum of three years (WTO 2004c). Safeguard measures can take the form of tariffs, quotas, TRQs, and import licenses, and they can be based on import price or volume.[16] Chapter 99 of the 2005 US Tariff Schedule lists safeguard measures on beef; sheep meat; milk and cream; butter; dried milk and cream; certain dairy products; cocoa powder and chocolate; infant formulas; rough cotton; peanuts, peanut butter, and peanut paste; and sugars, syrups, and molasses. Measures are also levied on multiple cheeses—blue mold, cheddar, American-type, Edam and Gouda, Italian, Swiss, and Emmental (HS code 0406.90.97; see USITC 2005b, chapter 99, 55–81). The top Swiss agricultural export to the United States, certain food preparations containing over 10 percent of sugars (HS code 2106.90.97), is currently subject to Article 5 safeguard measures.

As a general rule, the United States does not invoke WTO safeguard measures on goods originating in bilateral FTA partner countries.[17] Thus, in December 2001, President Bush excluded Mexican, Canadian, Israeli, and Jordanian steel from its safeguard regime. Third countries, including Switzerland, challenged this exclusion. The WTO Appellate Body held that bilateral FTA partners can be excluded from a safeguards remedy, but that the products from excluded countries must not be counted in the findings of injury—contrary to what happened in the steel case (WTO 2002a).[18]

The United States reserves the right to apply special safeguards to products originating in FTA partner countries, including agricultural

---

15. Current safeguard measures are listed in Chapter 99 of the US Tariff Schedule (USITC 2005d). US notifications of safeguard measures to the WTO are also available online; see WTO (2002c).

16. Price-based safeguards are applied on a shipment-by-shipment basis. Importers of goods in an over-quota tariff line must declare a price range applicable to the product. If the price range corresponds to a level that triggers a safeguard duty, additional charges are levied. Volume-based safeguards have been invoked in the past for products for which the United States did not have a TRQ system. Some of these measures were terminated after they were challenged in WTO proceedings (WTO 2004c).

17. At the time of writing, US bilateral FTA partners are Israel, Canada, Mexico, Jordan, Singapore, Chile, Morocco, Australia, and CAFTA-DR members.

18. In WTO (2000a), the Appellate Body concluded that the US practice of including certain countries in determining injury while excluding others from the application of the measure was inconsistent with the Agreement on Safeguards. WTO (2002d) further clarifies that the competent authorities must "establish explicitly" that imports from the sources covered by the measure must by themselves satisfy the conditions for applying safeguards, and WTO (2003c) reaffirms this interpretation.

products subject to preferential TRQs.[19] The special agricultural safe-guard provision, a standard clause in US FTAs, allows additional tariffs to be applied (sometimes automatically) when over-quota imports pass certain thresholds of price or quantity; these often target dairy products, beef, and fruits and vegetables and their products.[20] Typically, the special safeguard provision is a transition measure, but in some instances, the United States and its partner countries have agreed to continue it post-transition. In a similar spirit, US unilateral preference schemes include "competitive need" provisions, whereby products can lose eligibility when imports exceed certain thresholds.

Antidumping and Countervailing Duties (AD and CVD)

Though AD measures are typically associated with certain manufactured products, the United States applies them on agricultural and food imports. In fact, AD measures on agriculture and food are applied to a greater extent than their share in total US imports. In recent years, US AD measures have targeted honey, sugar, frozen apple and orange juices, raspberries, fresh garlic, preserved mushrooms, live swine, and canned pineapple fruit.[21] However, as of December 2004, no product originating in Switzerland was subject to AD measures.

Other Measures

In addition to tariffs, TRQs, duties, and AD and CVD measures, the United States upholds other policies that amount to barriers in agricultural trade, ranging from domestic support in the form of subsides and other programs, to custom procedures.[22]

Domestic Support

The Organization for Economic Cooperation and Development (OECD 2003) concludes, "Agricultural policy in the United States is characterized by levels of support below the OECD average."[23] It also notes a long-term

---

19. For a full description of the actual application of special safeguards in US bilateral FTAs, see the later section on phaseouts.

20. See Chapter 99 of the 2005 US Tariff Schedule.

21. See WTO document G/ADP/N/126/USA.

22. Sanitary and phytosanitary issues and standards are explored at length in chapter 3.

23. Domestic support is rarely a topic treated in bilateral FTAs. We do not anticipate that it will be addressed in negotiations between Switzerland and the United States. Therefore, our discussion does not delve into details.

**Table 2.5 Production, consumption, and support of the
agricultural sector, 2004**

	Switzerland (billions of Swiss francs)	United States (billions of US dollars)
Total value of production (at farm gate)	7.3	225.4
Total value of consumption of domestic produce (at farm gate)[a]	8.9	206.6
Total value of agricultural imports[b]	8.9	47.4
Total support estimate (TSE)	7.8	108.7
Producer support estimate (PSE)	7.2	46.5
Of which market price supports	4.0	16.2
General services support estimate (GSSE)	0.5	34.1
Share of production (percent)		
TSE	87.0	53.0
PSE	81.0	23.0
Of which market price supports	45.0	8.0
GSSE	0.1	0.2

a. Does not include imports.
b. 2003 CIF import values.

Sources: OECD (2004e), USDA (2004f), and USDA Grain Report E34042, 2004.
Exchange rates were obtained from the IMF.

tendency toward reduced support payments; however, support under the Farm Act of 2002 is higher, and the extent of market orientation is lower, than when the preceding Farm Act of 1996 was in force.

Most US subsidy payments are channeled directly to individual producers, reflected in the OECD producer support estimate (PSE) indicator in table 2.5. However, government expenditures on marketing promotion and infrastructure also constitute important sources of support (see general services support estimate in table 2.5). After two years of substantial decline, the PSE increased sharply in 2004 to about $46 billion, but remained below the record values of government assistance to individual producers posted in 1999 and 2000. It should be noted that PSE figures include the price-raising consequences of market-access barriers, as well as direct subsidy payments.

Through different means and at different levels of commitment, the United States supports the production of cereals, rice and upland cotton, oilseeds, peanuts, pulses, sugar, milk and dairy products, lamb meat, white wool, mohair, and honey (table 2.6). Based on 1999 figures, which are now dated, the WTO estimated that US trade-distorting domestic support was approximately $25 billion annually (WTO 2004c, 107).

**Table 2.6 Producer support estimates (PSE),
for top 10 products, 2003**

Rank	Product	Value	Share
Swiss value (millions of Swiss francs)			
1	Milk	2,902	0.39
2	Beef and veal	1,209	0.16
3	Pigmeat	1,003	0.13
4	Wheat	225	0.03
5	Poultry	202	0.03
6	Sugar	142	0.02
7	Other grains	114	0.02
8	Eggs	106	0.01
9	Oilseeds	98	0.01
10	Maize (corn)	63	0.01
	Total	7,529	1.00
US value (millions of US dollars)			
1	Milk	10,992	0.28
2	Maize (corn)	4,316	0.11
3	Oilseeds	4,095	0.11
4	Soybeans	4,095	0.11
5	Wheat	2,657	0.07
6	Sugar	1,354	0.03
7	Beef and veal	1,197	0.03
8	Rice	744	0.02
9	Other grains	733	0.02
10	Poultry	677	0.02
	Total	38,878	1.00

Source: OECD, PSE/CSE database 2004.

Export Subsidies

Agricultural export subsidies have received limited or no attention in US bilateral FTAs. Recent FTAs, such as US-Chile, US-Australia, CAFTA, and US-Morocco, include the reciprocal commitment not to subsidize agricultural sales in the partner country's home market, unless subsidies are necessary to meet the export subsidies of a third party, notably, the European Union. We anticipate that the Swiss-US FTA will follow the norm and either ignore export subsidies altogether or contain a similar "non-aggression" clause. However, since export subsidies clearly distort markets, we present a brief overview of their magnitudes and trends.

Under the WTO Agreement on Agriculture, the United States committed to discipline export subsidies to total outlays not exceeding $594 million per annum. In addition, the United States pledged to reduce that amount over time, identifying 13 agricultural product groups in its schedule that receive export subsidies, including cereals, oilseeds, dairy products, and vegetables.

The actual amount of export subsidies granted yearly by the US government is much lower than the agreed cap. According to the latest figures reported to the WTO, the United States distributed $32 million in 2002, a significantly lower figure than the $147 million estimate for 1998. While export subsidies under $150 million are insignificant compared with total US agricultural exports, subsidies can be important for particular commodities. The WTO (2004c) mentions that, in 2000, "91 percent of total exports of skim milk powder were subsidized."

While perhaps not technically export subsidies—the characterization is still debated—US export finance, insurance, and guarantee programs also play a role in promoting exports. Export finance and kindred systems provide short-, medium-, and long-term credit lines, guaranteed by the Commodity Credit Corporation (CCC). The value of officially supported export credits stood at $3.4 billion in 2002. According to the WTO (2004c, 111), "government-guaranteed export financing confers an export advantage, because the interest rates charged does [sic] not reflect the actual risk of the transaction, but rather the credit rating of the underlying guarantee." Few government-financed exports are shipped to Switzerland; typical destinations are South America, Mexico, Turkey, and South Korea.

Customs Procedures

Foreign reports on US barriers have frequently voiced concerns over US licensing systems, invoice requirements, customs fees, and other charges.[24] More recently, foreign governments have objected to higher transaction costs and delays associated with the Homeland Security Act of 2002.[25]

---

24. Title 19 of the US Code contains provisions on fees for custom services (WTO, 2004c). Fees include the Harbor Maintenance Act (with an ad valorem levy of 0.125 percent).

25. This Act established new and stricter customs procedures, and given the perceived threat of terrorism, these procedures are not subject to negotiation in an FTA. Under the Container Security Initiative (CSI), the US Customs Service, renamed the Customs and Border Protection Service (CBP), now operates container screening checks in ports of departure, 24-hour pre-shipment vessel cargo declarations, and supply chain guidelines for businesses desiring to export goods to the United States. The CBP has selected the main ports of continental Europe—Rotterdam, Antwerp, Le Havre, and Genoa, among others—to participate in a CSI-related program that uses new technology to speed up pre-shipment inspection. Switzerland benefits from this program. According to the CBP, no complaints of cargo delayed due to the CSI system have been received (WTO 2004c). Foreign reports, however, highlight the unilateral nature of US measures, as well as business concerns (European Commission 2004a). On the other hand, it has been argued that there are some offsetting gains in efficiency arising from efforts to meet the new US security requirements.

Table 2.7 Swiss agricultural production, 1997–2003
(millions of Swiss francs)

Branch	1997–99	2003[a]	Share 2003 (percent)
Total vegetable production	4,817	4,067	45
Cereals	715	428	5
Fruits	575	534	6
Plants and flowers	923	790	9
Potatoes	207	178	2
Sugar beets	152	151	2
Vegetables	472	536	6
Wine	366	388	4
Total animal production	5,241	4,933	55
Bovines	1,003	1,016	11
Eggs	184	184	2
Milk	2,665	2,360	26
Porcines	1,124	1,082	12
Poultry	169	202	2
Total agricultural production	10,058	9,000	100

a. Provisional figures.

Source: WTO (2004b).

Switzerland: Barriers to Agricultural Trade

As far as agriculture is concerned, Switzerland ranks among the most highly protected countries in the industrial world, with levels comparable to Japan, Korea, and Norway. Swiss barriers to agricultural trade result from policies designed to ensure the conservation of rural areas, promote the decentralized use of territory through income generation, and contribute to food security through national self-sufficiency in agriculture (see table 2.7 for Swiss agricultural production).

Historically, trade protection has been the most important (but not the only) instrument Switzerland has chosen to achieve these multifunctional goals. Apart from agricultural self-sufficiency, the other goals of Swiss agricultural policy could be achieved, at least according to the United States, by alternative policy measures. Box 2.1 briefly reviews the multifunctional debate, summarizing US and Swiss positions. In any event, Switzerland implements its trade barriers mostly through tariffs and TRQs, supplemented by other trade barriers, such as domestic subsidies, standards, and technical regulations.[26] US officials have stated repeatedly that Switzerland

26. In some instances, standards and technical regulations (SPS measures) are more restrictive than tariffs and quotas.

Box 2.1 Multifunctional nature of agriculture

The multiple functions of agriculture attract attention when trade liberalization is negotiated, within both the WTO and bilateral agreements. Debate centers on the links between agricultural production and associated noncommodity values. Since Swiss and US positions differ substantially, Swiss-US FTA talks may be an opportunity to find common ground on selected aspects of the wider debate.

Both countries agree that agriculture contributes to society beyond the value of food and fiber produced. Externalities include the maintenance of open space, environmental benefits such as erosion control and wild animal habitats, the preservation of a cultural heritage and rural communities, and the assurance of food supply ("food security," in Swiss terminology). Article 104 of the Swiss Constitution stipulates that domestic agriculture should provide a "substantial contribution" to the food consumed by the Swiss population, the conservation of rural areas, and the decentralized use of territory. Between 1992 and 2002, 60 percent of all calories consumed in Switzerland were in fact produced domestically. Apart from the food security issue, the agricultural policies of both the United States and Switzerland foster externalities through various policies that run the gamut from subsidies to regulation to trade barriers.

Switzerland fears that full liberalization would lead to a substantial drop in domestic prices and undermine external benefits. By contrast, the United States believes that the multifunctional benefits of agriculture can be achieved by targeted and transparent policies that have little trade-distorting impact. As a general rule (with exceptions) the United States argues that subsidies should be limited to "green box" measures that are not coupled with agricultural production or price levels. Moreover, the United States believes that public food stocks, not self-sufficiency goals, best ensure food security.

is a "difficult market" for many US agricultural products. US agricultural producers trying to sell into the Swiss market often face high tariffs; in addition, they must compete with third-country firms that enjoy preferential access and overcome negative public attitudes toward biotechnology (USTR 2005b).

Tariffs

Estimates of the simple average tariff equivalent for Swiss agricultural imports in 2004 range from 28.6 percent (using major division 1 of the International Standard Industrial Classification, or ISIC) to 36.2 percent (WTO definition), as table 2.8 and chapter appendix table 2A.5 show. Switzerland's tariff peaks are concentrated in the agricultural sector. Even the ISIC estimate of 28.6 percent is nearly triple the corresponding level of US

Table 2.8 Summary of Swiss MFN tariffs, 2004

Product description	Number of lines	Lines used[a]	Average tariff (AVE, percent)	Standard deviation (percent)	Imports, 2003 (millions of dollars)
			Applied rates		
Agriculture[b]	1,947	1,613	36.2	87.9	6,336
Beverages and spirits	104	100	23.2	40.5	1,226
Coffee and tea, cocoa, sugar, etc.	413	345	29.7	48.0	1,428
Cut flowers and plants	77	73	23.3	69.4	463
Dairy products	55	52	77.4	113.7	236
Fruits and vegetables	488	427	34.1	64.4	1,287
Grains	82	54	42.8	63.5	150
Live animals and products thereof	150	131	109.0	229.4	528
Oil seeds, fats, oils, and their products	350	217	34.4	49.5	237
Tobacco	15	13	10.0	11.0	200
Other agricultural products	213	201	6.6	23.9	580
Nonagriculture[c]	6,233	6,137	2.3	4.1	85,452
By stage of processing					
Fully processed products	4,465	4329	9.7	48.2	71,237
Raw materials	1,255	1052	18.6	54.4	6,207
Semiprocessed products	2,479	2388	4.5	17.2	17,759
Total	8,199	7,769	9.3	42.5	95,204

a. Lines with no ad valorem equivalents are excluded.
b. WTO definition.
c. Excludes petroleum.
Source: WTO (2004b).

applied MFN tariffs on agricultural imports (9.3 percent). Switzerland's highest average tariffs are applied to animals and products thereof, dairy products, and grains (table 2.8). However, various high peaks are also found for certain vegetables (e.g., lettuce and carrots), fruits and fruit juice, oilseeds, and vegetable oils (chapter appendix table 2A.6).

The WTO tariff definition is expressed in AVE terms, since Switzerland applies specific tariffs and TRQs. It is worth noting that, when dealing with specific tariffs, exchange rate fluctuations affect the analysis of AVE levels: For example, when the Swiss franc is strong, specific tariffs translate into higher AVE figures.

Despite high tariff and quota barriers, many agricultural products enter Switzerland at reduced rates, often close to zero, depending on when they are imported or what their final use is. According to Confoederatio Helvetica (2005a), eligible agricultural products include live swine, animal products, fruit cereals, fodder goods, oilseeds, and edible oils.[27] The purpose of the low rates is to boost the competitiveness of Swiss food processing and pharmaceutical firms, which otherwise would be hampered by costly inputs. Yet Swiss retail prices substantially exceed the average prices for most agricultural products found in neighboring countries (chapter appendix table 2A.7).

Reducing these price differentials to be consistent with Article 104 of the Swiss Constitution has preoccupied Swiss agricultural policy since the early 1990s. Article 104 requires that domestic agriculture provide a "substantial contribution" to the food needs of the Swiss population, the conservation of rural areas, and the decentralized use of territory. Since 1990, Swiss agricultural producers have contributed about 60 percent of the total caloric intake of the Swiss population. The contribution is higher for animal products than those of vegetable origin (94 percent versus 45 percent).

According to the Swiss Federal Office for Agriculture, Agricultural Policy 2011 will consist essentially of policies that contribute to reducing price differentials at both the producer and consumer levels. This will be done by reallocating subsidies toward direct payments rather than production-based or price-based supports, reducing tariffs on animal feed, and implementing measures to make Swiss producers more competitive.[28] Improving the productivity of Swiss farmers and reducing costs are seen as "the only means of attenuating the risks related to the reduction of border protection" (Swiss Federal Office for Agriculture 2005). The new agricultural policy is expected to provide some maneuvering room for Swiss officials as they tackle the challenging negotiating agenda in the Doha Development Round as well as bilateral negotiations with the European

---

27. The complete list of eligible products is listed in the 20-page annex of the ordinance (Confoederatio Helvetica 2005a).

28. For example, tariffs on fodder cereals are scheduled to decrease from Sfr 43 to Sfr 36/quintal.

Table 2.9 US agricultural exports to the European Union that fare poorly in the Swiss market[a]

HS code	Product	Rank in US agricultural exports to European Union	Average tariff, 2001	Tariff-rate quotas
1201.00.00.40	Soybeans, broken or not	1	21.5	No
2303.10.00.10	Corn gluten feed, in pellets or not	4	14.0	Yes[b]
1001.90.20.55	Wheat and meslin, except seed, nesoi	8	118.7	Yes[c]
0802.11.00.00	Almonds, fresh or dried, in shell (kg)	10	0.0	No
0101.10.00.00	Purebred breeding horses and asses, live	17	n.a.	Yes[d]

nesoi = not elsewhere specified or included
n.a. = not available
a. US exports of the product are not in the top 30 of US agricultural exports to Switzerland.
b. See quota 28 in table 2.5.
c. See quota 26 in table 2.5.
d. See quota 01 in table 2.5.
Source: FAS (2005).

Union, the United States, and major agricultural producers such as the Southern Cone Common Market (Mercosur) and the Southern African Customs Union (SACU).

So far, Switzerland has not used its extensive network of bilateral FTAs, including agreements with its European Free Trade Association (EFTA) partners and the European Union, to reduce the average level of agricultural protection, though the Bilateral Agreement on Agriculture and recent modifications to Protocol 2 of the 1972 FTA between the European Union and Switzerland significantly liberalized certain products.[29]

Despite high tariffs, many existing US agricultural exports are subject to low tariffs. In fact, about half of US top 30 agricultural exports to Switzerland enter duty free or pay nuisance tariffs (chapter appendix table 2A.8). Meats, asparagus, wine, and bovine semen are subject to stiff tariffs. This analysis, however, doesn't take into account the prohibitive effect of the highest peaks. For example, many top US agricultural exports to the European Union and the world, such as wheat, corn, and soybeans, fare quite poorly in the Swiss market: Table 2.9 shows that high tariffs and quotas partly explain the low volumes registered for exports of these products to Switzerland.

---

29. See the section below on phaseout schedules in Swiss bilateral FTAs.

Tariff-Rate Quotas

Switzerland currently applies 28 TRQs to 282 tariff lines (WTO, 2004b). Chapter appendix table 2A.9 lists the broader product categories, not the specific tariff lines.[30] The simple average in-quota and out-of-quota tariff rates on products subject to TRQs are 11.2 percent and 118.8 percent respectively. Switzerland has among the highest average out-of-quota TRQ rates in the world. Cut flowers lead the way (336 percent), followed by durum wheat (200 percent), pork and poultry (153 percent), grapes and grape juice (143 percent), vegetables (125 percent), cereals (120 percent), and grains (113 percent).

In recent years, utilization rates of TRQs scheduled in the WTO have increased, reaching or surpassing 100 percent in most categories, especially cereals for making bread and dairy products. Red meats and fresh vegetables have also experienced out-of-quota imports.

Swiss TRQs may affect 4 out of the top 30 US agricultural exports. These products are bovine semen, meat of horses and mules, bovine meat, and asparagus. Moreover, many of the top US exports to the European Union fare rather poorly in bilateral trade between the United States and Switzerland. Some of these products—wheat, poultry, cereals, and grains—also face prohibitive out-of-quota barriers. Swiss TRQs are administered by different allocation systems, such as *prise en charge*, auctions, and first-come-first-served systems.[31] In recent years, some US exporters, such as potato producers, have complained about the allocation of quotas. On the other hand, the auctioning of the white wine quota from 1996 to 2000 led to considerable increases in the US share of the white wine market, a product that is relatively expensive.

Safeguards, Antidumping Measures, and Countervailing Duties

Switzerland does not have any AD, CVD, or safeguard measures in place, nor do they intend to establish any.[32] But it reserves the right to impose special safeguards (SSG) for all imports subject to TRQs when domestic prices fall below, or import quantities exceed, certain thresholds.[33] This

---

30. The list of the 282 tariff lines affected by TRQs is available at www.tares.ch.

31. The *prise en charge* system requires traders to purchase domestic production to use the quota on foreign imports (e.g., potato products, milk powder, and poultry). Recent reforms have replaced the *prise en charge* system with the first-come-first-served system in some instances (e.g., eggs) or the auctioning system (e.g., beef, pork, and poultry).

32. See WTO (2004b). While AD and CVD measures are theoretically possible, Swiss legislation enabling penalty duties has not been updated since the Tokyo Round.

33. One legal basis is Article 7 of the Customs Law, which allows any tariff modification when the "national interest is at stake." Other articles allow temporary increases in agricultural tariff products, consistent with international agreements. The Switzerland Ministry of Economy is the competent Swiss authority for AD and CVD investigations (WTO 2004b).

prerogative has not been invoked since 2000, and only once before then, for pork meat.

Other Barriers

Like the United States, Switzerland employs considerable domestic support and export subsidies that amount to barriers to trade. In addition, it also uses price controls, export refunds, and import prohibitions, which are likely to be a part of FTA negotiations.

Domestic Support Measures

According to an OECD (2003) report, "Agriculture in Switzerland is characterized by high support levels and limited market orientation."[34] In 2004, producer support was estimated at 68 percent of gross receipts from agriculture, more than twice the OECD average and double the EU level. Switzerland ranks among the top OECD countries in per capita support to agricultural producers. From 1995 to 2003, the per capita PSE estimates were €293 for the European Union, €122 for the United States, and €683 for Switzerland.

As estimated by the OECD, the level of producer supports stood at 7.2 billion Swiss francs in 2004 (see tables 2.5 and 2.10). Of that amount, government support totaled about 4 billion Swiss francs; the remaining amount essentially reflected transfers from consumers to producers through high prices induced by tariff and quota protection. Agricultural support in Switzerland remained broadly unchanged between 1995 and 2001, but increased in dollar terms after 2001 due to the appreciation of the Swiss franc.[35] Since the reorientation of agricultural policy in 1992, Switzerland has progressed in switching domestic subsidies from production-based and price-based payments to direct producer-based payments.[36] Between

---

34. Domestic support is rarely treated in bilateral FTAs, and we do not anticipate it will be addressed in negotiations between Switzerland and the United States. Therefore, our discussion does not delve into details.

35. Agricultural support in Switzerland largely consists of product-specific market-price supports, mainly through border barriers and producer-specific subsidies (payments based on historical entitlements, the so-called ecological payments distributed on the basis of planted area or number of animals). As shown in tables 2.6 and 2.10, in 2003, support through market prices represented about 60 percent of total support to individual farmers, while support for historical entitlements and planted area/number of animals made up 30 percent. The milk subsector receives the largest share of support, about 40 percent of the total, while beef and pig meat also command large entitlements of 16 and 13 percent respectively. See table 2.7 for estimates of agricultural production in Switzerland.

36. Direct payments not related to production or price targets are less distorting, as they allow for more room for market forces in setting domestic supply and demand. They also pave the way for reducing border barriers.

Table 2.10 Composition of producer support estimate, 2003[a]
(average percentage share in total value of PSE)

Type of payment	Switzerland	United States	OECD
Market price supports[b]	57	38	62
Based on output	5	8	4
Based on area planted/ animal numbers	13	5	16
Based on historical entitlements	17	13	4
Based on input use	4	19	9
Based on input constraints	2	5	3
Based on overall farm income	0	6	2
Miscellaneous	3	0	0
Countercyclical[c]	—	6	—
Producer support estimate	100	100	100

a. Provisional figures.
b. Market price supports reflect the impact of tariffs on domestic prices.
c. Reported only for US data.
Source: OECD, PSE/CSE database 2004.

1992 and 2004, direct payments jumped from 29 to 71 percent of total subsidies.

Price Controls, Export Refunds, and Export Subsidies

Government intervention through target prices has now been replaced by market-determined prices, bolstered by restrictive TRQs.[37] The price compensation scheme provides "export refunds" to compensate domestic food processors for the high input costs resulting from agricultural protection. Dairy and milling products when exported in processed agricultural products falling under HS chapters 15–22, sugar confectionery, preparations of cereals, and other food preparations are eligible, and comprise most of the top 20 Swiss agricultural exports to the United States.

According to the WTO (2004b), total export subsidies granted by the Swiss government to agricultural producers declined 30 percent between 1996 and 2000, dropping to 318 million Swiss francs (roughly $190 million).

---

37. The WTO *Trade Policy Review* notices that the *Ordonnance sur les produits agricoles* (Confoederatio Helvetica 2003) maintained a complex system of price brackets for certain agricultural goods, including duty-inclusive imports. The system currently applies to animal feed and seeds.

More recent data from the Swiss Federal Office for Agriculture (2005) confirms the decline, with export subsidies reaching 200 million Swiss francs in 2004. Part of the decrease in Swiss agricultural export subsidies can be traced to the implementation of the Swiss-EU Bilateral Agreement on Agriculture, which eliminated export subsidies for cheese trade between the parties.

The draft version of Agricultural Policy 2011 indicates that export subsidies will continue to decrease over the next five years.[38] The Swiss government is considering fully eliminating export subsidies distributed under the *loi sur l'agriculture* by 2009, which affects exports of cheese destined to non-EU countries, other dairy products, certain live animals, fresh and processed fruit products, and potatoes. Agricultural Policy 2011, however, will not affect export subsidies dispensed under the *Loi Chocolatière*.[39]

While the reported level of export subsidies is small compared with domestic support to agriculture, their relevance lies in the high ratio of export subsidies to the value of agricultural exports. Based on figures from 2000 that are now dated, the CBO (2005) estimated that the ratio of export subsidies to exports in Swiss agriculture was nearly 7 percent, making Switzerland the highest provider of export subsidies in the world, surpassing even the European Union (4 percent in 2000). Using 2004 data, however, the ratio of agricultural export subsidies to agricultural exports for Switzerland stood at 5 percent.

Given the affected trade volumes, Swiss agricultural export subsidies are not nearly as disruptive as those of larger players, such as the European Union. However, the 2004 WTO (2004b, 90) concludes that "Swiss export subsidies, when they were last notified in 1998 . . . were likely to distort world markets of mainly cheese." This conclusion was based on data preceding the Swiss-EU Bilateral Agreement on Agriculture that eliminated export subsidies on cheese trade between the parties.

Import Prohibitions

The Ordinance on Plant Protection prohibits imports, on the grounds of plant protection, of the following products: potatoes, potato plants, vines, fruit trees from non-European countries, and certain soils (Confoederatio Helvetica 2001).

Phaseout Schedules for Agricultural Barriers in US FTAs

This section describes US and partner country agricultural phaseout schedules, and correspondingly, agricultural market access commitments in

---

38. Revisions to Protocol 2 to the Swiss-EC FTA of 1972 could also limit Swiss export subsidies on a number of processed agricultural products sold in the European Union.

39. These export subsidies will be eliminated over the medium term.

selected FTAs. We consider the North American Free Trade Agreement (NAFTA), US-Australia, US-Chile, US-Morocco, and the Central American-Dominican Republic Free Trade Agreement (CAFTA-DR). The material is divided between the text of this chapter and Appendix A. The chapter text presents a general overview of market access commitments in the selected FTAs, focusing on tariffs, TRQs, and safeguards.[40] Appendix A gives a detailed description of phaseouts for 15 selected categories of agricultural products, and includes a summary table of concessions on selected products across the different FTAs (table A.1).

With the exception of US bilateral relations with Mexico and Chile, all other US bilateral FTAs fall short of full liberalization for both parties. Products that were excluded, or phased-out over more than 20 years in one or more agreements, include sugar, some dairy items, beef, wheat, poultry, eggs, margarine, ethanol, potatoes, and onions. In addition, US bilateral FTAs establish quantity- or price-based special safeguards for certain agricultural products. In a few cases, parties have agreed to extend, or review the possibility of extending, the application of special agricultural safeguards beyond the transition period.

NAFTA

NAFTA includes three sets of bilateral market access commitments: US-Mexico, US-Canada, and Canada-Mexico. We cover the first two relationships in that order. In general, Canada-Mexico commitments are similar to US-Mexico commitments, but they fall short of full liberalization.[41]

US-Mexico

When NAFTA went into effect in 1994, immediately more than half the value of bilateral US-Mexico agricultural trade became duty free. The remaining tariffs and nontariff barriers (NTBs) are being phased-out over transition periods of 5, 10, or 15 years. Once the 15-year transition period

---

40. The specific US sources are NAFTA Agricultural Fact Sheets (USDA-FAS); US-Australia Free Trade Agreement: Commodity Fact Sheets" (USDA-FAS); US-Central America-Dominican Republic Free Trade Agreement: Overall Agriculture Fact Sheet (USDA-FAS); US-Chile Free Trade Agreement: Commodity Fact Sheets (USDA-FAS); and US-Morocco Free Trade Agreement Agriculture Provisions (USTR). All sources are listed under references. Other sources consulted include The Australia-US Free Trade Agreement: Advancing Australian Agricultural Exports (Australian Department of Foreign Affairs and Trade); Principales Logros y Resultados (Department of Foreign Trade of Costa Rica); and Tratado de Libre Comercio Chile-Estados Unidos" (Chile Foreign Affairs Ministry). Chapter 3 discusses commitments on SPS matters in US and Swiss FTAs.

41. Important exceptions to full liberalization are in dairy products, poultry, eggs, and the sugar sector.

is ended, free trade between the US and Mexico will prevail for all agricultural products.[42]

Quota barriers affecting agricultural trade between the United States and Mexico were immediately converted to preferential tariffs or TRQs. NAFTA established preferential TRQs that provide in-quota duty-free access, while the initial over-quota tariffs are equivalent to the border protection of previous quantitative restrictions. The over-quota tariffs are phased out over 10- or 15-year periods.[43] The United States established NAFTA TRQs to replace US section 22 TRQs for imports of cotton, dairy products, certain fruit juices, peanuts, and sugar from Mexico. Mexico replaced its import licensing system with NAFTA TRQs on imports of corn, dry beans, milk powder, poultry, barley/malt, animal fats, potatoes, eggs, and some lumber products from the United States.[44]

NAFTA's agricultural safeguards are quantity-based. Once the threshold is met, the importing country may apply the tariff rate in place when the agreement went into effect, or the then-current MFN rate, whichever is lower. The threshold level grows at an annual rate of 3 percent throughout the transition period (see USDA 2004b for threshold details). A special agricultural safeguard provision is included in NAFTA for certain import-sensitive products: The United States may apply them on seasonal horticultural imports, for example, while Mexico may do the same on certain meats, vegetables, and fruits.[45]

US-Canada

Tariff elimination schedules in the Canada-US Free Trade Agreement (CUSFTA) remained in place for US-Canadian agricultural trade under NAFTA.[46] Many tariffs on agricultural products were eliminated over nine years after CUSFTA entered into force, but there are important exceptions for US imports of dairy products, peanuts, peanut butter, sugar, sugar-containing products, and cotton. Canadian over-quota tariffs remain in place for dairy, poultry, eggs, and margarine.

---

42. This is not the final outcome of Mexico's other bilateral FTAs, including, for example, the Mexico-EU FTA and Mexico's NAFTA relations with Canada.

43. Over-quota tariffs lasting 15 years are applied to corn, dry beans, peanuts, and powdered milk.

44. Additionally, Mexico's import licenses on wheat, grapes, tobacco, certain cheeses, evaporated milk, and day-old chicks imported from the United States were replaced by tariffs, which were phased out over a 10-year period.

45. The special safeguards products for the United States are fresh tomatoes, eggplant, chili peppers, squash, watermelon, and onions; for Mexico, live swine, pork, potato products, fresh apples, and coffee extract.

46. The CUSFTA entered into force in January 1, 1989.

CUSFTA's "snap-back provision" allows both countries to invoke priced-based special safeguards on fresh fruits and vegetables for 20 years after the entry in force of the agreement.[47] Safeguard measures must satisfy two conditions: For each of five consecutive days, the import price of the product must be below 90 percent of the corresponding five-year average monthly import price; and the planted acreage for the product in the importing country must be no higher than the average planted acreage over the preceding five years (excluding the years with the highest and lowest acreage). If these conditions are met, a partner country may restore MFN duties on imports of the product.[48]

US-Australia

When the US-Australia agreement was ratified in 2004, Australia immediately eliminated nearly all its agricultural tariffs.[49] The United States eliminated almost two-thirds of its agricultural tariffs, and it will reduce a further 9 percent of tariff lines to zero within four years. It will liberalize duties on products that are subject only to tariffs (not TRQs) either immediately or in 4, 10, or 18 years. However, the agreement falls short of complete liberalization. Sugar was excluded altogether from the agreement, and tariffs on some dairy products, such as certain cheeses, will remain at base year rates throughout phase-out periods that will go beyond 18 years (for details, see USDA 2004c, Australia Department of Foreign Affairs and Trade 2005).

The United States will establish preferential TRQs with duty-free in-quota volumes on several products: beef, cotton, peanuts, avocados, tobacco, milk, powder and other milk products, cream, ice cream, butter and butterfat, and cheddar, American, Swiss, European, and other types of cheeses.[50] Over-quota tariffs will be phased-out over 18 years, except for certain dairy products, where the in-quota tariff-free level will grow at constant fixed rates after year 18 of the agreement.

Both countries agreed not to subsidize their agricultural exports to the partner's market but preserved "the right to respond" to third-country use

---

47. The snap-back provision remains in force until 2008.

48. Safeguards may remain in place 180 days, or until the price of the product exceeds 90 percent of the five-year price average, whichever comes first.

49. With the exception of dairy products, Australia's agricultural tariffs were already low. Australia, however, will preserve its single-desk (state-managed) arrangements for marketing Australian commodities such as sugar, rice, wheat, and barley; Australia will also maintain its "best practice" quarantine and food safety regime.

50. The Australian government will administer FTA dairy quotas through a system of certification not available under the existing WTO cheese quota system of access into the US market. Australia's administration of quotas allows the Australian dairy industry to retain the financial gains (quota rents) derived from additional FTA access.

of export subsidies that displace their own products in the partner's market. The agreement establishes a system of recourse to special agricultural safeguards, but they may not be applied concurrently on the same product with general FTA safeguards or WTO Article 19 safeguards. The United States may invoke automatic, price-based agricultural safeguard measures on imports of beef, vegetables, and fruits.[51] Beef is subject to both a volume-based safeguard during the transition period and the continuation of price-based safeguards in the post-transition period. The price-based safeguard trigger is based on US market prices, and there is no requirement that imported beef affect US prices. The threshold prices for commodities subject to safeguards are programmed into the US customs and border protection computers, which automatically assess the tariff uplift if the import value of the commodity falls below the trigger price established in the agreement. However, the United States has the option to waive application of the safeguard.[52]

US-Chile

By value, more than three-quarters of US agricultural exports to Chile will be duty free within four years of the agreement's entry into force (January 2004).[53] The analogous figure for Chile is nearly 85 percent.[54] The remaining tariffs will be phased-out over the course of 8, 10, or 12 years. Some 12-year phaseouts will apply a nonlinear formula. At the end of the twelfth year, all agricultural products, with no exceptions, will be duty free.[55] Sugar was not a problematic product in US-Chile negotiations, in large part because Chile does not export sugar (Rosales 2003). According to the USTR (2002b), "US farmers will have access to Chile that is as good as or better than the EU or Canada, both of which already have FTAs with Chile."[56]

---

51. The actual list of products includes beef, onions, garlic, canned fruits, grape juice, orange juice, and tomato paste and puree.

52. More information available at the Australian Department of Agriculture, Fisheries and Forestry, available at www.affa.gov.au.

53. For more information, see Rosales (2003).

54. It is worth noting that, by value, tariffs on 13.7 percent of Chilean agricultural exports to the United States will be eliminated according to the 12-year phaseout category.

55. This was not the case in Chile's other bilateral agreements.

56. Chile has committed to eliminate its price band mechanism as it relates to the United States over a 12-year transition period. Eliminating price bands was not part of the EU or Canadian FTAs with Chile. In the transition period, Chile also guarantees to treat the United States no less favorably than any other trading partner. The United States has agreed not to subsidize US agricultural exports to Chile, but preserves the right to respond to third countries' (e.g., European Union) use of export subsidies to displace US products in the Chilean market. See USDA (2003a) for more information.

The agreement provides for the establishment of preferential TRQs. In-quota volumes will be duty free and all quotas removed at the end of 12-year phaseouts. The United States may apply TRQs on Chilean beef, turkey, poultry, avocados, sugar, tobacco, processed artichokes, cheeses, condensed and powdered milk, butter, and other dairy products, including some chocolates. Chile may apply quotas to US exports of beef, poultry, turkey, and dairy products.

The agreement stipulates that special agricultural safeguards may not be applied concurrently for the same product as general safeguards under the FTA agreement or WTO safeguards under Article 19. It contemplates using price-based special safeguards in 50 tariff lines. The United States may apply safeguard measures on canned or processed fruits, grape juice, orange juice, artichokes, mushrooms, tomato products, garlic, spinach, broccoli, avocados, asparagus, and cherries from Chile. Chile may invoke safeguards on eggs, several varieties of rice, and wheat grains. Safeguards are automatically imposed once the price of imports drops below a certain threshold. Import prices will be calculated for each shipment. Any differential from the reference price will be used as a basis for assessing additional duties, as long as overall duties do not exceed the MFN rate. The United States and Chile may use this recourse only during the 12-year transition period.

US-Morocco

The United States and Morocco will provide preferential market access on all agricultural products. The agreement falls short of full liberalization, as the United States only achieved limited access to the Moroccan market on beef, wheat, certain pasta products, and poultry.[57] The United States, on the other hand, will phase-out all agricultural tariffs under the agreement, most within 15 years.

Besides immediate elimination, preferential tariff phaseouts will take place over periods of 5, 8, 10, 12, 15, and 18 years. Some US tariffs in the 18-year period will be phased-out using a nonlinear formula. Moroccan tariffs on certain US products will be phased-out using nonlinear formulas applied over 6, 18, 19, and 25 years (see USDA 2004d, US Department of State 2004a).

The US-Morocco FTA establishes preferential TRQs. In-quota volumes are zero duty, while out-of-quota tariffs are gradually eliminated over 15 years. The United States will apply TRQs on beef, dairy products,

---

57. Katherine Novelli, assistant USTR, said that for these products, Moroccan concessions to US producers consist of "extremely small quantities that could in no way disrupt the Moroccan market" (US Department of State 2004b).

peanuts, cotton, tobacco, sugar and sugar-containing products, tomato products, tomato sauces, dried onions, and dried garlic. Sugar and sugar-containing products are subject to a net surplus exporter methodology and an 18-year phaseout. Morocco established preferential TRQs for US beef, whole birds, leg quarters, durum and nondurum wheat, almonds, and apples. Moroccan TRQs on beef and wheat are quite limited. Moreover, in-quota volumes of wheat and beef will still be subject to duties. Out-of quota tariffs are not eliminated for some beef, wheat, and certain pasta products.[58]

The agreement contains an automatic "preference clause"[59] whereby US exporters of wheat, beef, poultry, corn, and soybeans obtain better market access than Morocco gives other trading partners, notably the European Union. As in the US-Chile FTA and CAFTA-DR, the United States has agreed not to subsidize US agricultural exports to Morocco but preserves "the right to respond" to third parties—again, such as the European Union—using export subsidies to displace US products in the Moroccan market.

Like other agreements, this agreement stipulates that special agricultural safeguards may not be applied with general FTA safeguards or WTO Article 19 safeguards concurrently for the same product. During the implementation period, Morocco may apply quantity-based safeguards on chickpeas, lentils, almonds, dried prunes, poultry, and turkeys. The margin of extra duty permitted by the agreement is calculated as a variable percentage of the difference between the MFN rate and the preferential rate under the agreement, and is phased-out over the transition period. The United States may apply price-based safeguards on certain fruits, vegetables, and fruit juices,[60] and can invoke them if import prices drop below certain thresholds. The extra duty applied is proportional to the price differential, but may not exceed MFN rates. Morocco and the United States will evaluate the need for post-transition safeguards on certain products, such as poultry.

---

58. Talking about the limited access provided to certain agricultural products, Katherine Novelli, assistant USTR, stated that "We have never agreed to limit our access in this way, but we did this willingly because we understand how vital it is to preserve rural income in Morocco and we wanted to also have a free trade agreement that covers all products . . . but do it in a way that would in no way have a negative impact on Morocco's farmers or its citizens" (US Department of State 2004b).

59. Annex 1 of the agreement states: "In the event that Morocco grants or maintains with respect to any other trading partner market access better than that granted to the United States under this Agreement for any good listed in subparagraph (b) below, Morocco shall immediately grant such better market access to the United States" (US Department of State 2004a).

60. The actual products are dried onions; dried garlic; preserved tomato products; tomato pastes/purees; canned asparagus; certain canned black olives; canned pears, apricots, peaches, and fruit mixtures; and orange juice.

CAFTA-DR

Under prior unilateral arrangements, notably the Caribbean Basin Initiative, the United States already allowed duty-free entry to over 99 percent of Central American exports, measured by tariff lines. However, the most sensitive products with the greatest export potential belonged to the remaining 1 percent of tariff lines.

Under CAFTA-DR, the United States will provide the same tariff treatment to each of the six countries, but its partners need not apply the same tariffs to the United States.[61] Tariff phaseouts will be immediate, or in 5, 10, 12, 15, 17, or 20 years. As a general rule, tariffs will be linearly reduced as they are phased-out. For a few products, tariff reductions will be backloaded, but tariffs will eventually be eliminated for all products, except sugar and ethanol for the United States, fresh potatoes and fresh onions for Costa Rica, and white corn for other Central American countries.[62]

The CAFTA countries will create preferential TRQs with duty-free access for all in-quota imports. The United States will establish different initial volumes for each country as well as different growth rates for in-quota volumes.[63] Exceptions aside, the longest phaseout for over-quota tariffs will be 20 years. The United States will apply TRQs on beef, dairy products, peanuts, ethyl alcohol, and sugar; CAFTA countries will apply TRQs on poultry, beef, rice, dairy products, and corn (USDA 2005b).

The United States has agreed not to subsidize US agricultural exports to CAFTA-DR countries, but it reserves the right to respond to third-country export subsidies that displace US products in Central American or Dominican markets. As in other agreements, CAFTA-DR stipulates that special agricultural safeguards may not be applied concurrently for the same product as general safeguards under the agreement FTA or WTO Article 19 safeguards. The special safeguards will be volume-based, activated by specific triggers. The sum of any additional import duties and other customs duties cannot exceed the lesser of the prevailing MFN applied rates, or the MFN rate applied before the agreement entered into force.

The United States may invoke safeguards on out-of-quota imports of peanuts, peanut butter, cheese, butter, ice cream, fluid fresh and sour cream, some milk items, and other dairy products. All CAFTA-DR countries can apply safeguards on US poultry products, dairy items, milled rice, rough

---

61. US quotas, however, are determined on a country-by-country basis.

62. In the United States, white corn is considered a food-grade corn, while yellow corn is primarily used for animal feed. The distinction is rather arbitrary, and price differentials partly explain the different usages of corn varieties.

63. Typically, lower growth rates for Central American countries and faster growth for imports from the Dominican Republic.

rice, onions, pork cuts, corn, and corn syrups. In addition, certain country-specific safeguards are remitted. For example, US fresh tomatoes and potatoes will face agricultural safeguards only in Costa Rica and Guatemala. Though the possibility of employing safeguards will expire at the end of the transition period, safeguard coverage can be extended beyond the tariff phaseout if all parties agree.

Phaseout Schedules for Agricultural Barriers in Swiss FTAs

As mentioned earlier, Switzerland has not used its extensive network of bilateral FTAs, including agreements with its EFTA partners and the European Union, to sharply reduce the average level of agricultural protection. While Switzerland has granted duty-free entry to 99.8 percent of nonagricultural goods in its bilateral agreements, the lowest FTA average preferential agricultural tariff, per the WTO definition, applies to EFTA partners: 34.5 percent, a slight reduction compared with an average MFN agricultural tariff of 36.2 percent (table 2.11). However, since April 2004, Swiss agricultural imports from LDCs are entitled to unilateral tariff reductions that range between 55 and 75 percent, thereby bringing the average AVE rate on these imports down to 24.1 percent. A complete phaseout of all tariffs and TRQs for LDCs has been decided in principle, along the lines of the EC's "Everything but Arms" initiative.

Swiss-EU Agreement on Trade in Agricultural Products

Though Switzerland and the European Union have a long record of trade agreements that extends as far back as 1972, for the most part, these agreements excluded agricultural liberalization.[64] However, in June 1999, Switzerland and the European Union addressed the issue in their Bilateral Agreement on Agriculture.[65] Entered into force in June 2002, this agreement aims to reduce tariff barriers and eliminate nontariff barriers arising, for example, from differences in sanitary measures. In May 2004, the scope of the agreement was expanded to include the 10 new members of the European Union. In this section, we discuss the agreement as it concerns

---

64. Protocol 2 of the 1972 Swiss-EC FTA included partial concessions on processed agricultural products (for the most part, products falling in HS chapters 19 through 22). This protocol subsequently underwent an important revision that entered into force in early 2005. We discuss this revision in more detail later.

65. The BAA was one of seven bilateral agreements signed by the European Union and Switzerland in June 1999. The others covered free movement of persons, overland transport, air transport, research, technical barriers to trade, and public procurement.

Table 2.11 Swiss preferential tariffs by country as AVEs, 2004
(percent)

Country or group	Agriculture		Nonagriculture	
	Average	Free lines out of total	Average	Free lines out of total
Bulgaria	35.2	21.2	0.0	99.8
Croatia	35.7	19.8	0.0	99.8
EFTA	34.5	25.0	0.0	99.9
European Union	34.6	22.0	0.0	99.3
Macedonia	35.1	22.2	0.0	99.8
Israel	34.7	25.2	0.0	99.8
Jordan	35.2	21.9	0.0	99.8
Mexico	35.4	25.1	0.0	99.8
Morocco	34.9	23.9	0.0	99.8
Faeroe Islands	36.1	17.2	0.0	99.8
Romania	35.2	21.1	0.0	99.8
Singapore	35.1	23.0	0.0	99.8
Turkey	34.8	25.6	0.0	99.8
West Bank and Gaza Strip	35.3	19.3	0.0	99.8
Generalized System of Preferences (GSP)	34.2	31.9	0.5	82.8
Less developed countries (LDCs)	24.1	45.8	0.0	99.8
Most-favored nation (MFN)	36.2	15.9	2.3	18.0

EFTA = European Free Trade Association

Note: AVE refers to ad valorem equivalent of specific tariffs and nontariff barriers.

Source: WTO (2004b).

tariff barriers and export subsidies. Chapter 3 discusses the agreement's treatment of sanitary measures, standards, and geographical indications (GIs). We also discuss the revisions to Protocol 2 of the 1972 Swiss-EC FTA in the context of the second series of bilateral negotiations between Switzerland and the European Union (Bilateral II).

The reduction in custom duties was limited to those agricultural products in which both parties have a particular interest. Switzerland gained full access in cheese, plus additional (but not full) access in other dairy products as well as fresh vegetables and fruits. The European Union also obtained full access in cheese and concessions on products exported during nonharvesting periods, and for foodstuffs that are either not produced or produced in small quantities in Switzerland. The agreement did not reduce custom duties on fresh meat, wheat, and milk.

The agreement, however, is more forward-looking than implied by the narrow scope of coverage. It includes an evolutionary clause that calls for new tariff reductions "on a reciprocal preferential and mutually advantageous basis" (Switzerland Integration Office 2005a). The draft version of the Agricultural Policy 2011 implies that Switzerland might extend further preferential treatment to EU products over the medium term.[66] The document lists fresh milk, other milk products, and certain meat specialties as Swiss offensive interests in case the scope of product coverage is extended.

Cheese and Dairy

Trade in cheese products will be fully liberalized at the end of the five-year transition period (January 1, 2007). All tariff and quotas on cheeses of all kinds are eliminated at the end of the transition period. The parties also agreed to fully eliminate export subsidies affecting their cheese trade. Switzerland gains access on certain creams and yogurts through a duty-free TRQ of 2,000 metric tons. Out-of-quota shipments will be subject to the EU common external tariff. So far, Swiss producers have not taken full advantage of these concessions, as indicated by a quota utilization of 60 percent for yogurts and less than 50 percent for cheese. Switzerland did not make reciprocal commitments on these products.

Plants and Flowers

Switzerland gains unlimited free access for bouquets (HS 0603.10) and certain ornamental plants (HS 0602). The European Union gains free access to the Swiss market on ornamental plants and bouquets from October 26 until April 30, but only TRQ access for bouquets during other periods.

Fruits and Vegetables

Switzerland obtained several duty-free TRQs on many fresh or chilled fruits and vegetables,[67] and the EU common external tariff will apply to out-of-quota shipments of these products. In addition, Switzerland gained unlimited access for champignons and powders for certain fruit juices. So far, Swiss producers have not benefited from these concessions, as indicated by negligible quota-utilization rates. For its part, the European Union

---

66. The Swiss Federal Office for Agriculture (2005) characterizes invocation of the evolutionary clause as the most moderate scenario for its impact on Swiss agriculture. Two other scenarios considered include a comprehensive Swiss FTA with the European Union and full Swiss membership in the European Union.

67. Namely, seed potatoes, tomatoes, onions, cabbages, lettuce, carrots, beets, cucumbers, beans, eggplants, spinach, celeries, apples, apricots, pears, cherries, prunes, and raspberries.

obtained free and unlimited access on a variety of products,[68] certain nuts, and certain fruit products (with or without sugars or spirit), such as peach or citrus fruits. Switzerland established several duty-free TRQs for EU exports of apricots, strawberries, lettuce, and tomatoes, and maintained reduced tariffs on certain fruit products of apricots.

Dried Meat

Within one year of the agreement's entry into force, Switzerland obtained a duty-free TRQ of 1,200 metric tons on dried boneless meat of bovine animals. The European Union obtained a TRQ of 200 metric tons on dried boneless meat of bovine animals and a duty-free TRQ of 1,000 metric tons on boneless dried hams. Both concessions were conditional on the solution of outstanding bovine spongiform encephalopathy (BSE) issues, which have since been addressed by the Joint Committee on Agriculture. Swiss producers have rapidly taken advantage of the concessions, using the full preferential quota volume provided in the agreement.

Other Products

Switzerland granted the European Union a 50 percent tariff reduction on olive oil and a duty-free TRQ of 1,000 metric tons on EU exports of port wine. The European Union gained preferential access (though not full liberalization) on sweet wines and Retsina wine from Greece. The European Union did not grant reciprocal concessions on these products.

Revisions to Protocol 2 of the 1972 Swiss-EC FTA

Protocol 2 of the 1972 Swiss-EC FTA contained provisions regarding trade in processed agricultural products (e.g., chocolate, pasta, soups, sweets, and biscuits).[69] Under the protocol, Switzerland and the European Union granted duty-free treatment to the industrial component of the processed products and allowed a price compensation mechanism to offset price differentials in the agricultural raw materials.

In 2002, within the context of the second series of bilateral negotiations, Switzerland and the European Union agreed to revise the provisions under Protocol 2 to improve market access for processed agricultural products. The new protocol entered into force in February 2005.[70] The

---

68. Namely, citrus, kiwis, saffron, oranges, mandarins, melons, olives, certain processed tomato products, asparagus, and mushrooms.

69. This section is partly based on information provided by the Swiss Integration Office (2005).

70. Unlike many other bilateral agreements, these new provisions did not require public consultation in Switzerland, since they modified an existing agreement.

revisions simplified the price compensation mechanism and extended the scope of products covered under the agreement. Moreover, the revisions offer the potential for further liberalization. According to the Swiss Integration Office (2005c and 2005d), while Swiss concessions under the 1999 bilateral agreement amounted to an annual loss of nearly 115 million Swiss francs in tariff revenue, Swiss concessions under the new calculation of price differentials will amount to a loss of an additional 100 million Swiss francs.

The principle behind the price compensation mechanism, however, remains unchanged. The party with the higher price for agricultural raw materials (typically Switzerland) will be allowed to use a combination of tariffs and export subsidies to compensate producers of certain processed agricultural products for the use of higher-priced agricultural raw materials. However, under the revised protocol, only processed products based on specific raw materials—flour, dried milk, butter, and vegetable fat—will qualify for the mechanism. The revision also calculates the price-differential margin using bilateral rather than world prices as the benchmark. This change resulted in decreased tariffs faced by EU producers of processed agricultural products sold to Switzerland, and reduced export subsidies for Swiss processed agricultural products sold to the European Union. In exchange, the European Union agreed to fully eliminate tariffs and grant no further export subsidies for products listed under the revised protocol.

Many processed agricultural products still qualify for the compensating price mechanism under the revised protocol,[71] and several of these products receive exports subsidies under the *Loi Chocolatière*. Switzerland will grant duty-free treatment and eliminate export subsidies for all other processed food products listed under the revised protocol.[72]

Recommendations on Agricultural Market Access Barriers

It is useful to preview the calculations reported in chapter 8 on the possible gains in bilateral agricultural trade resulting from a Swiss-US FTA. Based on gravity model estimates, two-way agriculture trade might increase

---

71. Namely, butter and buttermilk, margarine, sugar confectionery, chocolate, malt extract, roasted cereals and corn flakes, preserved potatoes, nuts and peanut butter, tomato pastes and ketchup, pasta, biscuits, bread, cakes, pastries, ice cream, and ethyl alcohol.

72. Other processed agricultural products listed under the protocol are animal hairs and feathers, sweet corn, coffee, tea, mate, certain fresh and preserved vegetable products (HS 1401–1404 and HS 2001–08), certain oils and waxes, cocoa, mineral and other waters, beer, vermouths, spirits, and vinegar.

by as much as 140 percent if both partners totally eliminate their trade barriers. Based on computable general equilibrium model estimates, again assuming total elimination of market-access barriers, US exports to Switzerland of broadly defined agricultural products[73]—which are starting from a small base—might increase by more than five times, for a dollar increase of about $1.5 billion (see table 8.6). Similarly, Swiss agricultural exports to the United States—which start from a substantial base—might increase by about 100 percent, for a dollar increase of about $150 million (see again table 8.6). Of course, total elimination of agricultural trade barriers will not happen immediately, and phase-in periods will often be lengthy. Nevertheless, the prize, in expanded trade, is very large. We turn now to ambitious but still feasible recommendations for eventually eliminating many agricultural barriers.

The place to begin is to recognize that certain measures that indirectly limit imports are beyond the reach of a bilateral FTA, such as agricultural subsidies, whether the WTO "box" that categorizes them is amber, blue, or green. Subsidies will be reduced in size or shifted between boxes (e.g., from amber to green) only in the larger context of the WTO Doha Round. Based on precedent, neither EFTA nor US bilateral FTAs have any prospect of altering the size or changing the composition of agricultural subsidies.

Other market access barriers have a long history and are fiercely protected by domestic agricultural lobbies, however great the costs to society at large. In Switzerland, cows grazing at altitude fit this category.[74] In the United States, extremely restrictive cheese quotas are another classic example. Many previous trade agreements—the General Agreement on Tariffs and Trade (GATT), the WTO, and bilateral treaties—have failed to ease these barriers, which will certainly give Swiss-US FTA negotiators reason to pause. But past failures should not be an excuse for abandoning the quest. Rather, the most difficult agricultural products should be liberalized on very long timetables. Long phaseouts will give farm owners and workers time to find alternative land use and employment, and the government time to implement green payments as a means of income support. With

---

73. Namely, grains, oil seeds, fibers, other crops, animal products, wool, forestry, dairy, and food products.

74. A classic example, not of Swiss protection, but of German willingness to liberalize beef trade in a way that would pose no competitive threat in the German market, was the Swiss-German Commercial Treaty of 12 April 1904. A new German tariff concession was granted for "large dapple mountain cattle or brown cattle reared at a spot at least 300 meters above sea level and having at least one month's grazing each year at a spot at least 800 meters above sea level." Curzon (1965, 60) describes this provision as a "grotesque reclassification [designed to deprive Germany's other trading partners of] their most-favored-nation advantages [in existing trade agreements]."

these cautions in mind, we offer the following recommendations, starting with the United States and then Switzerland.

Recommendations for the United States

- The highest tariffs and most severe quotas in the US agricultural sector strictly limit imports of tobacco, peanuts, raw sugar, confectionary, cheese, and dairy (chapter appendix tables 2A.1, 2A.2, and 2A.3 and table 2.4). Apart from confectionary, cheese, and gourmet dairy, these measures have little commercial relevance to Switzerland because the products are neither present nor prospective Swiss exports. Nevertheless, to establish the right precedent, the United States should agree to phaseout all of its tariffs and quotas over a period of 20 years, while retaining special safeguards to deal with harm to US farmers during the transition period.

- Confectionary products are of considerable interest to Switzerland, but high tariffs and strict quotas limit US imports. For the next 10 years, Switzerland should be granted access for candy and confectionary that has sugar content over 10 percent, according to the best current FTA terms (the CUSFTA). Existing US quotas very possibly restrict imports of chocolate from Switzerland (chapter appendix table 2A.4). These should be aligned with quotas applied to candy imports from Canada. After 10 years, US duties on in-quota Swiss candy and confectionary should be removed, on a linear schedule, over the succeeding ten years. Quotas should be expanded by 10 percent of the base amount annually to double in 10 years. At that point, they should be abolished, so that within 20 years, Swiss candy and confectionary face no US market access barriers.

- Among agricultural exports, US market access barriers are highest for Swiss cheeses. Cheese tariffs generally range between 6 and 10 percent for in-quota imports (chapter appendix table 2A.3). These should be reduced to zero when the FTA is implemented.[75] The tariffs do transfer revenue from Swiss cheese producers to the US Treasury, but this sum is approximately $4.5 million annually, which the US Treasury can easily forego. Meanwhile, these tariffs have little protective effect, because US protection is largely accomplished by cheese quotas. For the three items listed in table 2A.3, quotas permit imports of 7,200

---

75. The US tariff on cheeses and substitutes with cows milk and butterfat, HTS 0406.90.97.00, is a relatively high $1.509 per kilogram. This HTS line item, which corresponds to common household cheeses that compete directly with US products, is also subject to safeguards.

metric tons annually. This figure should be increased by 10 percent of the base amount per year for the next 20 years, thereby tripling the quota to 21,600 metric tons. This corresponds to the phaseout for TRQs in CAFTA-DR, and is twice as fast as the agreed phaseout in the Australia-US FTA; however, rapid liberalization for Swiss cheese exports will play a central role in a balanced Swiss-US FTA. After 20 years, US quotas on Swiss cheese exports should be abolished, so that US cheese imports from Switzerland face no market access barriers. Similar tariff and quota terms should apply to other Swiss dairy exports.[76]

- Tobacco, peanuts, and other ultrasensitive agricultural products that have little or no commercial interest for Switzerland should be admitted on terms aligned with NAFTA and other US FTAs.[77] After 20 years, all US barriers should be abolished.

- Turning to the other extreme of protective barriers, among the top 30 products, the remaining Swiss agricultural exports to the United States face tariffs under 8 percent and are not limited by quotas (table 2A.3). Within five years, on a linear schedule, the United States should eliminate these duties on Swiss exports of these "other" agricultural exports—including products not listed in chapter appendix table 2A.3. An exception would be made when special circumstances bracket "other" exports in the same sensitive camp as tobacco, peanuts, raw sugar, confectionary, cheese, and dairy.

- To achieve a significant volume of trade, the United States and Switzerland will also need to reach a mutual recognition agreement as to the certification of "organic" products. These should benefit Swiss and US exports of dairy and other fresh items that were seen as potential Swiss exports and were scheduled in the Swiss-EU Bilateral Agreement on agriculture (e.g., fruits and vegetables).

- We acknowledge that the recommended phaseout of 20 years for the most important agricultural products is twice as long as the norm agreed to in the WTO Understanding on the Interpretation of Article

76. At present, dairy exports do not appear among the top 30 products exported by Switzerland to the United States. However, the potential US market for epicurean Swiss milk, cream, and butter is substantial; like cheese, these imports are strictly limited by high tariffs and strict quotas. Since common butterfat and milk powder are particularly sensitive for both countries, TRQ liberalization for these products might be back-loaded.

77. Chapter appendix table 2A.3 shows that exports of cigarettes (HS 2402) are the third-most important Swiss export to the world at the 6-digit HTS level. The US tariffs on these imports are high, and may be affecting trade, but they are not as high as they are for other tobacco-based products. In previous bilateral FTAs, the United States has dealt with tobacco through long TRQs.

XXIV. However, sensitive agricultural products, such as confectionary, cheese, and dairy, have been heavily protected since World War II, so a 10-year phaseout is unrealistically short. As explained in the text and appendix A, longer phaseouts are now customary in FTAs.

Recommendations for Switzerland

- Our recommendations are based on the proposition that Swiss citizens will accept that a free trade agreement with the United States commits both parties to eventual free trade in nearly all agricultural products. Exceptions will be strictly limited. In previous FTA negotiations, the United States has accepted (and imposed) indefinite protection on a very short list of agricultural items. Everything else is liberalized eventually, but often on long timetables. Special safeguards would be retained to redress harm to Swiss farmers during the transition period.

- The outer limit of agricultural exceptions in a Swiss-US FTA is probably defined by analogies to the exceptions and long phaseouts that the United States itself negotiated for sensitive products in prior FTA agreements (see appendix table A.1). NAFTA, the US-Australia FTA, and CAFTA-DR provide useful benchmarks for sensitivities, both in the United States and partner countries. In all three agreements, US liberalization of sugar is either very slow (with Mexico, 15 years and counting), or strictly limited (in CAFTA-DR, starting at 109,000 additional metric tons, relative to US annual consumption in excess of 9 million tons), or zero (in the Australia FTA). Cheese and dairy products are liberalized over very long periods (approximately 20 years) in the Australia FTA and in CAFTA-DR. Moreover, US imports are susceptible to hair-trigger safeguards. Finally, several FTAs liberalize US beef imports over long periods of time (approximately 15 to 18 years, most notably the Australia FTA), and again, imports are susceptible to hair-trigger safeguards.

- While all of Swiss agriculture is highly protected, beef and dairy appear to be the most sensitive products. Tariffs on the beef–dairy sector are high, and quotas are strict. The two are closely linked because in Switzerland, the same cows are often used for both dairy and meat. Domestic milk and butter sales both exceed beef sales in value. The sensitivity also reflects the multiple roles served by grazing cattle at high altitudes beyond their agricultural production, namely environmental care against mountain erosion and maintaining decentralized settlement in remote areas. Pork and poultry are almost as sensitive as the beef–dairy sector, though the "multifunctional" arguments are not nearly as strong.

- Swiss imports of dairy and meat products from the United States are quite modest, totaling under $30 million annually.[78] We recommend that Switzerland establish duty-free TRQs for US beef, most dairy items, and pork and poultry products that gradually expand to agreed percentages of the Swiss market over a 20-year time horizon. During this period, special agricultural safeguards would be available. At the end of the 20-year period, the market share caps would be subject to renegotiation.

- Corn, soybeans, and wheat are highly protected in the Swiss market. The Swiss-EU Bilateral Agricultural Agreement excludes them. Tariffs range high into double digits, and corn and wheat face quotas. Reflecting its own comparative advantage, the United States is very demanding on these products. Appendix table A.1 shows that the United States tries to obtain immediate free access, but did allow exceptions to Morocco and some CAFTA partners. The rationale for these exceptions does not apply to Switzerland.[79]

- In the case of Switzerland, however, protection for animal feeds (corn and soybeans) is closely linked to protection of livestock (cattle, pigs, and poultry). Therefore, we recommend that animal feed imports be liberalized, only somewhat faster (in line with Agricultural Policy 2011 recommendations) than liberalization of the beef–dairy, pork, and poultry markets. The idea is to reduce costs for livestock producers, but avoid a sharp dislocation in the relation between input prices (feedstuffs) and output prices (dairy and meats), so as to avoid excessively fast adjustment for grain farmers. Again, however, the goal should be substantial liberalization over 20 years, subject to special agricultural safeguards.

- Switzerland also applies TRQs to other agricultural products that are potentially interesting to US exporters—fruits, vegetables, wheat, and bread (chapter appendix table 2A.9). We recommend that all Swiss in-quota tariffs on US exports be decreased by 10 percent of the base level

---

78. For example, the US share of Switzerland's beef imports (HTS 0201 and 0202) decreased from $10.5 million in 2002 to $8.5 million in 2004, largely because of the beef hormone issue. Meanwhile, total Swiss imports of beef increased from $37 million to $58 million over the same period; Brazilian exports were particularly strong, rising from $20 million to $34 million. As a further comparison, the value of Swiss beef at the farm gate is about $365 annually, so total imports are less than 20 percent of domestic production.

79. For Morocco, the cited reason was that the Moroccan economy is heavily dependent on its agricultural sector to provide jobs and income; moreover, the Moroccan FTA was prompted by US concerns for stability and democracy in the Middle East. Exceptions under CAFTA reflect US recognition of the possible adverse impact of free trade on subsistence farmers.

each year, until they are phased-out in 10 years. We also recommend that the corresponding quotas assigned to US exports be expanded by 10 percent of the base amount each year, starting in year 10 and running until year 20—the same approach we suggest for US cheese imports. At the end of 20 years, the quotas should be abolished.

- That leaves a number of agricultural imports with varying tariff levels and no quotas. Most of the tariffs on the top 30 US exports are specific duties, expressed as Swiss francs per kilogram (chapter appendix table 2A.8). In many cases, the ad valorem equivalent exceeds 60 percent (chapter appendix table 2A.9). As before, we recommend that these tariffs be cut by 10 percent of the base amount annually until they are eliminated in 10 years.

- In previous negotiations, the United States has striven for at least equal preferential treatment that the FTA partner has previously granted to third parties, notably the European Union. Our recommendation on the "parity issue" is that Switzerland should, for the most part, immediately extend the same preference to the United States that it has already extended to the European Union. Exceptions to the principle of parity might be invoked when the United States cannot reciprocate the market access preference granted by Switzerland. However, these exceptions should apply to a limited number of products, such as cheese.

- We recognize that, for Swiss farmers, several of our recommendations may seem drastic, even though liberalization is phased over two decades. Hence, it is important to underline that we recommend special agricultural safeguards, with both price-based and volume-based triggers, so that the Swiss government can respond quickly to undue distress among its farmers and food processors. The FTA safeguards should be available for the entire 20-year transition period.

- After 20 years, the agricultural sector would still have recourse to WTO safeguards. In addition, we recommend that the agreement should offer the possibility, upon mutual agreement, of extending special safeguards beyond the transition period for products that are still highly sensitive. If special safeguards are granted an extended life after the transition period, however, their use should be accompanied by trade compensation to the other party.

- Finally, to accommodate concerns strongly felt by the Swiss public, we recommend that "food security," appropriately defined, should be a legitimate ground for invoking special safeguards by either party, both during the 20-year transition period and beyond. However, when food security is cited as a ground for limiting imports under the FTA, trade compensation should be paid to the other party.

As this chapter shows, both the United States and Switzerland protect agriculture in multiple ways, using barriers that have no ostensible purpose aside from protecting the agricultural sector. To a considerable extent, these restrictions limit bilateral trade in basic agricultural goods and processed foods, and reducing them will be at the core of the Swiss-US FTA, because they stick out like Alpine peaks and hinder substantial volumes of commerce at great cost to both countries. Related to these, however, are SPS measures and GIs, which are discussed in the next chapter.

Appendix 2A

Table 2A.1 US applied MFN tariffs for agricultural products, 2002 (HS 2-digit)

HS chapter	Product description	Number of lines		Simple average (percent)[a]	Standard deviation (percent)
		Ad valorem	Non ad valorem		
1	Live animals	20	8	1.1	2.0
2	Meat, edible offal	54	45	6.1	8.1
4	Dairy products	125	126	12.4	5.0
5	Animal products nes	20	1	0.6	1.4
6	Live trees, plants	20	8	2.9	2.5
7	Edible vegetables	78	89	9.0	7.4
8	Edible fruit, nuts	55	63	5.3	7.7
9	Coffee, tea, spices	40	7	0.7	1.7
10	Cereals	7	14	2.2	4.1
11	Milling products	19	19	4.2	4.2
12	Oil seeds	37	24	8.2	34.0
13	Lac, gums, resins	14	1	0.7	1.3
14	Vegetable plaiting	11	2	1.1	1.6
15	Fats, animal and vegetable	37	31	3.6	5.3
16	Meat, fish, preparations	81	9	4.2	5.5
17	Sugars	32	34	6.4	2.9
18	Cocoa and cocoa preparations	44	34	5.8	3.6
19	Cereal, flour, starch	52	18	9.0	5.9
20	Vegetable, fruit, preparations	106	77	11.1	21.5
21	Miscellaneous edible preparations	50	39	7.8	5.4
22	Beverages, vinegar	37	36	1.5	4.8
23	Residues, wastes	24	13	1.8	2.7
24	Tobacco	27	29	90.7	156.3
41[b]	Raw hides and skins	122	n.a.	2.4	1.6
43[b]	Furskins	22	n.a.	2.3	2.1
50[b]	Silk	13	n.a.	1.5	1.6
51[b]	Wool, animal hair	73	26	6.1	8.0
52[b]	Cotton	221	12	9.0	3.7
	Totals and averages	1,441	765	9.8	9.4

n.a. = not available; nes = not elsewhere specified. a. Includes ad valorem equivalents; b. All lines considered, including agricultural and nonagricultural products.

Source: WTO (2004c).

Table 2A.2 US tariff peaks in agriculture, 2002[a]

HS chapter	Product description	Number of tariff lines above 15 percent	Average peak[b]
52	Cotton (HS 5201–5203 only)	3	34.5
24	Tobacco and manufactured tobacco substitutes	14	187.5
23	Residues and prepared animal feed	1	17.0
22	Beverages, spirits, and vinegar	7	25.3
21	Miscellaneous edible preparations	23	33.8
20	Preparations of vegetables, fruit, nuts or other	24	36.2
19	Preparations of cereals, flour, starch, or milk	24	32.2
18	Cocoa and cocoa preparations	16	31.7
17	Sugars and sugar confectionery	12	49.0
16	Preparations of meat, fish, crustaceans, or other	5	36.5
15	Animal or vegetable fats, oils, and waxes	3	18.7
12	Oil seeds and oleaginous fruits and other	2	147.8
07	Edible fruit and nuts; peel of citrus fruit or melons	7	23.8
07	Edible vegetables and certain roots and tubers	16	22.1
04	Dairy items, of which	117	35.6
	Cheese	83	33.4
	Milk and cream	14	30.9
	Other dairy	20	47.8
02	Meat and edible meat offal	7	25.0

a. Tariff peaks are defined as tariffs above 15 percent on an ad valorem equivalent basis.
b. Average of all tariff lines above 15 percent, including on ad valorem equivalents.

Source: USITC (2005b).

Table 2A.3 US barriers on top 30 Swiss agricultural exports to the United States, 2004

Rank	HS code	Product description	Tariff rate (specific and ad valorem)	Quota (metric tons)	Swiss exports (millions of dollars)	Share (percent)	Cumulative share (percent)
1	2106.90.97	Food preparations, n/o 10 percent milk solids, o/10 percent sugar	13.2[a]	no	33.3	15	15
2	2101.11.29	Coffee, extracts, essences, and concentrates	Free	no	30.7	13	28
3	0406.90.95	Cheese and substitutes for cheese	10.0	1,720	20.1	9	37
4	0406.90.46	Swiss or Emmentaler cheese with eye formation	6.4	3,630	16.4	7	44
5	1806.90.90	Chocolate and preps w/cocoa, not for retail sale	6.0	no	12.0	5	50
6	1704.90.25	Cough drops, sugar confectionery, w/o cocoa	Free	no	8.1	4	53
7	3302.10.10	Mixtures of odoriferous substances	Free	no	7.9	3	57
8	2106.90.99	Other food preparations, not canned/frozen	6.4	no	6.4	3	59
9	1806.90.90	Chocolate and preps w/cocoa, not for retail sale	6.0	no	6.1	3	62
10	0406.90.97	Cheeses and substitutes with cow's milk and butterfat	23.2[a]	no	4.9	2	64
11	1806.31.00	Chocolate and other cocoa preparations in blocks/bars	5.6	no	4.1	2	66
12	1806.32.30	Chocolate, not filled, in blocks/bars	4.3	no	3.9	2	68
13	1905.31.00	Sweet biscuits	Free	no	3.7	2	69
14	1704.90.35	Sugar confections for consumption, w/cocoa	5.6	no	3.5	2	71
15	2104.10.00	Soups and broths and preparations thereof	3.2	no	2.9	1	72
16	0406.30.51	Gruyere cheese, processed, not grated/powdered	6.4	no	2.5	1	73
17	0406.90.90	Cheeses and substitutes for cheese	10.0	1,850	2.5	1	74
18	1905.90.10	Bread, pastry, cake, biscuits, and similar products	Free	no	2.2	1	75
19	1302.19.40	Ginseng; with anesthetic or therapeutic properties	1.0	no	2.1	1	76

(table continues next page)

Table 2A.3 US barriers on top 30 Swiss agricultural exports to the United States, 2004 *(continued)*

Rank	HS code	Product description	Tariff rate (specific and ad valorem)	Quota (metric tons)	Swiss exports (millions of dollars)	Share (percent)	Cumulative share (percent)
20	1803.10.00	Cocoa paste, not defatted	5.6	no	2.1	1	77
21	3301.12.00	Essential oils, of range	2.7	no	2.0	1	78
22	1302.19.90	Other vegetable saps and extracts	Free	no	2.0	1	70
23	2102.20.20	Yeasts, inactive (except dried brewers' yeast)	6.4	no	1.8	1	80
24	1806.32.90	Other chocolate, not filled in blocks/bars	6.0	no	1.7	1	80
25	3301.13.00	Lemon oil	3.8	no	1.7	1	81
26	0901.12.00	Coffee, decaffeinated, not roasted	Free	no	1.6	1	82
27	0901.21.00	Coffee, roasted, not decaffeinated	Free	no	1.6	1	83
28	1904.20.10	Preparations from cereal flakes, airtight containers	5.6	no	1.5	1	83
29	1515.90.20	Nut oils	Free	no	1.3	1	84
30	0712.90.74	Tomatoes, dried, in powder	7.8	no	1.3	1	84
		Subtotal of top 30 agricultural products			192.0	84	84
		All other agricultural products			36.7	16	100
		Total agricultural products			228.6	100	100

a. These figures are 2002 ad valorem equivalents, as the United States applies specific tariffs. Safeguards pursuant to Article 5 of the Agreement on Agriculture have been invoked for imports of these products. Information on additional rates is available in Chapter 99 of the 2005 US Tariff Schedule.

Sources: FAS (2005) and USITC (2005b).

Table 2A.4 US tariff-rate quotas, 2002[a] (metric tons unless otherwise stated)

Product description	Average out-of-quota tariff rate (percent)[b]	Bound import quota	Fill ratio (percent)[c]
Beef: Fresh, chilled, or frozen	26.4	696,621	83
Cream (hectolitres)	26.8	6,695	65
Evaporated/condensed milk	26.6	6,857	87
Nonfat dried milk	52.6	5,261	98
Dried whole milk	53.8	3,321	96
Dried whey/buttermilk	6.8	296	22
Butter	59.5	6,977	98
Butter oil/substitutes	98.0	6,080	100
Dairy mixtures	37.0	4,105	100
Blue cheese	39.0	2,911	97
Cheddar cheese	30.5	13,256	98
American-type cheese	58.4	3,523	99
Edam and Gouda cheese	50.3	6,816	98
Italian-type cheese	48.1	13,481	99
Swiss/Emmental cheese[d]	42.4	34,475	83
Gruyere process cheese[e]	46.7	7,855	86
Other cheese NSPF[f]	35.7	48,628	99
Lowfat cheese	32.9	5,475	65
Peanuts	139.8	52,906	100
Chocolate crumbs	15.1	26,168	79
Infant formula containing oligo saccharides	64.8	100	100
Place-packed stuffed olives	2.0	2,700	31
Green olives, other	2.7	550	69
Green whole olives	4.3	4,400	19
Mandarin oranges (Satsuma)	0.4	40,000	100
Peanut butter and paste	131.8	20,000	78
Ice cream (hectolitres)	30.4	5,668	57
Raw cane sugar	48.8	1,117,000	81
Other cane or beet sugars or syrups	49.8	22,000	151
Other mixtures over 10 percent sugar	19.6	64,709	99
Sweetened cocoa powder	18.8	2,313	15
Mixes and doughs	25.8	5,398	100
Mixed condiments and seasonings	13.1	689	45
Tobacco	350.0	150,700	75
Long staple cotton	3.0	40,100	13
Cotton, processed but not spun	29.0	3	100

NSPF = not specifically provided for

a. Listing of tariff with 2002 fill ratios above 10 percent. Quotas with 2002 fill rates below 10 percent applied to dried cream, low-fat chocolate, green olives, animal feed containing milk, four different types of cotton.
b. Average based on ad valorem rates or on ad valorem equivalents provided by the authorities.
c. Calculated as ratio of actual import volumes to bound import quota.
d. Switzerland is allocated 10.6 percent of bound import quota.
e. Switzerland is allocated 16 percent of bound import quota.
f. Switzerland is allocated 3.6 percent of bound import quota.

Source: WTO (2004c).

Table 2A.5 Swiss applied MFN tariffs for agriculture, 2004

HS chapter	Product	Total number of 2-digit lines	Average tariff (AVE, percent)	Standard deviation (percent)
1	Live animals	32	47.1	81.4
2	Meat, edible offal	99	143.6	280.1
3	Fish, crustaceans	106	0.2	0.6
4	Dairy products	62	72.0	107.8
5	Animal products	30	3.2	9.9
6	Live trees, plants	51	34.1	82.8
7	Edible vegetables	277	47.9	77.1
8	Edible fruit, nuts	112	14.6	38.5
9	Coffee, tea, spices	38	1.9	4.1
10	Cereals	82	42.8	63.5
11	Milling products	156	65.7	79.1
12	Oil seed	211	6.9	15.6
13	Lac, gums, resins	18	2.1	7.9
14	Vegetable plaiting	10	0.3	0.8
15	Fats, animal, and vegetable	175	48.7	54.7
16	Meat, fish, preparations	43	25.6	39.4
17	Sugars	56	15.3	20.0
18	Cocoa and cocoa preparations	35	13.3	11.4
19	Cereal, flour, starch	88	31.4	35.6
20	Vegetable, fruit, preparations	134	22.5	39.1
21	Miscellaneous edible preparations	46	12.1	9.9
22	Beverages, vinegar	58	14.9	15.3
23	Residues, wastes	72	12.2	30.6
24	Tobacco	15	10.0	11.0
41[a]	Raw hides and skins	38	1.1	2.0
43[a]	Furskins	14	0.9	1.7
44[a]	Wood	92	3.1	3.4
50[a]	Silk	18	1.8	1.9
51[a]	Wool, animal hair	56	1.8	1.8
52[a]	Cotton	180	3.7	2.0

AVE = ad valorem equivalent

a. All lines considered, including nonagricultural products.

Source: WTO (2004b).

Table 2A.6 Swiss tariff peaks in agriculture, 2004

Harmonized system number	Product description	Number of tariff lines above 50 percent	Average peak, AVE basis[a]
0101	Live horses, asses, mules, and hinnies	3	148.7
0102	Live bovine animals	3	78.2
0103	Live swine	2	226.0
0104	Live sheep and goats	1	59.0
0201	Meat of bovine animals	5	109.1
0202	Meat of bovine animals	3	334.7
0203	Meat of swine	3	150.9
0204	Meat of sheep or goats	3	79.3
0206	Edible offal, fresh	12	346.1
0207	Meat and edible offal, of poultry	16	261.8
0210	Meat offal, salted, dried, or smoked	5	116.0
0401	Milk and cream, no sugar	2	348.8
0402	Milk and cream, with sugar	8	170.9
0403	Buttermilk, cream, and yogurt	6	159.2
0404	Whey and dairy products not elsewhere specified	1	100.0
0405	Butter, oils, and other fats derived from milk	3	72.4
0406	Cheese and curd	2	54.6
0408	Birds' eggs, not in shell, and egg yolks	1	60.5
0511	Animal products not elsewhere included	1	50.0
0602	Other live plants, cuttings, and slips	5	129.0
0603	Cut flowers for bouquets or ornamental purposes	3	278.0
0701	Potatoes, fresh or chilled	1	63.9
0702	Tomatoes, fresh or chilled	4	144.7
0703	Onions, shallots, garlic, leeks, etc.	9	178.8
0704	Cabbages, cauliflowers, kohlrabi, kale, etc.	9	103.9
0705	Lettuce and chicory	15	146.7
0706	Carrots, turnips, and similar edible roots	7	152.9
0707	Cucumbers and gherkins	3	107.3
0709	Other vegetables	2	124.9
0710	Vegetables, uncooked or boiled	8	93.1
0806	Grapes	1	295.3
0808	Apples, pears, and quinces	5	96.1
0809	Apricots, cherries, peaches, plums, and sloes	4	67.4
0810	Other fruit	2	62.2
1001	Wheat and meslin	5	147.4
1002	Rye	3	106.0
1003	Barley	3	151.5

(table continues next page)

Table 2A.6 Swiss tariff peaks in agriculture, 2004 *(continued)*

Harmonized system number	Product description	Number of tariff lines above 50 percent	Average peak, AVE basis[a]
1004	Oats	2	68.5
1005	Maize (corn)	1	70.9
1006	Rice	1	65.7
1007	Grain sorghum	1	72.1
1008	Buckwheat, seeds, other cereals	6	59.1
1101	Wheat or meslin flour	1	381.8
1102	Cereal flours other than of wheat or meslin	5	91.6
1103	Cereal groats, meal, and pellets	8	133.1
1104	Cereal grains otherwise worked	19	111.3
1105	Flour, meal, powder, flakes, of potatoes	2	236.8
1107	Malt, roasted or not	7	127.9
1205	Rape or colza seeds, broken or not	1	79.6
1206	Sunflower seeds, whether or not broken	1	79.5
1214	Forage products	1	57.3
1501	Pig fat and poultry fat	3	67.4
1502	Fats of bovine animals, sheep, or goats	2	137.3
1503	Lard stearin, lard oil, oleostearin, and tallow oil	2	99.7
1504	Fats and oils, of fish or marine mammals	2	72.9
1507	Soybean oil	5	136.8
1508	Ground-nut oil	4	83.7
1511	Palm oil	5	113.4
1512	Sunflower-seed, safflower, or cottonseed oil	6	113.3
1513	Coconut, palm kernel, or babassu oil	9	132.9
1514	Rape, colza, or mustard oil	5	116.7
1515	Other fixed vegetable fats and oils	6	105.4
1516	Animal or vegetable fats and oils	3	95.0
1517	Margarine; edible preparations of fats or oils	4	76.7
1601	Sausages of meat, meat offal, or blood	3	118.1
1602	Other prepared meat, meat offal, or blood	9	70.2
1701	Cane or beet sugar and pure sucrose, solid	2	97.0
1806	Chocolate; food preparations with cocoa	1	50.9
1901	Malt extract; flour and starch preparations with cocoa	9	91.6
1904	Food preparations from swelling or roasting cereal	1	168.5

(table continues next page)

Table 2A.6 *(continued)*

Harmonized system number	Product description	Number of tariff lines above 50 percent	Average peak, AVE basis[a]
1905	Bread, pastry, cakes, biscuits, etc.	1	100.4
2004	Other vegetables, preserved by vinegar	2	101.6
2005	Other vegetables, not preserved by vinegar	2	119.3
2009	Fruit and vegetable juices	7	146.4
2202	Waters; mineral and aerated, with sugar	1	54.7
2204	Wine of fresh grapes	1	58.0
2302	Bran, sharps, and other residues	1	72.5
2303	Residues of starch manufacture	1	88.2
2308	Vegetable materials, waste, residues	1	130.8
2309	Animal feeding preparations	1	167.6
3501	Casein, caseinates, and derivatives	1	65.2
3502	Albumins, albuminates, and derivatives	1	208.2
	Average	4.0	125.3

a. Average of all tariff lines above 50 percent within 4-digit category. Ad valorem equivalents (AVEs) reported.

Source: WTO estimates, based on data provided by the Swiss authorities; WTO (2004b).

Table 2A.7 Swiss consumer prices of selected agricultural products, 2003 (Swiss francs per kilogram, unless specified)

Product	Switzerland	EU-4[a]	United States	Swiss price as percent of EU-4 = 100	Swiss price as percent of US = 100
Apples, Golden Delicious	3.67	2.76	2.91	133	126
Bananas	3.06	2.15	1.51	142	203
Butter	11.97	7.94	8.34	151	144
Carrots	2.26	1.44	n.a.	157	n.a.
Cheese	20.89	12.82	11.71	163	178
Cream	2.91	0.95	n.a.	306	n.a.
Eggs	0.61	0.26	0.12	235	508
Fresh chicken	8.90	5.20	3.07	171	290
Ham	29.99	21.01	8.57	143	350
Milk (Swiss francs per litre)	1.53	1.16	0.98	132	156
Onions	2.39	1.70	2.42	141	99
Pears	3.69	2.97	2.94	124	126
Pork chops	21.32	9.65	9.27	221	230
Potatoes	2.16	1.16	1.36	186	159
Roast beef	27.16	15.37	10.94	177	248
Roast pork	19.90	11.44	n.a.	174	n.a.
Sugar	1.59	1.51	1.25	105	127
Tomatoes	3.67	3.60	4.48	102	82
Vegetable oil	4.30	2.48	3.37	173	128
White bread	1.80	1.56	1.48	115	122
White flour	1.71	0.94	0.92	182	186
Unweighted average				163	192

n.a. = not available

a. The EU-4 are Switzerland's neighboring countries: Austria, France, Germany, and Italy.

Source: WTO (2004b).

Table 2A.8 Swiss barriers on the top 30 US agricultural exports to Switzerland, 2004

Rank	HS code	Product description	Tariff rate[a] Swiss francs per 100 kilograms	Ad valorem equivalent (percent)	Quota[b]	US exports (millions of dollars)	Share (percent)	Cumulative share (percent)
1	5201.00.10	Cotton, not carded or combed, length 25 to 28mm	Free	Free	No	23.5	15	15
2	2401.20.80	Tobacco, flue-cured, threshed or similarly processed	25	3.7	No	19.2	13	28
3	2204.21.40	Wine of fresh grapes, alcoholic strength below 14 percent	47.2	26.9	Yes[c]	13.7	9	37
4	2401.20.80	Tobacco, burley, threshed, stemmed/stripped	25	3.7	No	10.5	7	44
5	0205.00.00	Meat of horses, asses, mules	740	154.4	Yes[d]	9.2	6	50
6	0709.20.00	Asparagus, fresh or chilled	370	56.9	Yes[e]	7.0	5	54
7	0802.12.00	Almonds, fresh or dried, shelled	Free	Free	No	6.0	4	58
8	0201.30.35	Meat of bovine animals, boneless	1210	183.2	Yes[d]	4.8	3	61
9	3302.10.00	Mixture of odoriferous substance and mixture	37	1.6	No	4.8	3	65
10	3301.12.00	Essential citrus fruit oils	1	0.3	No	3.8	3	67
11	0806.20.00	Grapes, dried	Free	Free	No	3.5	2	69
12	1515.90.80	Fixed vegetable fats and oils not chemically modified	153	33.8	No	3.4	2	72
13	0802.32.00	Walnuts, fresh or dried, shelled	19	1.6	No	2.7	2	73
14	3301.29.60	Essential oils, except those of citrus fruit	7	0.3	No	2.5	2	75
15	1006.30.10	Rice, semi- or wholly milled, parboiled	15	4.0	No	2.0	1	76
16	1006.20.40	Rice, long grain, husked (brown)	14	5.8	No	1.8	1	78
17	0804.10.00	Dates, fresh or dried	5	1.6	No	1.6	1	79
18	3301.19.00	Essential oils of citrus fruit	1	0.0	No	1.4	1	80

(table continues next page)

Table 2A.8 Swiss barriers on the top 30 US agricultural exports to Switzerland, 2004 *(continued)*

Rank	HS code	Product description	Tariff rate[a] Swiss francs per 100 kilograms	Tariff rate[a] Ad valorem equivalent (percent)	Quota[b]	US exports (millions of dollars)	Share (percent)	Cumulative share (percent)
19	0511.10.00	Bovine semen	3	33.1	Yes[f]	1.4	1	80
20	3301.24.00	Essential oils of peppermint	3	0.1	No	1.3	1	81
21	2401.20.80	Tobacco, partly or wholly stemmed/stripped	25	3.1	No	1.3	1	82
22	2005.80.00	Sweet corn	Free	Free	No	1.3	1	83
23	3507.90.70	Enzymes; prepared, not elsewhere specified	24	1.1	No	1.1	1	84
24	0802.50.20	Pistachios	Free	Free	No	0.9	1	84
25	0805.40.00	Grapefruit, fresh	2	1.82	No	0.9	1	85
26	2309.10.00	Dog and cat food	5.9	48.1	No	0.9	1	85
27	0202.20.60	Meat of bovine animals, with bone	721	132.6	Yes[d]	0.8	1	86
28	1006.30.10	Rice, semi- or wholly milled	15.3	4.0	No	0.8	1	86
29	1704.90.30	Sugar confectionery, not containing cocoa	103.5	31.5	No	0.7	0	87
30	4101.50.10	Raw hides and skins of bovine or equine, above 16kg	Free	Free	No	0.7	0	87
		Subtotal of top 30 agricultural products				133.4	87	87
		Total agricultural products				151.6	100	100

a. Average of 6-digit level lines in the Swiss schedule, corresponding to US product at 6-digit level. In instances when the position was not available at digits, 4-digit averages were used. The ad valorem equivalents correspond to data at 6-digit level reported by UNCTAD.

b. The 6-digit level of the Swiss schedule lists a number of lines subject to quotas.

c. See quotas 23, 24, or 25 in table 2A.9.

d. See quota 05 in table 2A.9.

e. See quota 15 in table 2A.9.

f. See quota 12 in table 2A.9.

Sources: FAS (2005), Switzerland Customs (2005), UNCTAD (2005).

Table 2A.9 Swiss over-quota tariff rates for TRQ imports, 2004

Quota number	Product description	Average out-of-quota rate[a] (percent)	Fill ratio, 2002[b] (percent)
01	Live horses, asses, mules, and hinnies	85.6	88
02	Live bovines	59.4	2,465
03	Live swine	226.0	0
04	Live goats and sheep	46.4	110
05	Meat (beef, sheep, goat, horse)	173.5	115
06	Other meat (pork and poultry)	153.1	96
07	Dairy products, in milk equivalent	71.7	84
08	Casein	33.5	60
09	Birds' eggs, in shell	34.2	81
10	Dried egg products	36.8	90
11	Other egg products	94.8	170
12	Bull sperm	50.0	3,095
13	Cut flowers	335.9	161
14	Potatoes and products	80.7	132
15	Vegetables	125.4	126
16	Frozen vegetables	105.0	119
17	Fresh apples, pears, quinces	85.8	109
18	Fresh apricots, cherries, plums, etc.	58.5	109
19	Other fresh fruit	45.4	90
20	Fruit for cider	78.4	62
21	Products from fruit with pips	57.1	269
22	Grapes for pressing and grape juice	143.3	87
23	White wine in bottles	39.7	106
24	Red wine, other than industrial wine	13.2	106
25	White wine, in bulk	58.0	106
26	Durum wheat, undenatured	199.7	95
27	Bread and other cereals for human consumption	120.4	82
28	Coarse grains for human consumption	112.6	60

a. Averages are based on ad valorem equivalents.
b. The fill ratio expresses imports as a percentage of in-quota import limit. A fill ratio above 100 percent indicates that the out-of quota tariff rates are determining prices within Switzerland.
Source: WTO (2004b).

3

Issues Linked to Agriculture

Sanitary and phytosanitary (SPS) and geographical indication (GI) issues are both closely related to agricultural trade. Though SPS and GI measures reflect nontrade-related objectives—notably, ensuring animal and human health, and safeguarding know-how and high standards of product quality—at times, they are viewed as behind-the-border or nontariff barriers. The United States and Switzerland have searched for common ground on SPS and GI issues, both in the framework of the World Trade Organization (WTO), other international organizations (e.g., World Organization for Annual Health, known in French as Office International des Epizooties [OIE]) and with their bilateral partners in free trade agreements (FTAs). However, both countries have well-established doctrines, and their differing stances are buttressed by commercial interests and entrenched bureaucracies.

These differences have led, on a few occasions, to disputes between Switzerland and the United States. This chapter illuminates regulatory differences and examines US and Swiss approaches to SPS and GI issues. We address SPS measures first and then focus on GI issues, offering recommendations at the end of each section.

Sanitary and Phytosanitary Measures

As mentioned above, SPS measures are sometimes viewed as behind-the-border trade barriers. The WTO *Trade Policy Review* (WTO 2004c) on the United States cites "actions targeted to safeguard consumer health one of the most frequent reasons behind most US quantitative restrictions and controls on trade." Likewise, some countries, including the United States, have voiced concerns about certain Swiss SPS measures.

Modern FTAs have typically addressed SPS matters, and if the Swiss-US FTA is to be a forward-looking agreement, it will also have to tackle this topic. In the following sections, we present each country's approach to dealing with SPS matters in past trade agreements. Then we discuss current SPS, labeling, and standards issues that affect agricultural trade. Finally, we offer recommendations for addressing these matters in the Swiss-US FTA. Unlike the section on GIs, we do not describe the SPS regimes of each country, as this has been done already and in detail by the WTO in its *Trade Policy Reviews* for both countries.

SPS Measures in US Trade Agreements

The United States has addressed SPS matters through various approaches that, on top of WTO multilateral agreements, include bilateral FTAs, veterinary agreements, memoranda of understanding (MoUs), and institutionalized dialogue. Appendix B deals with the fine print of the SPS chapters of selected examples of those documents. Here, we present a general overview of the US negotiating stance on SPS matters.

The SPS chapter in the North American Free Trade Agreement (NAFTA) constitutes the most comprehensive set of commitments that the United States has agreed to on a bilateral basis. NAFTA's SPS provisions encourage equivalent SPS measures and the use of international or North American standards for risk assessment, establish rules regarding pest-free areas, and require transparency in adopting and modifying SPS measures. At the same time, NAFTA reaffirms each party's right to adopt the level of SPS protection that it considers necessary. However, measures must be based on scientific principles and proper risk assessment, be applied only to the extent necessary to secure the desired level of protection, and should not result in unfair discrimination.

Recent US bilateral FTAs are generally less ambitious in their treatment of SPS questions, though they differ from one another. Regarding agriculture matters in FTA negotiations, the United States has been primarily interested in reducing traditional tariff and quota barriers, while SPS issues have received secondary attention. When the United States does attend to them, it has concentrated on outstanding SPS issues rather than raising new issues of possible future concern. The US Animal and Plant Health Inspection Service (APHIS) concludes that SPS issues typically raised by US partners "exceed the number of issues that APHIS can realistically deal with given other priorities" (US APHIS 2004, 2). By contrast, US partners often put a higher priority on SPS issues.

Reflecting the US negotiating stance, US bilateral FTAs generally reaffirm the parties' obligations under the WTO SPS Agreement, and establish the WTO dispute settlement mechanism as the appropriate body for bilateral SPS disputes. Since SPS chapters in recent US bilateral FTAs create no new SPS rights or obligations, US officials believe that there is no need for a bilateral dispute settlement mechanism.

In most negotiations, the United States and its negotiating partner instead established an ad hoc special group to focus on outstanding SPS issues.[1] These special groups worked to find technical solutions to specific SPS measures prior to congressional ratification of the FTA. Some of these groups made considerable progress.[2]

The United States views the actual existence of irritating SPS measures as a prerequisite to establishing ad hoc bodies.[3] As pointed out later in this section, such irritants appear in bilateral trade relations between the United States and Switzerland. Examples of concrete SPS issues addressed by previous SPS bodies include recognition of equivalence of regulatory requirements for specific products, mutual recognition of inspection systems, recognition of pest-free status, and acceptance of product inspection in the exporting country.[4]

The SPS chapters in US bilateral FTAs often establish bodies, named SPS Committees, to create a shared understanding of regulatory procedures and resolve outstanding bilateral SPS issues. These bodies continue the efforts of the ad hoc working groups formed during FTA negotiations; such committees have formed for the Central American–Dominican Republic Free Trade Agreement (CAFTA-DR) as well as the US-Chile and US-Australia FTAs. The US-Morocco FTA did not establish an SPS committee due to the relatively small volume of bilateral agricultural trade and low frequency of bilateral SPS issues.

Though SPS Committees are not decision making bodies, they are expected to "provide a forum for the parties to engage at the earliest appropriate time in each other's regulatory processes on and to cooperate in developing science-based measures that facilitate trade between them" (US APHIS 2004, 3). The US-Australia FTA contains some of the strongest language on the attributes of an SPS Committee, mandating it to review progress and resolve specific SPS matters.

US authorities sometimes cite different levels of SPS infrastructure in partner countries as an impediment to progress in dealing with outstanding SPS issues, arguing that countries without strong SPS infrastructure cannot meet the requirements of US SPS regulations or fully implement the WTO agreement.[5] This is evidently not the situation with Switzerland. But

---

1. For the most part, ad hoc SPS groups were not considered negotiating groups, though they held meetings in the same time frame as negotiating groups did.

2. For example, the ad hoc special group on SPS matters established for the US-Chile negotiations resolved several outstanding issues (see appendix B).

3. The "lack of substantive issues" was cited as the reason for the US reluctance to establish formal mechanisms to address SPS measures with Morocco (US APHIS 2004, 8).

4. Appendix B gives more information.

5. Negotiations with countries that have a relatively poor SPS infrastructure often involve some commitment of US aid to upgrade the local SPS regime.

it is worth noting that FTA negotiations with countries that enjoy stronger SPS infrastructure, such as Chile and Australia, delivered comparatively better results.

The US-EU Veterinary Agreement also establishes a committee to oversee SPS matters. However, the scope of this committee reflects the more limited nature of the agreement, which is largely confined to trade in certain live animals and bovine and swine meat. For these products, the agreement recognizes the equivalence of regulatory requirements and the health status of regions as determined by the exporting country.[6] The United States and European Union have also addressed outstanding SPS matters on products not covered by the agreement in the Positive Economic Agenda Initiative.

The United States has also dealt bilaterally with SPS issues through MoUs. Some memoranda establish consultative committees on agriculture, with mandates to resolve trade issues and increase cooperation in a number of areas, including sanitary and phytosanitary measures.

SPS Measures in Swiss Trade Agreements

Switzerland has dealt with SPS matters at the multilateral, regional, and bilateral level. At the multilateral level, Switzerland has implemented the SPS Agreement under the WTO Agreement. At the regional level, it has made substantial progress in harmonizing its SPS regime with the European Union's. And at the bilateral level, as a member of the European Free Trade Association (EFTA), Switzerland has reaffirmed its commitments under the WTO.

Switzerland's decision to harmonize aspects of its SPS regime with the European Union's has to be seen as an important component of the broader context of special relations.

The European Union is the principal source of Swiss imports and destination for Swiss exports, and though Switzerland has fostered economic integration with its neighbors, it has stopped short of full EU membership.[7] Formal links between the European Union and Switzerland are governed by a large number of agreements; indeed, no other third country has as many agreements with the European Union as Switzerland does.[8] In addition to facilitating trade, harmonizing SPS regimes in Europe has promoted

---

6. The recognition of the health status of regions as determined by the exporting country is limited to the list of diseases included in Annex III. Bovine spongiform encephalopathy (BSE) is not listed in that annex. Nevertheless, the European Commission (2004a, 36) argues that, "the United States has failed repeatedly to apply the regionalisation provisions of the Veterinary Agreement."

7. In 2004, the European Union was the destination for more than 60 percent of Swiss exports and the source of nearly 80 percent of Swiss imports.

8. The Web site of the Swiss Integration Office provides a vast selection of official documents and a brief explanation of Switzerland's European policy, available at www.europa.admin.ch.

the adoption of international standards. There are very few regional phytosanitary standards left in Europe that differ from the International Plant Protection Convention (IPPC) standards and procedures.

Annexes 4 and 6 (on plant health and seeds) and Annex 11 (veterinary) in the Swiss-EU Agreement on Trade in Agricultural Products regulate trade in certain plants, seeds, live animals, animal products, foods of animal origin, and animal waste. Both annexes recognize the equivalence of SPS protection levels resulting from the parties' domestic legislation for many of these products, notably dairy items. Additionally, Annex 5 (on feed products) aims to recognize legislative equivalence to facilitate trade in feed products. This annex, however, is still under negotiation.

The veterinary annex eliminates border checks. Controls other than mere inspection of accompanying certificates will now be conducted within the country. The annex on plant health also limits the scope of border checks to low percentages of consignments. Plants designated under Annex 4 will obtain a "plant passport," certifying conformity with domestic legislation.

When the agreement entered into force in June 2002, the recognition of equivalence of legislation did not apply to all of the products covered under the agreement. Milk and dairy products were the only foods of animal origin for which the European Union recognized the equivalence of Swiss legislation. Progress in recognizing equivalence of SPS legislation for a number of products required adapting certain aspects of Swiss legislation to the format and substance of EU legislation (WTO 2004b).

Joint committees will oversee the application and functioning of Annexes 4, 6, and 11 of the agreement. A working group on bovine spongiform encephalopathy (BSE) was established by the Joint Committee under the Veterinary Annex to analyze alternatives to the EU ban on Swiss exports of cattle. At the end of 2003, the EU Council of Agricultural Ministers recognized the equivalence of Swiss regulations regarding BSE.

Recent bilateral FTAs negotiated by EFTA include, for the most part, much weaker approaches to tackling SPS matters. SPS provisions in many EFTA agreements involve reaffirmation of the WTO agreement, commitments to apply SPS regulations in a nondiscriminatory fashion, and pledges not to introduce new measures that may have the effect of "unduly obstructing trade"(EFTA 2002a). The EFTA approach to SPS matters probably reflects the absence of outstanding SPS issues and the small volume of bilateral agricultural trade between EFTA and its partners. Also, agricultural liberalization has not been a high concern for Switzerland in its bilateral FTAs through EFTA, as evidenced by the low wedge between applied preferential and MFN tariff rates. (Appendix B gives more detail on the bilateral EFTA agreements.)

The EFTA-Chile FTA goes beyond other EFTA bilateral FTAs, as parties pledge to strengthen their cooperation in the field of SPS measures with a view toward increasing mutual understanding of their respective systems. The EFTA-Chile FTA also establishes an ad hoc mechanism to review SPS measures that parties believe have an effect on market access. Still, the text establishing that mechanism is weaker than similar mechanisms established in US bilateral FTAs.

Summing up, the US and Swiss approach to SPS matters on bilateral FTAs share a number of important similarities. Leaving aside the Swiss relation with the European Union, both countries have avoided introducing new SPS-related rights and obligations in bilateral agreements, as they both believe that the WTO remains the central forum for discussing SPS issues and settling SPS disputes. The United States, however, favors SPS chapters that reflect a stronger commitment to dealing with outstanding bilateral SPS issues. In this respect, it is worth highlighting the EFTA-Chile FTA as an important precedent for EFTA efforts to address SPS measures. The Swiss-US FTA should include similar commitments. With that objective in mind, we turn now to a review of issues that need to be tackled.

Outstanding SPS Issues on the Bilateral Swiss-US Agenda

Given that the United States and Switzerland both view the WTO as the central forum for discussing SPS matters, it is important to recognize that many outstanding SPS issues on the bilateral agenda are already being addressed. In the WTO, both countries are currently engaged in reaching common approaches on hormone-treated beef, genetically modified organisms (GMOs), and process and production methods (PPM).

FTA negotiations between Switzerland and the United States could search for common ground on these topics. It is unrealistic to expect that the FTA itself can resolve these issues, but recognizing this need not devalue the SPS chapter in the Swiss-US FTA. We first review the most relevant SPS issues on the bilateral agenda, then recommend ways to address them.

Some US products derived from biotechnology face case-by-case Swiss approval, requiring detailed information on the process for creating biotech products. Swiss certificates for approval of agricultural biotechnology products are valid for five years, and then must be renewed. Under this system, some US firms, such as those in the animal feed industry, have enjoyed market access for bioengineered products, while others, such as those in the creation of biotech crops, face difficult approval hurdles.[9]

The United States considers that Swiss regulations on meat from animals treated with hormones, antibiotics, and similar products are not

---

9. Even so, the most significant barriers for biotechnology products in Switzerland stem from the attitudes of highly skeptical consumers, farmers, and food retailers—not the Swiss government. In recent years, a coalition of environmental groups, consumers, and farmers has actively petitioned for a five-year moratorium on genetically modified (GM) crops in Switzerland. The Swiss Parliament has rejected this petition twice on grounds that the existing legislation adequately protects humans, animals, and the environment. However, the initiative was put to popular vote in November 27, 2005, and almost 56 percent of voters supported the interdiction. Swiss farmers will not be allowed to grow GM crops until 2010. For more information see www.lemonde.fr.

based on sound science or proper risk assessment. Moreover, the United States argues that, since tougher requirements are applied to out-of-quota meat imported under the tariff rate quota (TRQ), there is a question mark on the validity of the public health objective (WTO 2004a, 2005b).

Some US producers complain that the Swiss Veterinary Agency refuses to list new US meatpacking facilities as eligible to export beef to Switzerland. The United States Trade Representative (USTR 2005b) mentions that "despite repeated requests, has not produced science-based reasons for this position. Swiss inaction has blocked three plants that the United States requested be listed since early 2002."

A potential source of disagreement might result from Switzerland's sympathy for the precautionary principle as a legitimate risk management approach to protect human, animal, and plant health.[10] Powerful players in the US private sector[11] are highly skeptical of the precautionary principle, and the US government "has often charged against its implementation" (Graham 2003). However, no bilateral SPS issues have resulted from Swiss SPS measures based on it. In fact, Switzerland has not invoked the precautionary principle in its own SPS system, and though the possibility is not foreclosed, differences regarding the application of this principle should not stand in the way of successful negotiations. Both Switzerland and the United States have avoided discussion of the rights and obligations raised by the precautionary principle in their previous FTA negotiations.

Meanwhile, Switzerland objects to US import restrictions on meat and meat products. Following the BSE outbreak in Switzerland, the United States banned imports of Swiss meat and meat products (WTO 2002b). The Swiss government questions many elements of that measure: the disregard of international standards, the application of a double inspection procedure, and the US failures to recognize Switzerland's low incidence of BSE

---

10. The Swiss Agricultural Act revised as part of the 2007 Agricultural Policy defines the precautionary principle as follows:

> Precautionary measures may be adopted if it appears plausible that a farming product or plant material, which can be a carrier of particularly dangerous pests, can have an unacceptable side-effect for human, animal or plant health or the environment, and the likelihood of occurrence is assessed as considerable or the corresponding consequences are far-reaching yet the scientific information for a comprehensive risk assessment of the agricultural product or plant material is insufficient (Swiss Federal Office of Public Health 2003, 9).

11. The US Chamber of Commerce's strategy is to "oppose the domestic and international adoption of the precautionary principle as a basis for regulatory decision making" (US Chamber of Commerce 2004).

12. Switzerland is not the only country to voice concerns regarding BSE-related measures in the United States. The European Union largely shares Swiss views, while Canadian authorities have criticized the United States for slow rule-making to resume trade in live cattle (USDA 2005a).

and to stick to the agreed road map.[12] The Swiss government also believes that the US measure is unwarranted now that original circumstances have changed and homegrown cases of BSE have been discovered in the United States. It notes that nowadays, Switzerland and the United States share the same OIE category regarding BSE risk.

In previous FTAs, such as the US-Australia FTA, the United States has agreed to work towards common solutions on BSE risk to food safety and animal health in Codex and other forums. More recently, the United States has recognized Canada as a "minimum-risk country." The recent discovery of the first homegrown case of BSE in the United States should advance the effort to find common ground on BSE quarantine measures.

The WTO Secretariat reports that "bilateral consultations had clarified some of the questions raised by Switzerland. The United States noted that there was a further complication pertaining to the foot and mouth disease status of certain countries providing meat to Switzerland for processing and subsequent export to the United States" (WTO 2005b, 129).

Another Swiss concern relates to the tighter US food safety requirements under the Bioterrorism Act of 2002.[13] A number of Swiss exporters have been affected by measures related to its implementation. The Switzerland Ministry of Economy (2004) notes difficulties in both the process of approving Swiss food consignments to the United States and the treatment of confidential records regarding exported products.[14]

Despite differences, these various SPS issues on the bilateral agenda do not appear to pose a major obstacle to an FTA between Switzerland and the United States. The Agricultural Attaché of the US Mission to the WTO reports that "there are some US concerns with SPS relative to Swiss market access, but generally these concerns have been at a much lower level compared with other neighboring European country policies."[15] Swiss authorities have also been more accommodating than neighboring European countries have: They have allowed access for US beef with growth promoter treatment and US poultry products packed under current US water treatment methods.

---

13. The act introduces new requirements, including registration of food manufacturing facilities; prior notice to FDA of all food consignments; maintenance of records regarding distribution of food; and permission to detain any food that is suspected of posing a threat to the health of humans or animals. See US FDA (2002) for additional information.

14. The report states: *"Les programmes de lutte contre le bioterrorisme (formalités pour les importations de produits alimentaires), l'initiative des conteneurs (annonce 24 heures à l'avance pour le fret maritime) et l'application de nouvelles procédures pour entrer aux Etats-Unis ont eu des répercussions en Suisse. Des difficultés sont apparues dans l'expédition des denrées alimentaires et dans le traitement des données confidentielles transmises par les cargos"* (Switzerland Ministry of Economy 2004, 88).

15. Information gathered through exchange of e-mails with Gregg Young, USDA Agricultural Attaché to the United Nations in Geneva.

Labeling and Equivalent Standards

Switzerland and the United States disagree as to the adequate scope of labeling requirements for certain agricultural products.[16] While Switzerland favors a consumer "right-to-know" rationale for labeling, the United States believes that labels are only justified for safety-related issues. The positions of both governments reflect the attitudes of domestic constituencies. A large and visible segment of the Swiss public supports strong regulation, including labeling requirements, particularly for products derived from biotechnology. By contrast, consumer research in the United States shows that while a substantial majority of American consumers want more information about their food (including genetically engineered products), biotechnology labeling is rarely mentioned unless consumers are specifically asked (USDA 2005e). Meanwhile, agricultural firms fear that additional labeling requirements will be effectively turned into campaigns against their products. The basic disagreement on the proper content of labels has affected market access. US agricultural producers have found it increasingly difficult to access the Swiss market, and the US government has raised concerns over specific Swiss mandatory labeling requirements.[17]

The United States has questioned Swiss labeling requirements for foodstuffs not produced according to certain Swiss standards. Special labeling requirements apply to beef, pork, and eggs, when production includes the use of growth hormones, antibiotics, certain other substances in the raising of beef and pork, or in the case of eggs, the manner of caging.[18] Swiss authorities, however, claim that the United States has failed to pursue the bilateral consultations that took place on the issue of foodstuff PPM.

Switzerland and the United States have addressed labeling issues in the WTO Doha Round and other international forums, but their positions continue to differ. Their respective positions in the WTO illustrate the divide. In the Doha Round of agricultural negotiations, Switzerland has questioned whether the current technical barriers to trade (TBT) agreement sufficiently addresses consumer needs. Switzerland backs more stringent

---

16. While we address standards and technical barriers more generally in chapter 4 on manufactures trade, this section presents two standards and TBT issues that are intimately related to trade in agricultural products, and could be examined in the context of a Swiss-US FTA—namely, labeling measures and the mutual recognition of standards for organic products.

17. For a discussion of the impact of labeling and standards on trade, see chapter 6 of Josling, Roberts, and Orden (2004, 127–46).

18. In the Doha Round, Switzerland has advocated stronger labeling requirements. The Swiss proposal would increase consumer information to encompass production methods, food safety, and animal protection. Switzerland believes that consumers need more information so they can make choices based on ethical and moral convictions, as well as taste. It argues that these information needs extend to the identification of GMOs, respect for the environment, and animal welfare. All this would entail a revision of the SPS Agreement (WTO 2000b).

labeling requirements on production methods—particularly regarding the presence of GMOs—and respect for the environment and animal welfare. In the Swiss view, proper labeling allows consumers to make informed choices based on their own preferences and ethical and moral convictions.

The United States does not object to a "right to know" policy per se, but it does object to labeling requirements independent of product risk assessments or scientific justification. The United States believes that labeling requirements designed solely in response to moral and ethical concerns will impose additional costs and risks for the food and feed supply chain, and may sharply limit the world market for US agriculture. It is unclear whether US and Swiss FTA negotiators will be able to find common ground amid their countries' divergent views on these issues.

A more tractable and somewhat related issue—one that could be tackled in FTA talks—is the equivalence of standards for organic products. In previous US FTA pacts, parties have agreed to give positive consideration to accepting, as equivalent, each other's technical regulations, provided that they adequately fulfill the objectives of domestic regulations. However, imported organic agricultural produce may only be sold, labeled, or represented in the United States as organic when it is certified by a US Department of Agriculture (USDA) accredited certifying agent, when the USDA recognizes the ability of a foreign government to assess and accredit certifying agents as meeting the requirements of the USDA National Organic Program (NOP), or when the USDA has determined a foreign government's organic certification program to be equivalent to the NOP. Currently, two USDA-accredited certifying agents operate in Switzerland.

Likewise, imported organic products must meet the minimum requirements laid down in the Swiss Federal Ordinance on Organic Farming and the Labeling of Organically Produced Products and Foodstuffs to be labeled "organic" in Switzerland. Organic imports originating in countries with regulations not recognized as equivalent to Swiss legislation need to be registered with an approved Swiss certification or inspection body to demonstrate their compliance with Swiss legislation. Switzerland does not recognize the NOP as equivalent, but it has granted import permits for a few US organic products on an individual basis.

Trade in organic products would be facilitated if both countries could, within the context of the FTA, establish equivalent standards for organic products. Moreover, it could level the playing field with third countries that already have established equivalence of organic standards with Switzerland or the United States. The United States has already recognized conformity assessment systems in Denmark, Israel, Japan, New Zealand, the United Kingdom, and two Canadian provinces, Quebec and British Columbia; it is working towards recognizing Spain and the rest of Canada. It is also working towards establishing the equivalence of organic standards with Australia, Japan, India, and the European Union. Switzerland has established equivalence of the production rules and inspection systems for certain organic products from Argentina, Australia, Costa Rica, all members of the European Union, Israel, and New Zealand (Confoederatio Helvetica 1997).

Recommendations for SPS and Related Issues

Given current US and Swiss regulations and attitudes toward SPS and related issues, we offer the following suggestions:

- Negotiators should recognize that, while some outstanding issues may be addressed in the context of a Swiss-US FTA, others are best left to the WTO. This is particularly true for issues that engage core principles in each country's approach toward SPS.

- Switzerland and the United States both have veterinary agreements with the European Union, and Switzerland has plant health and seed agreements. Given the central role of the European Union in SPS matters, for both the United States and Switzerland, it makes sense for the Swiss-US FTA to borrow heavily from the best parts of their respective EU agreements. In particular, both countries could build on their prior recognition of equivalency between their own SPS measures and those adopted by the European Union for live animals, meats, foods of animal origin, and plants.

- As a separate matter, the United States and Switzerland should reach an understanding on BSE. As in the US-Australia FTA, the United States and Switzerland should agree to work cooperatively in the OIE, Codex, and other appropriate forums to ensure consistency in BSE standards and guidelines. Also, the United States should instruct its responsible agencies to work toward recognizing Switzerland as a minimum-risk country with the shortest possible delay.

- As in the US-Australia FTA, Switzerland and the United States should establish both an SPS committee and a standing technical working group on animal and plant health measures. Meeting at a senior level, the SPS committee should have two broad mandates: to further mutual understanding about national SPS regulatory processes, and to promote the convergence of US and Swiss SPS rules, giving appropriate consideration to EU rules.

- The working group should be instructed to resolve conflicting animal, meat, and plant standards and tests conducted in the exporting countries to the maximum extent. Whenever possible, working group members should be the same persons who handle the Swiss-EU and the US-EU files on SPS questions.

- Certain issues should be awarded priority attention in the working group: US BSE measures; Swiss certification of US slaughter plants; and labeling requirements that provide information on production methods, food safety, and animal protection.

- In addition, the SPS committee should evaluate the approval hurdles faced by US firms that ship biotech foodstuffs to Switzerland, as well as concerns stemming from the US implementation of the Bioterrorism Act. However, in dealing with these matters, representatives from both countries may sometimes find rather limited scope for accommodation, as differences may spring from fundamental societal choices. In such instances, the SPS Committee could still contribute to mutual understanding of each country's regulatory processes.

- The WTO is perhaps the most natural forum to reach a solution to the labeling issue that takes its global context into account. However, the Swiss-US FTA could allow both countries to work towards bridging the divide. The working group could be instructed to find mutually acceptable labels that would facilitate access to the Swiss market for sensitive products. The SPS committee should aim to limit the risks and costs faced by producers, for example, by reducing the time needed to comply with domestic regulations.

- Within the context of the FTA, Switzerland and the United States should reach a mutual agreement to recognize equivalent standards for organic products. This will promote trade in high-value produce and level the playing field regarding third countries that already have established equivalence of organic standards with Switzerland or the United States.

- As in the prior FTA agreements signed by both Switzerland and the United States, any disputes that cannot be resolved by the working group or SPS committee should be consigned to the WTO dispute settlement mechanism. To expedite disputes that may arise, the parties should agree in advance, in consultation with the WTO Secretariat, on a short roster of qualified panelists.

Geographical Indications

According to the Agreement on Trade-Related Aspects of Intellectual Property Rights (TRIPS), GIs "identify a good as originating in the territory of a Member, or a region or locality in that territory, where a given quality, reputation or other characteristic of the good is essentially attributable to its geographical origin" (www.sice.oas.org). GIs have spawned a certain amount of trans-Atlantic controversy, with Europe generally and Switzerland specifically. The Swiss and US approaches to GIs differ substantially. We first explain the regimes protecting GIs in Switzerland and the United

States; we then examine the Swiss and US positions in the Doha Round and in bilateral agreements. Finally, we suggest how GI issues could be addressed in the Swiss-US bilateral FTA.

Geographical Indications in the United States

Whether they are of domestic or foreign origin, the United States protects GIs through its trademark system, in the category of certification, collective marks, or common law (unregistered) versions of such marks.[19] The United States links GIs and trademarks because both are source identifiers, marks of a certain quality or standard (mandatory for GIs), and indicators of particular business interests.[20] However, there are differences between trademarks and GIs. The function of trademarks is to indicate the commercial origin of goods or services. To register or protect a trademark, it is normally not necessary to specify the quality or standard of the good or service it identifies. By contrast, to register or protect a GI, it is necessary to establish a quality, reputation, or other characteristic of the product that is linked to its geographical origin.

GIs may be registered as certification marks, but registration is not necessary to enforce GI rights against infringement if the GI qualifies as a common-law (unregistered) certification mark. Certain statutes and regulations related to spirits, such as wine-labeling laws and USDA inspection standards, may have the incidental effect of additionally protecting GIs. These pieces of legislation are not intellectual-property laws, and consequently, they do not establish a particular sign as a GI.

Roquefort, Parma ham, Stilton, Darjeeling, and cognac are examples of foreign GIs protected in the United States through certification marks. Within the United States, GIs include Florida for oranges, Idaho for potatoes, Washington state for apples, Tennessee for whiskey, and Napa for wine. Anecdotal evidence suggests that some Swiss GIs already enjoy protection in the United States, registered as protected appellations of origin (PAOs) or protected geographical indications (PGIs). Tête de Moine Fromage de Bellelay is registered as a certification mark in the United States.[21]

---

19. The paragraphs in this section draw extensively on the US Patent and Trademark Office (2005).

20. A collective mark indicates the commercial origin of goods or services in a product for which no single individual owns the trademark. A certification mark has two peculiar characteristics. First, the owner of the mark does not use it. Second, it does not indicate commercial source, nor distinguish goods or services within users of the certification mark. A certification mark can take the form of any word, symbol, or name used by a person other than its owner to certify, for instance, a certain origin, quality, accuracy, or production process. Any entity that meets the certifying standards is entitled to use the certification mark.

21. Between 2000 and 2004, Swiss residents filled 14,122 trademark applications and obtained 5,025 trademarks in the United States. These figures include all trademarks, and do not indicate the extent of protection of Swiss GIs in the United States.

Even so, the US trademark system falls short of Swiss expectations, since it only protects Swiss product GIs (other than wines and spirits) from misleading use, not from simply incorrect use or confusingly similar labels. It is common to find domestic products in the United States with labels that evoke Swiss origin through confusing readings, such as "Swiss-style" or pictures of snow-covered mountains.

Recent US bilateral FTAs, such as US-Chile, US-Australia, and CAFTA-DR, include provisions on GI protection. Typically, these agreements reinforce the commitment of parties to treat GIs as trademarks, but expressly refuse GI protection in the event that they correspond to preexisting trademarks. The US-Chile FTA, US-Australia FTA, and CAFTA-DR, as well as the US-EU Agreement on Distilled Spirits/Spirit Drinks, provide mutual recognition of certain spirits. These bilateral FTAs introduce the concept of "distinctive products" that may only be manufactured in a certain region of a country, in accordance with the country's laws governing manufacture, consumption, sale, or export. The FTAs explicitly forbid the sale, under a "distinctive product" label, of any product that does not qualify for such distinction.

Geographical Indications in Switzerland

Switzerland has a tradition dating from the 19th century of protecting GIs for all goods and services.[22] Until the adoption of special rules for registering GIs for agricultural products in 1997, legal protection for agricultural GIs was exclusively granted under the federal law on the protection of trademarks and indications of source.[23] Under this law, known as the LPM, GI protection is granted automatically, without a formal notification or registration procedure, provided that certain conditions are satisfied.

In addition to the protection granted by the LPM, since 1997, producers of agricultural products can enter their GIs in a national registry.[24] The

---

22. This section draws mostly on publications of the Swiss Federal Institute of Intellectual Property (2005). We thank Institute staff members for their comments.

23. The Federal Law on the Protection of Trademarks and Indications of Source of 28 August 1992 (LPM; RS 232.11) provides general protection to trademarks and GIs. A number of ordinances complete the general protection of GI for different products such as watches (Ordinance on the Use of the Designation "Swiss" for Watches of December 1971; RS 232.119), wine (Ordinance on Viticulture and the Importation of Wine of 7 December 1998; RS 916.140), and agricultural products (Ordinance on the Protection of Appellations of Origin and Geographical Indications in respect of Agricultural Products and Processed Agricultural Products of 28 May 1997; Ordinance on PAOs and PGIs; RS 910.12).

24. See the Ordinance on the Protection of Appellations of Origin and Geographical Indications with respect to Agricultural Products and Processed Agricultural Products.

first GI for such products was registered in January 2000. The Ordinance on PAOs and PGIs distinguishes two different types of GIs, the *Appellation d'origine contrôle* (AOC/PAO) and the *Indication géographique protégée* (IGP/PGI).

The AOC constitutes the name of a place, region, or traditional denomination used to designate an agricultural product whose quality and character draw essentially or exclusively from the surrounding geographical environment, including both human and natural factors. As of May 2005, some 13 products had successfully completed AOC registration, including, for the most part, cheeses, spirits, bakery products, and other products of vegetable origin.[25]

The IGP concept is based on a slightly weaker link between the product and the territory of origin. This concept applies to products for which the quality, reputation, or other characteristic may be attributed to the region or place of origin. As of May 2005, five products enjoyed IGP protection, including, for the most part, meats and sausages.[26]

An important difference from the US approach lies in the range of protection GIs enjoy. For registered AOCs and IGPs, the direct or indirect use of protected denominations for commercial purposes is strictly prohibited for similar products that do not comply with the specification. The same protection also extends to dissimilar products if the use exploits the reputation of the protected denomination.[27] Also, unlike the US trademark system, GI protection in Switzerland extends widely to imitations; fallacious indications; misleading packaging; translations; abusive labeling, such as "like," "type," and "according to the recipes;" and "other recourses to the distinctive shape of the product" even if the true origin of the product is identified.[28]

Registering AOCs or IGPs is not an easy process, as petitions for protection undergo a thorough review by Swiss authorities. Currently, six cheese products, five meat products, one plant-based product, two alcohol-based products, and one forestry product are undergoing evaluation. Chal-

---

25. These products included cheeses such as L'Etivaz, Tête de Moine, Gruyère, Sbrinz, Formaggio d'Alpe Ticinese, Vacherin Mont-d'Or, and Berner Alpkäse/Hobelkase; spirits such as Abricotine and Eau-de-vie de poires du Valais; vegetable products such as Rheintaler Ribelmais (corn), Safran de Mund (spice), and Cardon épineux genevois (vegetable); and bakery products such as pain de seigle valaisan (bread).

26. The five products are Viande des Grisons, Viande séchée du Valais, Saucisse d'Ajoie, Saucisse and Saucisson neuchâteloise, Saucisse aux choux, and Saucisson vaudois.

27. The most relevant laws are the Ordinance on the Protection of Appellations of Origin and Geographical Indications with respect to Agricultural Products and Processed Agricultural Products, and the Federal Law on the Protection of Trademarks and Indications of Source.

28. Article 16.6 of the Law on Agriculture allows an exception for prior trademarks, and Article 17a of the Ordinance does so for products that have been commercialized under a protected denomination at least five years prior to the demand for registration of the GI.

lenges against the decision to register "Emmentaler" as an AOC are still pending. Registered GIs, both AOCs and IGPs, also undergo surprise inspections and other controls to ensure respect for traditional production methods, traceability, and authenticity.

Under Swiss legislation, foreign GIs, including those of US origin, are granted the same protection as Swiss GIs. Thus, US GIs may benefit from the general protection provided by Law 232.11, and may apply for AOC or IGP registration under Ordinance 910.12. The 2003 US Commerce Department Country Commercial Guide stated that "Switzerland has one of the best regimes in the world for the protection of intellectual property, and protection is afforded equally to foreign and domestic rights holders." (US Department of Commerce 2003). The US concern that US GI owners face systematic discrimination in the European Union does not apply to Switzerland.

All bilateral FTAs negotiated by EFTA include provisions whereby parties "ensure in their national legislations adequate and effective means to protect GIs with regard to all products, including appellations of origin" (EFTA 2003). In some of these agreements, GI protection is also granted to services. The negotiated text within EFTA reinforces, but does not go much beyond, the commitments incorporated in the TRIPS Agreement. In some FTAs (e.g., with Mexico), a separate annex deals exclusively with the protection of GIs. Annexes 7 and 8 of the Bilateral Agreement on Agriculture between the European Community and Switzerland ensure mutual protection for GI names, without recipes or enological practices, for wines, spirits, and wine-based drinks. A joint declaration also calls for the mutual protection of designations of origin and GIs for agricultural products and foodstuffs. Currently, the ad hoc working group is discussing the list of denominations that should be protected under the agreement.

US and Swiss Views of GI Protection in the TRIPS Agreement

Articles 22 and 23 of the TRIPS Agreement grant two types of protection to GIs, namely regular and "additional protection." Regular protection for GIs that identify any type of product aims at protecting consumers and producers by preventing the use of indications that mislead the public or constitute unfair competition. "Additional protection" forbids the use of indications that do not originate in the place designated by the GI, regardless of any risk that their use might mislead the public or constitute unfair competition. "Additional protection" applies only to GIs identifying wines and spirits. Regular protection allows labeling such as "Sbrinz from Argentina," but additional protection bans the use of that expression or kindred phrases, such as "Bordeaux produced in Australia" or "Australian wine, Bordeaux style."

The Swiss government has actively participated in GI talks at the WTO since the Uruguay Round, and especially in the ongoing Doha Round. Switzerland considers that the TRIPS Agreement is the appropriate framework to establish minimum standards for more effective protection of GIs for all products at the multilateral level.[29]

Swiss authorities believe that the regular protection of TRIPS Article 22 is less effective than that of TRIPS Article 23, since Article 22 is based on an inappropriate test (consumer deception or unfair competition). Protection through Article 22 of TRIPS for products other than wines and spirits does not secure GIs from abusive use in translated form, or in conjunction with modifiers such as "like," "type," or "style."[30] Thus, producers from any other region can evoke the region of origin in a label such as "Gruyere-style cheese, made in Spain." If this practice continues to be permitted, Swiss officials argue, GIs risk becoming generic concepts with the passage of time, loosening even the limited protection granted by Article 22.

Swiss authorities also worry that Article 22 of TRIPS distributes the burden of proof in GI disputes unfairly. GI-protected producers not only have to prove incorrect use of the disputed label but also intent to mislead the public, a difficult claim to establish. Fine print on labels, seldom read by consumers, may correctly state the origin, while the headline type conveys a false impression. Swiss officials thus conclude that, for products other than wines and spirits, GI rights are difficult to enforce under the TRIPS Agreement's current standards of protection.

Swiss negotiators, supported by other delegations, have proposed extending "additional protection" (TRIPS Article 23) to all products as part of the Doha Round package. This would lead, in their view, to a better protection system—one that ensures the exclusivity and better enforceability of rights, eliminates abusive exploitation of certain GIs, maximizes the value of GIs as a marketing tool, creates conditions for the sustained development of certain regions, and better protects consumers from misleading labeling.

US negotiators, supported by other delegations, reject the Swiss proposal, as they consider that the current level of protection available under the TRIPS Agreement is sufficient. They argue that the Swiss proposal would tip the balance between trademark and GI protection in favor of the latter, which the US views as "a hidden subsidy" (Melzer 2002). Moreover, the United States interprets the Swiss proposal as leading to the creation of a supranational registry for GIs, and the United States believes that registration should remain a national prerogative.

---

29. Swiss GI-based producers have also been in the front line in advocating the creation of an international organization, such as ORIGIN (Organisation for an International Geographical Indications Network), to protect GIs more effectively at the international level, and in the WTO in particular.

30. "Additional protection" under Article 23 of TRIPS prevents this sort of abusive modifier.

Some US officials consider the Swiss proposal a vehicle for "taking back" generic terms.[31] They worry that adopting stronger GI protection could adversely affect certain production carried out by immigrants, or descendants of immigrants, in the United States.

Recommendations for GI Issues

- To balance the political economy of Swiss market access liberalization in agriculture, the FTA will need US concessions on GIs, an area of considerable commercial value not only to Swiss farmers and food processors, but also to Swiss industry (e.g., watches, textiles, machinery, and medical devices).

- A unique feature of the Swiss food sector is its production of epicurean specialties, notably cheese and chocolate. Switzerland is also reputed for its luxury and technical industry (e.g., watches, textiles, machinery, medical devices). All of these items embody Swiss comparative advantage, but to access the US market to the maximum extent, Swiss producers need adequate GI protection. Contrary to its stance on other intellectual property rights (IPR) issues, the United States has adopted a defensive posture on the GI question.

- Nevertheless, in bilateral agreements with the European Union, Chile, Australia, and Central American countries, the United States obtained specific recognition of bourbon whiskey and Tennessee whiskey, and in turn recognized certain GIs of the partner country (e.g., Scotch whiskey, Irish whiskey, *pisco chileno,* and *pajarete*). In other words, the United States has established a precedent for recognizing particular GIs in the context of bilateral agreements.

- Based on these precedents, in the context of the Swiss-US FTA, the United States should ensure better protection of Swiss GIs for all goods and services (i.e., an agreement on the protection of GIs) and expressly recognize protection for a list of Swiss GIs (after the Annex to the Agreement on the Protection of GIs). As part of the same bargain, Switzerland should recognize the same level of protection for US GIs for all products, and expressly for the GIs listed in the agreement, such as Florida oranges, Idaho potatoes, Washington State apples, Tennessee whiskey, bourbon whiskey, and Napa wine.

---

31. The TRIPS Agreement allows countries to exempt from GI protection indicators that correspond to a "generic" term or preexisting trademark. Since the United States considers "Chablis" a generic term, US producers are still permitted to use that word in the United States as a synonym for white wine. The European Union disagrees, arguing that "Chablis" is a GI.

- As a collateral agreement, in the context of the Doha Development Round, the United States should accede to the request of Switzerland and other countries that Article 23 of the TRIPS Agreement be amended to state that additional protection should apply to all products. The use of words such as "like," "style," or "type," or label information that, in relatively small print, correctly states the origin of the product, would then be prohibited. This amendment to Article 23 would also give Swiss producers better grounds for challenging the words "Swiss-style."

- Finally, in the context of the Swiss-US FTA, the parties should form a standing working group on intellectual property to consult on issues concerning GIs or other intellectual property rights that arise from time to time. Disputes would continue to be handled by the WTO dispute settlement mechanism, but the working group might head off some disagreements at an early stage.

Addressing SPS and GI issues in the Swiss-US FTA could aid negotiations in agricultural trade overall. However, though the agriculture sector is quite protected on both sides, it is dwarfed in volume by manufacturing and services. These areas could see impressive gains should trade between the United States and Switzerland become more open, and it is to them that subsequent chapters turn.

4

Manufactures Trade

Manufactured goods (also referred to as industrial products) dominate merchandise trade between the United States and Switzerland, accounting for more than 95 percent of two-way commerce.[1] In 2004, two-way trade between Switzerland and the United States in manufactured goods, excluding gold (HS 7108), reached nearly $17 billion (table 4.1). Swiss manufactured exports to the United States reached $10.4 billion, while US manufactured exports to Switzerland were $6.6 billion (table 4.1). In the last decade, the US bilateral deficit with Switzerland has widened, reflecting the ballooning US merchandise trade deficit globally.

While both countries have very low average tariffs on manufactured imports, they maintain significant barriers on selected products.[2] According to data from the US International Trade Commission (USITC) Dataweb, based on current sales figures to the United States (table 4.2), Switzerland will be most interested in exporting boilers, machinery, and mechanical appliances (HS chapter 84); clocks and watches (HS chapter 91); optical, measuring, precision, and medical instruments and apparatus (HS chapter 90); organic chemicals (HS chapter 29); and pharmaceuticals (HS chapter 30).

---

1. Throughout this chapter, manufactured goods are defined as all products comprised in HS chapters 25 through 97.

2. Because our goal is to present an overall picture of industrial protection, the analysis of Swiss tariffs presented in this chapter is not based on data at the finest level of tariff detail. Another word of caution: We base US export figures on data compiled by the United States at the moment of export. According to Swiss authorities, figures compiled by Swiss Customs Revenue based on import data often differ significantly. Evidently, US exporters often divert shipments en route to Switzerland to other destinations (principally in Europe).

Table 4.1 Manufactured goods in US-Swiss bilateral trade, 1996–2004 (millions of current dollars)

	1996	2000	2004
Trade in manufactured products[a]			
US exports	5,598	6,136	6,607
Swiss exports	7,023	9,123	10,388
Trade balance (US-Swiss)	−1,425	−2,987	−3,781
Total bilateral trade			
US exports	5,832	6,488	6,759
Swiss exports	7,162	9,272	10,617
Trade balance (US-Swiss)	−1,330	−2,784	−3,858
Share of manufactures in bilateral trade[b]	0.97	0.97	0.98

a. Trade in manufactures was estimated as total trade in HS chapters 25 through 97, with the exclusion of gold (HS 7108).
b. (US + Swiss industrial exports) / (US + Swiss total exports).
Sources: USITC (2005d).

Likewise, based on current US exports to Switzerland (table 4.2), the United States will be most interested in boilers, machinery, and mechanical appliances (HS chapter 84); optical, measuring, precision, and medical instruments and apparatus (HS chapter 90); pharmaceuticals (HS chapter 30); precious metals (HS chapter 71); and works of art (HS chapter 97). In most of these industries, trade between the United States and Switzerland is either tariff-free or pays only nuisance duties. However, tariffs or other barriers are significant for a few tariff lines, and those are the cases that attract our attention.

This chapter is divided into six sections. The first section deals with tariffs and tariff-rate quotas. The second reviews safeguard, antidumping (AD), and countervailing duties (CVDs). The third examines technical barriers as they relate to industrial products. The fourth reviews tariff phaseout schedules in selected US bilateral free trade agreements (FTAs). The fifth addresses rules of origin in industrial products. Finally, the sixth presents recommendations for liberalizing industrial trade.

Tariffs and Tariff-Rate Quotas

Both Switzerland and the United States are among the most open economies in the world for trade in industrial products. According to recent World Trade Organization (WTO) *Trade Policy Reviews* (2004b and 2004c), the average applied tariff for manufactured imports was 2.3 percent for Switzerland and 4.2 percent for the United States. World Bank trade-

Table 4.2   Manufactured exports in leading 2-digit HS chapters, 2004
(millions of current dollars)

HS chapter	Description	Swiss manufactured exports to the United States	US manufactured exports to Switzerland
HS-91	Clocks, watches, and parts thereof	1,695	120
HS-84	Nuclear reactors, boilers, machinery, and parts	1,675	906
HS-90	Optical, cinematographic, medical instruments, and parts	1,590	731
HS-30	Pharmaceutical products	1,289	1,305
HS-29	Organic chemicals	1,191	163
HS-85	Machinery, electrical apparatus and instruments; parts	765	322
HS-71	Precious stones, metals, pearls, and articles thereof	446	812
HS-39	Plastics and articles thereof	182	76
HS-88	Aircraft, spacecraft, and parts thereof	164	344
HS-97	Works of art, collectors' pieces, and antiques	155	936
HS-82	Tools, implements, cutlery, and parts	153	21
HS-32	Tanning or dyeing extracts; dyes, pigments, paints, varnishes	120	107
HS-73	Articles of iron or steel	101	68
HS-33	Essential oils; perfumery, cosmetic, or toilet preparations	88	102
HS-48	Paper and paperboard; articles of paper pulp	83	15
HS-38	Miscellaneous chemical products	62	105
HS-95	Toys, games, and sports requisites; parts	52	19
All manufactured exports, excluding gold (HS 7108) and special provisions		10,388	6,607
HS 7108	Gold	15	2,283
HS-98	Special classification provisions[a]	832	280
HS-99	Temporary legislation; additional import restrictions[b]	191	0

a. Trade under "special classification provisions" includes repairs and alterations of previously imported products; donated pharmaceuticals, textiles, and food products; nonidentified military equipment; small transactions; and US goods returned without having been advanced in value or improved in condition while abroad.
b. Not all restrictions correspond to manufactured products.

Source: USITC (2005b).

weighted averages, reported in the 2005 Index of Economic Freedom, indicate that the tariff burden on actual trade is even lower—0.8 percent in Switzerland and 2.6 percent in the United States. Hence, on average, the United States imposes higher tariffs on industrial products than Switzerland does.[3]

Swiss and US principal manufactured exports to each other are subject to low rates. Analyzed at the harmonized tariff schedule (HTS) 10-digit and 6-digit levels, simple average tariff rates for all industrial exports above $10 million to the other party were 2.4 percent for Swiss exports to the United States, and 2.6 percent for US exports to Switzerland (chapter appendix tables 4A.1 and 4A.2).[4] Trade-weighted average tariffs were also lower, at 0.8 percent for Swiss exports to the United States, and 1.2 percent for US exports to Switzerland (table 4.3).[5]

Nevertheless, several high tariffs remain, and the affected products will be of great interest to Swiss-US FTA negotiators. According to Swiss authorities, in 2004, high tariffs—those exceeding 5 percent—obstructed about 10 percent of Swiss industrial exports to the United States, and less than 1 percent of US industrial exports to Switzerland. The United States applies high tariffs on leading Swiss exports, such as clocks, watches, and chemicals, excluding pharmaceuticals (chapter appendix table 4A.1).

By contrast, high tariffs (above 5 percent) do not affect any of the current leading US industrial exports to Switzerland. Chapter appendix table 4A.2, however, identifies a number of tariff lines for which potential US exports of chemicals, printed materials, clocks, watches, and machinery, and electrical apparatus would face high tariffs. In fact, as chapter appendix table 4A.3 shows, high Swiss tariffs are not rare, and may limit imports of selected industrial products.

Generally, the mutual elimination of all industrial tariffs could boost trade in products for which current volumes are modest, as the very low trade-weighted tariff averages compared with simple tariff averages on bilateral trade suggest. The highest industrial tariffs apply to those products where bilateral trade volumes are small. Currently, no products facing

---

3. Some analysts object to the use of trade-weighted tariff averages, arguing that frequently understate the protective effect of tariffs, since (other things being equal) imports of items with higher tariffs will be lower relative to production or consumption. These analysts would prefer the use of production-weighted or consumption-weighted tariff averages. However, these alternative weighting schemes are very time-consuming and costly to implement. In our view, given the low level of Swiss and US tariff barriers on manufactured goods, the weighting scheme is not critical to evaluate average tariff levels.

4. The cutoff at $10 million of exports covers 64 percent of Swiss manufactured exports to the United States, and 77 percent of US manufactured exports to Switzerland.

5. Another way of looking at protection is to calculate average collected duties. According to estimates by Swiss authorities, the average customs duty paid for industrial imports from the United States was 0.2 percent, while the figure for industrial exports from Switzerland to the United States was 1.5 percent (personal communication with Thomas Zimmerman).

Table 4.3 Trade-weighted tariffs on bilateral trade[a]

Description	US exports Millions of dollars	Share	Swiss exports Millions of dollars	Share	Weighted average tariff (percent) United States	Switzerland[b]
Works of art (Ch. 97)	927	0.14	121	0.01	0.0	0.0
Clocks and watches (Ch. 91)	83	0.01	1,448	0.14	3.8	0.3
Optical, measuring and medical instruments (Ch. 90)	519	0.08	1,141	0.11	0.1	0.3
Aircraft (Ch. 88)	385	0.06	139	0.01	0.0	0.2
Machinery, electrical apparatus, and instruments (Ch. 85)	117	0.02	360	0.03	0.0	2.5
Boilers, machinery, and mechanical appliances (Ch. 84)	640	0.10	632	0.06	1.1	3.3
Pearls, precious metals and stones (Ch. 71)	756	0.11	360	0.03	1.0	n.a.[c]
Other chemicals and plastics (Ch. 32–40)	238	0.04	174	0.02	3.8	4.4
Pharmaceuticals (Ch. 30)	1,259	0.19	1,263	0.12	0.0	0.0
Organic chemicals (Ch. 29)	77	0.01	788	0.08	5.5	0.0
Subtotal	5,001	0.76	6,427	0.62	1.2	0.8
Total manufactured exports to each party	6,607	1.00	10,388	1.00	—	—

a. Calculations for Switzerland are at the 6-digit level; those for the United States are at the 10-digit level.
b. Based on ad valorem equivalents at the 6-digit level as reported by UNCTAD.
c. Ad valorem equivalents not reported by UNCTAD.

Sources: USITC (2005d), UNCTAD (2005).

tariffs of over 10 percent record imports over $15 million at the 6-digit level (Switzerland) or the 10-digit level (United States).

Chapter appendix table 4A.4 presents a list of manufactured goods subject to US tariffs above 10 percent ad valorem at the 6-digit HTS level. The table excludes textiles, clothing, and footwear, sectors where hundreds of tariff lines are routinely subject to high tariffs. Chapter appendix table 4A.5 presents a list of 4-digit HTS categories where the simple average tariff exceeds 5 percent (averaging tariffs at the 6-digit level). Nearly $2 billion of Swiss exports to the United States arrive in these high-tariff 4-digit HTS categories. It is worth pointing out that Switzerland has no quantitative restrictions on manufactured products (WTO 2004b). For example, under a US TRQ, Swiss exports of card strips made from cotton with a staple length of under 30.1625 mm (HS 5202.99.10) are guaranteed a minimum access of just 6,711 kilograms.[6]

Comparable detail is not available for high Swiss tariffs. However, chapter appendix table 4A.3, drawn from WTO sources, lists several 2-digit HS categories where tariffs on 6-digit items exceed 10 percent of their ad valorem equivalents.[7] This table excludes textiles and clothing, sectors where high tariffs are the rule, as they are in the United States.

According to estimates from a static computable general equilibrium (CGE) model, a comprehensive Swiss-US FTA might increase two-way manufactures trade by about 20 percent; gravity model estimates suggest that trade could more than double (see chapter 8). These robust estimates reflect that nuisance tariffs drag down trade to a far greater extent than simple models, based on the elasticity of demand, might imply that they do.[8] They also reflect that high tariffs can choke off manufactures trade altogether, especially when alternative sources of supply are readily available, or when firms forego industrial investments because trade barriers burden imported inputs.

Safeguards

According to the WTO (2004b), Switzerland and Liechtenstein do not maintain or intend to establish any safeguard measures as envisaged under

---

6. As a minor but not negligible barrier, the United States applies quantitative restrictions on imports of certain cotton-based products (see USITC 2005b, chapter 52, page 3).

7. In the Swiss tariff schedule, specific duties are common, and these need to be converted to ad valorem equivalents for meaningful evaluation.

8. Before the advent of gravity and CGE models, it was common to estimate the impact of tariffs by applying the estimated demand elasticity (a value, for example, between −1.0 and −3.0) to the ad valorem tariff. If the tariff on an item was 2 percent, and the demand elasticity was −3.0, eliminating the tariff would supposedly result in a trade volume increase of 6 percent. The recent literature on free trade areas (e.g., DeRosa and Gilbert 2005) suggests that this approach badly understates the effect of a free trade area in augmenting trade.

Article 19 of the General Agreement on Tariffs and Trade (GATT) 1994.[9] However, existing legislation permits safeguards consistent with the WTO, and they could be invoked without new legislation.

At present, the United States has no safeguards on imports of manufactured goods from Switzerland, and while US law has long permitted their application, they are not frequently imposed. But one safeguard issue concerns Switzerland: the US practice of excluding the North American Free Trade Agreement (NAFTA) and other FTA partners from application of its safeguard measures.[10] Switzerland participated in a group of countries that, in March 2002, challenged US safeguard measures on steel, arguing that, among other defects, the United States "did not respect the requirement of parallelism between the scope of the investigation of the injury arising from imported products and the scope of the safeguard measures"[11] (WTO 2003c). The WTO Panel and Appellate Body found the US safeguard measures to be inconsistent with the Agreement on Safeguards and GATT-1994, citing the absence of parallelism among a long list of defects. The United States revoked the steel safeguard in December 2003. Of course, if a Swiss-US FTA is concluded, the Swiss concern over parallelism will be moot.

Antidumping and Countervailing Duties

According to its latest notification to the WTO (2005d), the United States does not apply AD duties to any product originating in Switzerland[12]—but if it does so in the future, the Byrd Amendment could be a matter of concern. Akin to a damage award, this amendment distributes a large portion of the revenues collected from AD measures to firms in the affected US industry that supported the AD petition. The Byrd Amendment was ruled illegal by the WTO Appellate Body, but Congress remains strongly opposed to its repeal.[13]

In recent years, Switzerland has not applied AD measures against any country.[14] Moreover, Swiss exporting firms are infrequently involved as

---

9. Safeguards are also discussed in chapter 2 on agricultural barriers, where they have greater relevance.

10. Under US practice, NAFTA and FTA partners are included only when they contribute in a significant way to total imports, and to the injury suffered by the domestic industry.

11. In other words, the United States did not justify excluding Canada and Mexico from its safeguard measures.

12. See WTO (2005d). Nor is the United States considering applying AD duties.

13. Many observers believe that the Byrd Amendment will remain on the US law books at least until the WTO Doha Development Round is concluded and the package is ratified by Congress.

14. There is no current legislation in Swiss law on applying AD duties. The last reference in Swiss legislation dates from the Tokyo Round of multilateral trade negotiations. For more information, see WTO (1995a).

targets of AD investigations: Since 1995, Swiss firms have faced just five, of which only one ended in applying definitive duties, and none of these cases involved the United States. This record is all the more remarkable given that an important share of Swiss exports corresponds to sectors with a moderate incidence of AD investigations, such as chemicals and machinery.[15]

There are no outstanding issues on the bilateral agenda with respect to CVDs. Switzerland has not applied them in recent years,[16] and though the United States is the world's most frequent user of CVDs, Switzerland rarely subsidizes industrial production that would necessitate them.[17]

Technical Barriers

Standards and technical regulations, conformity assessment, and mutual recognition can constitute technical barriers to trade, particularly since such regulations differ not only between Switzerland and the United States, but within them. As these barriers can be complex, the United States and Switzerland are each discussed in turn.

Standards and Technical Regulations

Voluntary standards are usually developed by private-sector associations in a given industry, profession, or academic field (WTO 2004c). By contrast, mandatory standards can be established at either the federal or state level (WTO 2004c). While Congress retains the power to write product regulations, "it usually delegates enabling legislation to regulatory agencies, generally pursuant to broad guidance as to the factors considered and policy goals to be achieved" (WTO 2004c). An agency may also develop standards and technical regulations on its own if Congress has previously conferred broad authority to do so.

The United States is often criticized for ignoring international standards. Its domestic standards sometimes contradict them; other times, it

---

15. About 57 percent of US AD initiations between 1995 and 2004 corresponded to base metals and articles thereof (HS chapters 72 through 83), and Swiss exports to the United States are small in these sectors, only 2 percent of total trade. US AD initiations on chemicals and machinery and apparatus, over that same period, represented about 18 percent of total AD measures.

16. Switzerland has no current legislation on the application of countervailing measures. The last reference in Swiss legislation dates from the Tokyo Round of multilateral trade negotiations. For more information, see WTO (1995b).

17. Moreover, between 1995 and 2004, 60 percent of US CVD investigations targeted base metals and articles thereof (HS chapters 72 through 83), not products that Switzerland exports in large volume.

purposefully does not adopt them. US standards on electrical and electronic products differ from international standards (European Commission 2004a). Likewise, US standards for nondestructive testing (NDT) require that the personnel be certified twice, while the international standard is a single certification (European Commission 2004a). It annoys other countries when US officials argue that US standards, such as those for pressure containers, are "international" because they are widely used abroad.

In the pharmaceutical area, the European Union claims that FDA approval of new medicinal products takes much longer for new non-US drugs than it does for new US drugs. The European Union attributes this delay to the investigational new drug (IND) system, which allows "the FDA advanced knowledge of medicinal products tested in clinical trials in the United States" (European Commission 2004a). The European Union also takes exception to the US "over the counter" (OTC) procedure, in which active substances that have been approved for an array of medicinal products by the FDA are put on an approved list (European Commission 2004a). The approved active substances can then be sold without a prescription. However, this procedure is only available for active substances that have a US market history. This limits market access for OTC products from the European Union and Switzerland, despite their equivalent regulatory system for pharmaceuticals.

For textiles and leather, custom formalities are costly. Textile, clothing, and footwear imports require detailed and voluminous information that sometimes entails disclosure of confidential processing methods, such as type of finishing or dyeing.[18] As a result, "liquidation" (i.e., final determination) of custom duties may take 210 days or longer. The European Commission (2004a) argues that this practice constitutes an important barrier, since apparel articles often have a short shelf life.[19]

The American Society of Mechanical Engineers (ASME) sets basic standards for pressure equipment in the United States. In addition, however, local jurisdictions may regulate that equipment, leading to a multiplicity of standards from state to state. If foreign manufacturers want to use a particular material for the US market not listed in the ASME code, they have to initiate a "code case" procedure, which is extremely costly and lengthy. The ASME also requires an authorized authority to inspect each manufacturing firm; this authority must be an insurance company authorized to write pressure equipment insurance in at least one US jurisdiction.

---

18. Moreover, imported textile fabrics have to be marked with generic names, and when constituent fibers are more than 5 percent, their percentages by weight must be identified. Products with woolen fiber need to be clearly marked to comply with the Wool Products Labeling Act of 1939 (European Commission 2004a).

19. If the importer is not in a position to redeliver the goods when US Customs requests, the importer faces a large penalty, which usually amounts to 100 percent of the value of the good (European Commission 2004a).

Finally, the European Union contends that the very complexity of the US regulatory system is itself an additional import barrier, not only for pressure equipment, but for many other products as well. Products entering the United States are often subject to an array of standards and technical regulations regarding consumer and environmental protection. The European Commission (2004a, 32) complains that "equipment for use in the workplace is subject to US Department of Labor certification, [national] electrical equipment standards, specific regulations imposed by municipalities, and other product safety requirements as determined by insurance companies." Swiss exporters have similar complaints.

For Switzerland, possibly because the Swiss market is small, or because Swiss standards and technical regulations are closely aligned with international practice, few complaints are heard from trading partners. As in the United States, Swiss federal departments and agencies develop standards and technical regulations if Parliament grants authority. In 1996, the Federal Law on Technical Barriers to Trade entered into force. This law, which applies to regulations at the federal level, states that technical legislation has to be drafted in such a way that it does not create trade barriers. To this end, product standards must be harmonized with Switzerland's most important trading partners.

Today, the legal competence for all technical regulations resides at the federal level, not at the cantonal level as in former times. The WTO (2004b) reports that Swiss efforts to harmonize technical requirements across cantons and with the European Union have been successful, particularly for motor vehicles and telecommunications.

Conformity Assessment

To ensure that manufactures meet standards and technical regulations, the United States often relies on third-party conformity assessment procedures for industrial products, so that it often requires third party certification rather than self-certification for telecommunications equipment, electrical equipment, and domestic appliances (European Commission 2004a). By contrast, the norm in other countries is usually self-assessment. Third-party assessment can imply additional costs for foreign suppliers of industrial goods.

Switzerland's Federal Law on Technical Barriers to Trade does not require third-party assessment. According to the WTO (2004a), "the LETC states that several conformity assessment procedures should be proposed when a technical regulation is established, and that at least one procedure should allow producers or suppliers self-assessment."

Mutual Recognition

As a general rule, the United States does not follow the EU norm of mutual recognition of product standards established by EU member states, nor has it embarked on a large-scale effort to harmonize its product standards with international ones. However, on a case-by-case basis, the United States has accredited foreign testing agencies. In December 1998, the European Union and United States signed a mutual recognition agreement (MRA) dealing more broadly with conformity assessment. The EU-US MRA aims to allow manufacturers in both countries "to test and certify their products with a domestic conformity assessment body (CAB) according to the requirements of the other Party" (European Commission 2004a).

The US-EU MRA was initially targeted at manufacturers of computers and medical devices but encompassed other sectors as well. The European Commission (2004a, 26), however, considers that the United States "has not made a sufficient commitment to implementing [the US-EU MRA], particularly in the areas of electrical safety and pharmaceutical good manufacturing practice." These areas are of significant interest to Switzerland. The European Union complains that, in 2003, it was obligated to suspend its MRA with the United States regarding electrical safety because the US Occupational Safety and Health Administration (OSHA) refused to grant European authorities the right to designate European laboratories as acceptable conformity assessment bodies (European Commission 2004a). Switzerland had the same experience when it tried to have OSHA recognize Swiss conformity assessment bodies in 1998. Not only do Switzerland and the United States have different accreditation requirements, but product marking requirements create another barrier, since smaller certification bodies have difficulty promoting their own trademarks.

The Swiss-American Chamber of Commerce (2002) reports that the United States initiated a proposal to negotiate a conformity assessment MRA with three European Free Trade Association (EFTA) countries, Norway, Iceland, and Liechtenstein. The contemplated agreement was supposed to match the provisions of the US-EU MRA, but would be restricted to telecommunications equipment, electromagnetic compatibility, and recreational craft. In April 2002, the Swiss-American Chamber of Commerce (2002) submitted a letter to the USTR suggesting that Switzerland be part of this agreement, arguing that it was "in the best interest of US business to also facilitate access to the three proposed sectors in the Swiss market." Negotiations are under way, but apparently not at a brisk pace.

Unlike the United States, Switzerland has entered into MRAs dealing with both product standards and conformity assessment.[20] Switzerland has concluded MRAs with Canada (1999), the European Union (2002), and the EFTA/European Economic Area (EEA) states (2002), and is negotiating with Australia, New Zealand, and the United States.

The MRA between Switzerland and the European Union deals with both product standards and conformity assessment, and covers 15 product

---

20. The following discussion is based on information in Switzerland Ministry of Economy (2005).

areas and assessment subjects.[21] For product sectors in which EC and Swiss legislation are equivalent, the agreement enables conformity assessment to be carried out by a recognized Swiss body according to Swiss technical legislation. For products without equivalent legislation (e.g., boilers and certain measuring instruments), conformity assessment procedures must be based on EC technical regulations. However, a Swiss body that is recognized by both parties may deliver an attestation of conformity (also based on EC regulations). Finally, while the Swiss-EU MRA facilitates trade in pharmaceuticals by providing mutual recognition of good manufacturing practice (GMP) inspection and batch certification by manufacturers, each party retains responsibility for authorizing the sale of pharmaceuticals in its territory.

The MRA between Switzerland and Canada does not cover as many products as the Swiss-EC MRA does. However, the Swiss-Canada MRA allows conformity assessment to be achieved by a Swiss body recognized by both parties.

Independent of future FTA negotiations, regulatory cooperation already exists between Swiss and US health authorities in the field of GMP for pharmaceuticals (Swiss Federal Department of Foreign Affairs 2003). Swiss authorities believe that this cooperation might eventually lead to mutual recognition.

Tariff Phaseouts in US and Swiss FTAs

As mentioned in chapter 1, the Swiss-US FTA could set a new standard for liberalization, but much depends on the phaseout regime. To hazard an estimate as what such a regime might look like, it is instructive to look at past FTAs for both the United States and Switzerland—particularly the former, since its FTA experience with phaseout regimes on manufacturing is considerably broader. To that end, selected US FTAs are discussed individually, followed by a shorter discussion of Swiss FTAs.

US-Singapore FTA

Tariffs on most products exchanged were already low before the agreement. Despite the modest agenda on tariffs, and possibly due to the ease of negotiations in this area, progress on other issues, such as rules of origin

---

21. Those subjects are machinery; personal protective equipment; toys; medical devices; gas appliances and boilers; pressure vessels; telecommunications terminal equipment, equipment and protective systems intended for use in potentially explosive atmospheres, electrical equipment, and electromagnetic compatibility; measuring instruments and prepackaging; motor vehicles; agricultural or forestry tractors; good laboratory practice (GLP) for chemicals and pharmaceuticals; and good manufacturing practice (GMP) inspection and batch certification.

and customs procedures, achieved results that the USTR characterizes as "ground-breaking."[22]

Under the US-Singapore FTA, Singapore committed to apply zero tariffs for all manufactured imports upon entry into force. Since Singapore already applied zero tariffs on almost all manufactured goods, the agreement entailed eliminating tariffs on very few products, such as beer, stout, samsoo, and medicated samsoo.

In negotiating market access for industrial products, the United States secured the longest phaseouts (8 to 10 years) for products that enjoy the highest most favored nation (MFN) tariff protection (above 8 percent). Products with moderate MFN tariff protection (5 to 8 percent) typically obtained shorter phaseouts (4 years), while products with low MFN tariff protection (below 5 percent) were granted, for the most part, immediate access to the US market.

According to the US Trade Representative (USTR), the United States committed to eliminate 92 percent of its tariffs on Singaporean manufactured exports immediately, leaving only 8 percent of tariff lines for longer phaseouts. However, chapter appendix table 4A.6 shows a larger percentage of phaseout tariffs affecting important product-categories, such as organic chemicals, starches, and enzymes, clocks, optical, and medical instruments, and certain vehicles. In fact, for the selection of products listed in chapter appendix table 4A.6, only 77 percent of the tariff lines will qualify for immediate duty-free access. Most of the remaining US tariffs will be phased-out within 4 years (16 percent); but very sensitive US products qualify for 8- to 10-year phaseouts (7 percent).

Unlike the US-Australia FTA, many textiles and apparel under the US-Singapore FTA enjoy immediate duty-free entry into the US market if they meet the agreement's special rules of origin.[23] The Web site of the Ministry of Trade and Industry of Singapore, however, does not include textiles among the sectors that stand to benefit from US tariff liberalization. The "benefit" sectors identified by the ministry are electronics, information technology equipment, chemicals and petrochemicals, instrumentation equipment, processed foods, and minerals.[24]

US-Australia FTA

Similar to US trade relations with Switzerland, manufactured exports account for almost 95 percent of US merchandise exports to Australia. Before the agreement, Australia applied higher tariffs to US manufactured products

---

22. The US-Singapore FTA is among the first US trade agreements with specific obligations on the conduct of customs procedures. See USTR (2002a).

23. Rules of origin are discussed below.

24. For more information, see the section on the US-Singapore FTA in Singapore Ministry of Trade and Industry (2003).

than the United States did on similar products originating in Australia.[25] Balancing this situation was an important US objective. For its part, Australia wanted to give its exporters equal footing with competitors that already benefited from preferential access to the US market.

Australia will grant immediate duty-free access to more than 99 percent of manufactured imports from the United States. Indeed, chapter appendix table 4A.7 shows that, leaving textiles aside, Australia only managed to apply phaseouts (6 years) on about 15 tariff lines that correspond to secondhand passenger vehicles. According to the USTR, autos and auto parts, chemicals and plastics, construction equipment, electrical equipment and appliances, fabricated metal products, furniture and fixtures, medical and scientific equipment, nonelectrical machinery, and paper and wood products manufactured in the United States will benefit immediately.

Though the United States will grant immediate duty-free access to 97 percent of nonagricultural tariff lines, it insisted on phaseouts for a substantial number of sensitive products. Chapter appendix table 4A.7 shows that US phaseouts will apply to tariff lines in ceramic products, glassware, certain tools used in construction, optical and medical instruments, and electrical machinery. Tariffs on most of these products will be phased-out over 4 to 10 years. Tariffs on a few milk proteins and casein will be phased-out over 18 years.

Despite these long phaseouts, the Australian Department of Foreign Affairs and Trade (2005b) highlights that the automotive, metals, minerals, seafood, paper, and chemical sectors, as well as sectors that use US inputs, stand to benefit immediately. Australia expects benefits to its textiles, clothing, and footwear sectors over a longer time frame, since many tariffs will be eliminated over 15 years (Australia Department of Foreign Affairs and Trade, 2005). The agreement also establishes a Committee on Trade in Goods to address market access concerns (mainly on the part of Australia), particularly those relating to nontariff barriers (NTBs).

In all, the USITC expects that FTA concessions will result in gains for the following US manufactured exports, listed in decreasing order of projected gain: coal, oil, and gas; processed food; textile, apparel, and leather products; motor vehicles and parts; ferrous metals; and wood products. Also listed in decreasing order of projected gain, Australian manufactured exports projected to increase are: textiles; chemicals, rubber, and plastic; and motor vehicles and parts (USITC 2004b).

US-Chile FTA

Trade in manufacturing plays a smaller role between the United States and Chile than it does in US trade relations with more highly developed coun-

---

25. The difference was particularly noticeable for durable goods, which accounted for about three-quarters of US exports to Australia.

tries. Industrial products represented less than 60 percent of Chilean exports to the United States, and many Chilean industrial exports are food or forest-based products, though Chile's chemical exports are rapidly expanding. More than 85 percent of bilateral trade in consumer and industrial products became duty free immediately upon entry into force, and most of the remaining tariffs will be eliminated within four years.[26] Tariffs on textile products were eliminated immediately on both sides. However, Chile does not export large amounts of these products to the United States.[27]

Before the FTA, many Chilean industrial-based exports entered the United States duty-free under the Generalized System of Preferences (GSP). Hence, the FTA tariff cuts will have a comparatively small effect on Chilean manufactured exports. However, the United States will apply 4- to 10-year phaseouts on certain tariff lines.[28] In addition, the United States established two duty-free TRQs on Chilean exports of radial tires and certain ceramic products, such as hotel or restaurant chinaware. Out-of-quota tariffs will be phased out over 8 to 10 years. Textiles and footwear, with a few exceptions for wool-based products and certain shoes, receive immediate duty-free treatment.

Selected Swiss FTAs

Switzerland approaches negotiations differently than the United States does. For one thing, to date, Switzerland has negotiated all of its bilateral FTAs as a member of EFTA, excluding Switzerland's agreements with the

---

26. US manufactured exports gaining immediate duty-free access to Chile include: agricultural and construction equipment; autos and auto parts; computers and other information technology products; medical equipment; and paper products. Chile retained 4- to 10-year phaseouts on certain tariff lines in organic chemicals (HS 2905, 2915, 2917, and 2930), fertilizers (HS 3102), tanning colors (HS 3204, 3207–09, and 2314), cosmetics (HS 3303–05), enzymes (HS 3501–06); miscellaneous products of the chemical industry (HS 38), plastics (HS 3901–02; 3905–09; 3519–20, and 3926), rubbers (HS 4005–08, 4010 and 4012), certain shoes (HS 6403), stones used in construction (HS 68) including brick or ceramic, glassware (HS 7004–7018), certain machinery and mechanical appliances (HS 8419–26), and vehicles and parts thereof, including HS 8702 and parts listed in other chapters. However, Chile applies an almost perfectly uniform MFN tariff of 6 percent, and for none of the phaseout products does the MFN tariff exceed that level.

27. In 2002, Chilean textile exports were just over $10 million.

28. Egg albumin and indelible gelatin (HS 3502 and 3503), trunks and suitcases (HS 4202), gloves (HS 4203), luggage (HS 4602), glazed ceramic tiles (HS 6907 and 6908), drinking glasses (HS 7013), articles of metal such as knives, scissors, joint pliers, etc. (HS 8203–8208, HS 8214, and 8215), bicycles and parts (HS 8714), watches (HS 9101–9114), and brooms and whiskbrooms (HS 9602 and 9603). Only 62 percent of the tariff lines in chapter 91 of the US schedule (watches) qualify for immediate duty-free treatment. Tariffs on the remaining tariff lines will be phased out over four years (23 percent) or eight years (15 percent).

European Union. EFTA's bilateral agreements require very few exceptions in nonagricultural products,[29] and do not require long phaseouts on the EFTA side for market access barriers.[30] However, they do not seriously cover agriculture, and so do not significantly reduce high agricultural protection in the EFTA countries.

As an illustration, the EFTA-Singapore FTA immediately abolishes practically all customs duties on products listed in HS chapters 25 through 97 upon entry into force. A few exceptions are listed in Annex V (EFTA 2002a). For Switzerland, excluded products are casein and albumin (ex chapter 35), and feeding stuffs for production animals in chapter 35 (dextrin, other modified starches, and prepared glues) and chapter 38 (finishing agents, fatty oils, alcohols, acid oils, prepared binders for foundry moulds, and residual products of the chemical industry).

The EFTA-Chile FTA recognizes the asymmetry in development levels between parties,[31] and Annex VI allows Chile to establish phaseouts on certain manufactured products (EFTA 2003). The phaseouts for more than three-fourths of the products listed there are indefinite, but this provision could be renegotiated two years after the agreement entered into force.[32] Chile will allow EFTA partners to propose changes to the phaseouts, to the extent that Chile grants better access for the same products originating in the European Union. For its part, Switzerland only excluded from immediate duty-free treatment those same tariff lines that were reserved in the EFTA-Singapore accord (Annex III).

Rules of Origin

Rules of origin determine which goods are eligible for preferential FTA tariff rates, and defining these rules will be a crucial aspect of the negotiation.[33] Many sectors in Switzerland rely heavily on foreign inputs to pro-

---

29. In most of these EFTA bilateral agreements, Switzerland has excluded only 13 nonagricultural tariff lines.

30. Recognizing asymmetries, EFTA has allowed long phaseouts for developing countries. From the standpoint of promoting growth, most developing countries would benefit from faster rather than slower trade liberalization. However, the asymmetry argument is regularly invoked for protectionist purposes, and advanced countries (such as EFTA members) often accept it for political rather than economic reasons.

31. See the preceding note.

32. Affected products include organic chemicals, fertilizers, certain tanning products, cosmetics, other chemicals, plastics and rubbers, raw fur skins, bricks and other ceramic products, certain glassware, a few articles of iron and base metals, some electrical and mechanical appliances, and vehicles and parts thereof. This listing is very similar to the list of products that received 4- to 8-year phaseouts in the US-Chile FTA.

duce exported goods. Producer associations have commented that the benefit of reduced and zero tariffs on manufactured goods will critically depend on whether the FTA contains liberal rules of origin.

This is all the more important because, for the majority of traded goods, FTA preferences will be meaningful only if the cost of complying with the rules of origin is modest. Otherwise, firms will simply pay the MFN tariff and avoid the hassle. We focus this section on rules of origin for sectors where high MFN tariffs prevail, such as textiles and apparel, and sectors where using imported inputs is an important part of industrial production. Before turning to details, as revealed in past FTA negotiations, it is worth calling out three general issues that are sure to arise in negotiating the rules of origin: cumulation, rules on remanufactures, and methods of certification.

The cumulation issue centers on the designation of countries whose products qualify for meeting the rules of origin set forth in the FTA. Will only goods manufactured in the two partner countries qualify? Or will goods manufactured in third-country FTA partners also be allowed? The answer is critical in a world where components from several countries are assembled to make many final products, from shoes and clothing to computers.

EFTA's approach to the cumulation issue often agrees with the EU model, under which rules of origin permit goods from a number of countries that are linked by trade agreements with identical rules of origin to qualify; the result is called "diagonal cumulation." Under one version of diagonal cumulation, if both the United States and Switzerland had FTAs with identical rules of origin as a given third country, that country's products would qualify for meeting the rule of origin test in preferential Swiss-US trade.[34] Some EFTA bilateral FTAs follow the principle of diagonal cumulation, though FTAs with non-Euro-Mediterranean partners do not.

By contrast, as a normal practice, the United States has adopted a "bilateral cumulation" approach in its FTAs, meaning that only products manufactured in the partner country, whether sold as final goods or as inputs, qualify for the rules of origin. Following a "bilateral cumulation" rule, inputs made in Chile, Singapore, or Australia—all countries with which the

---

33. The legitimate purpose of rules of origin is to avert "trade deflection"—the practice of routing third-country imports into the FTA partner with the lowest MFN tariff, then exporting the same goods into the partner with the higher MFN tariff, taking advantage of the FTA preferential tariff rate.

34. Under a strict interpretation, diagonal cumulation with third partners linked to both the United States and Switzerland by bilateral FTAs (such as Chile, Singapore, or Mexico) would not be possible, since the regimes of origin established by the FTAs differ. However, as we suggest in our recommendations, a considerably less strict interpretation would have substantial benefits.

United States has negotiated FTAs—would not qualify if they were embedded as components of a Swiss product shipped to the United States.

Remanufactures are industrial products assembled from "recovered goods," typically made from items listed in HS chapters 84, 85, and 87. Parts resulting from disassembling a product do not constitute a "recovered good" unless they are cleaned, inspected, and tested. In producing a remanufactured good, the parts must be subjected to welding, flame spraying, surface machining, knurling, plating, sleeving, or rewinding. The United States contends that remanufactured products should qualify under rules of origin regardless of their original source. The US auto industry is particularly interested in this provision.

Switzerland has adopted procedures for certification of origin that are significantly different from those of the United States. While US bilateral FTAs establish declaration of origin by the importer, Switzerland requires certification by the exporter.

Rules of Origin in US Bilateral FTAs

Many US bilateral FTAs require that preferred imports be wholly made in the partner country, or that the "substantial transformation" of components that originated elsewhere occur there. The underlying principles that define "substantial transformation" are similar in the US-Chile, US-Australia, and US-Singapore FTAs, as well as the Central American–Dominican Republic Free Trade Agreement (CAFTA-DR).

Substantial transformation can be achieved when activity in the territory of the FTA exporter changes the tariff classification between inputs from a third country and the exported product. Depending on the product, that requirement could correspond to a change involving different HS chapters at the 4-digit or 6-digit level. US bilateral FTAs include a de minimis exception to HS classification change tests when the product contains 10 percent or less of nonoriginating material.

An alternative requirement, which is sometimes combined with the change-of-tariff-heading rule, is a minimum share of local value added in the free on board (f.o.b.) value of the product. Typically, the minimum local content is 35 percent using the "build-up" method, and 45 percent using the "build-down" method.[35] Chemical products (HS 28 through 40) are subject to specific rules defining substantial transformation based on the place where specific chemical reactions occur.

---

35. The "build-down" method estimates the share of the local value added in the f.o.b. price by subtracting overhead, transportation, and similar costs. The "build-up" method estimates the share of local value added by combining the cost of originating materials used in making the final product. The US-Australia FTA uses a variant, a net cost method, for certain automotive products.

The agreements allow cumulation of origin for inputs from in the territory of either party. Thus, Singaporean inputs can be counted as American in US exports to Singapore, and vice versa.

The US-Singapore FTA makes an important effort to give the rules of origin greater flexibility. It does this through its integrated sourcing initiative (ISI), which applies to specific products designated in Annex 3B of the agreement (USTR 2003a). ISI coverage extends to more than 250 US tariff lines, representing almost 30 percent of US imports from Singapore in 2004.[36] For the most part, these are information technology products and medical devices.[37] The US-Singapore FTA allows new products to be added to the ISI list by mutual agreement of the parties.

Regarding verification, the agreements require importers to declare the origin of products, allowing importers to argue for preferential treatment based on "the importer's knowledge or on information in the importer's possession that the good qualifies as an originating good"(USTR 2003a). The agreements stipulate that each party will grant any properly filed claim for preferential treatment, unless a party possesses information that the claim is invalid.

Many US bilateral FTAs include special textile and clothing rules of origin, one of which is the "yarn-forward rule." For fabrics to be conferred origin, the yarns (cotton, wool, and most man-made fibers) must be produced in one of the parties to the agreement. The transformation (fabric-making, cutting or knitting, sewing, and finishing activities) must also take place in one of the parties. The yarn-forward rule is obviously designed to ensure that the maximum amount of manufacturing activity takes place in the territory of the FTA partners, and not in third countries. Some Australian textile producers correctly complain that the yarn rule does not allow them to reap the full benefits of the agreement, since they will not be able to source yarn from cheaper Asian suppliers.[38]

---

36. Based on 2004 data, more than 90 percent of US imports from Singapore of designated ISI products take place in the following four-digit HS categories: 8470, 8471, 8473, 8479, 8517, 8525, 8534, 8541, 8542, 9021, 9027, and 9030.

37. The actual description for these HS categories are calculating and data processing machines, magnetic or optical readers, telecommunication and sound and image transmitting apparatus, semiconductor devices, electronic integrated circuits, orthopedic appliances, instruments and apparatus for physical or chemical analysis, and instruments and apparatus for measuring or checking electrical quantities.

38. The Australian Textile, Clothing, and Footwear (TCF) Union stated to the Senate Commission on the Australia-US Free Trade Agreement (AUSFTA) that "whilst there was potential for considerable benefits to the Australian TCF industry from this agreement, the US insistence on maintaining 'yarn forward' rules of origin has significantly reduced, if not eliminated, any potential up-side for industry and created a considerable down-side." The TCF representatives also pointed out that the regime of origin for textiles in AUSFTA is very different from the one of Australia–New Zealand Closer Economic Relations Trade Agreement (ANZCERTA), which only requires 50 percent value added (Woolgar 2004).

There are exceptions to the yarn rule. Under the US-Singapore FTA, silk garments only need to undergo cutting, knitting, sewing, and finishing in Singapore to qualify.[39] A special provision in that same agreement stipulates that if a particular type of yarn is designated as "short supply" in the United States, Singaporean textiles based on yarn from third countries can claim origin if the yarn is transformed in Singapore.[40]

Rules of Origin in Swiss Agreements

Switzerland applies different regimes of origin in various trade agreements: the Swiss-EU FTA of 1972, the EFTA Convention, EFTA's bilateral FTAs, and nonreciprocal preferential schemes.

The rules of origin in the Swiss-EU FTA (SEFTA) and EFTA conventions are very similar; in fact, the definitions of origin as they apply to Switzerland is the same.[41] They stipulate that wholly obtained or substantially transformed products may qualify. The principles used are change of tariff classification (generally a change of heading)[42] and a maximum amount of third-party content (typically between 40 and 50 percent of the ex-works price).[43] For sensitive products, more complex rules combine both principles.

Both regimes facilitate the use of third-country inputs through a 10 percent of value tolerance rule, and by allowing transformation in third countries as long as there is less than 10 percent value added.[44] Textile products in HS chapters 50 through 63, however, are excluded from these exceptions.[45]

In both regimes, the proof of origin requires presenting a certificate or submitting an invoice declaration describing the products "in sufficient detail" (European Commission 2004b). The exporter, or his authorized representative, is responsible for submitting information on the origin of products.

---

39. For a full treatment of textile rules of origin in US-Singapore, see Singapore Customs (2003).

40. Textile rules of origin also include a modified version of the de minimis provision. Products that fail to meet the requisite HS classification change, but contain nonoriginating material of not more than 7 percent of the total weight, can still qualify.

41. The definition of origin is also the same in EFTA bilateral FTAs with Bulgaria, Morocco, Romania, Tunisia, and Turkey.

42. A tariff heading refers to an HS classification at the 4-digit level.

43. The ex-works price equals the f.o.b. price of a good as it leaves a factory for export.

44. The 10 percent general tolerance rule allows the use of nonoriginating products up to 10 percent of the ex-works price.

45. However, note 5 to Annex 1 introduces a different exception for third-country basic textile materials, which, when used in the manufacture of certain textile products, represents 10 percent or less of the total weight of all the basic textile materials used (European Commission 2004b).

In 1992, the Swiss population rejected Swiss participation in the European Economic Area (EEA), which prevented the unification of several rules of origin regimes that are applied concurrently in Switzerland (Nell 1994). However, according to the WTO (2004b, 55), "the only fundamental difference between the EEA origin regime and the SEFTA is the full cumulation which can be used within the EEA."[46]

Instead of full cumulation, since 1997, Switzerland has enjoyed diagonal cumulation under the Pan-European Cumulation System, meaning that Swiss firms can use inputs from all of the system's members. All members operate identical origin rules concerning the working or processing of nonoriginating materials, and they all consent to cumulate inputs from other members. All EU and EFTA members, plus Turkey—more than 30 countries—participate in this system, and many partners to EFTA bilateral FTAs, such as Israel, Jordan, and Lebanon, are also adopting it.

Most EFTA bilateral FTAs define origin in a similar fashion. However, differences among agreements remain, since EFTA bilateral FTAs with countries such as Chile, Mexico, and Singapore have tried to include more liberal rules of origin taking into account the trade flows between the parties. These agreements have tried to include more liberal rules, particularly in those sectors where "either party is faced with a lack of raw materials" (EFTA 2002b).[47]

Recommendations for Manufactures Trade

The Swiss-US FTA should aim to eliminate tariffs on manufactured products to the maximum extent and reduce NTBs arising from technical standards, conformity assessment practices, and restrictive rules of origin. As the gravity and CGE models reported in chapter 8 suggest, tariff elimination could expand bilateral trade by at least 20 percent ($3.4 billion) and perhaps more than 100 percent ($17 billion). The US-Singapore and US-Australia FTAs illustrate what an FTA can achieve, but the Swiss agreement should be more ambitious. In this context, we offer the following recommendations:

- Switzerland should grant immediate duty-free access to nearly all of the products to which Australia gave immediate duty-free access to the

---

46. According to the European Commission (2004b), "full cumulation means that all operations carried out in the EEA are taken into account when assessing the final origin. It does not require that the goods be originating in one of the EEA partner countries before being exported for further working or processing in other EEA partners but it does require that all the working or processing necessary to confer origin is carried out on the product."

47. See, for example, the EFTA Secretariat's description of the rules of origin regime in the EFTA-Mexico FTA (EFTA 2002b).

United States in 2004. Those sectors would include autos and auto parts, chemicals and plastics, metal products, electrical equipment, and medical and scientific equipment.

■ The United States should immediately eliminate nearly all of its tariffs on watches, chemicals and pharmaceuticals, and optical and medical instruments. As in the US-Singapore FTA, the United States should also immediately eliminate nearly all of its tariffs on Swiss textiles and apparel.

■ Phaseouts of 4 years should apply to no more than 3 percent of tariff lines, and phaseouts of 5 to 10 years should apply to no more than 2 percent of tariff lines. In other words, US and Swiss tariffs on 95 percent of manufactures tariff lines should be eliminated immediately. No phaseout of manufactures tariffs should last longer than 10 years.

■ In the context of the FTA negotiations, each party should accord mutual recognition to approved conformity assessment bodies based in the other country. The mutual recognition process should be open ended, so that additional bodies can be recognized at a later date.

■ The parties should establish a working group on standards to do two things. First, on a periodic basis, it should recommend products for which US and Swiss technical standards should be harmonized, and products where the mutual recognition principle should apply. It should begin in areas in which Switzerland has already achieved harmonization or mutual recognition with the European Union. Second, the working group should identify products where manufacturer self-assessment can replace—if the firm desires—third-party conformity assessment by an independent body.

■ Diagonal cumulation is clearly the preferable approach to rules of origin, because it reduces their protective impact and opens up a wider array of sources for purchased inputs. However, since the United States has no experience with this approach, it would be too ambitious in the context of the Swiss-US FTA. Instead, the FTA should establish a working party to examine both US and Swiss FTA networks, with a mandate to identify third countries with products that could qualify as inputs under the bilateral rules of origin. The qualifying third countries need not be limited to countries that are partners of both the United States and Switzerland. Inputs from Canada and Mexico (NAFTA partners) might qualify, along with inputs from selected EFTA partners.

■ Swiss firms very often rely on purchased inputs beyond Swiss borders. The same is true of US firms, but to a lesser extent. A forward-looking Swiss-US FTA should accommodate, and indeed encourage, integration of the world economy, in which links of the value-added chain are made in different countries. This goal can be accomplished by liberal interpretation of the "substantial transformation" principle. Allow remanufactures, provide for low "build-down" and "build-up" thresholds, and avoid stringent change-of-tariff-heading rules. The least burdensome certification method should be adopted.

- Additionally, for products with low or zero tariffs on an MFN basis, the Swiss-US FTA should eliminate origin requirements so that firms can benefit from simplified bookkeeping and customs procedures. The ISI devised in the US-Singapore FTA is an excellent model.

In following these recommendations, both Switzerland and the United States can augment the already robust trade in manufactures between them. Of course, trade is not limited to goods; there is also considerable trade in services, which is covered in the next chapter.

Appendix 4A

Table 4A.1 Top Swiss exports of manufactures to the United States

HS-10	Description	2004 Millions of dollars	Share (percent)	2005 US tariff (percent)	Weighted average (percent)
Works of art (Ch. 97)		**121.5**	**0.012**	**Free**	**Free**
9703.00.00.00	Original sculptures and statuary, in any material	14.1	0.001	Free	
9701.10.00.00	Paintings, drawing, and pastels other than of heading 4906	107.4	0.010	Free	
Clocks and watches (Ch. 91)		**1,448.2**	**0.139**	**4.5**	**3.8**
9114.90.40.00	Parts for watches, nesoi	12.8	0.001	8.8	
9102.21.90.30	Straps, bands, or bracelets for wristwatches, not battery powered, over 17 jewels, nesoi	52.8	0.005	1.9[e]	
9102.21.90.20	Cases for wristwatches, over 17 jewels, nesoi	54.3	0.005	1.9[e]	
9102.21.90.10	Movements for wristwatches, over 17 jewels, nesoi	121.7	0.012	1.9[e]	
9102.21.70.30	Straps, bands or bracelets for wristwatches, over 17 jewels, with band of textile or base metal	38.0	0.004	3.8[d]	
9102.21.70.20	Cases for wristwatches, not battery powered, over 17 jewels, with band of textile or base metal	78.1	0.008	3.8[d]	
9102.21.70.10	Movements for wristwatches, not battery powered, over 17 jewels, with band of textile or base metal	150.1	0.014	3.8[d]	
9102.11.95.20	Cases for wristwatches, battery powered, with mechanical display only, more than 1 jewel, nesoi	56.7	0.005	4.7[c]	
9102.11.95.10	Movements for wristwatches, battery powered, with mechanical display only, more than 1 jewel, nesoi	60.8	0.006	4.7[c]	

124

9102.11.65.30	Straps, bands, or bracelets for wristwatches, with mechanical display only, more than 1 jewel	59.2	0.006	6.6[b]
9102.11.65.20	Cases for wristwatches, battery powered, with mechanical display only, more than 1 jewel	91.4	0.009	6.6[b]
9102.11.65.10	Movements for wristwatches, battery powered, with mechanical display only, more than 1 jewel	106.7	0.010	6.6[b]
9102.11.50.30	Straps, bands, or bracelets for wristwatches, more than 1 jewel, gold/silver plated cases	12.8	0.001	6.7[f]
9102.11.50.20	Cases for wristwatches, more than 1 jewel with band of textile or base metal, gold/silver plated cases	13.6	0.001	6.7[f]
9102.11.50.10	Movements for wristwatches, more than 1 jewel, band of textile or base metal, gold/silver plated cases	16.0	0.002	6.7[f]
9102.11.45.20	Cases for wristwatches, 1 jewel or none, with base metal case, nesoi	12.9	0.001	10.2[g]
9102.11.25.10	Movements for wristwatches, 1 jewel or none, band of textile or base metal case	18.9	0.002	9.7[h]
9101.29.90.20	Cases for wristwatches, not battery powered, over 17 jewels, without automatic winding, nesoi	18.6	0.002	Free
9101.29.90.10	Movements for wristwatches, not battery powered, over 17 jewels, without automatic winding, nesoi	36.1	0.003	Free
9101.21.50.20	Cases for wristwatches, no strap, not battery powered, with automatic winding, over 17 jewels, nesoi	87.5	0.008	Free
9101.21.50.10	Movements for wristwatches, bands, or bracelets, not battery powered, over 17 jewels, nesoi	109.2	0.011	Free
9101.21.30.00	Straps, bands, or bracelets for wristwatches not textile, not battery powered, over 17 jewels, nesoi	17.9	0.002	3.1
9101.21.10.00	Straps, bands, or bracelets for wristwatches textile, not battery powered, over 17 jewels	46.1	0.004	3.1
9101.11.80.30	Straps, bands, or bracelets for wristwatches, with mechanical display only, more than 1 jewel	35.6	0.003	4.9[a]

(table continues next page)

Table 4A.1 Top Swiss exports of manufactures to the United States *(continued)*

HS-10	Description	2004 Millions of dollars	2004 Share (percent)	2005 US tariff (percent)	Weighted average (percent)
9101.11.80.20	Cases for wristwatches, battery powered, with mechanical display only, more than 1 jewel	53.8	0.005	4.9a	
9101.11.80.10	Wristwatches, battery powered, with mechanical display only, more than 1 jewel	76.3	0.007	4.9a	
9101.11.40.20	Cases for wristwatches, with mechanical display only, 1 jewel or none	10.3	0.001	5.4l	
Optical, measuring precision, medical instruments and apparatus (Ch. 90)		**1,141.2**	**0.110**	**0.2**	**0.1**
9031.90.90.95	Parts and accessories	18.6	0.002	1.7	
9030.39.00.40	Apparatus to test voltage, and current, or resistance	11.9	0.001	1.7	
9027.90.54.30	Parts and accessories of 90273040	17.5	0.002	Free	
9027.80.25.00	Nuclear magnetic resonance instruments	10.8	0.001	Free	
9027.30.40.80	Spectrometers and spectrographs, electrical, nesoi	13.2	0.001	Free	
9022.90.60.00	Parts/accessories of apparatus based on X-ray use	41.7	0.004	0.8	
9021.90.80.00	Other appliances worn, carried, or implanted in the body	422.5	0.041	Free	
9021.50.00.00	Pacemakers stimulating heart muscles (excluding parts and accessories)	62.6	0.006	Free	
9021.40.00.00	Hearing aids, excluding parts and accessories	79.9	0.008	Free	
9021.39.00.00	Other artificial body parts and parts and accessories	16.0	0.002	Free	
9021.29.80.00	Dental fittings, except of plastic, and parts and accessories	45.6	0.004	Free	
9021.10.00.90	Other orthopedic or fracture appliances and parts or accessories, nesoi	10.3	0.001	Free	
9021.10.00.50	Bone plates, screws and nails, and other internal fixation devices or appliances	156.4	0.015	Free	
9018.90.80.00	Other instruments and appliances used in medical, surgical, dental, or veterinary sciences, nesoi	111.8	0.011	Free	

9018.50.00.00	Other ophthalmic instruments or appliances and parts or accessories	16.6	0.002	Free	
9018.49.80.80	Other instruments and appliances, used in dental sciences, and parts and accessories, nesoi	17.5	0.002	Free	
9018.49.80.40	Dental hand instruments and parts and accessories	40.7	0.004	Free	
9018.41.00.00	Dental drill engines, whether or not combined on a single base with other dental equipment, and parts and accessories	11.4	0.001	Free	
9018.39.00.50	Cannulae and the like and parts and accessories	11.2	0.001	Free	
9015.20.40.00	Electrical theodolites and tachymeters	12.6	0.001	Free	
9015.10.40.00	Electrical rangefinders	12.5	0.001	Free	
Aircraft (Ch. 88)		**139.0**	**0.013**	**Free**	**Free**
8803.30.00.60	Other airplane or helicopter parts used in military aircraft (not propellers, rotors, undercarriages, or parts thereof)	11.3	0.001	Free	
8802.30.00.60	New airplanes, other than multiple engines, nonmilitary, of an unladen weight exceeding 2,000 kg but not exceeding 15,000 kg	127.7	0.012	Free	
Machinery, electrical apparatus, and instruments; parts (Ch. 85)		**360.5**	**0.035**	**1.7**	**0.0**
8543.89.96.95	Electric machines and apparatus nspf	13.3	0.001	2.6	
8543.81.00.00	Machines and apparatus, proximity cards, and tags	10.1	0.001	Free	
8542.21.80.60	Monolithic integrated circuits, digital, silicon, memory	49.5	0.005	Free	
8542.10.00.00	Cards incorporating an electronic integrated circuit ("smart cards")	76.0	0.007	Free	
8538.90.80.40	Electrical metal contacts for heading 8535–37	12.3	0.001	3.5	
8536.90.80.85	Electrical equipment for switch circuits	25.9	0.002	Free	
8536.69.80.00	Lampholders, plugs, sockets, other	18.1	0.002	2.7	
8536.69.40.10	Coaxial connectors for switches	16.4	0.002	Free	
8536.50.90.65	Switches for electrical circuits, other	12.8	0.001	2.7	
8536.49.00.65	Contactors for voltage exceeding 60 v but not exceeding 1,000 v	30.1	0.003	2.7	
8535.21.00.00	Automatic circuit breakers for voltage exceeding 1000 v but less than 72.5 kv	10.2	0.001	2.7	

(table continues next page)

Table 4A.1 Top Swiss exports of manufactures to the United States *(continued)*

HS-10	Description	2004 Millions of dollars	2004 Share (percent)	2005 US tariff (percent)	Weighted average (percent)
8534.00.00.20	Printed circuits, base of plastic with glass, three or more layers of conducting materials	13.3	0.001	Free	
8516.71.00.80	Electric tea makers, domestic	10.5	0.001	3.7	
8515.90.30.00	Welding machine and apparatus and parts	17.0	0.002	1.6	
8515.80.00.80	Electric welding machines, nesoi; machines for hot spraying of metals	11.4	0.001	Free	
8501.10.40.60	Electric motors under 18.65w, with other brushes	33.4	0.003	4.4	
Boilers, machinery, and mechanical appliances (Ch. 84)		**632.0**	**0.061**	**1.1**	**1.1**
8481.90.90.80	Parts, nesoi, of taps, cocks, valves, similar appliances	33.3	0.003	Free	
8479.90.94.95	Other parts of machines and mechanical appliances having individual functions, nesoi	63.1	0.006	Free	
8479.89.98.97	Other machines and mechanical appliances having individual functions, parts thereof	48.1	0.005	2.5	
8479.89.84.90	Machines nesoi for production and assembly of diodes, transistors, and similar semiconductor devices	11.8	0.001	Free	
8473.30.50.00	Parts and accessories of heading 8471 machines, nesoi	10.4	0.001	Free	
8466.94.85.85	Machine parts, noniron, nonmechanical trans	13.1	0.001	4.7	
8466.93.95.85	Machine parts, noniron, metal, other	16.7	0.002	4.7	
8461.40.50.70	Gear grinding or finishing machines, metal removing, valued $3,025 and over, nesoi, new	11.8	0.001	4.4	
8456.30.10.20	Machine tools for working metal, by electro-discharge processes, traveling wire (wire-cut) type	27.1	0.003	3.5	

8456.10.10.10	Machine tools for working metal, by laser or other light/photon beam processes, of numerical control	31.2	0.003	3.5
8452.10.00.90	Sewing machines, household type, over $20 each	26.9	0.003	Free
8443.90.90.00	Parts of printing machinery, except textile, and machines for uses ancillary to printing	14.1	0.001	Free
8443.60.00.00	Machines for uses ancillary to printing	35.6	0.003	Free
8443.30.00.00	Flexographic printing machinery	11.5	0.001	2.2
8441.90.00.00	Parts of machinery for making up paper, pulp, paper, or paperboard, including cutting machines	13.5	0.001	Free
8441.30.00.00	Machines for making cartons, boxes, cases, tubes, drums, or similar containers, other than by molding	62.8	0.006	Free
8441.10.00.00	Cutting machines for paper products	10.9	0.001	Free
8431.39.00.10	Parts of pneumatic elevators and conveyors	18.5	0.002	Free
8422.40.91.80	Packing or wrapping machinery, nesoi	15.0	0.001	Free
8419.89.95.85	Industrial machinery, plant/equipment for treatment of materials, with change in temperature, nesoi	10.1	0.001	Free
8419.81.90.40	Industrial machinery and equipment used in restaurants or hotels for making hot drinks or cooking, nesoi	43.9	0.004	Free
8415.90.80.85	Parts of air conditioning machines, nesoi	15.5	0.001	1.4
8414.90.41.75	Parts of compressors, except compressor housings, nesoi	18.7	0.002	Free
8413.91.90.80	Parts of pumps for liquids, nesoi	11.0	0.001	Free
8411.99.90.60	Nonaircraft gas turbines parts, except turbojets and turbopropellers	57.4	0.006	2.4
Pearls, precious metals, and stones (Ch. 71)		**360.5**	**0.035**	**1.0**
7118.90.00.19	Gold coin, nesoi	20.0	0.002	Free
7115.90.05.30	Articles of precious metal, in rectangular shapes, 99.5 percent or more by weight of precious metal, gold	18.7	0.002	Free

(table continues next page)

Table 4A.1 Top Swiss exports of manufactures to the United States (*continued*)

HS-10	Description	2004 Millions of dollars	2004 Share (percent)	2005 US tariff (percent)	Weighted average (percent)
7114.11.70.00	Silver articles nesoi for office, desk, religious uses; smokers requisites nesoi	10.5	0.001	3.0	
7113.19.50.00	Gold or platinum jewelry, whether plated, clad, or not, nesoi	57.3	0.006	5.5	
7110.31.00.00	Rhodium, unwrought or in powder form	17.4	0.002	Free	
7110.21.00.00	Palladium, unwrought or in powder form	32.5	0.003	Free	
7110.11.00.20	Sponge of the metal platinum	26.1	0.003	Free	
7103.91.00.20	Sapphires cut but not set for jewelry	11.1	0.001	Free	
7103.91.00.10	Rubies cut but not set for jewelry	11.4	0.001	Free	
7102.39.00.50	Diamonds, nonindustrial, (cut, faceted, set, or mounted) weighing 0.5 carat and over each	155.4	0.015	Free	
Other chemicals and plastics (Ch. 32–40)		**173.8**	**0.017**	**4.6**	**3.8**
3926.90.98.80	Other articles of plastic, nesoi	16.4	0.002	5.3	
3921.12.50.00	Plates, sheets, film, foil and strip, cellular, of polymers of vinyl chloride, nesoi	10.6	0.001	6.5	
3907.99.00.50	Other polyesters, nesoi	10.7	0.001	6.5	
3907.30.00.00	Epoxide resins	12.1	0.001	6.1	
3824.90.91.50ʲ	Chemical products and preparations, residual products of chemical or allied industries, nesoi	10.9	0.001	5.0	
3707.90.32.90	Chemical preparations for photographic uses, nesoi	11.4	0.001	6.5	
3304.99.50.00	Beauty or make up preparations and preparations for skin care (other than medicaments), nesoi	15.5	0.001	Free	
3303.00.30.00	Perfumes and toilet waters containing alcohol	39.6	0.004	Free	
3215.19.00.50	Printing ink, not black, offset lithographic	15.3	0.001	1.8	

3204.17.04.85	Pigments and preparations based thereon, pigment black 1, etc.	16.2	0.002	6.5	Free
3204.16.30.00	Reactive dyes and preparations based thereon	15.0	0.001	6.5	
Pharmaceuticals (Ch. 30)		**1263.0**	**0.122**	**Free**	
3006.40.00.00	Dental cements and other dental fillings; bone reconstruction cements	13.3	0.001	Free	
3004.90.91.90	Medicaments put up in measured doses or in forms or packings for retail sale, nesoi	280.5	0.027	Free	
3004.90.91.85	Medicaments primarily affecting the eyes, ears, or respiratory system, nesoi	15.5	0.001	Free	
3004.90.91.60	Medicaments primarily affecting the digestive system put up in measured doses or in forms for retail sale	65.8	0.006	Free	
3004.90.91.40	Medicaments affecting the central nervous system, in measured doses or packings for retail sale, nesoi	13.7	0.001	Free	
3004.90.91.30	Anticonvulsants, hypnotics, and sedatives, affecting central nervous system, in doses for retail sale	27.3	0.003	Free	
3004.90.91.20	Cardiovascular medicaments put up in measured doses or in forms for retail sale, nesoi	229.7	0.022	Free	
3004.90.91.15	Antineoplastic and immunosuppressive medicaments, in doses or packings for retail sale, nesoi	31.5	0.003	Free	
3004.90.91.10	Antiinfective medicaments, in measured doses or packings for retail sale	28.1	0.003	Free	
3004.39.00.50	Products of heading 2937 but not containing antibiotics, not for veterinary use	123.5	0.012	Free	
3003.90.00.00	Other medicaments consisting of two or more constituents mixed together, etc.	149.9	0.014	Free	
3002.10.01.90	Blood fractions, nesoi	84.0	0.008	Free	
3002.10.01.10	Human blood plasma	200.1	0.019	Free	
Organic chemicals (Ch. 29)		**787.9**	**0.076**	**4.8**	**5.5**
2941.90.50.00	Other antibiotics (excluding natural, aromatic, or modified aromatic antibiotics)	17.3	0.002	Free	
2937.90.00.00	Hormones, prostaglandins, thromboxanes, and leukotrienes, natural or synthetic, nesoi	10.8	0.001	Free	

(table continues next page)

Table 4A.1 Top Swiss exports of manufactures to the United States *(continued)*

HS-10	Description	2004 Millions of dollars	2004 Share (percent)	2005 US tariff (percent)	Weighted average (percent)
2936.28.00.00	Vitamin E (tocopherols and related compounds with vitamin E activity) and its derivatives	50.0	0.005	Free	
2936.21.00.00	Vitamins A and its derivatives unmixed	15.5	0.001	Free	
2935.00.60.00	Other sulfonamide drugs (not anti-infective agents)	15.4	0.001	6.5	
2934.99.30.00	Heterocyclic compounds used as drugs, nesoi	66.9	0.006	6.5	
2934.99.12.00	Heterocyclic compounds used as fungicides, nesoi	19.5	0.002	6.5	
2933.99.65.00	Anticonvulsants, hypnotics, and sedatives with heterocyclic compounds and nitrogen hetero-atom(s) only	50.9	0.005	6.5	
2933.99.53.00	Cardiovascular drugs, not elsewhere specified	234.4	0.023	6.5	
2933.69.60.50	Other compounds containing an unfused triazine ring (whether or not hydrogenated) in their structure	11.3	0.001	3.5	
2933.59.46.00	Antidepressants, tranquilizers, and other psychotherapeutic agents, with pyrimidine or piperazine ring	14.2	0.001	6.5	
2933.49.70.00	Compounds with quinoline/isoquinoline ring system	10.1	0.001	6.5	
2933.29.20.00	Aromatic or modified aromatic drugs containing an unfused imidazole ring in the structure	19.2	0.002	6.0	
2932.99.90.90	Other heterocyclic compounds with hetero-atom(s)	16.4	0.002	3.7	
2930.90.90.90	Nonaromatic organo-sulfur compounds, nesoi	10.3	0.001	3.7	
2929.90.15.00	Other aromatic compounds with other nitrogen function of products in US note 3 to section 6	15.6	0.002	6.5	

2924.29.47.00	Other cyclic amides used as pesticides	83.2	0.008	6.5
2924.19.80.00	Acyclic amide derivatives, salts thereof	10.8	0.001	6.5
2922.50.25.00	Other aromatic amino-alcohol-phenol drugs	45.5	0.004	6.5
2921.49.43.00	Aromatic monoamine drugs, nesoi	26.2	0.003	6.5
2914.29.50.00	Other cyclanic, cyclenic, cycloterpenic ketones without other oxygen	16.2	0.002	4.8
2914.23.00.00	Iones and methyliones	16.9	0.002	5.5
2912.29.60.00	Other cyclic aldehydes without oxygen function	11.3	0.001	5.5
Other industrial products		**204.0**	**0.020**	**3.2** **2.9**
9503.30.00.00	Other construction set/toy/parts, other	15.8	0.002	Free
8211.93.00.30	Penknives, pocketknives and others with folding blades	19.6	0.002	7.7[k]
8202.99.00.00	Other saw blades and parts, base metal	19.5	0.002	Free
8202.40.60.60	Chainsaw blades and parts, base metal other, not continuous lengths	18.4	0.002	Free
8202.40.60.30	Chainsaw blades, base metal other, continuous lengths	12.4	0.001	7.2
7324.10.00.00	Sinks and wash basins of stainless steel	11.4	0.001	3.4
7306.30.50.15	Tubes, pipes, and hollow profiles, welded, nesoi, iron or nonalloy steel, 165mm, cold-drawn, not for boilers	14.2	0.001	Free
6203.11.90.00	M/b suits of wool lt 30% slk, nt knt/crchtd nesoi	11.2	0.001	17.5
5911.20.10.00	Textile products and articles for technical uses, bolting cloth, whether made up or not	12.6	0.001	3.3
4811.51.60.00	Paper and paperboard, coated, impregnated, or covered with plastics, bleached, over 150 g/m², nesoi	12.6	0.001	Free
4811.51.40.00	Paper and paperboard, coated, with plastics, bleached, over 150 g/m², 15×36×15cm, max 3mm thick, in strips or rolls	19.8	0.002	Free
4202.91.00.90	Containers, with outer surface of leather, composition leather, or patent leather, nesoi	10.8	0.001	4.5
2710.11.15.14	Unleaded gasoline, reformulated	13.1	0.001	1.8[l]

(table continues next page)

Table 4A.1 Top Swiss exports of manufactures to the United States *(continued)*

| HS-10 | Description | 2004 | | 2005 US tariff (percent) | Weighted average (percent) |
		Millions of dollars	Share (percent)		
2707.10.00.00	Benzene, weight of aromatic constituents greater than nonaromatic	12.7	0.001	Free	1.2
Subtotal		6,632	0.638	2.4	1.2
Total Swiss manufactured exports to the United States		10,388	1.000	n.a.	n.a.
Total US manufactured imports from all countries		1,353,654	n.a.	4.3	2.6[m]

n.a. = not available

nesoi = not otherwise available

a. 2002 ad valorem equivalent of 87¢ each + 6.25 percent on the case and strap, band, or bracelet + 5.3 percent on the battery.
b. 2002 ad valorem equivalent of 76¢ each + 8.5 percent on the case + 14 percent on the strap, band, or bracelet + 5.3 percent on the battery.
c. 2002 ad valorem equivalent of 76¢ each + 8.5 percent on the case + 2.8 percent on the strap, band, or bracelet + 5.3 percent on the battery.
d. 2002 ad valorem equivalent of $1.53 each + 4.2 percent on the case + 9.8 percent on the strap, band, or bracelet.
e. 2002 ad valorem equivalent of $1.53 each + 4.2 percent on the case + 2 percent on the strap, band, or bracelet.
f. 2002 ad valorem equivalent of 80¢ each + 6 percent on the case + 14 percent on the strap, band, or bracelet + 5.3 percent on the battery.
g. 2002 ad valorem equivalent of 40¢ each + 8.5 percent on the case + 2.8 percent on the strap, band, or bracelet + 5.3 percent on the battery.
h. 2002 ad valorem equivalent of 40¢ each + 8.5 percent on the case + 14 percent on the strap, band, or bracelet + 5.3 percent on the battery.
i. 2002 ad valorem equivalent of 51¢ each + 6.25 percent on the case, strap, band, or bracelet + 5.3 percent on the battery.
j. This number does not match a position at 10-digit level in the 2005 US HTS; thus we only use the first 8 digits.
k. 2002 ad valorem equivalent of 3¢ each + 5.4 percent.
l. 2002 ad valorem equivalent of 52.5¢/bbl.
m. 2002 World Bank Figure cited in 2005 Index of Economic Freedom, www.heritage.org.

Note: Some descriptions have been slightly abbreviated for formatting purposes.

Sources: USITC (2005b, d).

Table 4A.2 Top US exports of manufactures to Switzerland, 2004

HS-6	Description	Millions of dollars	Share (percent)	Average Swiss tariff[a] (percent) Simple	Weighted
Works of art (Ch. 97)		**926.6**	**0.140**	**Free**	**Free**
9706.00	Antiques of an age exceeding one hundred years	37.8	0.006	Free	
9703.00	Original sculptures and statuary, in any material	87.0	0.013	Free	
9702.00	Original engravings, prints and lithographs, framed or not	13.3	0.002	Free	
9701.10	Paintings, drawings, and pastels, hand-executed works of art, framed or not	788.5	0.119	Free	
Clocks and watches (Ch. 91)		**82.7**	**0.013**	**1.3**	**0.3**
9101.99	Pocketwatches and other watches, except wristwatches, with cases of precious metal, not battery powered	10.6	0.002	3.6[b]	
9101.21	Wristwatches, not battery powered, with cases of precious metal (or of metal clad with precious metal), with automatic winding	14.2	0.002	0.1	
9101.11	Wristwatches, battery powered, with cases of precious metal (or of metal clad with precious metal), with mechanical display only	57.9	0.009	0.3	
Optical, measuring precision, and medical instruments and apparatus (Ch. 90)		**518.7**	**0.079**	**0.9**	**0.3**
9031.80	Measuring or checking instruments, appliances, and machines, nesoi	12.6	0.002	9.4	
9027.80	Instruments and apparatus for physical or chemical analysis, nesoi	16.4	0.003	Free	
9027.30	Spectrometers, spectrophotometers, and spectrographs using optical radiations (ultraviolet, visible, infrared)	10.3	0.002	Free	
9022.14	Apparatus based on the use of X-rays for medical, surgical, or veterinary uses, including radiography or radiotherapy apparatus, nesoi	14.8	0.002	Free	
9021.90	Appliances worn, carried, or implanted in the body, to compensate for a defect or disability; parts and accessories thereof	177.8	0.027	Free	

(table continues next page)

Table 4A.2 Top US exports of manufactures to Switzerland, 2004 *(continued)*

HS-6	Description	Millions of dollars	Share (percent)	Average Swiss tariff[a] (percent) Simple	Weighted
9021.39	Artificial parts of the body (other than artificial joints) and parts and accessories thereof, nesoi	32.0	0.005	Free	
9021.31	Artificial joints and parts, and accessories thereof	15.1	0.002	n.a.	
9021.10	Orthopedic or fracture appliances, and parts and accessories thereof	81.0	0.012	Free	
9018.90	Instruments and appliances for medical, surgical, or veterinary sciences, nesoi, and parts and accessories thereof	83.7	0.013	Free	
9018.49	Instruments and appliances used in dental sciences, nesoi, and parts and accessories thereof	11.3	0.002	Free	
9018.39	Medical etc. needles nesoi, catheters, cannulae, and the like; parts and accessories thereof	10.9	0.002	Free	
9018.19	Electro-diagnostic apparatus (and apparatus for functional exploratory examination) nesoi, and parts, etc.	19.7	0.003	Free	
9014.20	Instruments and appliances for aeronautical or space navigation (other than compasses)	22.6	0.003	Free	
9001.90	Lenses, prisms, mirrors, and other optical elements, unmounted, other than elements of glass not optically worked	10.5	0.002	2.6[c]	
Motor vehicles and aircraft (Chs. 87 and 88)		**385.2**	**0.058**	**0.5**	**0.2**
8803.30	Parts of airplanes or helicopters, nesoi	189.8	0.029	Free	
8802.40	Airplanes and other aircraft nesoi, unladen weight exceeding 15,000 kg	124.9	0.019	0.1	
8802.30	Airplanes and other aircraft nesoi, of an unladen weight exceeding 2,000 kg, but not exceeding 15,000 kg	11.8	0.002	0.1	
8703.24	Passenger motor vehicles with spark-ignition internal combustion reciprocating piston engine, cylinder capacity over 3,000 cc	30.8	0.005	1.3	

8703.23	Passenger motor vehicles with spark-ignition internal combustion reciprocating piston engine, cylinder capacity over 1,500 cc, but not over 3,000 cc	27.9	0.004	0.9[c]	2.5
Machinery, electrical apparatus, and instruments; parts (Ch. 85)		117.1	0.018	2.9	
8542.21	Electronic monolithic digital integrated circuits	38.9	0.006	Free	
8541.40	Photosensitive semiconductor devices, including photovoltaic cells; light-emitting diodes	11.7	0.002	Free	
8529.90	Parts (except antennas and reflectors) for use with radio transmission, radar, radio navigational aid, reception, and television apparatus, nesoi	14.5	0.002	9.7[c]	
8522.90	Parts and accessories, except pickup cartridges, for sound reproducing, sound recording, and video recording or reproducing apparatus	20.7	0.003	6.4[d]	
8517.50	Electrical telecommunication apparatus for carrier-current line systems or for digital line systems, nesoi	12.3	0.002	Free	
8504.40	Electrical static converters; power supplies for adapter machines or units of 8471	19.0	0.003	1.0[d]	
Boilers, machinery, and mechanical appliances (Ch. 84)		640.2	0.097	1.6	3.3
8481.80	Taps, cocks, valves, and similar appliances for pipes, vats, including thermostatically controlled valves, nesoi	21.9	0.003	8.6[d]	
8479.90	Parts of machines and mechanical appliances having individual functions	18.5	0.003	0.8[d]	
8473.30	Parts and accessories for automatic data processing machines and units thereof, magnetic or optical readers, transcribing machines, etc., nesoi	56.3	0.009	Free	
8471.80	Automatic data processing units, nesoi	19.5	0.003	Free	
8471.70	Automatic data processing storage units, nesoi	10.8	0.002	Free	
8471.60	Automatic data processing input or output units, containing storage units in the same housing or not, nesoi	13.6	0.002	Free	
8471.49	Digital automatic data processing machines and units thereof presented in the form of systems, nesoi	10.6	0.002	Free	
8440.10	Bookbinding machinery, including book-sewing machines	16.4	0.002	0.1	
8411.99	Parts of gas turbines, nesoi (not parts for turbojets or turbopropellers)	52.8	0.008	0.2	
8411.91	Parts of turbojets or turbopropellers	187.0	0.028	0.1	

(table continues next page)

Table 4A.2 Top US exports of manufactures to Switzerland, 2004 (continued)

HS-6	Description	Millions of dollars	Share (percent)	Average Swiss tariff[a] (percent) Simple	Weighted
8411.82	Gas turbines, not turbojets or turbopropellers, of power over 5,000 kw	31.9	0.005	0.0	
8411.12	Turbojets of a thrust exceeding 25 kn	20.1	0.003	0.1	
8409.91	Parts for use with spark-ignition internal combustion piston engines (including rotary engines), nesoi	180.9	0.027	10.4	
Pearls, precious metals, and stones (Ch. 71)		**756.1**	**0.114**	**n.a.**	**n.a.**
7118.90	Coin, nesoi	16.8	0.003	Free	
7116.20	Articles of precious/semiprecious stones—natural, synthetic, reconstructed	19.6	0.003	3999 Sfr/100kg	
7113.19	Jewelry and parts thereof, of precious metal other than silver	256.7	0.039	0.7	
7112.91	Gold waste and scrap, including metal clad with gold, but excluding sweepings containing other precious metals	49.4	0.007	8 Sfr/100kg	
7110.21	Palladium, unwrought or in powder form	32.3	0.005	80 Sfr/100kg	
7106.91	Silver, unwrought nesoi (other than powder)	17.3	0.003	7 Sfr/100kg	
7103.91	Rubies, sapphires, and emeralds, otherwise worked	32.1	0.005	n.a.	
7102.39	Diamonds, nonindustrial, worked, including polished or drilled	331.9	0.050	800 Sfr/100kg	
Other chemicals and plastics (Ch. 32–40)		**238.1**	**0.036**	**3.3**	**4.4**
3824.90	Chemical products and preparations of the chemical or allied industries, nesoi; residual products of the chemical or allied industries, nesoi	70.1	0.011	7.8[d]	
3822.00	Composite diagnostic or laboratory reagents, not heading 3002/3006 pharmas; certified reference materials	16.8	0.003	Free	
3304.99	Beauty or makeup preparations and preparations for skin care (excluding medicaments) nesoi, including sunscreens and suntan preparations	26.5	0.004	8.1	
3303.00	Perfumes and toilet waters	41.0	0.006	4.4	

3206.49	Coloring matter of a kind used for coloring any material or used in the manufacture of coloring preparations (other than paints or enamels), nesoi	50.8	0.008	1.8	
3204.19	Synthetic organic coloring matter and specified preparations based thereon, nesoi	14.5	0.002	0.3[d]	
3204.17	Pigments and preparations based thereon	18.5	0.003	0.6	
Pharmaceuticals (Ch. 30)		**1259.1**	**0.191**	**Free**	**Free**
3004.90	Medicaments, in measured doses (excluding vaccines, coated bandages, and pharmaceutical goods), nesoi	347.9	0.053	Free	
3004.40	Medicaments, containing alkaloids or derivatives thereof, but not containing hormones and similar steroids or antibiotics	72.6	0.011	Free	
3004.39	Medicaments, containing hormones or other steroids used primarily as hormones, but not containing antibiotics, nesoi	28.3	0.004	Free	
3003.39	Medicaments, containing hormones or other steroids, but not containing antibiotics, not in measured doses, etc.	486.9	0.074	Free	
3002.90	Human blood; animal blood prepared for therapeutic, etc. uses; toxins, cultures of micro-organisms, and similar products, nesoi	121.0	0.018	Free	
3002.20	Vaccines for human medicine	70.0	0.011	Free	
3002.10	Antisera and other blood fractions, and modified immunological products	132.3	0.020	Free	
Organic chemicals (Ch. 29)		**76.8**	**0.012**	**0.1**	**0.0**
2941.90	Antibiotics, nesoi	25.1	0.004	Free	
2933.99	Heterocyclic compounds with nitrogen hetero-atom(s) only, nesoi	26.1	0.004	n.a.	
2930.90	Organo-sulfur compounds, nesoi	14.6	0.002	0.1[d]	
2918.30	Carboxylic acids with aldehyde or ketone function, but no other oxygen function, their anhydrides, halides, peroxides, etc.	11.0	0.002	0.1[d]	
Other industrial products		**148.1**	**0.023**	**2.2**	**1.6**
8703.24	Passenger motor vehicles with spark-ignition internal combustion reciprocating piston engine, cyclinder capacity over 3,000 cc	30.8	0.005	1.3	

(table continues next page)

Table 4A.2 Top US exports of manufactures to Switzerland, 2004 *(continued)*

HS-6	Description	Millions of dollars	Share (percent)	Average Swiss tariff[a] (percent) Simple	Weighted
8703.23	Passenger motor vehicles, spark-ignition internal combustion reciprocating piston engine, cylinder capacity 1,500 cc to 3,000 cc	27.9	0.004	0.9[d]	
8108.90	Titanium and articles thereof, nesoi	10.6	0.002	2.1	
7602.00	Aluminum waste and scrap	11.1	0.002	Free	
7307.22	Pipe or tube fittings, nesoi, stainless-steel threaded elbows, bends, and sleeves	27.6	0.004	1.9[d]	
5201.00	Cotton, not carded or combed	24.1	0.004	Free	
4911.99	Printed matter, nesoi	16.1	0.002	8.9[e]	
	Subtotal	5,090	0.771	2.6	0.8
	Total US manufactured exports to Switzerland	6,607	1.000	—	—
	Total Swiss manufactured imports from all countries	88,704	2.3	0.8	

nesoi = not elsewhere specified or included

a. Values reported correspond to ad valorem equivalents for non–ad valorem tariffs. When more than one tariff line (at eight digits) corresponded to the position at six digits, simple averages were computed. Superscript character corresponding to footnote c indicates that such an approach was taken.

b. This value corresponds to the top value of the range for chapter 91 as reported by the WTO (2004b). According to UNCTAD, the ad valorem equivalent for those tariff lines is 20.4 percent. The Swiss Federal Customs Administration establishes that the specific tariff for this product is 1.10 Swiss francs for each unit.

c. This value corresponds to the top value of the range for chapter 85 as reported by the WTO (2004b). According to UNCTAD, the ad valorem equivalent for those tariff lines is 13.4 percent.

d. The tariff level is an average of several tariff lines, which vary depending on final use of the product.

e. This value corresponds to the top value of the range for chapter 49 as reported by the WTO (2004b). According to UNCTAD, the ad valorem equivalent for those tariff lines is 70.9 percent. The Swiss Federal Customs Administration establishes that the specific tariff for this product is 48 Swiss francs/100kg.

Sources: USITC (2005b) and UNCTAD (2002).

Table 4A.3 Selected Swiss ad valorem tariff peaks, 2004[a]

HS-2	Description	Highest tariff value
25	Salt, sulphur, earths and stone, plastering materials, lime and cement	15.5
28	Inorganic chemicals, organic or inorganic compounds of precious metals	16.2
32	Tanning or dyeing extracts and other coloring matter	16.0
33	Essential oils and resinoids, perfumery, cosmetic or toilet preparations	24.3
35	Albuminoidal substances, modified starches, glues, enzymes[b]	208.2
36	Explosives, pyrotechnic products, matches, pyrophoric alloys	17.8
38	Miscellaneous chemical products	20.7
39	Plastics and articles thereof	15.1
40	Rubber and articles thereof	16.1
42	Articles of animal gut (other than silk worm gut)	16.5
44	Wood and articles of wood, wood charcoal	18.3
48	Paper and paperboard	23.9
66	Umbrellas, sun umbrellas, walking sticks, seat sticks, whips	10.0
67	Prepared feathers and down, articles made of feathers or down	13.4
70	Glass and glassware	25.8
72	Iron and steel	13.2
73	Articles of iron or steel	20.2
76	Aluminum and articles thereof	10.1
81	Other base metals, cermets, articles thereof	30.7
83	Miscellaneous articles of base metal	15.1
84	Nuclear reactors, boilers, machinery, and mechanical appliances	16.9
87	Vehicles other than railway or tramway rolling stock	10.5
96	Miscellaneous manufactured articles	11.2

a. Shipment data are not available, nor are numbers of 6-digit tariff lines. Peaks in textile and clothing HS chapters are numerous but were excluded.
b. Products with HS codes 35011090 and 35021990 are the only two nontextile industrial products in the Swiss schedule subject to tariffs higher than 50 percent. Only 6 tariff lines in the entire Swiss schedule have rates above 50 percent.

Source: WTO (2004b).

Table 4A.4 Selected US ad valorem tariff peaks, 2002[a]

HS-6	Tariff item	Ad valorem lines	Simple average[b] (percent)
8704.21	G.v.w. not exceeding 5 tonnes	1	25.0
8704.23	G.v.w. exceeding 20 tonnes	1	25.0
8704.31	G.v.w. not exceeding 5 tonnes	1	25.0
8704.32	G.v.w. exceeding 5 tonnes	1	25.0
8704.90	Other	1	25.0
4202.19	Other	1	20.0
7013.10	Of glass-ceramics	2	16.5
7013.99	Other	10	15.4
8605.00	Railway or tramway passenger coaches, not self-propelled; luggage vans, post office coaches, and other special purpose railway or tramway coaches, not self-propelled, excluding those of heading no. 86.04	1	14.8
8606.10	Tank wagons and the like	1	14.8
8606.20	Insulated or refrigerated vans and wagons, other than those of subheading no. 8606.10	1	14.8
8606.30	Self-discharging vans and wagons, other than those of subheading no. 8606.10 or 8606.20	1	14.8
8606.91	Covered and closed	1	14.8
8606.92	Open, with nonremovable sides of a height exceeding 60 cm	1	14.8
8606.99	Other	1	14.8
8704.22	G.v.w. exceeding 5 tonnes but not exceeding 20 tonnes	2	14.5
9603.10	Brooms and brushes, consisting of twigs or other vegetable materials bound together, with handles or none	5	14.4
9102.29	Other	1	14.0
7013.29	Other	7	13.9
7013.32	Of glass having a linear coefficient of expansion not exceeding 5×10^{-6} per kelvin, within a temperature range of 0 to 300°C	4	13.9
6905.10	Roofing tiles	1	13.5
4203.29	Other	8	13.3
6911.10	Tableware and kitchenware	12	13.3
7013.39	Other	6	13.0
9607.19	Other	1	13.0
8540.11	Color	7	12.9

(table continues next page)

Table 4A.4 Selected US ad valorem tariff peaks, 2002 *(continued)*

HS-6	Tariff item	Ad valorem lines	Simple average[b] (percent)
4202.12	With outer surface of plastics or textile materials	4	12.6
7013.91	Of lead crystal	4	12.6
7318.11	Coach screws	1	12.5
7318.12	Other wood screws	1	12.5
6907.10	Tiles, cubes, and similar articles, rectangular or not, the largest surface area of which is capable of being enclosed in a square, the side of which is less than 7 cm	1	12.0
6907.90	Other	1	12.0
7013.31	Of lead crystal	4	11.6
6908.10	Tiles, cubes, and similar articles, rectangular or not, the largest surface area of which is capable of being enclosed in a square the side of which is less than 7 cm	3	11.5
9607.20	Parts	1	11.5
9615.19	Other	1	11.0
4202.32	With outer surface of plastic sheeting or textile materials	5	10.9
6908.90	Other	1	10.6
8108.90	Other	2	10.3
6702.90	Of other materials	3	10.2
7013.21	Of lead crystal	4	10.1
4202.22	With outer surface of plastic sheeting or textile materials	7	10.0
4202.92	With outer surface of plastic sheeting or textile materials	9	10.0
7111.00	Base metals, silver or gold, clad with platinum, not further worked than semimanufactured	1	10.0
7202.50	Ferro-silico-chromium	1	10.0
9113.20	Of base metal, whether or not gold- or silver-plated	4	10.0
9607.11	Fitted with chain scoops of base metal	1	10.0

G.v.w. = gross vehicle weight

a. Tariff peak is defined as tariff above 10 percent. Textiles, clothing, and footwear tariff lines are excluded. About 326 6-digit level headings in HS chapters 50 through 64 of the US tariff schedule (textiles, clothing, and footwear) are subject to average tariffs exceeding 10 percent. They were excluded to save space.
b. Simple average of tariff lines subject to tariffs above 15 percent only.

Source: IDB, Hemispheric Trade and Tariff Database.

Table 4A.5 High US tariffs on selected Swiss manufactured exports at four-digit level

HS-4	Tariff item	2002 average tariff	US tariff lines > 5 percent	2004 Swiss exports to United States (millions of dollars)
6203	Men's suits, ensembles, suit-type jackets, trousers, not knitted or crocheted	14.1	39	20
6204	Women's suits, ensembles, dresses, trousers, not knitted or crocheted	12.4	61	19
4202	Travel goods, cases, handbags, and other containers, of various materials	10.3	63	17
9108	Watch movements, complete and assembled	8.3	11	11
9113	Watch straps, watch bands, and watch bracelets, and parts thereof	7.6	5	29
2710	Petroleum and oils from bituminous minerals and certain derivatives	6.8	15	14
3204	Synthetic organic coloring matter and preparations	6.6	46	76
8211	Knives with cutting blades	6.5	14	32
3809	Finishing agents, dye carriers, and preparations for textiles and papers	6.3	5	13
7113	Articles of jewelry and parts, of or with precious metal	6.3	15	65
2929	Nitrogen function compounds nesoi	6.3	10	27
2921	Amine-function compounds	6.0	46	34
3907	Polyacetals, polycarbonates, alkyds, and other polyesters, in primary forms	6.0	9	26
9011	Compound optical microscopes and parts and accessories thereof	5.7	4	15

HS-4	Description			
9013	Liquid crystal devices, lasers, optical appliances, and instruments	5.6	5	11
9102	Watches, wrist, pocket, and other, with other cases	5.6	18	1,108
2916	Monocarboxylic acids and their derivatives	5.5	23	25
3921	Plates, sheets, film, foil, and strip nesoi, of plastics	5.5	12	28
2934	Nucleic acids and their salts, other heterocyclic compounds	5.5	42	101
2922	Oxygen-function amino-compounds	5.3	50	58
2932	Heterocyclic compounds with oxygen hetero-atom(s) only	5.2	17	34
7010	Glass containers for packing of goods; jars, lids, and other glass closures	5.2	6	10
9114	Clock or watch parts, nesoi	5.2	6	23
2924	Carboxyamide and other amide-function compounds	5.1	29	116
2918	Carboxylic acids with oxygen function, their anhydrides, and derivatives	5.0	33	26
2912	Aldehydes; cyclic polymers of aldehydes; paraformaldehyde	5.0	16	22
	Subtotal for high-tariff HS-4 manufactured exports	6.7[a]	600	1,960
	Total HS-4 manufactured exports over $10 million	2.5[b]	914	6,632

a. Simple average of all observations in the column.

b. Simple average of tariffs for Swiss HS-4 exports to the United States exceeding $10 million. By comparison, in 2002, the simple average US MFN tariff for nonagricultural products (WTO definition) was 4.2 percent.

Note: 4-digit level headings facing average applied tariffs exceeding 5 percent.

Source: USITC (2005b).

Table 4A.6 Phaseouts for tariffs on manufactured goods, US-Singapore FTA[a]

Product	United States				Singapore	
	EDF	0	4	8 to 10	EDF	0 to 10
Chemicals						
Organic (Ch. 29)	254	160[b]	337[c]	207[d]	All	0
Pharmaceuticals (Ch. 30)	40	0	1	0	All	0
Fertilizers (Ch. 31)	25	0	0	0	All	0
Cosmetics (Ch. 33)	32	13	3	0	All	0
Starches, enzymes, et al. (Ch. 35)	5	12	4	1[e]	All	0
Construction materials						
Stone, cement, and ceramics (Chs. 68–69)	53	28	20	14[f]	All	0
Glass and glassware (Ch. 70)	39	47	44	28[g]	All	0
Tools and articles of metal (Chs. 82–83)	55	80	50	8[h]	All	0
Consumer goods						
Jewelry (Ch. 71)	48	33	16	8[i]	All	0
Clocks (Ch. 91)	24	39	95	19[k]	All	0
Electrical machinery						
Boilers, machinery; parts (Ch. 84)	547	273	31	0	All	0
Electrical apparatus; parts (Ch. 85)	247	316	39	7[l]	All	0
Optical and other instruments (Ch. 90)						
Optical (HTS 9001–05)	4	24	3	2[m]	All	0
Photographic (HTS 9006–10)	41	22	4	0	All	0
Medical and other (HTS 9011–30)	109	97	9	4[n]	All	0
Plastics						
Plastics (Ch. 39)	28	86	105	3[o]	All	0
Rubbers (Ch. 40)	58	78	10	1[p]	All	0
Textiles						
Articles of apparel (Chs. 61–62)	11[q]	557	0	0	All	0
Vehicles and transport goods						
Aircraft (Ch. 88)	17	1	0	0	All	0
Automobiles (Ch. 87)	80	61	7	14[r]	All	0
Railway and tramway (Ch. 86)	8	15	2	7[s]	All	0
Total	1725	1942	780	323	All	0
As percentage	36	41	16	7		

EDF = existing duty-free access

a. All tariff lines in the corresponding chapter were considered. Note that the number of lines in each chapter varies across countries. Before the agreement, Singapore applied tariffs only on beer (HTS 2203) and Samsu (2208.90).

(table continues next page)

b. Tariff lines enjoying protection lower than 5 percent are for the most part subject to immediate phaseout.

c. Medium phaseouts correspond to tariff lines enjoying moderate tariff protection, ranging between 5 and 8 percent.

d. Long phaseouts correspond to tariff lines enjoying high tariffs above 8 percent. These are fairly evenly distributed throughout the chapter. At 4 digits, the most problematic ones appear to be HTS: 2903–04, 2908, 2915–18, 2921–27, 2932–35, and 2942. The relation between existing tariff protection and phaseouts applies to most manufacturing chapters, with the exception of textiles.

e. Stage C (8 years): Other egg albumin (HTS 3502.19.00).

f. Most of these long phaseouts occur in HTS 6907.10 and 90; 6908.10; 6911.10; and 6912.00.

g. Most of these long phaseouts are related to glassware products (HTS 7113), and in particular: 7113.10; 21-39; 91; and 99.

h. Most of these long phaseouts occur in HTS 8203; 8206; 8211; and 8215.

i. Stage C (8 years): Unworked or cut but not set precious stones (HTS 7103.10.40 and 7103.9950); iridium (7110.49.00); ropes and chains of precious metal (HTS 7113.11.20, 7117.19.20, 7117.19.90, 7117.90.90); other articles of precious stones (7116.20.50).

j. Not used.

k. Most of these long phaseouts occurs in HTS 9101.29; 9102.29; 9106.90; 9108.90; and 9113.20.

l. Most of these long phaseouts occur is HTS: 8513.10; 8513.90; and 8540.11.

m. Stage C (8 years): Parts and accessories (HTS 9005.9040 and 9005.90.60).

n. Most of these long phaseouts occur in HTS: 9013.10 and 90; 9015.90 and 9017.90.

o. Most of these long phaseouts occur in HTS: 3907.40; 3912.90; and 3926.20.

p. HTS 4015.19.10.

q. This number differs substantially from the number of tariff-lines enjoying "existing duty-free" treatment in the US Tariff Schedule for the US-Australia FTA. A number of tariff-lines, for example 6103.19.15, changed status in the interval between negotiations.

r. Most of these long phaseouts correspond to motor vehicles for the transport of goods (HTS 8704.21 through 90), and bicycles (HTS 8712 through 14).

s. All of these long phaseouts correspond to railway or traimway passenger coaches or freight cars (HTS 8606 and 8607).

Notes: As a rule of thumb, there is a positive relation between existing MFN tariffs and phaseouts. See notes b, c, and d. Distribution of tariff lines according to phaseout periods for selected products.

Source: USTR (2003a).

Table 4A.7 Phaseouts for tariffs on manufactured goods, US-Australia FTA[a]

Product	United States			Australia		
	EDF	**0**	**4 to 18**	**EDF**	**0**	**4 to 10**
Chemicals						
Organic (Ch. 29)	264	723	1[b]	310	51	1[c]
Pharmaceuticals (Ch. 30)	40	1	0	26	8	0
Fertilizers (Ch. 31)	25	0	0	22	0	0
Cosmetics (Ch. 33)	32	15	1[d]	17	22	0
Starches, enzymes, et al. (Ch. 35)	5	12	5[e]	12	4	0
Consumer goods						
Jewelry (Ch. 71)	47	58	1[f]	34	11	0
Clocks (Ch. 91)	21	157	0	47	5	0
Construction materials						
Stone, cement, and ceramics (Chs. 68–69)	59	40	27[g]	20	58	0
Glass and glassware (Ch. 70)	43	93	32[h]	36	30	6[i]
Tools and articles of metal (Chs. 82–83)	52	115	19[k]	13	93	0
Electrical machinery						
Boilers, machinery; parts (Ch. 84)	568	289	16[l]	268	335	0
Electrical apparatus; parts (Ch. 85)	278	322	12[m]	165	184	0
Optical and other instruments (Ch. 90)						
Optical (HTS 9001-05)	4	27	2[n]	7	11	0
Photographic (HTS 9006-10)	39	20	4[o]	43	5	0
Medical and other (HTS 9011-30)	123	87	8[p]	108	19	0
Plastics						
Plastics (Ch. 39)	28	194	0	12	132	0
Rubbers (Ch. 40)	59	88	2[q]	8	85	0
Textiles						
Articles of apparel (Chs. 61–62)	45	126	404[r]	33	0	238[s]
Vehicles and transport goods						
Aircraft (Ch. 88)	17	1	0	14	0	0
Automobiles (Ch. 87)	81	87	0	40	100	15[t]

EDF = existing duty-free access

a. Distribution of tariff lines according to phaseout periods for selected products. All tariff lines in the corresponding chapter were considered. Note that the number of lines in each chapter varies across countries. In the chapters considered, the US tariff schedule has more entries than the Australian one does (4800 vs 2650).
b. US headnote, note 4: Tariffs on other chloride-based acid (HTS 2918.90.20) will be removed in equal annual stages over 5 years.
c. Stage L (6 years): Other carboloxylic acids with alcohol function (HTAS 2918.90.00).
d. Stage B (4 years): Essential oil of peppermint—mentha piperita (HTS 3301.24.00).

(table continues next page)

e. Stage F (18 years): Milk protein concentrate (HTS 3501.10.10) and other cassein (HTS 3501.90.60).
Stage B (4 years): Inedible gelatin and animal glue valued under 88 cents/kg (HTS 3503.00.20); dried egg albumin (HTS 3502.11.00); and casein glues (HTS 3501.90.20).
f. Stage C (8 years): Unworked precious stones, other than diamonds (HTS 7103.10.20).
g. Stage D (10 years): Porcelain or ceramic tableware, kitchenware, other household articles (HTS 6911.10.10, 6912.00.20, and 6912.00.20).
Stage C (8 years): Roofing tiles (HTS 6905.10.00); tiles, cubes, and similar articles (HTS 6907.10.00 and 6907.90.00); and glazed ceramic paving, wall tiles, and ceramic mosaic cubes (4 tariff lines in HTS 6908.10 through 6908.90).
Stage B (4 years): Ceramic sinks, washbasins, bidets (HTS 6910.90.00); porcelain tableware, kitchenware, other household articles (11 tariff lines in HTS 6911.10.15 through 10.80); ceramic tableware, kitchenware, other household articles (HTS 6912.00.35, 6912.00.46, and 6912.00.48); other ceramic statues, valued over $2.50 each and produced by professional sculptors (HTS 6913.90.50); and other ceramic articles (HTS 6914.10.80 and 6914.90.80).
h. Stage D (10 years): Glassware of a kind used for table, kitchen, toilet, office, indoor decoration, or similar purposes (7 tariff lines in HTS 7013).
Stage C (8 years): Glassware of a kind used for table, kitchen, toilet, office, indoor decoration, or similar purposes (11 tariff lines in HTS 7013).
Stage T1US (6 years): Glass fibers, including glass, wool, and articles thereof (14 tariff lines in HTS 7019).
i. Stage T1AU (6 years): Glass fibers, including glass, wool, and articles thereof (6 tariff lines in HTS 7019).
j. Not used.
k. Stage B (4 years): Axes and chainsaw blades (HTS 8201.40.60 and 8202.40.30); slip joint pliers (HTS 8203.20.40 and 8203.20.60); hand-operated spanners and wrenches (all tariff lines in HTS 8204); handtools, including glass cutters, nesoi (4 tariff lines in HTS 8205); tools for drilling (HTS 8207.50.40 and 8207.90.30); certain padlocks (HTS 8301.10.60); harness and saddlery (HTS 8302.49.20 and 8302.49.60); other paper clips (HTS 8305.90.60); bells and the like (HTS 8306.10.00).
l. Stage B (4 years): Ball or roller bearings, and parts thereof (all 14 tariff lines in HTS 8482); condensers for steam or other vapor power units (HTS 8404.20.00).
Stage C (8 years): Steam turbines for marine propulsion (HTS 8406.10.10).
m. Stage C (8 years): Color cathode-ray television picture tubes (HTS 8540.11.10, 8540.11.28, 8540.11.30, 8540.11.48, and 8540.11.50).
Stage B (4 years): Other parts of printed circuit assemblies of line telephone handsets (HTS 8518.90.40); other reception apparatus for radiotelephony, radiotelegraphy, or radio broadcasting (HTS 8527.90.95); color cathode-ray television picture tubes (HTS 8540.11.24 and 8540.11.44); and cathode-ray tubes and parts (HTS 8540.20.20, 8540.91.15, and 8540.91.50).
n. Stage B (4 years): Binoculars, monoculars, other optical telescopes, and parts (HTS 9005.80.60 and 90.40).
o. Stage B (4 years): Slide projectors (HTS 9008.10.00); photographic cameras valued at less than $10 (HTS 9006.52.60, 9006.59.60, and 9006.40.60).
p. Stage C (8 years): Telescopic sights for fitting to arms with infrared light (HTS 9013.10.10) and telescopic sights for rifles (HTS 9013.90.20).
Stage B (4 years): Taximeters (HTS 9029.10.40); drafting tables and machines, plotters, and other instruments (HTS 9017.20.70 and 9017.80.00); hand magnifiers, magnifying glasses, and door viewers (HTS 9013.80.20 and 9013.80.40); and telescopic sights for fitting to arms (HTS 9013.10.40).

(table continues next page)

Table 4A.7 Phaseouts for tariffs on manufactured goods, US-Australia FTA[a]
      (continued)

q. Stage C (8 years): Conveyor or transmission belts or belting, of vulcanized rubber with textile components in which vegetable fibers predominate by weight over any other single textile fiber (HTS 4010.19.10); and other gloves, mittens, and mitts of apparel and clothing and vulcanized rubber other than hard rubber (HTS 4015.19.50).

r. Nearly 87 percent of these 404 tariff lines retain tariffs of 15.5 percent during the 10-year transition period. The rest retain lower tariffs on 10 year phaseout, with the exception of 8 tariff lines that qualify for a five-year phaseout. Cuts will be backloaded.

s. Nearly 88 percent of these 238 tariff lines retain tariffs of 15.5 percent during the 10-year transition period. The rest retain lower tariffs on 10 year phaseout. Cuts will be backloaded.

t. Stage L (6 years): Used or secondhand passenger vehicles (HTS 8703.21 through 24; 31 through 33, and 90).

Sources: USTR (2004a).

5

Services Trade

By international norms, the service sectors of Switzerland and the United States are already open. However, Swiss and US barriers still persist in some industries, such as financial services, network industries, and the audiovisual complex, and assorted obstacles hinder the cross-border delivery of professional services. A Swiss-US free trade agreement (FTA) could push the envelope of service-sector liberalization, especially at the canton and state levels, and promote freer movement of personnel. By removing barriers, both countries could benefit from faster transmission of advanced technology and management skills. Moreover, US firms could take better advantage of Switzerland's geography and commercial expertise. Foreign companies—IBM and Citibank, to name two—tend to establish headquarters in Switzerland, not so much to access the Swiss market, but to locate in the heart of Europe and draw on a pool of qualified personnel (Owen 2005).

In 2004, Swiss-US two-way services trade amounted to $16.3 billion (table 5.1), only a little short of bilateral manufactures trade ($17.0 billion; see table 4.1). Royalties and license fees ($4.9 billion) and other private services ($8.7 billion) are the largest components of US-Swiss bilateral trade. Among other private services, financial services, insurance, telecommunications, and professional services represent the main components (table 5.2). A Swiss-US FTA will lead to greater values of bilateral trade.[1]

---

1. Results of the computable general equilibrium (CGE) model, presented in chapter 8, suggest that a Swiss-US FTA could lead to an expansion in bilateral trade in services of about 10 percent. This result provides a very conservative lower-bound estimate. Using a gravity model for trade in services, Ceglowski (2005) estimates that bilateral trade in services for

Table 5.1 Cross-border services trade between the United States and Switzerland (millions of current dollars)

Service category	US exports			US imports		
	2001	2002	2003	2001	2002	2003
Total private services	6,513	6,815	8,014	6,488	7,450	8,348
Travel	958	696	624	704	619	570
Other private services	3,192	3,548	4,005	2,646	3,814	4,700
Other transportation	510	353	485	611	422	525
Passenger fares	145	195	185	821	530	351
Royalties, license fees	1,708	2,023	2,715	1,706	2,065	2,202

Source: US BEA (2004b).

This chapter is divided into four sections. The first two analyze barriers to trade in the United States and Switzerland in the financial services, network industries (e.g., electricity, telecommunications), audiovisual complex, and professional services sectors. The third revisits services trade negotiations in selected US bilateral FTAs. The last section outlines our recommendations for further liberalization of services trade in the context of a prospective Swiss-US FTA.

A huge service sector not covered in this chapter is wholesale and retail trade. The advent of big-box self-serve retail outlets, such as Wal-Mart, Ikea, and Target, staffed by flexible nonunion employees—many of them part-time workers—has been a major source of efficiency in the US economy. Wholesale distribution has seen similar productivity gains, as supplies are routinely delivered to retail stores on a "just-in-time" basis, mainly at night, supported by sophisticated cash register systems that continuously report inventory needs.

While wholesale and retail productivity levels are generally much higher in the United States than they are in other countries in the Organization for Economic Cooperation and Development (OECD), in Switzerland, the difference from US distribution systems cannot be traced to trade or investment barriers. Swiss cities and cantons may, through zoning standards, restrict big-box retail outlets, and Swiss labor regulations may not

---

partners to a regional trade agreement is almost 40 percent higher than for nonpartners. The same researcher also estimates an expansion in two-way services trade by 6 to 7 percent for every 10 percent expansion in two-way merchandise trade. The gravity model for trade in goods presented in chapter 8 predicts a 100 percent expansion in two-way merchandise trade for a Swiss-US FTA. Hence Ceglowski's results would lead to an upper-bound estimate of 60 to 70 percent increase in two-way services trade resulting from a Swiss-US FTA. The CGE and gravity models and empirical results are explored in more detail in chapter 8.

Table 5.2 US-Swiss trade in services by industry, 2003 (millions of dollars)

Industry	US unaffiliated trade[a]			US affiliated trade[b]		
	Exports	Imports	Two-way	Exports	Imports	Two-way
Transport, fares, passengers	1,294	1,446	2,740	n.a.	n.a.	n.a.
Royalties and license fees	313	348	661	2,402	1,854	4,256
Other private services	1,529	3,140	4,669	2,475	1,561	4,036
Business, professional, and technical	799	193	992	n.a.	n.a.	n.a.
Advertising	18	16	34	n.a.	n.a.	n.a.
Computer/information	129	22	151	n.a.	n.a.	n.a.
Construction, architecture, engineering	9	4	13	n.a.	n.a.	n.a.
Industrial engineering	7	n.a.	n.a.	n.a.	n.a.	n.a.
Installation, maintenance, repair	89	3	92	n.a.	n.a.	n.a.
Legal services	179	20	199	n.a.	n.a.	n.a.
Management, consulting, public relations	46	10	56	n.a.	n.a.	n.a.
Operational leasing	(D)	n.a.	n.a.	n.a.	n.a.	n.a.
Others	(D)	34	n.a.	n.a.	n.a.	n.a.
Research, development, testing	137	59	196	n.a.	n.a.	n.a.
Education services	36	15	51	n.a.	n.a.	n.a.
Financial services	537	219	756	n.a.	n.a.	n.a.
Insurance	64	2,680	2,744	n.a.	n.a.	n.a.
Telecommunications	42	21	63	n.a.	n.a.	n.a.
Film, TV tape, rentals	51	12	63	n.a.	n.a.	n.a.
Total services	3,136	4,934	8,070	4,877	3,415	8,292

(D) = not disclosed
n.a. = not available

a. Unaffiliated trade represents transactions between independent companies.
b. Affiliated trade represents transactions between related companies.

Source: US BEA (2004b).

permit the sort of staffing arrangements common in the United States. But zoning standards and labor regulations are clearly beyond the scope of trade agreements. These are sensitive matters, reserved to national and local legislative bodies, under the principles of sovereignty and subsidiarity.

Barriers to Trade in Services: United States

The United States is the premier producer and exporter of services. Constituting some 64 percent of GDP, the service sector is the largest component of the US economy; in 2004, services constituted 30 percent of total US exports (USTR 2005a). The main service exports are business, professional, and technical services, travel services, royalties and license fees, and financial services. Royalties and license fees and transportation and travel services constitute the main US imports.

Liberalization of the services sector in the United States began in the 1970s, when the transportation, banking, and natural gas sectors were gradually deregulated. However, barriers to foreign entry still persist in several sectors, including, as mentioned above, financial services, telecommunications, transportation, and professional services. In the General Agreement on Trade in Services (GATS) negotiations, responding to requests from US trading partners, the United States Trade Representative (USTR 2003c) affirmed US intentions to further liberalize financial, telecommunications, environmental, energy, and express delivery services. But it pointedly noted that certain subjects would not be open to negotiations. Off-limit sectors included government monopolies (e.g., the US Postal Service and the Bureau of Engraving); areas of keen regulatory interest (e.g., consumer safety, healthcare, and education); programs restricted to US citizens and minority set-aside requirements (e.g., Overseas Private Investment Corporation guarantees, Trade and Development Agency financing, certain public contracts); and state and local education.

Financial Services

Two-way financial services trade between Switzerland and the United States is substantial, amounting to $750 million in 2003. However, barriers remain, particularly against foreign insurance firms and foreign participation in securities markets. The USTR (2003c) indicates that the United States is willing to curtail registration requirements that discriminate against foreign-owned banks.

Banking

The Findlay-Warren (2000) restrictiveness index indicates that barriers to banking services are somewhat higher in Switzerland than they are in the

Table 5.3 Restrictions on foreign banking firms

Country	Foreign restriction index
Switzerland	0.08
United States	0.06
Current US partners	
Australia	0.12
Canada	0.07
Chile	0.40
Mexico	0.17
Singapore	0.37
Prospective US partners	
Colombia	0.23
Indonesia	0.55
Malaysia	0.65
New Zealand	0.06
Philippines	0.53
South Africa	0.19
South Korea	0.43
Thailand	0.39

Note: Index based on restrictions on establishment (licensing requirements for new firms, restrictions on direct investment in existing firms and on the permanent movement of people) and restrictions on ongoing operations (on firms conducting their core business, the pricing of services, and the temporary movement of people). Index measures all restrictions that hinder foreign firms from entering and operating in an economy.

Source: Findlay and Warren (2000).

United States (table 5.3). This difference arises from disparities in ongoing operations, mostly limits on extending the network of branches, and restrictions on establishing a firm, mainly due to visa and work permit differences for professional personnel.

For the most part, legislation permits the cross-border supply of banking services. Accordingly, foreign banks without a commercial presence in the United States may deal directly with US customers. As a consequence of the US dual banking system—both federal and state governments can charter and supervise banks—foreign banks can establish a commercial presence by opening either a federal or a state-licensed branch, agency, or representative office, or by creating or acquiring a national or state bank as a corporate subsidiary (WTO 2004c).

Nevertheless, the EU Commission has identified US impediments to foreign participation in banking services. First, the majority of directors of national banks (i.e., federally chartered banks) must be US citizens; likewise, half of the states require either all or the majority of bank directors to be US citizens. Also, the federal regulator—the Office of the Comptroller of the Currency (OCC)—and some state banking supervisors require foreign banks to maintain "asset pledges" for funds readily available under US jurisdiction. These pledges are in addition to the paid-up capital that foreign banks are already bound to maintain in their home country. Legislation has been proposed that would permit the OCC to vary its asset pledge requirements to reflect the risk characteristics of different institutions (European Commission 2004a).

Another limitation is that banks cannot automatically expand through establishing or acquiring branches. Some states limit the issuance of branch licenses for foreign banks; others restrict the opening of representative offices by foreign banks (WTO 2003c). The European Union has requested that these restrictions be relaxed. Finally, US legislation prohibits a foreign bank branch from accepting a domestic retail deposit of less than $100,000 if the branch was established after 1991. The European Union has requested a reduction in this threshold.

Despite these various restrictions, representatives of both the Swiss Banking Association in Switzerland and Swiss banks operating in the United States question whether a Swiss-US FTA would bring much to the table for their industry, since Swiss banks are generally satisfied with US market access (Owen 2005). Moreover, given that bank secrecy is an important feature of the banking system, Swiss banks ask whether a Swiss-US FTA would disturb the existing arrangements for exchanging sensitive financial information. However, the US Treasury does not seem inclined to address the issues surrounding the exchange of financial information in an FTA.

Insurance

The United States has the largest insurance market in the world. It is also a net importer of insurance in its trade with Switzerland (Switzerland is especially prominent in the reinsurance market).[2] The US retail insurance market is highly segmented because regulations are made at the state level: Each insurance company must be licensed under the laws of each state where it intends to offer insurance (WTO 2004c). Hence, each company must deal with solvency, licensing, and operating requirements on a state-by-state basis. In addition, unlike banking, there is no such thing as a federally licensed or regulated insurance company. Market segmentation may impede

---

2. For unaffiliated companies, US insurance premiums paid to Switzerland from the United States amounted to $2.7 billion in 2003; US premium receipts from Switzerland amounted to $64 million.

foreign firms as it entails higher compliance costs. If a foreign insurer wants to offer nationwide services, the insurer would have to fulfill the licensing requirements of all 50 states.

The European Commission (2004a) notes that foreign insurance companies face discrimination on two main fronts. The first involves the absence of "port of entry" legislation in many states. If a foreign insurance company wants to underwrite risks in a state that does not offer a port of entry, it must first seek a license in another state that does offer such a port before seeking a license in the targeted state. Second, some states require their insurers to buy reinsurance from state-licensed companies before allowing reinsurance premiums to leave the state.

Most states do not allow insurance companies that are not licensed in the state to transact business there. Nevertheless, certain prominent insurers are exempted from licensing requirements and allowed to operate on a cross-border basis.[3] These prominent insurers, such as Lloyd's, are part of the $9 billion US "surplus lines" market. However, they face some important constraints. To participate in surplus lines business, foreign insurers and reinsurers have to be "white-listed" by the National Association of Insurance Commissioners (NAIC). In addition—and this is minor—they must name a US attorney and hold a local trust fund in a US bank of up to $60 million. That some foreign companies are effectively regulated in their home country carries little weight in the NAIC's determination (European Commission 2004a).

A federal excise tax on all insurance premiums ceded abroad is levied on companies that are not incorporated in either the United States or a country with which the United States has signed a double taxation treaty.[4] The European Union has requested the United States to eliminate this discriminatory tax. Since the United States and Switzerland have a double tax treaty, this is not a bilateral issue.

Most states also require US citizenship and in-state residency for key personnel in insurance companies. Some require that a majority of directors, lawyers, and brokers be US citizens or permanent US residents (Mexico and Canada are exempted). Moreover, local brokers must be used in all states where a risk has been underwritten.

Securities

Foreign and domestic security firms are both subject to regulation by the Securities and Exchange Commission (SEC). Broker-dealers and investment

---

3. By this means, various types of insurance related to maritime shipping, commercial aviation, space launchings, and other hard-to place risks are exempted from licensing requirements.

4. The tax rates are 1 percent for reinsurance and life insurance and 4 percent for nonlife insurance.

advisers are required to register with both the SEC and state regulatory authorities. Out of 25 "primary dealers"—a designation that the Federal Reserve gives to select firms that are eligible to participate in Treasury bill and bond auctions—two-thirds of them are US subsidiaries of foreign firms based in seven countries (WTO 2001a). In general, foreign securities firms are granted national treatment.[5]

Current legislation allows a foreign securities firm to establish a branch in the United States. However, this process is impractical for many foreign firms, since opening a branch subjects them to SEC regulation, which entails costs and might conflict with home-country regulation (European Commission 2004a). The Investment Company Act of 1940 (as amended) does not allow foreign investment companies, such as mutual funds, to conduct direct public offerings in the United States unless the SEC permits the company to register. Thus, few foreign funds are registered in the United States,[6] and the Act is a substantial barrier to foreign services trade in this regard.

However, foreign firms may register as investment advisers under the Investment Advisers Act of 1940. Thereafter, they may organize a mutual fund under US law and register the fund under the Investment Company Act. The managers and directors are not subject to residency or citizenship requirements, and the fund can be managed from abroad. Despite this end run, the European Union has requested the United States to open its market to foreign mutual fund sales, and has also sought US market access for foreign financial derivatives (European Commission 2004a).

Finally, regulatory requirements for listing on US stock exchanges became more burdensome in the aftermath of corporate scandals. The Sarbanes-Oxley Act of 2002 has increased the cost of access to the US market.[7] Several companies are said to have considered delisting from US stock exchanges. However, it is very difficult for foreign firms to delist under current SEC rules (European Commission 2004a). Moreover, firms that have more than 300 US shareholders would still be subject to SEC scrutiny even after delisting.

Telecommunications Services

The restrictiveness index for telecommunications services (table 5.4) shows that the United States has a more open market than its current and prospec-

---

5. However, the United States took a most favored nation (MFN) exemption in its General Agreement on Trade in Services (GATS) schedule for participation by foreign firms in the issuance of new government-debt securities, mainly Treasury bills and bonds (WTO 2004c).

6. Only 19 foreign funds, most of them from Canada, have been permitted to register. The last permission was issued in 1973 (European Commission 2004a).

7. It is claimed that Sarbanes-Oxley raises costs by imposing stiff accounting and disclosure requirements. Empirical evidence, however, remains scarce.

Table 5.4 Restrictiveness index for telecommunications services[a]

Country	Domestic index[b]	Foreign index[c]
Switzerland	0.10	0.20
United States	0.03	0.03
Current US partners		
Australia	0.02	0.04
Canada	0.13	0.44
Chile	0.08	0.09
Israel	0.15	0.53
Jordan	0.37	0.92
Mexico	0.21	0.53
Morocco	0.33	0.90
Singapore	0.19	0.44
Prospective US partners		
Bahrain	0.35	0.89
Bangladesh	0.23	0.58
Bolivia	0.15	0.49
Botswana	0.17	0.52
Colombia	0.17	0.46
Costa Rica	0.37	0.93
Ecuador	0.23	0.80
Egypt	0.27	0.63
Guatemala	0.17	0.33
Honduras	0.23	0.77
Indonesia	0.26	0.67
Jamaica	0.35	0.91
Malaysia	0.22	0.58
Namibia	0.30	0.65
New Zealand	0.03	0.03
Nicaragua	0.17	0.62
Oman	0.30	0.87
Pakistan	0.26	0.55
Panama	0.28	0.63
Peru	0.18	0.51
Philippines	0.13	0.45
Qatar	0.30	0.87
South Africa	0.26	0.59
South Korea	0.26	0.68
Swaziland	0.30	0.87
Thailand	0.27	0.79
Trinidad and Tobago	0.23	0.69
United Arab Emirates	0.29	0.84

a. Index based on restrictions on establishment (licensing requirements for new firms, restrictions on direct investment in existing firms and on the permanent movement of people) and restrictions on ongoing operations (on firms conducting their core business, the pricing of services, and the temporary movement of people).
b. Domestic index measures restrictions on domestic firms.
c. Foreign index measures restrictions on foreign firms.

Source: Findlay and Warren (2000).

tive FTA partners do. Moreover, the US telecommunications market is the largest in the world and highly competitive, with mobile, fixed line, cable, and VOIP (voice over Internet protocol) all fighting for market share. Table 5.2 indicates that, based on current accounting or settlement rates, the United States is a net exporter of telecommunications services to Switzerland and the rest of the world.[8] Given the volume of present and prospective traffic, conditions of access to the telecommunications sector will probably be an important issue in FTA talks between Switzerland and the United States.

The Federal Communications Commission (FCC), in cooperation with the USTR, began to liberalize internationally in 1996. One element of the US strategy was the General Agreement on Trade in Services (GATS) Basic Telecommunications Agreement, which entered into force in February 1998. That agreement committed the 69 signatory countries to significant market access. However, the European Community (EC) identifies important US barriers in the satellite and mobile sectors. These barriers include investment restrictions, lengthy regulatory proceedings, conditionality of market access, reciprocity procedures, and certain congressional attitudes (European Commission 2004a). In April 2003, the USTR stated that the United States will offer further liberalization in the telecommunications and information services in the Doha Round. This offer contemplates foreign ownership of cable television networks and direct broadcast by non-US satellite companies to American viewers. In May 2003, the FCC started a reform program aimed at faster licensing procedures in the satellite sector. The USTR also seems willing to push for expanding foreign companies' ability to provide information services directly to consumers (USTR 2005a).

Despite these offers and initiatives, US market access restrictions are still a matter of contention (European Commission 2004a). First, the US offer schedule in the GATS refers only to the liberalization of common carrier networks, excluding cable networks. Second, the United States maintains restrictions on foreign ownership. In 2002, the European Commission requested that restrictions on direct foreign ownership of common carrier radio licenses be removed.[9] Meanwhile, the US firm Comcast retains its exclusive right on satellite-based services that link up with Intelsat and Inmarsat (European Commission 2004a). Finally, the United States has retained its most favored nation (MFN) exemption on one-way transmis-

---

8. In 2003, US exports of telecommunications services amounted to $5.5 billion, while US imports amounted to $4.7 billion (US BEA 2004a). These payments represent "settlement charges" on incoming and outgoing telecommunications traffic respectively.

9. The EC claims that non-US citizens and any corporation that was not organized under US laws face restrictions on direct foreign ownership of a common carrier in the communication sector. For example, radio licenses may not be granted to these legal persons (European Commission 2004a).

sion of direct-to-home (DTH) and digital broadcast satellite (DBS) television services, as well as digital audio services (European Commission 2004a).[10]

Professional Services

In 2004, US professional services accounted for 11 percent of GDP and approximately 5 percent of US exports of goods and services. US exports of professional services are geographically diversified, with 25 percent of revenues originating from Asia and 16 percent from Latin America. Imports, however, are highly concentrated, the OECD being the main destination of US payments (WTO 2004c).

The Findlay-Warren (2000) restrictiveness index for professional services (table 5.5) indicates that trade barriers to accounting, architectural, and engineering services are higher in the United States than they are in Switzerland, though legal services are an important exception. Table 5.2 shows that, in 2003, the United States exported $800 million in professional services to Switzerland, with legal services being the largest single category. US imports of professional services from Switzerland amounted to $200 million and are highly diversified. The relative severity of restrictions may not be a major explanation for the favorable US trade balance, since US exports of legal services face higher barriers in Switzerland than vice versa (see table 5.5). For the most part, US net exports very likely reflect US comparative advantage (Mann 2006).

An important feature of service delivery to foreign markets is the fly in–fly out (FIFO) mode of professional services. Lawyers, accountants, engineers, and certain other professionals work with clients abroad predominantly through short-term visits.[11] This type of work raises distinctive issues, such as the unauthorized performance of professional duties, or malpractice that harms the client or the public at large. The question of how clients and the public can be protected internationally from unauthorized or incompetent lawyers and other professionals is gaining importance,[12] and by resolv-

---

10. However, the USTR has communicated its willingness to open a new round of negotiations on this issue.

11. This probably results in an understatement in official statistics of services exports. The US Bureau of Economic Analysis 2004 figures for the export of legal services are probably too low, since they do not include payments made by foreign clients for FIFO services.

12. "Rules of professional conduct," for example, relate to a lawyer's competence, requiring that a lawyer fully understand the factual basis for his advice and the legal principles to be applied. Bearing these rules in mind, the American Bar Association's Commission on Multi-Jurisdictional Practice has been concerned with the "unauthorized practice of law."

Table 5.5 Restrictiveness index for foreign professional services firms

Country	Engineering	Accountancy	Architecture	Legal
Switzerland	0.18	0.15	0.27	0.50
United States	0.23	0.19	0.33	0.48
Current US partners				
Australia	0.15	0.08	0.41	0.42
Canada	0.33	0.16	0.42	0.52
Chile	0.14	0.24	0.35	n.a.
Mexico	0.31	0.33	0.36	0.49
Singapore	0.08	0.11	0.41	0.42
Prospective US partners				
Indonesia	0.30	0.24	0.56	0.57
Malaysia	0.33	0.26	0.51	0.54
New Zealand	0.34	0.19	0.39	0.47
Philippines	0.33	0.15	0.63	0.54
South Africa	0.11	0.10	0.44	n.a.
South Korea	0.19	0.12	0.48	0.44
Thailand	0.12	0.11	0.49	0.44

Note: Index based on restrictions on establishment (licensing requirements for new firms, restrictions on direct investment in existing firms and on the permanent movement of people) and restrictions on ongoing operations (on firms conducting their core business, the pricing of services, and the temporary movement of people). Index measures restrictions on foreign firms.

Source: Findlay and Warren (2000).

ing these issues, the scope of two-way trade in professional services can be substantially increased.

The European Commission (2004a) notes that, since the implementation of the GATS schedules for professional services, access terms for foreign suppliers to the US market for professional services have improved. Freeman, Plascencia, and Setzler (2003) argue that citizenship requirements for these occupations have dropped significantly, and that requirements still on the statute books appear to be poorly enforced.[13] However, foreign access is still restrained by differing regulatory and licensing requirements from state to state. As the Commission report adds, "the application of Buy America and positive discrimination provisions as well as burdensome visa procedures for registration and for obtaining work permits, make it difficult for foreign suppliers of professional services to enter the US market" (European Commission 2004a).

---

13. This change is attributed to federal court decisions, advisory opinions of state attorneys general, and state legislative and administrative action.

Legal Services

In 2002, total cross-border exports of legal services amounted to $3.3 billion, while imports amounted to $1.2 billion (WTO 2004c). In 2000, the United States committed to liberalize its citizenship and residency requirements for licensing, scope of practice,[14] association of foreign-qualified lawyers with local lawyers (only possible in 24 states), and association of foreign partner law firms with local law firms (WTO 2004c). US courts have held that nationality requirements for licensing are prohibited by the US Constitution.[15] As of 2003, nine jurisdictions require in-state offices for licensing, and 16 require in-state or US residency of practitioners (WTO 2004c). The European Union has requested the United States to remove in-state residency requirements for commercial companies and natural persons (GATS modes 3 and 4) in Michigan, Texas, and Washington for consultancy practice on the law of foreign jurisdiction for which the service supplier is already a qualified lawyer (GATS 2002).

The market for legal services in the United States is currently segmented by different regulatory requirements across states. The US GATS schedule specifies that legal services must be supplied by a natural person as opposed to a company. In turn, this means that barriers to international labor mobility are important—and the United States is not disposed to grant additional work visas in the context of trade negotiations (WTO 2004c). However, the United States is willing to address barriers that take the form of state requirements for residency, minimum age, diploma or title, professional examinations, and registration with a professional body (WTO 2001a, 2004c).

Accounting and Auditing Services

Foreign accountants who wish to practice in the United States are required to pass the CPA Uniform Examination, comply with state laws (which differ across states), and meet state board educational or continuing professional education requirements. The European Union has challenged residency and citizenship requirements, and the obligation to create an in-state office, in several states (GATS 2002).

---

14. US willingness to liberalize citizenship and residency requirements does not, however, imply greater US willingness to extend work visas (e.g., H1-B visas) to foreign lawyers. It only means that, once legally admitted to the United States, foreign-born lawyers should not be denied the right to practice because they are not US citizens, or because they have not resided in a certain state for a period of years.

15. The California Supreme Court held in Raffaelli v. Committee of Bar Examiners, 7 Cal.3d 288, May 24, 1972. S.F. No. 22841. (1972) that the citizenship requirement for attorneys was unconstitutional. The US Supreme Court issued a similar finding in Application of Griffiths, 413 U.S. 717 (1973), holding that "Connecticut's exclusion of aliens from the practice of law violates the Equal Protection Clause of the Fourteenth Amendment."

The European Union may also challenge the requirement that accounting firms operating in the United States abide by US accounting standards, as opposed to the international standards used in Europe (European Commission 2004a). The SEC has rejected several requests to allow the domestic use of international accounting standards. The European Union argues that this "regulatory trade barrier" must be resolved (GATS 2002).

Finally, the Sarbanes-Oxley Act could have a substantial impact on US-listed Swiss companies and Swiss auditing firms. New provisions for audits and corporate governance might conflict with the laws that Swiss firms face at home (European Commission 2004a) and even if it does not, the Sarbanes-Oxley Act will likely entail higher costs. Essentially, foreign firms that list their shares on US security markets need to comply with US governance and auditing standards, as well as standards in their home country. Moreover, the law obliges all accounting firms that do business in the United States, such as by auditing foreign firms that list their shares on US security markets, to register with the Public Company Accounting Oversight Board (PCAOB). This requirement conveys an objectionable "extraterritorial" flavor to some foreign firms (WTO 2004c).

Engineering Services

As with other services, engineering services face market segmentation owing to different regulations from state to state, and several states have citizenship and in-state residency requirements. The European Union has requested the United States to abolish citizenship requirements in the District of Columbia and in-state residency requirements in Idaho, Iowa, Kansas, Maine, Mississippi, Nevada, Oklahoma, South Carolina, South Dakota, Tennessee, Texas, and West Virginia (GATS 2002).

Barriers to Trade in Services: Switzerland

Switzerland's service sector accounts for more than two-thirds of GDP, with financial services—banking and insurance—representing 11 percent, and tourism another 6 percent. However, certain service sectors are shielded from competition through market segmentation and border barriers. Switzerland's FTA with the European Union triggered some reforms, but further liberalization remains a goal. The conclusion of a Swiss-US FTA could prompt reforms in the Swiss market, to the benefit of both parties.

The analysis covers two network utilities, electricity and natural gas; two other network activities, the postal services and telecommunications; professional and audiovisual sectors; and financial services. Several of these have elements of natural monopoly, so we start with a discussion of competition law.

Switzerland's Competition Law

Compared with other industrial countries, Swiss legislation designed to increase market competition is relatively new. The main texts were adopted in the mid-1990s in the context of an economic "revitalization program" to align Switzerland with the European Union and other OECD members. The main pieces of legislation include the Federal Act on Cartels and Other Restraints of Competition (LCart, adopted in 1995); the Regulation on Business Merger Control (1996); the Domestic Market Act (DMA, 1995) and the Act on Technical Hindrances to Trade (1996).

LCart was the first legislation to give decision-making powers to competition authorities. It was amended in June 2003, and the new version entered into force in April 2004. One amendment enabled the authorities to immediately impose sanctions. Another gave them a leniency option. Prior to the 2003 amendments, sanctions could only be imposed in the event of repeated offences, which never occurred (OECD 2004a). In other words, before 2003, companies had a free pass to break the competition law, and be caught once or twice, before facing any penalty.

The competition authority comprises both the Competition Commission (Comco) and its Secretariat. The former is the decision-making body, while the latter conducts investigations. The authority is responsible for applying LCart by rendering decisions on antitrust and merger cases. Comco can make recommendations to the political authorities, and answer general questions relating to competition; it is also empowered to ensure that the Confederation, cantons, communes, and other bodies with public responsibilities comply with the provisions of the DMA.

Many areas are subject to additional regulation, such as imposing a state pricing system or granting special entitlements to certain companies to carry out public tasks. They are not formally excluded from LCart. The telecommunications incumbent Swisscom has faced several investigations by Comco.

Financial Services

One of the most stable and sophisticated countries in the world, Switzerland is a key financial center. Financial services represent approximately 11 percent of Swiss GDP. In 2004, Swiss-US commerce in financial services amounted to approximately $800 million in two-way trade.

Banking Services

Switzerland requires all branches, subsidiaries, and agencies of foreign banks to obtain a license from the Swiss Federal Banking Commission (SFBC) as a condition of operation. Once a license has been granted, foreign banks enjoy the same status that Swiss banks do (WTO 2004b). In 2000, the SFBC extended its licensing requirements to Internet-exclusive banks and securities dealers. While the SFBC has the right to supervise foreign banks, it also allows foreign supervisory agencies to inspect their banks in Switzerland. The Investment Fund Act (IFA) regulates investment funds. Foreign funds can be established if the representative agent is a Swiss resident and has a license (WTO 2004b).

Secrecy is important to the Swiss banking system, and while it does not affect market access, and lies well outside the scope of an FTA, the issue has come up in other international settings. The European Union in particular has pressured the Swiss government to modify its banking secrecy laws. In January 2003, EU members reached a political agreement to introduce a system of information exchange to avoid tax evasion within the European Union. Under the agreement, national regulators in Austria, Belgium, and Luxembourg will be allowed to maintain bank secrecy contingent on the collection of a withholding tax on interest and dividends paid to EU residents (OECD 2004a). The European Union and Switzerland reached a similar agreement that entered into force on July 1, 2005. The agreement was accepted by popular vote in a referendum. A prospective US-Swiss FTA could also face a referendum when dealing with the Swiss banking sector. However, the US Treasury seems disposed to deal with the tax-evasion and anti–money laundering aspects of information exchange outside of FTA negotiations.

Insurance Services

Since it has the highest per capita insurance expenditure in the world, Switzerland's insurance market is extremely appealing to foreign competitors. However, certain barriers to foreign entry persist. Foreign insurers attempting to do business in Switzerland are required to establish a subsidiary or a branch in Switzerland and may offer only the types of insurance for which they are licensed in their home countries. The manager of the foreign-owned branch must reside in Switzerland, and the majority of the board of directors of the Swiss subsidiary must have European Free Trade Association (EFTA) citizenship. However, foreign companies offering only reinsurance are not subject to oversight by the supervisory body, the Federal Office of Private Insurance (FOPI).

Public monopolies exist for fire and natural damage insurance in 19 cantons, and for the insurance of workplace accidents in certain industries (WTO 2004b). Private insurance firms must establish a fund, amounting to between 20 percent and 50 percent of their minimum capital requirement, available at short notice to cover potential losses. As part of Switzerland's bilateral agreement with the European Union, EU life insurers are required to deposit a certain percentage of their assets with the Swiss National Bank (SNB), though non-life insurers are not. All other non-EU insurers are required to make this deposit, and US insurers face this requirement (OECD 2004a).

Network Industries

Most network industries are only partially liberalized, and the degree of liberalization differs among them. The absence of competition abets higher prices that exceed the OECD average and probably limits productivity gains. As the Swiss-EU FTA concerns only goods, the liberalization process of services has been slower and pursued less aggressively in Switzerland than in the European Union. Nontrade barriers still insulate four of Switzerland's network industries: electricity, natural gas, telecommunications, and postal services.

Electricity

Electricity is the main source of energy produced in Switzerland. Switzerland counts 350 hydroelectric plants and five nuclear power plants. Electricity is considered as a good; imports are duty free and, like exports, they are not curtailed by licensing requirements. Production is competitive, but public monopolies dominate electricity transmission and distribution within Switzerland. As they are only factual monopolies as opposed to public legal monopolies, they are nullified by LCart, as the Swiss Supreme Court confirmed in 2003. Cantons and municipalities own 72 percent of capital invested in the electricity industry. Energy revenues are a substantial source of financing for local governments at 700 million Swiss francs a year, or some 0.2 percent of GDP. The noncompetitive character of this sector, along with the high taxes set by cantons and municipalities, make electricity rates for the Swiss industry the fourth highest among countries that belong to the International Energy Agency (WTO 2004b). Many regional and local activities are cross-subsidized by cantons, on the basis of revenues and taxes collected on electricity generation and transmission.

In a referendum launched by Swiss labor unions in 2002, the population rejected a proposed energy market law (EML) that would have permitted third-party access to the grid. In part, this reflected a general lack of confidence in liberalization, owing to private-sector management problems, particularly the collapse of Swissair and scandals in the United States (OECD 2003). However, most experts argue that lower energy power prices in neighboring countries will eventually force Switzerland to adapt, triggering a restructuring process. Consequently, the Federal Council proposed a new electricity supply law and an urgent temporary amendment to the Electricity Law (EIU 2005). The goal is to nest the Swiss electricity industry within the European Union. The proposals encompass two phases. The first, which is supposed to start in 2007, will allow commercial users to choose their electricity supplier (EIU 2005), and envisages legal unbundling of transmission from commercial activities; merging of transmission operators into a single system, Swissgrid; and establishing an independent regulatory agency for the electricity sector.

Originally, a second phase foresaw full market liberalization in 2012, unless it was defeated in a referendum. In the course of parliamentary debate, the second-phase proposal has now been modified. Full liberalization—regulated third party access (rTPA) according to the EU model—is proposed from the moment of entry into force of the law in 2007, accompanied both by extensive security of supply provisions (the so-called "Oregon model") for households and small business enterprises consuming less than 100 MWh per year, and by measures favoring electricity from renewable sources.

Natural Gas

The natural gas sector faces many of the same restrictions and challenges as the electricity sector does. Liberalization of the natural gas market is high on the Swiss government's reform agenda. However, after the failed attempt to restructure electricity, the project of liberalizing gas was aborted. Unlike the electricity sector, the legal regime governing the gas sector already applies negotiated third party access, by virtue of the law on pipelines. However, current initiatives by a few private companies to create a gas market and enable third-party access to the pipeline grid are making little headway. The initiatives do not provide for creating an independent regulator, and consequently, they could raise competition law issues. Moreover, the lack of unbundling between noncommercial and commercial activities, as well as the need to negotiate transport tariffs on a case-by-case basis, are both handicaps for gas trade.

Telecommunications

The telephone network in Switzerland is one of the densest in the world, and Internet usage is growing at a fast rate (WTO 2004b). The Swiss telecommunications sector was liberalized in 1998. After the sector was open to foreign investment and competition, three different operators—Swisscom, TDC Switzerland (sunrise), and Orange—became the main players in the mobile telephone market.[16] With a stake of about 63 percent in Swisscom's capital, the Swiss Confederation still plays a leading role (WTO 2004b). The foreign restrictiveness index for telecommunications services (Findlay and Warren 2000) indicates that discrimination against foreign firms persists in Switzerland, and that entry barriers are higher in Switzerland than they were in the United States (table 5.4). However, the values calculated in this study are based on 1996 barriers, which was before Switzerland's telecommunications liberalization. Most probably, Switzerland's barriers are nearly as low as US barriers today. Table 5.4 also shows that Switzerland's barriers to trade in

---

16. Since 1998, liberalization has attracted approximately 40 providers for mobile network services (WTO 2004b).

telecom services are low compared with most other current and prospective US FTA partners.[17]

New foreign entrants were able to gain substantial shares of the Swiss national long-distance and international markets for fixed-line services; in 2002, 32 and 46 percent respectively (WTO 2004b). However, Swisscom retains a dominant role in the local market.[18] In 2001, the independent regulator, the Federal Communications Commission (ComCom), attempted to unbundle the local loop and dismantle the federal monopoly on network infrastructure. Those efforts were defeated in Swiss courts. The Swiss Federal Council then approved a telecommunications reform package.

The first part of the reform proposal, which took effect in April 2003, gave ComCom the legal authority to order Swisscom to provide leased lines at cost-oriented prices. ComCom then ordered Swisscom to lower its interconnection rates by between 25 percent and 35 percent, starting in January 2004 (WTO 2004b). As the USTR report notes, "The ComCom decision is retroactive for the past three years and will ultimately force Swisscom to reimburse tens of millions of Swiss francs to Sunrise and MCI WorldCom, Swisscom's direct competitors" (USTR 2005c). However, claiming that its rates were already aligned with those of EU members, Swisscom took the ComCom decision to Federal Court, which approved the appeal for formal reasons in October 2004 and referred the matter back to ComCom for reassessment. In an order issued mid-June 2005, ComCom made a fresh decision that is, however, largely identical in content to its 2003 decision. Swisscom has announced that it will challenge this decision in Federal Court.

In the second part of the reform proposal, the Swiss Federal Council recommended amending the Law on Telecommunications to unbundle Swisscom's local loop, eliminate state authorization requirements for market access, and establish an independent body to resolve disputes between users and providers of telecommunications services simply and quickly. After deliberating on these proposals, in October 2004, the lower house of the Parliament (the National Council) passed legislation to allow telecom operators to set their own fees and charge their clients directly for the use of subscriber lines, to unbundle the local loop, and to allow operators physical access to the cabling network. In its resolution of June 2005, the Senate (Council of States) went a step further with liberalization. The two Parliamentary Councils will have to reconcile their differences in the coming months.

The USTR has evaluated the issue of termination charges for mobile calls in Switzerland. Switzerland's rates are said to be particularly high, and there is no regulatory oversight. Swisscom still retains substantial monopoly power, and has succeeded in blocking any attempts by ComCom to change

---

17. Rankings are better for Chile, Australia, and New Zealand.

18. According to the WTO (2004b), Swisscom operates 99 percent of subscriber lines and 72 percent of the local traffic.

the current regulation (USTR 2005c). However, Swisscom announced in May 2005 that it will reduce its termination charges.

Postal Services

Switzerland has a dense network of post offices of different sizes. Only a quarter of them record an accounting profit. Die Post/La Poste/La Posta has estimated its annual operating loss to be 500 million Swiss francs (OECD 2004a). This loss is covered by profitable business in reserved areas such as domestic first class mail and inbound international letters.[19] At prevailing exchange rates, postal service prices remain the highest in the OECD (2004a).

Swiss postal services are divided into three market segments: reserved services, offered exclusively by Swiss Post as a monopoly under its universal services obligations; nonreserved services, also offered by Swiss Post under its universal services obligations, but in competition with other suppliers; and liberalized services. The first segment, reserved to Die Post/ La Poste/La Posta, consists of domestic and incoming international mail for letters. In September 2005, the Federal Council of the Swiss Federation announced that the maximum weight of letters subject to the postal monopoly would be reduced to 100 grams, beginning in April 2006.[20]

The second market segment includes outbound international services for letters, and all postal services (domestic and international) for packages of up to 20 kilograms. Licenses are required for all nonreserved services if turnover exceeds 100,000 Swiss francs, newspaper and magazine subscriptions exempted (WTO 2004b). Smaller services are open to competition and do not require licensing. Unlike its private competitors, Die Post/La Poste/La Posta is obligated to provide universal service, implying that it must serve the reserved and nonreserved market segments in the whole country at the same price (OECD 2004a).

The third market segment includes express delivery services and parcels of more than 20 kilograms. This segment is already fully liberalized, and Die Post/La Poste/La Posta is not obliged to provide these services universally (OECD 2004a).

Audiovisual Services

Switzerland does not set quotas on non-Swiss or non-European programming. However, film distributors and cinema companies are expected to

---

19. Letters are defined as any mail of dimensions not exceeding 353 × 250 millimeters, a thickness of 2 centimeters, and a weight of 1 kilogram.

20. See Confoederatio Helvetica (2005b) for the announcement. At present, the incumbent firms in the EU member states and Switzerland retain monopoly rights over letters up to 100 grams (first-class mail, in US terminology). The EU limit is supposed to be reduced to 50 grams by 2006. Full liberalization of the market for EU letters is planned for 2012 (OECD 2004a).

maintain a certain diversity in the programs they offer. Since 2002, a law permits the government to levy a nominal development tax on tickets sold by a region's movie theater if the government judges that the content is not sufficiently diversified. The proceeds of the development tax will be redirected toward the financing of new theaters within the region that are willing to offer greater diversity (USTR 2005c).

Professional Services

The Swiss-EU Agreement on Free Movement of Persons, signed in 2002, marginally facilitated the employment of foreign workers by domestic Swiss firms.[21] However, professional services perfectly illustrate activities facing market access barriers within Switzerland. Professional services are subject to regulations in different cantons, leading to entry barriers not only against foreigners, but also between cantons. A Swiss-US FTA could have a positive impact on the free movement of people, as it would increase mobility between cantons (Owen 2005).

While barriers to entry differ from profession to profession, they are pervasive for accountants, lawyers, architects, and engineers. Barriers include compulsory certificates to exercise a profession, special permits to work in a given canton, and fixed or recommended prices. The cantons grant more certificates, but authorizations to exercise a profession are still required, often conditioned on solvency and insurance. Moreover, the Swiss Federal Tribunal has refused to recognize the right of establishment by professional firms, and supports cantonal decisions that reject certificates issued either by another canton or by a foreign government. Hence, a professional firm may not be able to practice in a given canton, even though the applicant has already been recognized in another one (WTO 2004b). All of this adds up to formidable entry barriers.

Fortunately, from a Swiss standpoint, it appears that all professional services can be negotiated in the FTA with the United States, except for the medical profession (Owen 2005). The Swiss health system entails compulsory health insurance and is heavily regulated. These features, along with medical licensing standards, will hamper any effort to liberalize the medical market.

Accounting and Auditing

Federal law stipulates that each audit firm must have at least one auditor with Swiss residency, and that the firm itself must be registered in the Swiss commercial register (WTO 2004b). Qualification of foreign professionals is

---

21. IMF (2005b) reports that the foreign labor force increased by 2 percent annually in 2003 and 2004.

contingent on Swiss recognition of foreign diplomas by the Office for Professional Education and Technology, although there is as yet no system of accreditation within Switzerland (WTO 2004b).

Legal Services

Access to the legal profession improved following a federal law, enacted in June 2002, aimed at harmonizing requirements across cantons. The law requires a period of practice of at least a year in Switzerland, and an equivalent law diploma for foreigners (WTO 2004b) awarded by a country that Switzerland recognizes: mainly EU and EFTA states. There is no indication that US legal diplomas are currently recognized.

Architecture and Engineering

Practicing architecture and engineering does not require a license. Entry may be difficult for foreigners, but under the law, they are accorded national treatment if they have worked for two years in Switzerland (WTO 2004b). However, prior practice requirements may differ across cantons. The European Union has requested the removal of prior practice requirements in the canton of Lucerne (European Commission 2002), and the federal government is now trying to harmonize requirements at the federal level to comply with EU standards (EIU 2005a). Recommended prices are published every year by the professional association, the Swiss Society of Engineers and Architects (SIA) (WTO 2004b).

Other Service Sectors

Other service sectors, such as taxis, restaurants, and hotels, are highly regulated. Licenses are exclusively valid in a given canton (OECD 2004a). For arts and crafts, a Switzerland Ministry of Economy report found that not one of the 15 different categories is harmonized across the 26 cantons (OECD 2004a). Finally, as mentioned above, the medical profession is protected by strong entry barriers, with fees usually fixed at the cantonal level (WTO 2004b).

Recent Developments

The process of changing Swiss legislation regarding the service sector was launched in 2002, and should continue in 2005 or 2006. While residency requirements are bound to persist, other restrictions are expected to be removed. Switzerland Ministry of Economy officials expect better terms for intracorporate transfers, allowing personnel to remain for five years in Switzerland (Owen 2005). In addition, the nationality requirement for the composition of boards may be lifted in the near future. The Swiss-American

Chamber of Commerce has recommended that members of a governing board have any nationality within the range of WTO members (Owen 2005).

Services Trade Negotiations in Selected US Bilateral FTAs

For the most part, we focus our analysis of phaseouts on those in US FTAs because the United States has pushed the envelope furthest in bilateral negotiations on services. In recent negotiations, such as US-Australia (2004) and US-Singapore (2003), the parties have used a "negative list" approach, meaning that all services are covered except for those specifically reserved. By contrast, Switzerland and EFTA have adopted the "positive list" approach, meaning the covered services must be specifically identified. The negative list approach inherently leads to broader coverage.[22] However, some of EFTA's bilateral pacts, such as EFTA-Singapore (2003), go well beyond commitments at the multilateral level.

As we hold high expectations for the potential liberalization of services in a Swiss-US FTA, we concentrate on US negotiating results to establish a benchmark. This section reviews the main points regarding services trade in the US-Australia and the US-Singapore FTAs. The first part reviews the critical points of the US-Australia FTA provisions related to audiovisual, financial, express delivery, telecommunications, and professional services. The second part reviews the US-Singapore FTA provisions for similar service industries, and compares selected features of the US-Singapore FTA with the EFTA-Singapore FTA.[23]

US-Australia

In broadcasting and audiovisual services, the Australian commitment to give US films and television programs some access to cable, satellite, and the Internet was seen as a major accomplishment (USTR 2004b). However, Australia's list of reservations ranked among the most detailed and complex of all negative lists in the audiovisual sector (Bernier 2004). Australia retains its existing commercial television quotas: 55 percent of programs must have Australian content. Content quotas for commercial radio remain at levels of up to 25 percent, and subscription television firms—pay TV—must spend 10 percent of their budgets for drama and general entertainment channels on new

---

22. The GATS uses a positive list approach.

23. We selected Singapore as the case study for comparison based on the statement by the EFTA Secretariat that Singapore is the most advanced EFTA agreement on services, and because both parties are developed countries.

Australian drama.[24] Finally, minimum "subquotas" for dramas and documentaries for adults and children are permitted to ensure the preservation of local culture (Bernier 2004). The only thing Australia conceded in the audiovisual sector was its ability to implement tighter quotas or more restrictive measures, especially with respect to new media services (USITC 2004b).

In financial services, the agreement guarantees that Australia will extend national treatment and MFN status to private-sector management of its civil service pension funds. It allows US asset management firms to sell portfolio management services to Australian mutual funds, and improves the transparency of financial services regulations (USTR 2004b). Australia retains the international investment screening mechanism embodied in its old foreign investment policy. As implemented by the Foreign Investment Review Board (FIRB), the policy creates modest barriers against inbound investment. However, investments in new financial services companies and acquisitions of existing ones of less than 800 million Australian dollars are exempted from the investment screening mechanism (the threshold was previously set at 50 million Australian dollars). Australia also agreed to lock in existing "good practice" regarding its review of acquisitions in the banking and insurance sectors. A side letter on financial services commits Australia to pursue the current practice of a restrained approach by the FIRB.[25]

In insurance, the FTA covers life, nonlife, reinsurance, intermediation (brokerage) for marine, aviation, and transport (MAT) services that are auxiliary to insurance but not covered by GATS, and key cross-border insurance products. Under the agreement, US life insurers may expand their branches in Australia, a practice that was previously prohibited.

The agreement recognizes express delivery services as a unique service sector, and makes important commitments to maintain market access. It also contains provisions to facilitate customs clearance, which is critical to the efficient operation of express carriers.

In telecommunications, the USITC (2004b) describes several important "WTO-plus" obligations for major suppliers included in the agreement, including resale, provisioning of leased circuits and co-location. The agreement guarantees the independence of regulatory bodies and ensures that the regulatory agency cannot have a financial interest in any supplier of public telecommunications services. It also commits Australian regulatory bodies to consult with interested parties before issuing regulations, to seek public remarks on prospective rules, and to publish all relevant regulations. Improved transparency is intended to ensure nondiscriminatory access for US firms on public telephone networks operated by major carriers. As with the Singapore FTA, however, the definition of "major

---

24. The agreement allows Australia to increase the funding requirement up to 20 percent, and to extend the 10 percent requirement to other genres.

25. The side letter encourages a process of government-to-government consultation and periodic revisions of the investment screening mechanism (USITC 2004b).

carriers" excludes mobile service providers, which means that cost-based interconnection rates are not the norm for these providers.[26] In fact, Australian mobile carriers have recently demanded higher termination rates (USITC 2004b).

In professional services, the agreement creates a working group that encourages the relevant bodies to harmonize their criteria for licensing and certifying professional service suppliers and recognizing professional credentials (USTR 2004b). However, the agreement does not directly alter state regulation of professional services in either Australia or the United States. Nor does it contain commitments for the temporary entry of businesspersons. The professional services commitments in the FTA are limited by its annexes, which reiterate that the two countries' commitments need not exceed those accepted under the market access provisions of Article XVI of the GATS (USTR 2004a).

In addition, the commitments made in the FTA are explicitly precluded from impinging on the existing rules of subfederal units. This limitation applies to commitments on national treatment, MFN treatment, local presence requirements, performance requirements, and senior management provisions (USTR 2004b). However, since the FTA makes no reference to new rules enacted by subfederal units after the FTA is ratified, there appears to be some scope for future federal-level agreements that could override new subfederal rules.

US-Singapore

In banking services, the US-Singapore chapter on financial services contains core obligations regarding nondiscrimination, MFN treatment, and additional market access obligations, and guarantees several conditions of access in the banking sector. Singapore must remove its ban on new licenses for full-service banks within 18 months, and within three years for wholesale banks. US banks must have access to Singapore's local ATM network within two and a half years for locally incorporated Singapore banks, and within four years for all other banks. Qualified US banks can open up to 30 branches and service locations; before the FTA, they could only open up to 15. US firms can offer asset and portfolio management and securities services in Singapore by establishing or acquiring local firms. Finally, US firms can offer pension services under Singapore's privatized social security system, with more liberal requirements regarding the number of portfolio managers who must reside in Singapore.

For insurance, all US and Singapore suppliers are assured fair and nondiscriminatory treatment and market access. Singapore has generally

---

26. However, mobile service providers are required to comply with the country's WTO commitments.

been recognized for its open insurance market. However, the FTA ensures further liberalization in the sector. It guarantees US firms access to customers in Singapore through subsidiary or branch offices located there; this covers life and nonlife insurance, reinsurance, insurance intermediation, and insurance auxiliary services. Significantly, the FTA also allows US insurance companies to sell MAT insurance, intermediation of reinsurance and MAT insurance, and insurance auxiliary services to customers in Singapore from offices in the United States. US firms can continue to sell reinsurance services to Singapore customers in the same manner. Finally, the FTA includes an innovative provision that allows licensed US insurers to provide new insurance products to their business customers in Singapore without prior regulatory approval. Meanwhile, the United States took a reservation: "The Overseas Private Investment Corporation insurance and loan guarantees are not available to certain aliens, foreign enterprises or foreign-controlled domestic enterprises" (USTR 2003a, Annex 8A).

In securities, the FTA guarantees market access, national treatment, and MFN treatment, opening Singapore's market to US investment firms. US investment firms that establish mutual funds in Singapore can use personnel based in the United States to manage the securities held in the fund portfolios. In addition, Singapore commits to easing the local staffing rules for US asset management and insurance companies that offer market access for their investment products to the Central Provident Fund, Singapore's mandatory national savings scheme (USITC 2003).

For telecommunications, the US-Singapore FTA addresses interconnection, resale of services, regulatory procedures, and nondiscriminatory access to the market. It ensures that all US telecommunication companies have market access to all of Singapore's telecommunications sectors,[27] and those companies are permitted to access the market in different ways: They can acquire or build local facilities, link their US network with a network in Singapore, or lease lines from Singapore firms. Singapore's telecom regulatory authorities commit to open and transparent administrative procedures (USITC 2003). However, the United States took a reservation to protect its restrictions on ownership of US radio licenses (USTR 2003a, Annex 8A).

The agreement guarantees that Singapore will improve market access to US providers of professional services and ease entry procedures for legal, architectural, engineering, and other professions. Singapore reduced the fraction of directors of engineering and architectural firms that must be professionally accredited in Singapore from two-thirds to more than half. It commits to entirely eliminate local ownership requirements for US land-surveying firms by 2004, to ease restrictions on US law firms that

---

27. By contrast, under the WTO, Singapore has committed to giving market access in select telecom markets to only three foreign telecom providers.

form joint law practices in Singapore, and to recognize degrees earned from certain US law schools to be able to admit their graduates to the Singapore bar (USTR 2003a, 2003e). However, it included reservations regarding the residency requirements of architects, registration and residency requirements for auditing services, and national treatment for engineering services.[28]

While Singapore took a reservation regarding its postal services, the FTA guarantees further liberalization of Singapore's express delivery services by giving market access to US services suppliers and improving customs administration.[29] The FTA guarantees national treatment and MFN status to all US audiovisual services.

However, Singapore took two reservations concerning cultural services in Annex 8B. These apply to basic obligations regarding national treatment, MFN treatment, and market access, and cover existing as well as future measures. The first reservation relates to broadcasting services, meaning that Singapore limits its obligation regarding television content broadcasts for local audiences (USTR 2003a). The second reservation applies to distribution and publication of printed media, meaning "any publication containing news, intelligence, reports of occurrences, or any remarks, observations or comments relating thereto or to any matter of public interest, printed in any language and published for sale or free distribution at intervals not exceeding one week" (Bernier 2004). The purpose of these reservations appears to be to protect Singapore's public from provocative US television shows or arguably defamatory media reports (Bernier 2004).

Comparing US-Singapore with EFTA-Singapore

The US and EFTA FTAs with Singapore are contemporary agreements, and in both cases, most of the negotiation took place in 2002. Both agreements address key service issues in a chapter of general commitments, accompanied by specific chapters or annexes dealing with financial services and telecommunications.[30] In their comments on services provisions, US and

---

28. The first reservation relates to restrictions on the temporary entry of professionals. The second reservation relates to the requirement for 51 percent local ownership of services in engineering corporations and, in the case of engineering partnerships, full local control of assets and profits. The USTR (2003e, 10) argues that these reservations "severely constrain US firms trying to open a Singaporean operation for single projects and requires them to give technical, managerial and financial control to outsiders in order to establish a long term presence."

29. For example, the agreement requires Singapore to prohibit its postal authority from subsidizing its express letter service in a way that gives the authority an unfair commercial advantage in express delivery services.

30. Unlike the EFTA-Singapore FTA, the treatment of "Temporary Entry of Business Persons" receives a full chapter in the US-Singapore FTA.

EFTA authorities stressed that they broke new ground, well beyond what has been achieved at the multilateral level. Chapter appendix table 5A.1 compares of the treatment of the core provisions on general services in both agreements. While the negotiated texts are quite similar, there are important differences in the scope of the two agreements.

As mentioned above, the US-Singapore FTA adopts a negative list approach to the core provisions, namely market access, national treatment, and MFN treatment. There are relatively few exclusions for domestic regulation and the entry of business persons. US-Singapore also goes beyond the EFTA-Singapore FTA in areas such as local presence and transparency measures (chapter appendix table 5A.1). By contrast, the core services provisions in EFTA-Singapore were negotiated on the basis of positive lists that identify sectors and measures where the commitments apply. EFTA-Singapore also applies the positive list approach to other provisions, such as the entry of businesspersons and domestic regulations (chapter appendix table 5A.1).

Recommendations for Services Trade

Working together, Switzerland and the United States can set a high standard for future bilateral FTAs as well as WTO negotiations in the Doha Round and beyond. With these ambitions in mind, we offer the following recommendations.

- Both countries should abolish citizenship and residency requirements for senior professionals, managers, and directors, except in very short (negative) lists of reserved activities. In particular, financial firms based in each country should be able to offer mutual funds and portfolio management services in the other country without establishing a physical presence there.

- As a general rule, again with negative lists, each country should extend umbrella national treatment and unconditional MFN rights to the other for their service sectors. The negative lists could contain state and cantonal exceptions to the national treatment requirement. However, a state and cantonal working group should be created to work on the progressive abolition of these subfederal exceptions.

- As in the US-Australia FTA, the Swiss-US FTA should establish a professional services working group to review professional diplomas and credentials, and recommend the mutual recognition of those degrees and standards that the working group determines are essentially equivalent. It should have an adequate budget to engage experts to assist in making these determinations.

- To deal with issues raised by FIFO delivery of professional services, the European Union is gradually adopting a "driver's license model" to facilitate the practice of law among member states.[31] American lawyers are generally excluded from the EU system.[32] However, something akin to the driver's license model might be adopted for FIFO services between the United States and Switzerland in the context of the FTA.

- The FTA should extend the scope of insurance and reinsurance that can be sold in one country by properly capitalized and regulated firms based in the other country, without additional capital or regulatory requirements. In other words, for designated lines of insurance, Switzerland and the United States should accord mutual recognition to firms based in the other country. For the United States, this provision will require the assent of key states, which should be obtained before the insurance mutual recognition clause comes into effect.

- Switzerland should commit to enacting its proposed new electricity supply law and comparable natural gas legislation as auxiliary provisions to the FTA. Similarly, it should commit to pursuing the initiatives launched by ComCom with respect to interconnection terms and rates.

- Although Swiss firms might have limited interest in enhanced access to the US telecommunications and information services market, nevertheless, the United States should use the FTA to advance its liberalizing agenda. In particular, the United States should permit ownership of cable networks, direct satellite broadcast, provision of satellite services, and provision of information services by bona fide Swiss firms.

- Although Switzerland does not set quotas on programming of non-Swiss origin, the new nominal development tax that was enacted in 2002 could have a negative impact on US film distributors and cinema companies. Switzerland should commit to consult with the United States before imposing this tax.

We believe that the Swiss-US FTA can push the envelope of services liberalization well beyond what has already been accomplished in GATS,

---

31. Once a driver's license is issued, it remains valid until it expires (a time limit) or until it is revoked (for bad driving). Following this approach, the EU approach allows lawyers to practice among the member states, once they pass a qualifying test. The legal license may need to be renewed periodically, and may be revoked upon a showing of incompetence or malpractice.

32. By contrast with continental Europe, Britain has a more open market for legal services.

and even beyond the US-Australia and US-Singapore FTAs. Both Switzerland and the United States have already reduced or eliminated the most obvious barriers to services trade, so the field is clear to attack the more subtle barriers. Both countries are also highly service-oriented, in shares in GDP, drivers of productivity, and prospective growth in international trade. Bilateral exchange of services can only flourish with further liberalization. But this includes the public as well as the private sector, and so we turn to the issue of government procurement.

Appendix 5A

Table 5A.1 Selected general provisions in services

Item	US-Singapore FTA	EFTA-Singapore FTA
Scope of measures	Measures by central, regional, or local government affecting cross-border trade in services (negative list).	Measures by central, regional, or local government affecting trade in services in committed sectors only (positive list).
Schedules	Annex 8A (measures) and 8B (sectors) include schedule-exceptions to national treatment and most favored nation treatment, market access, local presence, performance requirements, or senior management and boards of directors.	Each schedule specifies country-specific (a) terms, limitations, and conditions on market access. (b) conditions and qualifications on national treatment. (c) undertakings relating to additional commitments. (d) time frame for implementation of commitments.
Market access	Applies to all sectors except those specified in the agreement.	Applies to sectors in which specific commitments are undertaken.
	Removal of limitations on number of services providers; value of services transactions; quantity of services output; number of persons that may be employed in a particular sector; and measures that restrict or require specific types of legal entity or joint venture.	Removal of limitations on number of services providers; value of services transactions; quantity of services output; number of persons that may be employed in a particular sector; and measures that restrict or require specific types of legal entity or joint venture.
		Removal of limitations on the participation of foreign capital in terms of maximum percentage limit on foreign shareholding.

(table continues next page)

Table 5A.1 Selected general provisions in services *(continued)*

	US–Singapore FTA	EFTA–Singapore FTA
Most favored nation (MFN) treatment	Unconditional MFN treatment in like circumstances.	Exceptions to MFN: (a) Agreements and mutual recognition agreements (MRAs) in accordance with articles V and VII of GATS. (b) Annex VI.
National treatment	Yes, unless specified in Annexes 8A and 8B.	Only in sectors considered under the agreement.
Local presence	A party shall not require a service supplier of the other party to establish or maintain a representative office or any form of enterprise, or to be resident in its territory, as a condition for the cross-border supply of a service.	No equivalent provision other than general reference on market access.
Domestic regulations	Commitment to inform about status of requests and final decision in cases where a party requires authorization. Measures relating to qualification and license requirements should be based on objective and transparent criteria not more burdensome than necessary to ensure the quality of the service, and should not in themselves be restrictions to the provision of the service.	Applies to sectors in which specific commitments are undertaken. Commitment to inform about status of requests and final decision in cases where a party requires authorization. Measures relating to qualification and license requirements should be based on objective and transparent criteria not more burdensome than necessary to ensure the quality of the service, and should not in themselves be restrictions to the provision of the service. Each party establishes arbitral instance to review at the request of the party administrative decisions affecting trade in services. Joint review of results of negotiations pursuant to Article VI.4 of GATS.

Transparency measures	Establishment of mechanisms to respond to inquiries of persons regarding measures included in the chapter. Mandates publication of laws, regulations, procedures, and administrative rulings affecting trade in services or reasons for failure to comply with these mandates. Addresses substantive comments received from interested persons with respect to proposed regulations and allow reasonable time between publication of final regulations and their effective date.	No equivalent provision other than general references on other articles of the chapter.
Entry of business persons	Secures temporary access for business visitors and investors for up to 90 days without need for labor market tests. Additional grant, not subject to labor market tests, of 5,400 work visas for different categories of Singaporean professionals. This concession was reciprocated by Singapore.	Temporary access is granted to service suppliers and natural persons of a party who are employed by a service supplier of a party, with respect to the supply of a service. Commitments are based on conditions and qualifications stipulated under each national schedule.
Full set of provisions on services	Chapter 8 Trade in Services Chapter 9 Telecommunications Chapter 10 Financial Services Chapter 11 Temporary Entry of Business Persons Annexes to chapters 8, 10, and 11.	Articles 21–36 Annex on Telecommunications Annex on Financial Services Annex on Most-Favored-Nation Treatment Annexes with Country-Specific Commitments

Sources: USTR (2003a) and Singapore Ministry of Trade and Industry (2003).

6

Government Procurement

Switzerland and the United States have both signed the World Trade Organization (WTO) Government Procurement Agreement (GPA). Hence, one might think that a Swiss-US FTA would not open as many procurement opportunities as the US-Australia FTA, since Australia did not sign the GPA. However, Switzerland reserved its application of the GPA to US firms in important sectors, arguing that the United States had not given equivalent access to Swiss firms. The GPA does not cover all federal procurement. Finally, multiple restrictions persist at the subfederal level, in both Switzerland and the United States. Opening government procurement markets in both countries could thus deliver considerable benefits, and taxpayer dollars will be saved when states and cantons invite a larger number of bidders. As the largest public procurement body in the world, the US federal government too would benefit from Swiss bids, even in select market niches.

This chapter includes three sections. The first two sections review the regulatory environment and recent developments in the United States and Switzerland respectively. The third section outlines our recommendations for liberalizing government procurement in the context of a prospective Swiss-US FTA.

Government Procurement: United States

In 1996, the United States signed the WTO GPA along with 28 other nations. At the federal level, public procurement takes place through various departments supervised by the Office of Management and Budget (OMB) and two acquisition regulatory councils, the Defense Acquisition Regulations Council and the Civilian Agency Acquisition Council (WTO 2004b). The Federal Acquisition Regulation (FAR) furnishes umbrella regulation for all federal entities but permits them to follow their own internal guidelines (WTO 2004b).[1] Under the FAR, federal entities are obligated to publish their procurement requirements on a Web site known as FedBizOpps when the procurement exceeds $25,000.[2] The proposed contract must be published at least 15 days before bids begin; thereafter, prospective bidders must be given at least 30 days to place their bids (WTO 2004b).

At the subfederal level, state and local governments regulate procurement contacts. Contracts are subject to threshold values and other provisions specific to each state. Some states grant preferences to local suppliers and impose local-content requirements. However, 37 states have implemented the GPA provisions,[3] and are obligated to publish tender invitations on FedBizOpps for GPA-covered sectors.

The Buy America Act

The Buy America Act (BAA) of 1933 (as amended) is the core document governing US procurement of goods at the federal level. The act establishes discriminatory measures, also known as Buy America restrictions, for government-funded purchases, including supply and construction contracts (European Commission 2004a). These restrictive measures can take several forms, prohibiting government entities from purchasing foreign goods and services, requiring a certain amount of local content, and preferring domestic suppliers when evaluating bid prices.

The United States maintains a number of Buy America restrictions for procurement that are not covered by the GPA, the North American Free Trade Agreement (NAFTA), the WTO plurilateral Agreement on Trade in Civil Aircraft, or bilateral procurement agreements with Chile, Singapore, Australia, and Israel (WTO 2004c). Where in force, Buy America requirements apply to goods, not services. They require federal entities to procure only US-mined or US-produced unprocessed goods. In addition, only manufactured articles with at least 50 percent local content can be procured (European Commission 2004a).

Executive Order 10582 of 1954 goes beyond the scope of the BAA by carving out special status for procurement contracts with small businesses

---

1. The FAR was amended in 2001 to change aspects of electronic procurement and preferential access for small businesses, improve transparency of procedures, and alter bidding process and thresholds. Part 25 of the FAR deals with policies and procedures to acquire foreign supplies, services, and construction materials (WTO 2004b).

2. Exceptions are made for purchases of perishable supplies when delayed publication could be damaging (WTO 2004b).

3. The 37 states are listed in Annex 2 of the US GPA schedule (WTO 2002e).

and firms in areas with labor surpluses. The order also allows government entities to reject bids placed by foreign firms for national interest and security reasons (European Commission 2004a).

The Balance of Payments Program

The balance of payments program is a nonstatutory program that potentially restricts both purchases of supplies by government entities and contracts for construction, alteration, or repair of any public building outside the United States (WTO 2004c). Since 2001, this program no longer applies to civilian agency acquisitions, but it still applies to the Department of Defense for purchases of end products that are used abroad and exceed $100,000 in cost (WTO 2004c).

The Trade Agreements Act of 1979

The Trade Agreements Act of 1979 implemented the GATT Government Procurement Code agreed to in the Tokyo Round. Essentially, it overrides the BAA and kindred legislation by ensuring national treatment to signatories of the Code with respect to scheduled entities and above-threshold contracts (USITC 2004a). Thus, the act gives up BAA preferences regarding civil aircraft and related articles[4] as well as other end products for designated parties.[5]

Exemptions and Waivers

Exemptions and waivers to the BAA and balance of payments program are granted if it can be shown that domestic preferences are inconsistent with national interests, and if the supply of a particular material is either unavailable or too expensive in the United States (WTO 2004c).[6] BAA restrictions have been waived in acquiring defense equipment originating

---

4. Related articles are articles that "meet the substantial transformation test of the Act and originate in countries that are parties to the WTO Agreement on Trade in Civil Aircraft" (WTO 2004c).

5. Similar preferences are extended unilaterally to eligible countries through the GPA, NAFTA, other bilateral procurement agreements, and to less developed countries (WTO 2004c). For example, end products that are granted duty-free entry under the Caribbean Basin Economic Recovery Act (CBERA) are eligible for government contracts.

6. A domestic offer is judged too expensive if the foreign product is priced "below the lowest domestic offer when this offer is from a large business concern" (including import duty and a 6 percent added margin) (WTO 2004c). If the offer is from a small business, the added margin would be 12 percent, and for defense-related purchases, the price difference has to be a minimum of 50 percent.

Table 6.1 Threshold values in the WTO GPA and US bilateral FTAs (dollars)

	Supplies	Services	Construction
WTO	169,000	169,000	6,481,000
Canada	25,000	56,190	7,304,733
Mexico	56,190	56,190	7,304,733
Chile	56,190	56,190	6,481,000
Singapore	56,190	56,190	6,481,000

Source: WTO (2004c).

from countries with which the United States has a reciprocal procurement agreement, such as Switzerland.[7]

The goods listed in Subchapters VIII and X of Chapter 98 of the Buy America Act are not subject to custom duties when they are purchased for use in government contracts. Other supplies may also be eligible for duty-free entry if the contract price is reduced by the amount of duty that would prevail if the supplies did not enter duty free (WTO 2004c). Finally, excepting equipment, supplies aimed at government-operated vessels or aircraft are eligible for entering the United States duty free (WTO 2004c).

The WTO GPA and US Bilateral Agreements

As of 2004, the threshold values of procurement contracts covered under the GPA have been maintained at their 1996 levels (WTO 2004c). Table 6.1 shows the threshold values set by the United States in the WTO GPA Schedule, NAFTA, and its FTAs with Singapore and Chile. Table 6.2 shows the list of services that the United States has chosen to exclude from the GPA and in selected FTAs.

The US-Chile and US-Singapore FTAs opened additional state and federal agencies to foreign bids (Schott 2004b). However, under the US-Singapore FTA, state obligations do not expand beyond the sector obligations already committed under the GPA. Local procurement is not covered under either the GPA or the two FTAs. Under the US-Chile FTA, the 37 US states that have agreed to GPA provisions will treat Chilean suppliers in essentially the same manner (USTR 2003e). Finally, the US-Chile and US-Singapore FTAs specify high threshold values and exclude state set-aside programs for small and minority businesses (Salazar-Xirinachs and Granados 2004).

---

7. However, the secretary of defense retains the right to restrict or reject an offer from a qualifying country for national defense reasons.

Table 6.2 Services covered by the United States in the GPA and bilateral FTAs

Service	WTO	NAFTA/Chile	Singapore	Australia/ Morocco
Purchase of military services overseas	Excl.	Excl.	Excl.	Excl.
Automatic data processing, telecommunications and transmission	Excl.	Excl.	Incl.	Incl.
Telecom networks, automated news services, data services	Excl.	Excl.	Incl.	Incl.
Basic telecommunications network services	Incl.	Incl.	Excl.	Excl.
Dredging	Excl.	Excl.	Excl.	Excl.
Federally funded research and development centers	Excl.	Incl.	Excl.	Incl.
Department of defense, energy, aeronautics/ space facilities	Incl.	Excl.	Incl.	Excl.
Research and development	Excl.	Excl.	Excl.	Excl.
Transportation services	Excl.	Excl.	Excl.	Excl.
Utility services	Excl.	Excl.	Excl.	Excl.
Maintenance, repair, rebuilding, installation of equipment	Incl.	Excl.	Incl.	Excl.
Related to ships, including nonnuclear ship repair	Incl.	Excl.	Incl.	Excl.

Excl. = excluded
Incl. = included

Source: Acqnet (2005).

As with other FTAs, the procurement chapter (chapter 15) in the US-Australia FTA sets out specific rules and standards to achieve the objective of nondiscrimination.[8] The agreement requires the Australian government to eliminate industry development programs and limits selective tendering. These provisions will level the playing field for US firms that bid on public contracts. Australia will also become a designated country under the US Trade Agreements Act, meaning that Australian firms no longer have to establish operations in the United States or a designated country, or estab-

---

8. For example, the FTA requires each country to enact laws that make bribery of procurement officials a criminal or administrative offense.

lish partnering arrangements with US firms, to sell to the US government. Chapter 15 is complemented by eight annexes that determine the government entities covered and the types of procurements excluded by each party. A side letter deals with government procurement of blood plasma.

Government procurement was a source of concern in the debate over the Central American–Dominican Republic Free Trade Agreement (CAFTA-DR). Congressman Benjamin Cardin (D-MD) attempted to withdraw Maryland from the list of states subject to government procurement rules in the FTA package, but ultimately relented.[9]

Effect of Restrictions

In 2002, US government expenditures amounted to $1.98 trillion, or 19 percent of GDP. Defense-related expenditures were the largest component, at some $400 billion. Most expenditures, however, represent salaries and transfer payments. In 1999, the United States reported 56,598 procurement contracts, totaling $205 billion (WTO 2004c), though the EU Commission has estimated that BAA restrictions each year affect approximately $25 billion of those contracts—most noticeably in mass transport and airport improvements (European Commission 2004a).[10]

US public procurement restrictions take place in three different ways: federal restrictions on procurement by federal entities, state restrictions on state and local procurement contracts, and federal restrictions on how federal grant money can be used by state and local governments (USITC 2004a). At the federal level, major restrictions are placed on defense procurement contracts and small and minority-owned business contracts. At the state level, federal regulations—mostly BAA restrictions—prohibit using federal grant money in transportation and food assistance projects (USITC 2004a).

Public Transportation

The Department of Transportation (DOT) distributes federal aid to state and local governments under the Highway Administration Act, the Urban Mass Transit Act, and the Airports Improvements Act. The federal government may fund 40 to 80 percent of a project, leaving the state to fund the rest. All

---

9. Cardin dropped his demand after Deputy US Trade Representative Peter Allgeier gave him assurances that "if USTR found it acceptable, it would consult with DR-CAFTA parties in a way that would not delay congressional consideration of the free trade package." Subsequently, however, Allgeier informed Cardin that Maryland "will have to remain on the list of states subject to government procurement rules" in CAFTA-DR. See "Maryland to Remain on Government Procurement Annex for CAFTA," *Inside US Trade*, July 1, 2005, 5.

10. This figure is expected to increase to $35 billion in 2005 (European Commission 2004a).

projects are subject to local content requirements of 60 percent, or face a penalty of up to 25 percent of the price (European Commission 2004a).

Highway Construction

Federally assisted highway projects amounted to $46 billion in 2002, while federal grants to state and local governments totaled $26 billion (USITC 2004a). Under the BAA, highways must be constructed with domestically produced iron and steel. A waiver is possible but rarely granted.

Airport Construction

The Federal Aviation Administration (FAA) monitors BAA restrictions on state and local public procurement for airport construction projects. Some 80 to 90 percent of airport construction spending comes from the federal government. Airport construction projects are obligated to use steel and manufactured goods that are domestically produced, unless a waiver is invoked.

Food Assistance

The US Department of Agriculture and other federal entities (e.g., the Department of Health and Human Services) monitor a wide array of food assistance procurement programs. Those programs, such as the National School Lunch Program and the Child and Adult Care food program, give preference to local food suppliers. Even donated commodities must be of domestic origin. Some programs require that school food authorities buy domestic commodities to the maximum extent (USITC 2004a). Under NAFTA and the Uruguay Round agreements, the United States retained the right to exempt the "procurement of agricultural goods made in furtherance of agricultural support programs or human feeding programs" from its obligations (USITC 2004a).

Small-Business Set-Asides

The Small Business Act (SBA) of 1958 (as amended) governs federal grants and subcontracts for goods and services awarded to small business firms. Under the act, 23 percent of prime contracts must be awarded to small businesses; 5 percent of prime and subcontracts to minority-owned businesses; 5 percent to women-owned businesses; 3 percent to service-disabled veteran-owned businesses; and prime contracts for Historically Underutilized Business Zone firms (HUBZone) are phased in from 1 percent in fiscal year 1999, to 2.5 percent in fiscal year 2002, to 3 percent in fiscal year 2003 (USITC 2004a). All owners of small businesses must be US citizens to qualify for these preferential procurement programs. Because SBA regulations require that receipts of all domestic and foreign affiliates of the business be counted to qualify as a "small size business," most US affiliates of foreign-owned corporations cannot obtain small business status. Most federal purchases under the SBA programs face BAA restrictions, although a general waiver may be granted to federal purchases below $2,500 (USITC 2004a).

Defense Procurement

The BAA governs domestic sourcing requirements for defense procurement. In addition, the Defense Federal Acquisition Regulations System (DFARS) regulates defense-related procurement of specific products, such as food, clothing, fibers, vessel acquisition, and anchor chains (USITC 2004a). The DFARS regulations are intended to ensure that government procurement contracts comply with the memorandum of understanding (MoU) between Department of Defense (DOD) and SBA regarding the small-business goals mentioned above (USITC 2004a). North Atlantic Treaty Organization (NATO) countries that have ratified the MoU can obtain a waiver from DOD's domestic preferences (USITC 2004a).

State and Local Government Procurement

States impose procurement restrictions over and above the restrictions imposed by federal rules. So far, all negotiated US trade agreements have given states the choice to retain their state procurement rules or accede to the agreement. In response, some of the 50 states have chosen to relinquish state preferences. For a US FTA partner, the benefits of state accession are enhanced by the large number and diverse nature of state programs (USITC 2004a), though as of 2005, Ohio, Indiana, Virginia, Georgia, and New Jersey, among others, are still holding out.

Subfederal Selective Purchasing Laws

Selective purchasing laws at the subfederal level often impede foreign firms with links to "offensive" third countries, such as Burma. Such laws have been adopted by Massachusetts and 20 other cities and local authorities (European Commission 2004a). The Supreme Court ruled that the Massachusetts law was unconstitutional (US Supreme Court 2000), but the ruling was relatively narrow. Hence, municipal selective purchases on foreign policy grounds can still be a problem. In 2001, New York attempted to apply selective purchasing legislation based on the so-called MacBride principles (European Commission 2004a). While the proposal was dropped, it flagged a continuing concern.

Services

While the BAA is not supposed to apply to service procurement, the offshore outsourcing debate has inspired new legislative forays, mainly at state level. New Jersey in 2002, followed by Michigan in 2004, enacted leg-

islation stating that "only citizens of the United States and persons authorized to work in the United States pursuant to federal law may be employed
in the performance of services [funded by the states]" (European Commission 2004a). Connecticut, Florida, Maryland, Missouri, and Wisconsin have
announced the implementation of similar provisions (European Commission 2004a). The target of this legislation is to discourage "call centers" and
data-processing abroad (European Commission 2004a).

Recent Developments

Recent initiatives have attempted to make federal government procurement more efficient. The E-Government Act of 2002 led to the creation of
an Internet portal for government procurement known as the Integrated
Acquisition Environment (IAE) initiative. The General Services Administration (GSA) has promoted two new programs. GSA Global Supply (GGS)
identifies an array of goods and services that conform to government
acquisition policies and socioeconomic regulations (WTO 2004c). GSA
Advantage is an Internet program that allows interested parties to communicate with authorized contractors online. Under this program, 5,298
contracting foreign firms registered online in 2004 (WTO 2004c).

Government Procurement: Switzerland

Switzerland ratified the WTO GPA in 1994. The 1994 Federal Law on Government Procurement, however, deals only with federal procurement, not
cantonal procurement. The federal law "specifies the procurement regime;
it also provides for, *inter alia,* periodic adjustments of definitions and threshold values to the relevant GPA provisions" (WTO 2004b). Some 42 entities
have been designated for the purchase of goods. As for relevant services—
road and air transport, financial services, and certain professional services,
such as advertising, counseling, and publishing—these can be purchased
by each of the 42 designated federal entities (WTO 2004b). A 1995 ordinance
subsequent to the 1994 federal law covers remaining areas, such as procurements below the relevant WTO thresholds or purchases by entities not
included in Switzerland's commitment under the GPA (WTO 2004b).

The Swiss cantons passed the 1994 Inter-Cantonal Concordat, which
altered "previous cantonal arrangements that provided scope for buy-
local, buy-regional and buy-national preferences" (WTO 1996). The concordat covers contracts for construction projects in excess of 9.6 million
Swiss francs; contracts for goods and services in excess of 0.38 million Swiss
francs; and contracts for goods and services purchased by public water,
energy, and transport companies in excess of 0.77 million Swiss francs
(WTO 2004b). In 1995, the Swiss Parliament passed the Internal Market Law

(LMI), which explicitly created nondiscriminatory access to public procurement in cantons and municipalities.

Competition for public procurement contracts was enhanced in recent years, after Switzerland concluded a bilateral agreement with the European Union extending GPA coverage to the liberalization level of the EU internal market at EU thresholds. As a result, in March 2001, the Inter-Cantonal Agreement on Public Procurement (AIMP) was further revised, as was the federal ordinance in July 2002.[11] The AIMP was revised to harmonize thresholds and procedures of those contracts not governed by international treaties (OECD 2004a). The revised ordinance established a surveillance mechanism, the Commission des Marchés publics Confédération/Cantons (CCMC), which aims to enforce Switzerland's international commitments regarding public procurement contracts. To this effect, thresholds much lower than the WTO levels were established at the cantonal and communal levels, thereby seriously opening local procurement markets. These lower thresholds apply to Swiss-established bidders, while foreign bidders may bid on contracts that meet GATT/WTO thresholds.

Presently, the Swiss government is thoroughly revising the Swiss Federal Law on Public Procurement. The initiatives aim to simplify and harmonize public tender procedures (US Department of State 2005)[12] and attempt to improve the application of procurement procedures by federal purchasing entities (OECD 2004a).[13]

Swiss Reservations under the WTO GPA

Switzerland took reservations to the GPA for participants that do not provide similar and effective access for Swiss firms. Box 6.1 indicates that Switzerland's reservations apply mostly to the United States and Canada. Indeed, Switzerland made important reservations for US firms regarding communal entities—that is, public authorities that operate at the communal or district level—water, local transport, and airport authorities; service subsectors; and challenge procedures.[14]

---

11. The revised text of the AIMP was in force in 21 cantons at the end of June 2005.

12. Under the rules of the WTO Government Procurement Agreement, each canton was allowed to implement the agreement independently, leading to disparities across cantons (US Department of State 2005).

13. For example, the Swiss federal government created a database to track trends in procurement contracts and assess reforms (OECD 2004a).

14. Challenge procedures result from difficulties in honoring the recommendation in the WTO dispute settlement procedure that calls for "retrospective" remedies. The provisions on challenge procedures can be found in Article 20 of the WTO GPA. This article requires the parties to the GPA "to set up a domestic bid challenge system for the purpose of giving suppliers, who believe that procurement has been executed inconsistently with the requirements of the GPA, a right of recourse to an independent domestic tribunal" (WTO 2003).

Box 6.1 Swiss reservations to the Government Procurement Agreement

Country	Entities
United States	Communal bodies, water, electricity, local transports, airports, and ports Service subsectors Challenge procedures
Canada	Regional bodies, water, electricity, local transports, airports, and ports Service subsectors Challenge procedures
Japan	Communal bodies, electricity, and local transports Challenge procedures
South Korea	Communal bodies, local transports, and airports Challenge procedures
Israel	Communal bodies and local transports Service subsectors Challenge procedures
Singapore	Communal bodies, water, and electricity

Source: WTO (2003b).

Bilateral Agreements

Switzerland has signed bilateral procurement agreements with the United States (1996), the European Union (2002), Mexico (2001, as part of the European Free Trade Association (EFTA)–Mexico FTA), and Chile (2004, as part of the EFTA-Chile FTA). These agreements expand access to government procurement opportunities, including at the subfederal level.

The 1996 Swiss-US procurement agreement was incorporated into the WTO GPA; the Swiss-EU agreement draws and expands on WTO provisions. The GPA guarantees that the Swiss federal state and the cantons, as well as public companies in the water, urban transport, and energy sectors, will tender and award contracts for goods, services, and construction projects when they exceed certain threshold values (e.g., 250,000 Swiss francs, or about $211,000). The Swiss-EU agreement opens the public procurement market to tender in the rail transport sector, and allows contract awards to private companies that are working on the basis of exclusive rights, such as private utility companies (Switzerland Integration Office 2005b).

The Mexican procurement agreement, part of the EFTA-Mexico FTA (including Switzerland), was ratified in July 2001. The agreement guarantees that Mexico will grant EFTA suppliers the same access it provides to US, European, and Canadian suppliers (WTO 2004b). For their part, EFTA member countries will give Mexico access similar to their GPA commitments, except at the subfederal level (WTO 2004b).

In the EFTA-Chile FTA, both parties agreed to mutual nondiscriminatory access to their government procurement markets for goods, services, and public works at both the federal and subfederal government levels, as well as for certain utilities (WTO 2004b).

Effect of Restrictions

Despite the GPA and FTAs, the Organization for Economic Cooperation and Development (OECD) reports that competition for government procurement contracts is weak in Switzerland (OECD 2005). In 2000, total public spending on goods, services, and construction amounted to more than 30 billion Swiss francs, representing 25 percent of total government spending and 8 percent of GDP (WTO 2004b).[15] Cantons and municipalities play the major role in public procurement, which engenders a bias in favor of local firms (OECD 2005).[16]

This bias at the expense of foreign firms can be explained by three factors. First, most contracts for open public tenders are valued below the financial thresholds for international competition (OECD 2004a); they are, however, open to Swiss bidders. Second, the legislation on procurement contracting differs across cantons, and between the Swiss federation and the cantons.[17] These differences should, however, not be overstated, as they refer mainly to procedures and secondary issues: Each canton has its own remedy tribunal, and the decisions of the various tribunals may not be consistent across cantons or with federal remedies.[18] Third, when international thresholds are not

---

15. Swiss public procurement as a share of GDP is somewhat lower than it is in other industrial countries. The OECD reports that government procurement in the EU zone varies between 14 and 15 percent (OECD 2002).

16. More than 80 percent of the contracts are granted by cantons and municipalities (OECD 2004a).

17. The complexity of the legislation renders its application for both bidders and contracting authorities difficult. The incorporation of international agreements in domestic legislation is not harmonized between the Confederation and the cantons. For example, the OECD remarks, "Under federal law, negotiations with bidders are allowed during the procedure, which is not the case for the cantons" (OECD 2004a).

18. Similar differences exist in other federal countries.

reached, "the lower thresholds above which competition applies at national level have appreciably differed across cantons" (OECD 2004a), which hampers competition and transparency. However, with the revised AIMP, a uniform threshold has been set for the different procedures at the national level to harmonize procedures across Switzerland.

Recent Developments

The level of competition has improved thanks to recent initiatives. The cantons of Geneva and Vaud initiated a government procurement Web site to pool tenders at both the federal and cantonal levels, and unify the bidding system (OECD 2004a).[19] A new system is planned to go into effect in April 2006 under SIMAP II (Système d'information sur les marches publics) with the federal state and no less than 14 cantons. As the OECD argues, "The system should encourage scale economies on standard procurement contracts and a reduction in the management costs of tendering, which should lead to lower threshold values" (OECD 2004a).[20]

Some evidence indicates that the Internet portal, along with the AIMP revision and the Ordinance mentioned earlier, have created a more competitive environment. The OECD reports that, when comparing identical tenders in the Swiss federation between 2000 and 2002, figures show that prices have decreased by 25 percent on average (OECD 2004a).

Recommendations for Government Procurement

While the United States and Switzerland have different national competition policies, both countries permit state and cantonal regulations that impair competition. In the United States, the "state action doctrine" immunizes state and local governments from antitrust liability. Stemming from a US Supreme Court decision that allowed a state to sponsor a Depression-era cartel, US states can pursue anticompetitive regulation of transportation, hospitals, healthcare, and electric-power sectors (OECD 2004d). Likewise, despite Swiss federal efforts to gradually liberalize the electricity market, local and regional firms still continue as monopoly owners of the national

---

19. The site has 5,500 public contractors, over 98 percent of whom operate at the cantonal and communal level.

20. The OECD reports that "the maximum amount for contracts negotiable by mutual agreement was [recently] raised from 50,000 [Swiss francs] to 150,000 for a service or construction supply contract and to 300,000 [Swiss francs] for a contract on the shell of a building" (OECD 2004a). Higher thresholds are justified by the transactions costs incurred in public tendering, and these costs should be reduced by the new system.

electricity network, known as Swissgrid. To liberalize government procurement at the subfederal level, we offer the following recommendations for the United States and Switzerland.

For the United States

- The FTA should grant Swiss firms the best terms enjoyed under the GPA and by NAFTA partners, Chile, Singapore, Australia, and future US bilateral FTAs (an unconditional most favored nation [MFN] provision). The MFN provision should apply to both federal and state procurement.

- The United States should extend its procurement coverage to at least three additional sectors that were excluded from the WTO GPA: research and development (R&D), transportation services, and utility services. R&D contracts are likely to be of commercial interest to leading Swiss firms. Both US and Swiss firms may be interested in transportation and utility contracts in the other country.

- The United States Trade Representative (USTR) should seek to cover two or three holdout states in addition to states that have previously agreed to GPA or FTA procurement provisions. Likely candidates might be Atlantic Coast states New Jersey, Virginia, and Georgia.

- Additionally, the USTR should seek to cover a few metropolitan areas. Again, Atlantic Coast metropolitan areas seem most plausible because of their greater familiarity and proximity to Switzerland. Boston, New York, Washington, Charlotte, Savannah, and Miami come to mind.

For Switzerland

- Reciprocally with the recommended US provision, the FTA should grant US firms the best terms enjoyed under the GPA, and by EFTA partners and future Swiss bilateral FTAs (an unconditional MFN provision). The MFN provision should apply to both federal and cantonal procurement. This provision would eliminate most of Switzerland's GPA reservations with respect to the United States (communal bodies would still be excepted), and thus open both federal and cantonal procurement markets to US firms.

Subfederal practices that impede competition cannot be abolished overnight. Nevertheless, in the realm of public procurement, the Swiss-US FTA should be ambitious and forward-looking. For budget reasons alone, public authorities in both countries should welcome the precedent of greater competition. Our discussion now turns to investment—the final piece of the liberalization puzzle.

7

Direct and Portfolio Investment

The United States and Switzerland both figure prominently in foreign direct investment (FDI). They are known worldwide for their brand-name multinational enterprises (MNEs) and outward FDI stocks, which represented 112 percent of GDP for Switzerland in 2003 and 19 percent for the United States (UNCTAD 2004b). In performance index rankings for outward FDI between 2001 and 2003, Switzerland was ninth, and the United States thirtieth, among listed nations.[1] Both countries have also become important hosts to foreign MNEs and inward direct investment. Inward FDI stocks as a share of Swiss GDP increased from 8 percent in 1980 to 50 percent in 2003; for the United States, from 3 to 14 percent.[2]

For both countries, portfolio investment faces low barriers. Outward portfolio investment is particularly weighty for Switzerland, while inward portfolio investment is a major feature of the US economy. Portfolio investment exchanges between the two countries are substantial, with equity holdings as the dominant asset. The size of Swiss-US portfolio income flows is quite considerable, especially when benchmarked against flows to and from the European Union.

---

1. Based on data reported in UNCTAD (2004b).

2. From 2001 to 2003, Swiss and US inward "FDI performance," as measured by a three-year moving average of several indexes, ranked 49th and 112th respectively. According to a recent OECD report, Switzerland's gross fixed capital formation will rise by 3.6 percent in 2006, driven partly by inward FDI. This estimate is supported by UNCTAD, which argues that the short- and medium-term outlook for the Swiss economy seems brighter than it has in the past four years. See OECD (2005) and UNCTAD (2004b).

In most bilateral relationships, US outward direct investment outpaces the partner country's investment in the United States. The opposite is true, however, in the Swiss-US relationship: Swiss direct investment in the United States has historically exceeded US FDI in Switzerland. In 2003, the stock of Swiss FDI in the United States, based on US data, reached $113 billion, while the stock of US FDI in Switzerland was $86 billion (tables 7.1 and 7.2). In fact, the United States is the chief destination for Swiss direct investments abroad, making Switzerland the sixth-largest foreign direct investor in the United States, surpassing Canada. Conversely, Switzerland is the fourth most important destination for US direct investments, and US-based MNEs are the most important foreign investors in Switzerland. US companies prefer to have their European headquarters in Switzerland, because of its central location, good air access, and skilled multilingual personnel. A key Swiss objective in its free trade agreement (FTA) with the United States is to reinforce these advantages.

A recent OECD (2005) cross-country analysis examines the treatment of direct investment in international agreements, arguing that superior benefits result from addressing investment issues in multilateral and bilateral trade agreements rather than classic bilateral investment treaties (BITs), because of the former's broader scope. A Swiss-US FTA that addresses the small number of Swiss and US investment frictions should augment an already robust relationship.

Negotiating issues that might arise within the context of a Swiss-US FTA can be anticipated by analyzing each country's position. We first evaluate bilateral FDI within a larger transatlantic context, and sketch the industry and geographic breakdown of bilateral FDI stocks. The next two sections identify leading companies in the Swiss-US relation, the share of FDI in capital formation, and its relation to GDP. We address a handful of barriers facing FDI and then turn to portfolio investment. Portfolio investment channeled by Swiss financial institutions to the United States is huge and encounters very few obstacles. The chapter concludes with recommendations, mainly for FDI.

Foreign Direct Investment in Perspective

By year-end 2003, the global stock of outward US direct investment totaled $1.789 trillion (historical cost). Stock in the EU-15 totaled approximately $845 billion, and over $86 billion was placed in Switzerland (table 7.1). In US FDI, Switzerland thus hosts approximately 10 percent of the EU-15 level. Recent increases in US direct investment in Europe mainly reflect activity in the United Kingdom, Switzerland, the Netherlands, and Germany. Since 1999, US FDI stock in each of these countries has increased by at least $30 billion.

Table 7.1   US foreign direct investment stock abroad by industry, 2003[a]

Industry	Switzerland Billions of dollars	Switzerland Percent of total FDI	EU-15 Billions of dollars	EU-15 Percent of total FDI	World Billions of dollars	World Percent of total FDI
Depository institutions (banks)	7.1	8	27.8	3	63.7	4
Information	-2.7	-3	32.2	4	47.5	3
Finance (except banks) and insurance	3.3	4	110.8	13	299.8	17
Manufacturing						
Chemicals	3.0	3	48.3	6	90.3	5
Computers and electronic products	0.6	1	23.5	3	57.6	3
Electrical equipment, appliances, and components	(D)	(D)	4.3	1	9.7	1
Food	0.2	0	10.1	1	22.7	1
Machinery	0.5	1	10.2	1	21.4	1
Primary and fabricated metals	(D)	(D)	8.8	1	23.0	1
Transportation equipment	(D)	(D)	15.0	2	45.4	3
Subtotal	8.7	10	160.3	19	378.0	21
Mining	0.0	0	12.1	1	98.7	6
Professional, scientific, and technical services	0.5	1	19.8	2	40.6	2
Real estate, rental, and leasing	n.a.	n.a.	n.a.	n.a.	n.a.	n.a.
Retail trade	n.a.	n.a.	n.a.	n.a.	n.a.	n.a.
Utilities	0.0	0	7.9	1	26.9	2
Wholesale trade	11.9	14	75.9	9	140.6	8
Other industries[b]	57.6	67	397.8	47	693.1	39
Total	86.4	100	844.7	100	1,788.9	100

(D) = deleted to maintain data confidentiality

n.a. = not available

a. Historical cost basis, year-end 2003.
b. Holding companies (except banks) comprised 84 percent of the "other industries" share to the world.

Source: US BEA (2004a).

Table 7.2 Foreign direct investment stock in the United States by industry, 2003[a]

Industry	Switzerland Billions of dollars	Switzerland Percent of total FDI	EU-15 Billions of dollars	EU-15 Percent of total FDI	World Billions of dollars	World Percent of total FDI
Depository institutions (banks)	(D)	(D)	60.4	7	87.5	6
Information	11.7	10	76.8	9	120.1	9
Finance (except banks) and insurance	23.0	20	108.8	13	185.7	13
Manufacturing						
Chemicals	26.2	23	83.1	10	123.2	9
Computers and electronic products	0.6	1	26.1	3	45.9	3
Electrical equipment, appliances, and components	(D)	(D)	7.2	1	42.3	3
Food	5.3	5	10.3	1	19.1	1
Machinery	2.6	2	27.0	3	37.7	3
Primary and fabricated metals	1.3	1	11.7	1	19.4	1
Transportation equipment	(D)	(D)	36.3	4	63.7	5
Subtotal	72.3	64	291.8	34	475.5	35
Mining	(D)	(D)	(D)	(D)	(D)	(D)
Professional, scientific, and technical services	0.5	0	22.8	3	28.4	2
Real estate, rental, and leasing	0.6	1	18.7	2	47.0	3
Retail trade	0.3	0	17.6	2	24.2	2
Utilities	(D)	(D)	(D)	(D)	(D)	(D)
Wholesale trade	4.0	4	101.3	12	182.2	13
Other industries	(D)	(D)	157.4	18	227.5	17
Total	112.9	100	855.7	100	1,378.0	100

(D) = deleted to maintain data confidentiality

a. Historical cost basis, year-end 2003.

Source: US BEA (2004b).

By year-end 2003, the inward stock of FDI in the United States from all countries was valued at $1.378 trillion (historic cost). Of this total, $856 billion originated from the EU-15 and $113 billion from Switzerland (table 7.2). By country of origin, the United Kingdom holds first place, followed by Japan, Germany, the Netherlands, France, Switzerland, and Canada. For comparison, UK FDI is 16.7 percent of the US total inward stock, while Swiss FDI is 8.2 percent. Over the past five years, affiliates with parents in the United Kingdom, Germany, Luxembourg, the Netherlands, and Switzerland accounted for the largest dollar increases of inward investment positions in the United States.

Swiss-US FDI

The total stock of inward foreign direct investment in Switzerland reached 200 billion Swiss francs in 2003, or approximately $154 billion at end-2003 exchange rates (chapter appendix table 7A.1). This represents an 18-fold increase of inward FDI in Switzerland since 1980, and an almost fivefold increase since 1990.[3] In 2003, the United States was the largest single source of FDI in Switzerland, accounting for 40 percent of the country's total, up from 28 percent in 1998. EU member states taken together held 56 percent, with the Netherlands, Germany, and France constituting the largest EU sources of FDI in Switzerland. The recent growth in US FDI primarily reflects activity in the financial and management sector. Within this sector, holding companies play the most significant role by far (table 7.1). Investment in Swiss finance and holding companies, reaching nearly 50 percent in 2003, likewise accounts for the predominant share of global FDI in Switzerland (chapter appendix table 7A.1).

Total Swiss FDI in the United States reached almost $113 billion in 2003, which represents about 13 percent of the total EU-15 FDI stock in the United States (table 7.2). The stock of Swiss FDI in the European Union is about twice as large as Swiss FDI in the United States (chapter appendix table 7A.2). Switzerland's FDI in the United States is concentrated in the manufacturing sector, where pharmaceuticals and food are prominent. The US financial sector receives a fifth of total Swiss FDI (table 7.2). On a global level, Swiss firms allocate almost twice as much FDI to services as they do to manufacturing (chapter appendix table 7A.2).

As already mentioned, FDI in Switzerland is highly concentrated in finance and kindred activities. In 2003, out of a total inward FDI stock of 200 billion Swiss francs, 53 percent was attributed to financial and holding companies,[4] 15 percent to banks and insurance, and 10 percent to commerce

---

3. The stock of total FDI in Switzerland increased from $9 billion in 1980, to $34 billion in 1990, to $154 billion in 2003. See UNCTAD (2004b).

4. In 1998, the comparable figure was 44 percent.

(chapter appendix table 7A.1). The remainder is essentially divided between transport, chemicals and plastic, machinery and metalworking, electronics, energy, optics, and watches.[5]

The stock of Swiss FDI in the United States reflects major investments in pharmaceuticals, chemicals, food, equipment, finance, and banking (UNCTAD 2004b). As table 7.2 illustrates, Swiss FDI in the US manufacturing sector ($72 billion) accounted for about 64 percent of total Swiss FDI stock in the United States ($113 billion).

FDI Income Flows

FDI income flows—dividends, interest, and royalties—between the United States and Switzerland are significant in both directions. Flows from the United States to Switzerland are about $13 billion annually; from Switzerland to the United States, approximately $7 billion (table 7.3). By comparison, FDI income flows from the EU-15 to the United States are about $10 billion annually.

The Connection Between FTAs, FDI, and Exports

Appendix D summarizes several academic articles on the connection between FTAs and FDI. Most studies use variants of the gravity model. While different studies reach different numerical results, on the whole, FTAs are found to encourage inward FDI. Each country extends its own economic market to include the partner. Firms located in one FTA partner gain reliable access to markets in and inputs from the other partner. The FTA assures that firms can acquire industrial inputs from the partner country, free of tariffs and other barriers, and that goods and services can be readily sold to purchasers in the partner country.

The empirical studies suggest that, for Switzerland, the FDI-augmenting effect of an FTA could be substantial. Linked to the United States, Switzerland would extend its "economic market" by 4,700 percent, since US GDP is almost 47 times the size of Swiss GDP. Even applying an elasticity coefficient of 0.01—about the size of the smallest positive elasticity reported in appendix D—the increase in the inward Swiss FDI stock (from all sources) might eventually exceed 40 percent. Applied to US investment in Switzerland, a 40 percent increase suggests that the US FDI stock in Switzerland might eventually rise by $34 billion on account of the FTA, or to about $120 billion from its 2003 level of $86 billion.

---

5. Figures provided by the Swiss National Bank (2004).

Table 7.3 US income flows from FDI and portfolio investment, 2004
(billions of dollars)

	Switzerland		EU-15		World	
	To United States[a]	**From United States**[b]	**To United States**[a]	**From United States**[b]	**To United States**[a]	**From United States**[b]
FDI income[c]	6.8	13.0	9.9	n.a.	92.8	209.3
Portfolio income	9.3	38.2	61.9	75.2	143.4	235.1

n.a. = not available
a. US income from investments in Switzerland, EU-15, and world.
b. Payments to foreign owners (Swiss, EU-15, and world) from investments in the United States.
c. FDI income flows include dividends, interest, and royalties.
Source: US BEA (2004b).

Empirical analysis by Graham and Wada (2000) suggests that a 40 percent increase in the US FDI stock in Switzerland might boost US manufactured exports by 24 percent.[6] Assuming a 24 percent increase, US exports of manufactures might rise by $2.2 billion annually (from $9.2 billion to $11.4 billion) on account of the pull from a larger US FDI stock in Switzerland. While all these estimates are highly speculative and exceedingly rough, it seems likely that a Swiss-US FTA would sharply boost both direct investment in Switzerland and US exports to Switzerland. To a very much smaller extent, the FTA would inspire parallel effects in the other direction, as adding Switzerland to the US economic market represents an increase of only about 2 percent in US market size.

Chapter appendix table 7A.3 illustrates the complementary relationship between exports and outward direct investment. Over 1994–2004, positive correlations between FDI stocks and exports can be observed in both directions, as between Switzerland and the United States. For example, US FDI stock in Swiss manufacturing industries increased by 6.8 times, while US manufactured exports increased 1.7 times. Simple correlations such as these do not, of course, demonstrate causality, but they do suggest that Swiss-US experience supports the causal relationships found by Graham and Wada (2000) using sophisticated econometric techniques.

---

6. Graham's estimated coefficient is an increase of 6 percent in US manufactured exports for every 10 percent increase in the US stock of FDI. Hejazi and Safarian (1999), however, estimate a much smaller coefficient for the "pull" on Canadian exports. The higher US coefficient estimated by Graham may reflect the fact that the United States can supply a very wide array of manufactured goods.

Leading Companies in the Bilateral Relationship

Of the world's 100 largest nonfinancial MNEs, five are Swiss (Nestlé, ABB, Novartis, Roche Group, and Holcim), and 25 are American. The top Swiss firms, together with many others, are present in the United States (table 7.4). In 2004, Swiss-owned companies operating in the United States employed 500,000 people and paid an average compensation per employee of about $64,000 (US BLS 2005). Average US compensation per employee is approximately $53,000.[7] In 2002, Swiss firms spent over $4.3 billion on US research and development activities and imported $6.2 billion of goods from the United States. Nestlé appears to be the largest Swiss firm operating in the United States, employing almost 47,000 people in the food sector (table 7.4).

Swiss direct investment is largest in New Jersey ($5.5 billion), California ($4.9 billion), New York ($2.9 billion), Texas ($2.4 billion), and Illinois ($1.5 billion) (see UNCTAD 2004b). Illinois has the largest number of Swiss companies (147), followed by New York (96), Missouri (130), Pennsylvania (98), and Florida (68).

In 2004, US-owned companies in Switzerland employed 58,000 people. Of the 650 American companies in Switzerland, the largest employers are McDonald's, IBM, and Altria. Following suit, the principal sectors are food, technology, and consumer goods. Over the past two decades, US parent companies have increasingly used holding companies—essentially, management vehicles—to supervise their worldwide activities, and many of these companies are based in Switzerland.[8] The US parent companies of Swiss firms are mostly headquartered in New York, Nevada, California, Utah, and New Jersey.[9]

FDI Related to Capital Formation and GDP

Swiss inward and outward FDI flows are a substantial proportion of annual gross fixed capital formation. On average, between 1998 and 2003, they amounted to 22 and 44 percent respectively (table 7.5). The current

---

7. Based on the hourly compensation rate of $25.57 for the fourth quarter of 2004, as reported by the US BLS (2005).

8. In technical terms, a holding company is a company whose primary activity is holding the securities or financial assets of other companies. See US BEA (2004a, 2004b).

9. New York firms invest most heavily in miscellaneous manufactures, used merchandise, and chemical manufactures. Nevada comes next, with a focus on primary metals, particularly gold and silver. Following them are California (chemical manufactures, computer and electronic products, transportation equipment, including aircraft parts), Utah (primary metal manufactures essentially), and New Jersey (chemical manufactures, primary metal manufactures, computer and electronic products). For more information, see the Embassy of Switzerland (2005) in Washington, DC.

Table 7.4 Top 15 companies in the bilateral relationship, 2004

Rank	Name	Number of employees
Swiss companies in the United States		
1	Nestlé	46,600
2	UBS AG	25,000
3	Zürich Financial Services	21,100
4	Novartis	20,000
5	Crédit Suisse	18,500
6	Hoffmann-La Roche	17,000
7	ABB	11,000
8	Gate Gourmet	10,000
9	Schindler	6,500
10	Adecco	6,500
11	Scintilla	3,000
12	SGS	3,800
13	Syngenta	3,000
14	Holcim	2,300
15	Clariant	2,800
	Total employment	197,100
US companies in Switzerland		
1	McDonald's	7,200
2	IBM	3,400
3	Altria Group, Inc.	3,000
4	Johnson & Johnson	2,100
5	Hewlett-Packard	1,800
6	Synthes-Stratec	1,700
7	Texas Pacific	1,600
8	Procter & Gamble	1,500
9	Cablecom	1,450
10	Mettler-Toledo	1,250
11	General Electric	970
12	EDS	965
13	HCA Healthcare	900
14	Johnson Controls	900
15	Dow	830
	Total employment	29,565

Source: Swiss-American Chamber of Commerce (2005).

Table 7.5 FDI flows as share of gross fixed capital formation (percent)

Annual average during period	Inward FDI flows		Outward FDI flows	
	United States	Switzerland	United States	Switzerland
1992–97	5.4	4.7	7.1	21.3
1998–2003	9.1	22.0	7.7	43.9

Source: UNCTAD (2004b).

level of FDI flow into Switzerland reflects an almost fivefold increase since the early 1990s.[10] The current level for Swiss outward FDI represents a twofold increase over the same period, and constitutes a substantial share of Swiss gross fixed capital formation.

While Swiss inward and outward flows have reached a two-digit relationship to gross fixed capital formation, in the United States, both inward and outward flows remain at a one-digit relationship. US inward FDI as a percentage of gross fixed capital formation rose from about 5 percent in the early 1990s to about 9 percent in the late 1990s (table 7.5). Outward FDI has increased less, remaining in the range of 7 to 8 percent of gross fixed capital formation.

For both the United States and Switzerland, the size of the FDI stock has grown significantly relative to GDP. As portrayed in table 7.6, Swiss inward FDI rose from 8 percent of GDP in 1980 to nearly 50 percent in 2003. Swiss outward FDI escalated nearly sixfold relative to GDP since 1980, from 20 percent to 112 percent. Likewise, US inward FDI rose from 3 percent of GDP in 1980 to 14 percent in 2003. Relative to GDP, outward US FDI grew from 8 percent in 1980 to almost 19 percent in 2003.

In market value, FDI in the United States reached $2.435 trillion in 2003, reflecting both financial inflows and a substantial appreciation in share values. By comparison, historical-cost FDI in the United States was $1.378 trillion for 2003, less than two-thirds of the market value.

Impediments to FDI in Switzerland

Investment barriers are very low in Switzerland, and the country has a reputation for welcoming FDI. The freedom of trade and industry guaranteed by the Swiss Constitution allows anyone, including foreign nationals, to

---

10. Based on the indicated average of 4.7 percent for inward FDI as a share of gross fixed capital formation between 1992 and 1997.

Table 7.6 FDI stock as share of GDP^a (percent)

Year	Inward FDI stock		Outward FDI stock	
	United States	**Switzerland**	**United States**	**Switzerland**
1980	3.0	7.9	7.8	20.0
1990	6.9	15.0	7.5	28.9
2000	12.4	36.1	13.2	97.1
2003	14.1	49.7	18.8	112.0

a. Historical cost basis, year-end.

Source: UNCTAD (2004b).

operate a business in Switzerland, establish a company, or acquire a company. With few exceptions, establishing a business requires no approval from the government, chambers of commerce, or professional associations. Switzerland does not have a screening mechanism for foreign investments, nor does it have preferences or restrictions in sector or geography. Since 1997, permission has not been required to buy commercial or industrial real estate, or principal residences. Exchange control restrictions on capital flows are unknown.

However, there are Swiss investment restrictions in sectors dominated by public monopolies, including rail transport, postal services, certain insurance services, aspects of trade in alcoholic beverages, and salt (WTO 2004b). Special licensing provisions apply to banks, insurance companies, and investment brokers. They also affect hotels and restaurants in certain cantons. Physicians, dentists, pharmacists, and attorneys are licensed professions, as are certain mercantile and service businesses, such as wine merchants, private employment agencies, and temporary employment services.

Temporary Skilled Worker Visas

MNEs usually require foreign nationals, both permanent and temporary, to carry out key operations. If visas and work permits are difficult to obtain, the country becomes a less desirable location, especially for headquarters activity. Foreign nationals may perform skilled activities in Switzerland on a temporary basis, if they have the required permits (WTO 2004b). For some cases, visa approval requires demonstration of need. This situation will evolve, as residence qualifications for EU nationals will be completely liberalized by 2014 under the bilateral agreement with the European Union on free movement of persons.[11]

---

11. Similar terms apply to nationals of the European Economic Area (EEA).

In the nonfinancial sector, all corporate directors must be individuals (not other companies), and the majority of the board of directors of a stock corporation must be Swiss citizens, residing in Switzerland.[12] However, this latter requirement does not apply to holding companies. At least one managing director of a limited liability company must reside in Switzerland, and to establish a branch of a foreign company in Switzerland, an individual residing in Switzerland must be nominated as representative.[13] The Swiss parliament is considering repealing the nationality requirement, in line with Switzerland's initial offer in 2003 in the General Agreement on Trade in Services (GATS) negotiations. Draft legislation was originally published in the *Federal Journal* in July 2001, and the legislation is expected to enter into force by 2007.

Companies or their manufacturing facilities must be registered at cantonal or district levels. In certain regions, such as remote zones, the confederation and canton may provide investment incentives. Examples include tax exemptions for up to ten years, or a financial guarantee of up to one-third of the total cost of a project for eight years.

Impediments to FDI in the United States

As a general rule, foreign investors, like domestic firms, are not obligated to register with or seek approval from the federal government (EIU 2005b). Foreign firms are not subjected to local content requirements, ownership restrictions, or current transfer requirements, nor do they face controls on foreign exchange access or repatriation of profits. However, an important impediment that faces nearly all foreign firms is the difficulty and expense of obtaining work visas (e.g., H1-B visas) for temporary personnel.

Other barriers remain for foreign firms entering banking, mining, defense contracting, fishing, shipping, communications, aviation, and certain energy industries. The federal government also screens foreign

---

12. According to the WTO (2004b, 38), "Switzerland's revised Law on Stock Corporations, adopted in 1991, forms the basis of its investment legislation. Corporate governance (except in the banking sector) is generally based on a unitary system in which the board of directors has supreme strategic responsibility for the conduct of a company's affairs. Related powers may not be delegated, nor may they be withdrawn by the shareholders."

13. The WTO elaborates on Swiss establishment procedures in greater detail. For instance, it explains that "a permanent residence permit of the associate(s) is required under cantonal laws for the establishment of a commercial presence in the form of an enterprise without legal personality under Swiss law (i.e., in a form other than stock corporation, limited liability company or cooperative society), and for the establishment of a commercial presence by natural persons. (. . .) The minimum capital requirement ranges from Sfr 20,000 to Sfr 100,000 depending on the form of business; a maximum of Sfr 2 million is set for limited liability companies. (. . .) Establishment of a limited liability company does not normally take more than 10 days, substantially under the European average" (WTO 2004b, 39).

acquisitions that might threaten national security under the terms of the Exon-Florio amendment.[14] As a general rule, foreign nationals or firms are allowed to purchase US real estate, but some states restrict the purchase of land.[15] Foreign nationals or firms must report to the US Department of Agriculture when they purchase agricultural land (EIU 2005b).

A European Commission (2004a) report singled out three FDI limitations in the United States. The first involves the Exon-Florio amendment; the second deals with foreign ownership restrictions in areas such as defense, communications, and aviation; and the third concerns tax discrimination.

The Exon-Florio Amendment

To monitor the influence of foreign investment in the United States, a Committee on Foreign Investment in the United States (CFIUS)[16] was established in 1975. From its inception, the committee received notification of foreign acquisition of US companies, then determined whether such acquisitions raised national security concerns. The committee's authority was bolstered, in 1988, by passage of the Exon-Florio amendment,[17] which authorizes investigations into the national security dimensions of foreign acquisitions. This considerably expanded federal authority to obstruct foreign investment. While a threat to national security is the statutory justification for impeding FDI, "national security" is an elastic term that can be interpreted expansively, if the president wishes;[18] under Exon-Florio, CFIUS reports and advises the president, who makes a final determination.

---

14. In addition, restrictions exist on financial transactions with Cuba and Cuban nationals, Burma, Iran, Iraq, Sudan, the Taliban, specified terrorist groups, and specified drug traffickers. Those restrictions are strictly enforced (EIU 2005).

15. State restrictions are easily circumvented by establishing a US corporate presence.

16. The CFIUS is an interagency committee that is chaired by the Secretary of the Treasury and contains representation by the departments of state, defense, commerce, and justice; and the offices of management and budget, the US trade representative, and the Council of Economic Advisers. See Graham and Krugman (1995).

17. The Exon-Florio Amendment to the Defense Production Act (section 5021 of the 1988 Trade Act) encourages the president to investigate the potential national security impact of any merger, acquisition, or takeover leading to foreign ownership of legal persons engaged in interstate commerce. The president can block any foreign transaction on national security grounds.

18. According to Graham and Krugman (1995, 132), the role of the CFIUS "remains to be fully defined [and it is feared] that the direction of policy is toward ever broader definitions of national security concerns, [which would lead] the Exon-Florio amendment [to create] a de facto screening agency for FDI."

Apart from blocking a handful of transactions, the Exon-Florio amendment and CFIUS process can inflict delays and legal costs on foreign firms.[19] The United States has taken a reservation for Exon-Florio under the OECD Code of Liberalization of Capital Movements and the National Treatment Instruments, and after the terrorist attacks of September 11, 2001, the European Commission asserts that potential acquisitions in the telecommunications sector were deterred by the Exon-Florio amendment (European Commission 2004a).[20]

Foreign Ownership Restrictions

According to the OECD, the United States scores slightly below the OECD mean on an aggregate indicator of FDI restrictions (OECD 2004c). Foreign ownership restrictions usually involve limiting the share of foreign equity capital in selected sectors. In 2000, such equity restrictions were comparatively more stringent in the United States than they were in the European Union.

Equity restrictions are based on a mix of sovereignty and national security concerns. Most pertinent for Switzerland, the United States maintains restrictions on the share of foreign ownership in a few services sectors in the communications market, including broadcasting, common carrier radio licenses, and mobile phones. For example, a foreign investor can only own 20 percent of a US firm that holds common carrier radio licenses.

Tax Discrimination

Foreign investment in the US market may face discriminatory tax practices (European Commission 2004a). Tax discrimination arguably originates from burdensome reporting requirements, "earnings-stripping" provisions, and state "worldwide" unitary tax systems.[21] We merely note these issues

---

19. Over the past 18 years since the Exon-Florio amendment, the CFIUS has reviewed approximately 10 percent of all foreign acquisitions proposed in that period. These 1,560 reviews led to 25 investigations, of which 11 were approved. Of the remaining transactions, 13 investigations were cancelled by the parties, and only one was halted by the president (Bruce Stokes, "Tighter Control of Foreign Investment?" *National Journal*, July 23, 2005, 2389).

20. US agencies have allegedly used the Exon-Florio legislation to impose stringent corporate governance requirements "on companies seeking FCC approval of the foreign takeover of a US communications firm in the form of Network Security Arrangements going further than before" (European Commission 2004a).

21. US reporting rules obligate foreign controlled firms to keep books and records on related parties transactions, and to store the required documents in a location that the US tax authority specifies. Internal Revenue Code provisions on "earnings stripping" limit the extent of

without commenting on them. Historically, tax issues are addressed in tax treaties, not in FTAs, and the Swiss-US FTA is very unlikely to depart from historic practice. Moreover, US and Swiss withholding tax rates on direct investment income flows to parent companies based in the other country are very low because of the bilateral income tax treaty of 1996.[22] The statutory rate of Swiss withholding tax is 35 percent, while the statutory US rate is 30 percent. However, the bilateral Swiss-US withholding tax rates on FDI flows are only 5 percent for dividends, 5 percent for interest, and zero percent for royalties. Withholding taxes paid to the foreign jurisdiction can be credited against the parent firm's home country tax liability, which mitigates their force as an investment deterrent.

International Disputes

Investment disputes between the United States and Switzerland are rare.[23] No disputes involving both of them are listed among the cases addressed by the International Center for Settlement of Investment Disputes (ICSID). The United States is, however, involved in numerous cases, more often resulting from foreign demands for equal treatment in the United States than the other way around. For example, based on the 1978 US International Banking Act, all foreign-owned bank operations in the United States face constraints on interstate banking. Although domestic banks in the United States are subject to substantially similar restrictions, these controls remain more severe than parallel restrictions against US banks in Europe.[24]

The North American Free Trade Agreement (NAFTA) contained a major innovation in establishing a trilateral mechanism for handling investment disputes. Mexico had long been a champion of the Calvo doctrine, which called for strict regulation of foreign investment and required that disputes be adjudicated only in local courts. The NAFTA accord codified a major change in Mexican policy: It liberalized investment rules and created, in Chapter 11, a trilateral dispute resolution framework.[25] Mexico thus signaled to investors that it was committed to a new regime,

---

interest payments that can be made to a related party and still be deducted against US corporate income. State "worldwide" unitary tax systems can subject the foreign earnings of a Swiss MNE (for example) to taxation by a state (e.g., California).

22. This Swiss-US treaty became effective as of 1998. For complete details, see US IRS (1998).

23. This section draws on Hufbauer and Schott (2005).

24. Under pressure from the United States, the commission decided, in the spring of 1989, that it would apply a national treatment rather than a reciprocity standard for US banks operating in Europe. For more information, see ICSID (2005).

25. NAFTA's Chapter 11 refers to its dispute settlement mechanism.

and correspondingly opened many sectors to foreign investment (Vega-Cánovas and Winham 2002).[26]

Chapter 11 of NAFTA is unique among NAFTA provisions in allowing private investors to enforce government obligations.[27] For purposes of the NAFTA dispute settlement process, the definition of investment is broadened to include minority interests, portfolio investment, and real property. NAFTA's substantive rules include investment liberalization rights for foreign investors (Article 1101) and guarantees to protect existing investments established under conditions more favorable than those scheduled in the national reservations of individual NAFTA members (Article 1108).[28] However, the investor provisions that have sparked the most disputes filed under Chapter 11 are national treatment rights (Article 1102), most favored nation (MFN) rights (Article 1103), minimum international standards of treatment (Article 1105), performance requirements (Article 1106), and especially provisions for compensation in the event of expropriation (Article 1110). Article 1110 is the most criticized because it attempts to balance investor rights with government measures to protect public welfare.

In a joint statement, NAFTA member governments somewhat narrowed the scope of foreign investment protections under Chapter 11, and concurrently, the US government adopted more restrictive investor protection language in its FTAs with Chile, Singapore, and Central American countries (NAFTA Free Trade Commission 2005). The new language in the Chile and Singapore FTAs indicates that environmental or health regulations would rarely constitute indirect expropriation eligible for compensation.

Hufbauer and Schott (2005) recommend that NAFTA's Chapter 11 should add an appellate body for investor state disputes. A similar proce-

---

26. According to Vega-Cánovas and Winham (2002), industries opened to FDI included railroads, telecommunications, satellite transmission, banking, and some petrochemicals. However, the NAFTA accord did not mean North America was wide open to foreign investors. In fact, each country maintained investment thresholds or screening mechanisms. There are three types of reservations under NAFTA's Chapter 11: sectoral, reciprocal ("tit for tat"), and investment review reservations. Among the three NAFTA partners, the United States retained the longest list of "tit-for-tat" reservations.

27. Several principles embodied in NAFTA Chapter 11 are also found in the WTO Agreement on Trade Related Investment Measures (TRIMs). However, unlike NAFTA, the WTO TRIMs agreement does not grant private foreign investors the right to launch dispute settlement proceedings.

28. Under Article 1108 (4), no party may "require an investor of another Party, by reason of its nationality, to sell or otherwise dispose of an investment existing at the time the measure becomes effective." Other rights and obligations covered under Chapter 11 are prohibitions on senior management nationality requirements (Article 1107), and an environmental protection provision, under which members are not allowed to reduce environmental standards to attract investment (Article 1114) (Hufbauer and Schott 2005).

dure might be adopted in the Swiss-US FTA. An appellate body could help establish clear and uniform jurisprudence for arbitration panels.

Portfolio Investment

Table 7.7 gives an overview of portfolio securities holdings between the United States and Switzerland, the European Union (EU-15), and the world.[29] While the stock of total US inward portfolio investment was about $6 trillion in 2004, total outward portfolio investment was about $3.2 trillion. Similarly, in 2003, the stock of Swiss portfolio investment abroad totaled $650 billion, while the stock of inward portfolio investment in Switzerland amounted to about $450 billion (table 7.8).

The largest share of US inward portfolio investment is in long-term debt securities (59 percent), while equity investment constitutes the most important component of US portfolio investment abroad (66 percent). For Switzerland, equities are the largest share of inward portfolio investment (89 percent in 2003), while debt securities, specifically bonds, are the largest component of outward portfolio investment (55 percent) (table 7.8). Swiss holdings of US portfolio securities totaled approximately $200 billion in 2004, while US holdings of Swiss portfolio securities totaled $120 billion in 2003. Swiss portfolio investment in the United States represents 3 percent of total US inward portfolio investment.

Likewise, US holdings of Swiss portfolio securities represent 4 percent of the share of total US holdings of foreign portfolio securities. US holdings of Swiss securities are about 7 percent of US holdings of EU-15 securities. By contrast, Swiss portfolio investment in the United States is about 10 percent of EU-15 portfolio investment in the United States.

Equity Investment

Equity investment constitutes 98 percent of US portfolio investment in Switzerland and 60 percent of Swiss portfolio investment in the United States. By comparison, equities represent only 40 percent of EU portfolio investment in the United States, and 53 percent of US portfolio investment in the EU-15.

In 2003, Swiss holdings of US equities amounted to $120 billion, or 6 percent of total foreign equity investment in the United States (table 7.7).

---

29. Data on foreign holdings of US portfolio securities and US holdings of portfolio securities, by type and country, are available at US Department of the Treasury (2005). Data on Swiss portfolio investment abroad on a global basis can be found on the Swiss National Bank (2005b). However, Swiss data do not provide for a detailed picture of the Swiss position in the United States or Europe.

Table 7.7 US holdings of portfolio securities by partner and type, 2003–04 (billions of dollars)

	Switzerland		EU-15		World	
	To the United States, 2004	From the United States, 2003	To the United States, 2004	From the United States, 2003	To the United States, 2004	From the United States, 2003
Equity securities	120	118	843	977	1,904	2,079
Long-term debt securities	69	1	1,106	412	3,515	874
Treasury debt	33	n.a.	n.a.	n.a.	1,462	n.a.
Other long-term debt	36	1	n.a.	n.a.	2,052	n.a.
US agency debt	12	n.a.	n.a.	n.a.	623	n.a.
Corporate debt	24	n.a.	n.a.	n.a.	1,429	n.a.
Short-term debt securities	11	1	137.0	153	588	199
Total debt	80	2	1,243.0	442	4,103	874
Total equity and debt	199	120	2,086	1,832	6,007	3,152

n.a. = not available

Source: US Department of the Treasury (2005).

Table 7.8 Swiss holdings of portfolio securities (world totals), 2003[a]
(billions of Swiss francs and dollars)

	To Switzerland		From Switzerland	
	Dollars	Swiss francs	Dollars	Swiss francs
Equity securities	398.4	498.0	290.6	363.2
Shares	345.4	431.8	179.8	224.8
Investment fund certificates	53.0	66.2	138.4	173.0
Debt securities	58.8	73.5	360.1	450.1
Bonds	46.2	57.7	331.9	414.9
Money market paper	0.9	1.1	28.2	35.2
Total equity and debt	445.6	557.0	650.4	813.0

a. End = 2003, Sfr 1.00 = US$ 0.80, according to the IMF's *International Financial Statistics* database.

Source: Swiss National Bank (2005b).

US holdings of Swiss equities amounted to $118 billion, accounting for 6 percent of total US equity investment abroad. US inward and outward equity investments with Switzerland are thus about the same. This relationship also holds for equity investment between the United States and the European Union.[30]

Debt Securities

Long-term debt securities accounted for 35 percent of total Swiss portfolio securities in the United States but represented only 1 percent of US portfolio investment in Switzerland (table 7.7). In other words, investment in debt securities between Switzerland and the United States is heavily one-sided. Swiss holdings of US debt securities total approximately $80 billion, while US holdings of comparable Swiss securities amount to only $2 billion. This pattern is not unique to Switzerland, however. The United States has invested much more heavily in the EU debt market, with long-term debt securities representing 23 percent of overall US portfolio investment in the European Union. Nevertheless, EU outward debt investment in the United States ($1.106 trillion) is almost three times higher than EU inward investment from the United States ($412 billion) (table 7.7).

---

30. US holdings of EU equities amounted to $977 billion in 2003, while EU holdings of US equities amounted to $843 billion in 2004 (table 7.7).

In large part, the Swiss-US relationship is lopsided because Swiss banks act on behalf of investors around the world, many of whom want to acquire US debt securities. Meanwhile, most US investors who want to hold European debt securities prefer the larger and more liquid markets of Germany, France, and Italy.

Portfolio Income Flows

In 2004, US portfolio income receipts from Switzerland were around $9 billion, about 15 percent of US portfolio income receipt inflows from the EU-15. In the same year, Swiss portfolio income receipts from investments in the United States (US payments in table 7.3) reached $38 billion. This figure corresponds to half of the amount of EU-15 portfolio income receipts from investments in the United States, and underscores Switzerland's role as a financial center.

Portfolio Investment Issues

Barriers to portfolio investment in the United States and Switzerland are insignificant. They persisted in US real estate investment trusts (REITs) until President George W. Bush signed into law the American Jobs Creation Act of 2004, which gives foreign portfolio investors in listed US REITs the same favorable tax treatment that US corporations have (AFIRE 2004).

The rate of withholding taxes for Swiss-US portfolio investment is about half of the statutory rate. For both countries, the withholding tax rate is 15 percent of portfolio investment income flows (PWC 1999). However, these tax payments can be credited against the home country tax liability. This credit is important for portfolio investors that pay home country taxes, but it does not alleviate the tax burden for nonprofit investors and pension funds that pay no domestic taxes.

Swiss banks have raised concerns over the question of information exchange. However, the US Treasury appears to have no intention of raising exchange of information or money laundering issues in a Swiss-US FTA.[31]

---

31. A recent case involving Nigeria provides evidence that the Swiss government and banks are committed to fighting corrupt money laundering by national leaders. In September 2005, Switzerland started a process for returning $458 million that was stolen by General Sani Abacha (a former president of Nigeria) and deposited in Swiss banks. Speaking at the Institute for International Economics on September 27, 2005, Swiss Secretary of State for Economic Affairs Daniel Gerber pointed out that this agreement makes Switzerland "the first and so far the only country where a court of law ordered the transfer of Abacha funds back to Nigeria" (World Bank 2005a).

Recommendations for Investment

The very good Swiss-US commercial relationship can be improved, first and foremost, by eliminating barriers to merchandise and services trade, but secondly by addressing the modest frictions in investment relations described above. If liberalization proceeds, two-way commerce can flourish, and two-way investment expand beyond its already robust level. We offer recommendations for the investment frictions that could be fruitfully addressed in the Swiss-US FTA.

- Swiss investment restrictions in sectors dominated by public monopolies should be phased out within the broader framework of welcoming private investment by Swiss and foreign firms. Rail transport, postal services, certain insurance services, and alcoholic beverages all deserve attention.

- Swiss conditions for licensing selected professions and business activities deserve scrutiny. Some of the restrictions inhibit the operations of foreign MNEs—notably, licensing terms that affect banks, insurance companies, investment brokers, employment agencies, wine merchants, hotels, and restaurants. Restrictions on certain professionals, such as attorneys and accountants, may also have an inhibiting effect, and should be reviewed. Technically speaking, this recommendation can also be classified under services, as a Mode 3 recommendation in the parlance of GATS. We point it out here because of its importance for FDI, and Switzerland's attractiveness as a headquarters location.

- Easier access to temporary employee visas is particularly important for US-based MNEs with operations in Switzerland, and for Swiss-based MNEs with operations in the United States. Swiss legislation is expected to relax visa barriers by 2007, but the FTA should supplement the process. Spouses of accredited temporary employees should be allowed to work in Switzerland. The United States should apply similar principles to Swiss nationals working on a temporary basis in the United States (usually under H1-B visas).

- Impediments to FDI in the United States primarily involve foreign ownership restrictions in selected sectors, though they potentially include the CFIUS review process. The United States should liberalize its foreign ownership restrictions that inhibit bona fide Swiss investments in the communications sector, particularly in broadcasting services, common carrier radio licenses, and mobile phone services.

- As for the CFIUS process, the United States should agree that the sole ground for blocking a bona fide Swiss transaction would be national security. Further, the United States should commit to expeditious CFIUS reviews, including advisory opinions when requested.

- As an example to the world, the Swiss-US FTA should proclaim the rights of private investors with respect to national treatment, performance requirements, standards for the public taking of private property, and appropriate compensation in the event of expropriation. For obligations, the language in the US-Chile and US-Singapore FTAs is more relevant than that of NAFTA.

- As in NAFTA, the Central American–Dominican Republic Free Trade Agreement (CAFTA-DR), and the US-Chile, US-Australia, and US-Singapore FTAs, the Swiss-US FTA should contain procedures for resolving disputes between private investors and host states through arbitration, preferably under the auspices of the ICSID. The Swiss-US FTA should also provide for an appellate body to ensure that arbitration panels are faithful and consistent in applying legal principles.

- The main friction point for portfolio investment appears to be the withholding tax rate of 15 percent. While this tax is credited against the investor's home tax liability, some important investors—such as pension funds and charitable foundations—have no home country tax liability to absorb the credit. The FTA is not the place to negotiate withholding tax rates or other tax issues, but it can be an opportunity for the parties to indicate whether the time is ripe to revisit the 1996 bilateral income tax treaty.

It is no exaggeration to say that investment is the bedrock of Swiss-US commercial relations. On every investment question of global importance, Swiss and US policies are closely aligned. Both nations agree that direct and portfolio investment should be unfettered to the maximum extent; both respect property rights; both adhere to the principles of national treatment and MFN treatment; both are skeptical of state corporations; and both take a critical but not altogether hostile view of public subsidies for infant and senescent industries.

The synergy between direct investment and trade—a matter of common observation at least since the work of Reddaway (1967) and Hufbauer and Adler (1968)—has been established by econometric research (e.g., Graham and Wada 2000). US and Swiss two-way stocks of FDI exceed $200 billion. These powerful investment links foster $20 billion of two-way trade in manufactured goods annually, $16 billion in services, and another $20 billion in FDI income flows. This relatively free flow of two-way trade in goods, services, and income cycles back to promote further investment between the two countries. To facilitate this possible feedback loop, the Swiss-US FTA should liberalize across the board, as has been discussed in this and previous chapters. But what might be the economic returns from such a move? The next chapter, which simulates liberalization according to gravity and computable general equilibrium models, offers some encouraging estimates.

Appendix 7A

Table 7A.1 Foreign direct investment stock in Switzerland, 2003[a]

Industry	United States		European Union		World	
	Billions of Swiss francs	Percent of total FDI	Billions of Swiss francs	Percent of total FDI	Billions of Swiss francs	Percent of total FDI
Manufacturing						
Chemicals and plastics	n.a.	n.a.	n.a.	n.a.	11.7	5.8
Electronics, energy, optical, and watchmaking industries	n.a.	n.a.	n.a.	n.a.	9.8	4.9
Metals and machinery	n.a.	n.a.	n.a.	n.a.	4.8	2.4
Other manufacturing and construction	n.a.	n.a.	n.a.	n.a.	6.8	3.4
Textiles and clothing	n.a.	n.a.	n.a.	n.a.	n.a.	n.a.
Subtotal	n.a.	n.a.	n.a.	n.a.	33.0	16.5
Services						
Banks	n.a.	n.a.	n.a.	n.a.	26.1	13.1
Finance and holding companies	n.a.	n.a.	n.a.	n.a.	105.7	52.8
Insurance	n.a.	n.a.	n.a.	n.a.	4.0	2.0
Other services	n.a.	n.a.	n.a.	n.a.	4.3	2.1
Trade	n.a.	n.a.	n.a.	n.a.	20.6	10.3
Transportation and communications	n.a.	n.a.	n.a.	n.a.	6.4	3.2
Subtotal	n.a.	n.a.	n.a.	n.a.	167.2	83.5
Total	79.2	40	112.0	56	200.2	100

n.a. = not available

a. End = 2003, Sfr 1.00 = US$ 0.80, according to IFS database.

Source: Swiss National Bank (2004).

Table 7A.2 Swiss foreign direct investment stock abroad, 2003[a]

Industry	United States		European Union		World	
	Billions of Swiss francs	Percent of total FDI	Billions of Swiss francs	Percent of total FDI	Billions of Swiss francs	Percent of total FDI
Manufacturing						
Chemicals and plastics	n.a.	n.a.	n.a.	n.a.	62.2	14.7
Electronics, energy, optical, watchmaking industries	n.a.	n.a.	n.a.	n.a.	12.4	2.9
Metals and machinery	n.a.	n.a.	n.a.	n.a.	20.1	4.8
Other manufacturing and construction	n.a.	n.a.	n.a.	n.a.	38.6	9.1
Textiles and clothing	n.a.	n.a.	n.a.	n.a.	9.4	2.2
Subtotal	n.a.	n.a.	n.a.	n.a.	142.8	33.7
Services						
Banks	n.a.	n.a.	n.a.	n.a.	59.4	14.0
Finance and holding companies	n.a.	n.a.	n.a.	n.a.	116.2	27.4
Insurance	n.a.	n.a.	n.a.	n.a.	81.1	19.1
Other services	n.a.	n.a.	n.a.	n.a.	9.6	2.3
Trade	n.a.	n.a.	n.a.	n.a.	10.8	2.6
Transportation and communications	n.a.	n.a.	n.a.	n.a.	3.8	0.9
Subtotal	n.a.	n.a.	n.a.	n.a.	280.9	66.3
Total	81.6	19	181.6	43	423.7	100

n.a. = not available

a. End = 2003, Sfr 1.00 = US$ 0.80, according to IFS database.

Source: Swiss National Bank (2004).

Table 7A.3 FDI stock and exports, selected sectors, 1994–2004

	1994	1996	1998	2000	2002	2004
Part A (billions of dollars)						
US direct investment position in Switzerland						
Total FDI stock	27.9	30.7	38.2	55.4	74.2	100.7
All manufacturing	1.6	3.7	4.5	3.4	5.4	10.8
Chemicals	0.3	1.8	2.7	1.5	2.3	4.8
Swiss direct investment position in the United States						
Total FDI stock	24.9	30.4	48.3	64.7	123.9	122.9
All manufacturing	13.2	16.2	23.2	30.1	82.4	77.3
Chemicals	6.8	8.8	14.2	18.4	25.1	30.0
US exports to Switzerland						
Total manufacturing[a]	5.5	8.2	7.1	9.8	7.7	9.2
Chemicals[b]	0.8	0.6	0.9	1.4	1.4	1.8
Swiss exports to the United States						
Total manufacturing[a]	6.2	7.6	8.4	9.9	9.1	11.2
Chemicals[b]	1.5	2.0	2.0	2.2	2.5	2.8
Part B (index values, 1994 = 100)						
US direct investment position in Switzerland						
Total FDI stock	100	110	137	198	266	361
All manufacturing	100	234	288	218	342	687
Chemicals	100	540	811	462	685	1,437
Swiss direct investment position in the United States						
Total FDI stock	100	122	194	260	497	493
All manufacturing	100	123	176	228	624	585
Chemicals	100	129	209	271	369	441
US exports to Switzerland						
Total manufacturing[a]	100	150	130	179	140	167
Chemicals[b]	100	83	114	183	179	240
Swiss exports to the United States						
Total manufacturing[a]	100	123	136	160	147	182
Chemicals[b]	100	132	132	147	166	188

a. Manufacturing is defined as all trade in HTS chapters 24 through 98.
b. Chemicals are defined as all trade in HTS chapters 28 through 38.

Sources: US BEA (2005a) and USITC (2005d).

8

Estimates from Gravity and CGE Models

DEAN DeROSA and JOHN GILBERT

Quantitative assessments of the trade expansion and income gains fostered by a Swiss-US free trade agreement (FTA) require detailed consideration of economic structure and multilateral trade patterns. To carry out this task, we use both gravity and computable general equilibrium (CGE) models. Our gravity model is an augmented version of Rose's (2004) framework,[1] but while Rose analyzed total merchandise trade between multiple partner countries, we examine disaggregated merchandise trade. Our CGE model is the comparative static framework of world trade and economic activity designed by the Global Trade Analysis Project (GTAP). The GTAP model disaggregates world merchandise trade by sectors and also (unlike the gravity model) covers world trade in services. Using two models increases our confidence in the general tenor of the results. While the gravity model is grounded in the empirical tradition of trade analysis, the CGE model rests foremost on theoretical foundations. Hence, each model serves as a check on the other. The basic features and results of our gravity and CGE models are described in the sections that follow. Appendix E contains further technical details.

Before diving into the models, we must emphasize that the results of these exercises do not purport to track the details of the recommendations offered in previous chapters. The CGE model presents "before and after"

Dean A. DeRosa is a principal economist at ADR International Ltd., an economic research and policy consulting firm in Falls Church, Virginia. John P. Gilbert is associate professor of economics in the Department of Economics, Utah State University, Logan, Utah.

1. Andrew Rose is well known for his contentious questioning of the role of GATT/WTO membership in promoting trade. In this chapter, we cite Rose for his contribution to the technical gravity model and for his database—not for his analysis of the GATT/WTO system.

comparisons, assuming that all trade barriers that have been measured in the model's database are eliminated; it does not attempt the more exacting task of modeling the phaseout, over time, of tariffs, quotas, and other nontariff barriers. Similarly, the gravity model attempts to show what a Swiss-US FTA might accomplish in merchandise trade expansion, based on the average experience of prior FTAs and customs unions. Few of these agreements have achieved the extent of liberalization that we recommend for the Swiss-US FTA. Hence, the model results should not be read as precise forecasts as to what would happen if our recommendations were closely followed. They simply suggest, in broad terms, the quantitative outcome of an FTA.

Gravity Model: Construction and Results

With the proliferation of preferential trading arrangements during the last decade, the gravity model has become a widely utilized tool for analyzing the consequences of bilateral and regional trade agreements.[2] The basic gravity model evaluates thousands of two-way bilateral trade flows, measured in a common currency and adjusted for inflation, against the gravitational mass of explanatory variables describing the characteristics of bilateral trading partners. The core variables are distance and joint real GDP.[3] Most gravity models find that the shorter the distance between countries, and the larger their combined GDP, the greater the two-way trade is between them. Additional explanatory variables are specified as well, and these are of greatest interest: They show how much two-way trade is added or subtracted from the quantity predicted by the basic core variables because of the partners' institutions or policies. For instance, trading partners that share a common border, language, or currency are typically found to enjoy significantly greater mutual trade.

To analyze regional trade agreements, a dichotomous (0,1) explanatory variable—a dummy variable—is introduced to represent preferential arrangements, either individually or on a combined basis. If the coefficient on the dummy variable is positive and significant, then the regional trading arrangement is judged to expand mutual two-way trade between the arrangement members. The extent of trade expansion is usually measured in percentage terms, which can be derived from the estimated coefficient of the dummy variable. Given the log-linear specification of the gravity

---

2. Greenaway and Milner (2002) provide an excellent introduction to and review of the recent literature on the gravity model and its econometric applications for assessing the trade and other impacts of preferential trading arrangements among regional trading partners.

3. A third "core" variable is joint GDP per capita. A higher joint GDP per capita figure implies a smaller joint population figure (for a given joint GDP level). Less combined population tends to depress the bilateral level of trade; hence, the coefficient on joint GDP per capita is normally negative.

model regression equation,[4] the impact of an FTA on bilateral trade can be computed in percentage terms as $100*[\exp(b_{rta}) - 1.00]$. In this expression, b_{rta} is the estimated coefficient for the dummy variable representing the presence of a regional trade agreement, and $\exp(b_{rta})$ is the value of the natural number e raised to the exponent b_{rta}. If the coefficient b_{rta} is 0.33, then the value of $\exp(b_{rta})$ is 1.39, and the percentage expansion in trade is estimated as $100*[1.39 - 1.00]$, which equals 39 percent.

Swiss-US FTA Analytical Framework

We investigate the potential for expanding Swiss-US trade under an FTA following Frankel (1997) and Choi and Schott (2001), among others, using the general framework of the Rose (2004) gravity model. Our approach combines the existing regional trade agreements, and tries to account for the possibility that Swiss-US trade is already significantly greater than the level predicted by the basic explanatory variables of the gravity model in the absence of an FTA.

Our econometric results are based on bilateral trade flows worldwide from 1962 to 1999, compiled by Feenstra and Lipsey (Feenstra et al. 2005) and originally disaggregated according to the 4-digit Standard International Trade Classification (SITC). For the present analysis, the Feenstra-Lipsey trade data were aggregated to the 1-digit SITC level, and deflated by the US consumer price index. They were then concorded, by year and country pair, to the extensive set of explanatory variables compiled for the Rose (2004) gravity model.[5] The core explanatory variables in the Rose dataset include distance between trading partners, joint real GDP, and joint real GDP per capita. The Rose dataset also includes a number of country-specific variables, such as landlocked and island status, language, colonizers, and dates of independence. In all, the dataset constructed for the present analysis, using the augmented Rose gravity model, entails nearly 940,000 observations, covering bilateral trade for about 61,000 combinations of commodities and pairs of trading countries.[6]

To the core explanatory variables are added dummy variables representing bilateral, regional, and other preferential trade arrangements. These include an explanatory variable representing the generalized system of

---

4. In a log-linear regression, the dependent variable (here, two-way bilateral trade) is expressed in logarithmic terms, whereas some independent variables (notably, the discrete dummy variables) are expressed simply as linear numbers (e.g., 0 or 1), while others (notably, the continuous variables, such as distance or joint GDP) are expressed in logarithmic terms.

5. The complete set of regression variables constructed from the Feenstra-Lipsey and Rose datasets is described in appendix table E.1.

6. Notwithstanding its large size, the combined Feenstra-Lipsey and Rose dataset has some gaps, and excludes Taiwan and some centrally planned economies, because of holes in the two datasets individually.

preferences (GSP).[7] The regional trading arrangement (RTA) variable covers ten regional trade agreements around the world, treated on a combined basis in our analysis.[8] Combining the regional trade agreements allows the model to estimate a single coefficient for the impact of preferential trading arrangements on bilateral trade.

RTAs have, of course, proliferated in recent years. Schott (2004b) calculates that, as of May 2003, some 155 bilateral and regional trade agreements had been notified to the World Trade Organization (WTO) under Article 24 of the General Agreement on Tariffs and Trade (GATT).[9] Accordingly, in accounting for just 10 strong regional trade agreements, the Rose data upon which we rely does not reflect the breadth of recent experience with bilateral and regional trade agreements worldwide. This has uncertain implications for the magnitude of our estimated coefficient of the RTA variable. However, many of the 155 notified agreements are weak, in that they require considerably less than total free trade between the partners. Many others are quite recent—the 1990s were a boom period for FTAs—and their effects need time to flower. For those reasons, Rose's strategy of singling out the 10 strong and well-established RTAs to estimate the trade impact of bilateral and regional free trade has merit.

In our calculations, two Swiss-US trade integration and openness variables are specified in addition to Rose's set of explanatory variables. Actual trade integration between Switzerland and the United States is captured by a dummy variable for trade between the two countries, as if an FTA were already in place. Swiss and US "openness" are measured by separate dummy variables, one for each country. The dummy takes the value of one each time Switzerland (or the United States) is a trading partner with any other country in the world. The estimated coefficients for these "openness" variables suggest the degree to which Swiss (or US) trade with the world is greater or less than the norm established by the core gravity model variables.

---

7. The dummy variable is needed to distinguish between countries that receive GSP benefits and those that do not. Under the GSP system, a number of advanced countries extend preferences to less developed countries on a nonreciprocal basis. The GSP programs of major industrial and other countries are monitored by the UN Conference on Trade and Development (UNCTAD), including through a series of manuals describing the individual programs. See UNCTAD (2004a).

8. The Rose dataset includes indicators for the Association of Southeast Asian Nations (ASEAN), European Union (EU), US-Israel FTA, North American Free Trade Agreement (NAFTA), Caribbean Community (Caricom), Agreement on Trade and Commercial Relations between the Government of Australia and the Government of Papua New Guinea (PATCRA), Australia–New Zealand Closer Economic Relations Trade Agreement (ANZCERTA), Central American Common Market (CACM), South Pacific Regional Trade and Economic Cooperation Agreement (SPARTECA), and the Southern Cone Common Market (Mercosur).

9. As of July 2005, the WTO (2005e) features an illustrative list of 32 major regional trade agreements worldwide on its Web site, of which the majority are agreements between small developing countries or newly independent states of Eastern Europe.

Results from the Gravity Model

Tables 8.1 and 8.2 present the regression results for overall trade (SITC 0 through 9) and for trade by major commodity categories: food, beverages, and tobacco (SITC 0 and 1); raw materials (SITC 2 and 4); mineral fuels and lubricants (SITC 3); and manufactures (SITC 5 through 8). Regression coefficients are presented for the overall period 1962–99, and for two subperiods, 1990–99 and 1995–99. The two subperiods correspond to the decade of the 1990s and the post–Uruguay Round period respectively. Finally, the gravity model estimates are presented both with and without the Swiss-US trade integration and openness explanatory variables. As it turns out, the presence or absence of these additional variables makes surprisingly little difference to the other coefficients, including the estimated impact of a regional trade agreement.

The regression results for both total and disaggregated trade mirror the widely reported empirical robustness of the gravity model. In particular, the core explanatory variables, led by distance, joint real GDP, and joint real GDP per capita, bear the anticipated signs and are generally significant at high levels. Thus, for instance, bilateral trade is positively related to the joint GDP of the partner countries, and negatively related to the distance between them. Similarly, countries sharing a common border tend to trade significantly more with one another, whereas landlocked countries tend to trade significantly less than other pairs of countries.

The overall explanatory power of the gravity model using disaggregated bilateral trade data from the Feenstra-Lipsey dataset (R-squared generally about 0.30) is appreciably lower than that found by Rose (2004) using aggregate bilateral trade data (R-squared 0.50–0.60). An exception, however, is the impressive explanatory power of the regression results in table 8.2 for manufactures (R-squared about 0.50).

Gravity model studies by Rose (2004) and most other previous investigators, using aggregate bilateral trade, frequently report estimated coefficients near unity for the RTA variable. By contrast, in our analysis, the estimated coefficients for the RTA variable are generally less than 0.50, except for the post–Uruguay Round period, for which the RTA coefficient estimates generally exceed unity for both total trade and all commodity groups except mineral fuels. A regression coefficient of 0.50 implies that the RTA increases trade between the partners by 65 percent; a regression coefficient of 1.00 implies that the RTA increases trade by 172 percent.

As mentioned in chapter 1, Adams et al. (2003) counter these findings, reporting negative RTA coefficients after using an analytic framework in the spirit of the gravity model and a database that ends in 1997. Indeed, these authors at the Australia Productivity Commission (APC) claim that they find net trade diversion for 12 out of 16 recent RTAs. However, their technique for measuring diversion is poorly explained or justified in the paper, and for reasons explained in appendix E, we do not subscribe to their findings.

Table 8.1 Gravity model estimates for US-Swiss overall (SITC 0 through 9) trade, 1962–99

	1962–99		1990–99		1995–99	
	Without	With	Without	With	Without	With
Constant	−19.27***	−18.20***	−7.00***	−5.77***	−6.93***	−5.70***
Distance	−0.79***	−0.81***	−0.77***	−0.79***	−0.72***	−0.74***
Joint GDP	0.75***	0.74***	0.53***	0.51***	0.53***	0.51***
Joint GDP per capita	−0.10***	−0.10***	−0.25***	−0.25***	−0.28***	−0.28***
Common language	0.20***	0.13***	0.19***	0.08***	0.22***	0.12***
Common border	0.55***	0.57***	0.96***	0.98***	0.91***	0.93***
Landlocked	−0.19***	−0.25***	−0.50***	−0.62***	−0.53***	−0.66***
Island	0.11***	0.11***	0.34***	0.35***	0.31***	0.33***
Land area	−0.13***	−0.13***	−0.07***	−0.07***	−0.06***	−0.07***
Common colonizer	−0.06**	−0.03	−0.15***	−0.10**	−0.11**	−0.06
Colony	0.75***	0.76***	0.30*	0.30*	0.29	0.29
Ever a colony	1.67***	1.76***	1.00***	1.13***	0.95***	1.08***
Common country	0.22	0.20	−0.65	−0.75	−0.67	−0.77
Currency union	0.80***	0.79***	1.52***	0.66***	1.40***	0.48*
GSP	−0.14***	−0.15***	0.33***	0.26***	0.28***	0.22***
RTAs	0.33***	0.33***	0.32***	0.33***	1.19***	1.21***
US-Swiss trade		0.94*		1.63***		1.57***
US openness		1.46***		1.52***		1.50***
Swiss openness		0.51***		0.94***		1.01***
R-squared	0.40	0.41	0.34	0.35	0.36	0.36
Observations (thousands)	940	940	263	263	146	146
Groups (thousands)	61	61	44	44	41	41

***, **, * indicate that the coefficients are statistically significant at the 99, 95, and 90 percent levels, respectively.

Notes: Estimates are presented both with and without the Swiss-US trade integration and openness explanatory variables. Regressand is log real trade. Distance, GDP, GDP per capita, and land area are measured in log terms. Estimated year effects are not reported. Groups are numbers of country-pair-commodity combinations for which trade exists in the data sample.

Source: Authors' calculations based on generalized least squares estimation of the Rose (2004) gravity model with random effects, using a combined version of Rose (2004) and Feenstra-Lipsey (2005) datasets.

Table 8.2 Gravity model estimates by major commodity categories, 1962–99

| | Food, beverages, and tobacco (SITC 0 and 1) | | | | | | Raw materials (SITC 2 and 4) | | | | | |
| | 1962–99 | | 1990–99 | | 1995–99 | | 1962–99 | | 1990–99 | | 1995–99 | |
	Without	With	Without	With	Without	With	Without	With	Without	With	Without	With
Constant	-13.91***	-12.68***	-3.57***	-2.33***	-3.73***	-2.53***	-17.02***	-16.30***	-6.13***	-5.33***	-6.49***	-5.72***
Distance	-0.65***	-0.67***	-0.60***	-0.63***	-0.57***	-0.59***	-0.57***	-0.58***	-0.48***	-0.49***	-0.43***	-0.45***
Joint GDP	0.60***	0.58***	0.40***	0.38***	0.40***	0.38***	0.69***	0.68***	0.40***	0.39***	0.40***	0.39***
Joint GDP per capita	-0.13***	-0.13***	-0.22***	-0.22***	-0.23***	-0.23***	-0.25***	-0.25***	-0.20***	-0.20***	-0.21***	-0.21***
Common language	0.23***	0.15***	0.20***	0.10*	0.26***	0.16***	-0.01	-0.05	0.03	-0.03	0.06	0.00
Common border	0.60***	0.61***	0.97***	0.99***	0.93***	0.95***	0.37***	0.37***	0.97***	0.98***	0.94***	0.95***
Landlocked	-0.23***	-0.28***	-0.46***	-0.54***	-0.50***	-0.59***	-0.18***	-0.18***	-0.43***	-0.47***	-0.45***	-0.49***
Island	0.09**	0.08**	0.29***	0.30***	0.26***	0.28***	0.10**	0.09**	0.20***	0.21***	0.17***	0.18***
Land area	-0.07***	-0.08***	-0.03***	-0.04***	-0.02	-0.02**	-0.08***	-0.09***	0.01	0.00	0.02*	0.01
Common colonizer	-0.15*	-0.11*	-0.21**	-0.16*	-0.11	-0.07	-0.14**	-0.14**	0.16*	0.18**	0.21**	0.23**
Colony	0.51***	0.52***	0.54	0.54	0.49	0.49	0.44***	0.45***	0.09	0.09	0.27	0.27
Ever a colony	2.05***	2.14***	1.30***	1.41***	1.19***	1.30***	1.15***	1.19***	0.50***	0.57***	0.50***	0.56***
Common country	0.97	0.94	-0.67	-0.78	-0.85	-0.96	-0.20	-0.22	-1.61	-1.67	(dropped)	(dropped)
Currency union	0.83***	0.81***	1.88***	1.00*	1.90***	0.89	0.76***	0.75***	0.56	0.02	0.46	-0.12
GSP	-0.04***	-0.05***	0.42***	0.37***	0.42***	0.36***	-0.21***	-0.22***	0.06	0.04	0.08*	0.05
RTAs	0.55***	0.55***	0.56***	0.57***	1.32***	1.33***	0.36***	0.36***	0.36***	0.37***	1.14***	1.15***
US-Swiss trade		1.27		1.75		1.78		0.35		0.79		0.58
US openness		1.76***		1.56***		1.47***		0.92***		0.87***		0.83***
Swiss openness		0.39***		0.59***		0.67***		-0.09		0.30**		0.31**
R-squared	0.32	0.33	0.28	0.29	0.30	0.31	0.31	0.31	0.27	0.27	0.29	0.29
Observations (thousands)	194	194	53	53	29	29	162	162	43	43	24	24
Groups (thousands)	12	12	9	9	8	8	11	11	7	7	7	7

(table continues next page)

231

Table 8.2 Gravity model estimates by major commodity categories, 1962–99 (continued)

	Mineral fuels and lubricants (SITC 3)						Manufactures (SITC 5 through 8)					
	1962-99		1990-99		1995-99		1962-99		1990-99		1995-99	
	Without	With	Without	With	Without	With	Without	With	Without	With	Without	With
Constant	-11.26***	-10.57***	-3.35***	-2.25***	-3.52***	-2.40***	-25.04***	-23.96***	-11.08***	-9.85***	-10.60***	-9.33***
Distance	-1.02***	-1.03***	-0.82***	-0.84***	-0.80***	-0.83***	-0.98***	-1.00***	-1.03***	-1.05***	-0.98***	-1.00***
Joint GDP	0.31***	0.31***	0.27***	0.26***	0.29***	0.28***	0.98***	0.96***	0.73***	0.71***	0.72***	0.70***
Joint GDP per capita	0.41***	0.41***	0.03	0.02	-0.05	-0.05*	-0.12***	-0.13***	-0.32***	-0.33***	-0.37***	-0.37***
Common language	-0.25***	-0.28***	0.01	-0.07	0.05	-0.03	0.36***	0.27***	0.25***	0.14***	0.28***	0.17***
Common border	0.54***	0.53***	1.13***	1.15***	1.21***	1.22***	0.66***	0.68***	1.09***	1.10***	0.99***	0.99***
Landlocked	-1.34***	-1.21***	-1.28***	-1.34***	-1.30***	-1.37***	-0.07***	-0.21***	-0.50***	-0.66***	-0.56***	-0.72***
Island	0.50***	0.47***	0.58***	0.58***	0.65***	0.65***	0.02***	0.03	0.35***	0.37***	0.32***	0.35***
Land area	0.18***	0.17***	0.16***	0.15***	0.16***	0.15***	-0.24***	-0.23***	-0.15***	-0.15***	-0.15***	-0.15**
Common colonizer	0.74***	0.71***	0.79***	0.81***	1.11***	1.13***	-0.12***	-0.06*	-0.32***	-0.26***	-0.32***	-0.25***
Colony	0.69***	0.69***	-0.08	-0.08	0.32	0.32	0.82***	0.83***	0.39	0.39	0.33	0.33
Ever a colony	0.97***	0.98***	0.20	0.28	0.23	0.32	2.06***	2.16***	1.47***	1.62***	1.40***	1.54***
Common country	-0.75	-0.80	-1.10	-1.19	-1.43	-1.52	0.46***	0.47	-0.81	-0.90	-1.05	-1.15
Currency union	0.70***	0.69***	0.66	0.05	1.05	0.42	0.66***	0.65***	1.67***	0.75***	1.32***	0.33
GSP	-0.37***	-0.37***	-0.30***	-0.33***	-0.31***	-0.36***	-0.13***	-0.14***	0.54***	0.45***	0.46***	0.37***
RTAs	-0.28***	-0.28**	0.18**	0.18***	0.59***	0.60***	0.37***	0.37***	0.29***	0.31***	1.45***	1.48***
US-Swiss trade	1.43		-0.18		0.10		0.64		2.48***		2.44***	
US openness		0.91***		1.10***		1.12***		1.51***		1.32***		1.71***
Swiss openness		-0.95***		0.26		0.33		1.34***				1.37***
R-squared	0.33	0.33	0.26	0.27	0.27	0.28	0.57	0.58	0.50	0.51	0.52	0.53
Observations (thousands)	61	61	17	17	9	9	461	461	133	133	74	74
Groups (thousands)	5	5	3	3	3	3	28	28	21	21	20	20

***, **, * indicate that the coefficients are statistically significant at the 99, 95, and 90 percent levels, respectively.

Note: Estimates are presented both with and without the Swiss-US trade integration openness explanatory variables. Regressand is log real trade. Distance, GDP, GDP per capita, and land area are measured in log terms. Estimated year effects are not reported. Groups are numbers of country-pair/commodity combinations for which trade exists in the data sample.

Source: Authors' calculations based on generalized least squares estimation of the Rose (2004) gravity model with random effects, using a combined version of Rose

The regression coefficients for the US openness variable are always greater than those for the Swiss openness variable, suggesting that trade resistance forces are stronger in Switzerland than they are in the United States. Estimated coefficients for the Swiss-US trade integration variable on a sector-by-sector basis (table 8.2) generally have high positive values, suggesting that bilateral trade already exceeds the international norm. However, the coefficient is only significant for trade in manufactures in the 1990s. These results tend to suggest that US exports to Switzerland would expand more than Swiss exports to the United States under a Swiss-US FTA. They also suggest that agriculture is a prime candidate for trade expansion in both directions, probably because both countries currently have high levels of protection in place. Other evidence, reported shortly, suggests that there is also considerable room for expanded manufactures trade between Switzerland and the United States.

Table 8.3 reports the trade expansion effects implied by the various coefficient estimates for the RTA variables in tables 8.1 and 8.2.[10] The simple average column gives equal weight to the coefficients estimated for each of the overlapping periods. Based on the simple average percentage expansion for total trade (104 percent) and the four sectors taken together (102 percent), it appears that overall Swiss-US merchandise trade might expand, under an FTA, by a central estimate of about 100 percent, holding all other factors constant.[11] Both agriculture and manufactures two-way trade might expand by about 140 percent. Predicted expansion of Swiss-US trade in manufactures by more than 100 percent may seem implausible, given the relative openness of both Switzerland and the United States. However, a leap in bilateral foreign direct investment (FDI) could induce a great deal of bilateral trade expansion, as chapter 7 suggests.[12]

---

10. The figures in the tabulation are based on the regressions that include the dummy variables for Swiss-US trade integration and openness. However, as mentioned, the dummy variables make very little difference to the RTA coefficients.

11. Results of the CGE model, presented in this chapter, suggest that a Swiss-US FTA could lead to an expansion in bilateral trade in services of about 10 percent. However, based on Ceglowski (2005) estimates of the correlation coefficient between expansion in merchandise trade and in services trade, and the reported estimates of merchandise trade expansion, it is possible that a Swiss-US FTA could lead to as much as a 60 to 70 percent increase in bilateral trade in services.

12. Ignoring the other coefficients, and focusing only on post–Uruguay Round estimation results, suggests that overall Swiss-US trade might grow by 235 percent, led by expansion of manufactures (nearly 340 percent) and agriculture (nearly 280 percent). These results do seem implausible. However, given the array of hidden barriers to manufactures trade as well as overt barriers to agricultural trade, bilateral trade expansion could conceivably exceed 100 percent.

Table 8.3 Implied trade expansion effects (percent)

Category	1962–99	1990–99	1995–99	Simple average
Total trade (SITC 0–9)	39	39	235	104
Disaggregated trade				
Agriculture (SITC 0 and 1)	73	76	278	142
Raw material (SITC 2 and 4)	43	45	215	101
Fuels (SITC 3)	−25	20	82	26
Manufactured goods (SITC 5–8)	45	36	339	140
Simple average[a]	34	44	229	102

SITC = Standard International Trade Classification

a. The simple average excludes the estimate for total trade (SITC 0–9).

Source: Authors' calculations.

CGE Model: Construction and Results

CGE models are based on general equilibrium principles; they are built to turn abstract theories into practical tools. A number of features distinguish them from other widely used frameworks for trade policy analysis, especially gravity models. In particular, the actions of economic agents are modeled explicitly through utility- and profit-maximizing assumptions, while economy-wide resource and expenditure constraints are rigorously enforced. Because they gather markets into a single system, CGE techniques effectively capture feedback and flow-through effects induced by policy changes. Economic distortions often have repercussions beyond the sector in which they occur, which CGE models are designed to capture. They are particularly well-suited to examining FTAs, under which multisector liberalization is undertaken in at least two countries simultaneously and adverse consequences of discriminatory preferences may well arise (Panagariya 2000).

Against these significant advantages, CGE models are highly data-intensive, and subject to several uncertainties. How should equations be specified? What parameters should be used? How should the FTA experiment be designed? Because CGE results are sensitive to these decisions, they should be viewed cautiously. Our CGE model is the GTAP framework, a publicly available and widely adopted model. Multiregion and multisector, it assumes perfect competition and constant returns to scale. These assumptions are very strong, and in practice, tend to apply best to homogeneous goods and not so well to services, which are more heterogeneous and often entail large fixed costs. Other CGE frameworks assume that countries enjoy increasing returns to scale as they specialize, and that monopolistic markups are eroded by trade liberalization. Such models may also assume that freer trade spurs investment and productivity. Some also incorporate dynamic effects, such as fostered innovation due to greater competition. These additional assumptions typically result in significantly larger calculated trade and economic gains as a consequence of removing barriers. By contrast, the results reported here, using a comparative statics framework, are very conservative and may severely underestimate the benefits of an FTA—most notably in services, which command more than 70 percent of GDP in both the US and Switzerland, and for which products are in practice differentiated and knowledge-intensive. Accordingly, the expected gains of a Swiss-US FTA should come from returns to scale, competitive erosion of markup margins, and dynamic innovation. The GTAP model, however, does not capture these effects.

Experimental Design

The proposed FTA between Switzerland and the United States is first simulated independently of the existence of other FTAs. The results thus reflect the estimated effect of the proposal in isolation from any liberalization that occurred after the reference year for the GTAP6 database (2001), or that might be forthcoming. For services trade, the base year for the tariff equivalent values used in the analysis is 1996, reflecting barriers to trade in services as reported by Dee, Hanslow, and Phamduc (2003).

We then consider an all-partners experiment, in which the proposed Swiss-US FTA is implemented simultaneously with other, newer US FTAs—those ratified after the GTAP6 database—and prospective US FTAs that might come in force by the end of 2006. The newer US FTAs are those with Chile, Australia, Singapore, and Morocco; the prospective FTAs, apart from the Swiss-US FTA, are the Central American Free Trade Agreement (CAFTA) as well as FTAs with Thailand and the Southern African Customs Union (SACU).

In all cases, arrangements are assumed to be implemented "clean," meaning that all participating economies eventually reduce their import tariffs to zero on a bilateral preferential basis. Services trade barriers are also eliminated.[13] However, all other tariffs and barriers, such as those applied to nonparticipating economies, are left in place. In other words, possible liberalization negotiated in the WTO Doha Development Round is not taken into consideration. Moreover, in the experiment with all free trade areas, it is assumed that the FTAs are implemented only with the United States. Preferential liberalization among proposed partner regions is not considered.

As an additional benchmark for the implications of bilateral FTAs, beyond the status quo benchmark of the CGE model baseline, we also consider unilateral trade reform scenarios for Switzerland and the United States. In these scenarios, each economy is assumed to unilaterally remove

---

13. Estimates of barriers to services are those reported by Dee, Hanslow, and Phamduc (2003), which reflects barriers as of 1996.

all tariffs on a nondiscriminatory basis, thereby indicating the extent to which an FTA either improves upon, or falls short of, the usual textbook optimum of free trade.

All of the simulations are run as exercises in comparative statics. This entails "before" and "after" pictures, allowing all of the agreed bilateral liberalization to take place and all industries to adjust, but with no attempt to profile the time path of adjustment. Factor market "closure" conditions allow full mobility of capital and labor across domestic industries; in other words, all capital and labor, both skilled and unskilled, are assumed to be fully employed once the adjustment process is complete.[14] The implicit time frame is the long run, typically regarded as an adjustment period of about 10 years. However, the adjustment path is not directly modeled. Land is treated as imperfectly mobile across agricultural activities, while other natural resources are assumed to be committed to individual industries as specific factors.

Results from the CGE Model

Table 8.4 presents estimates of the overall effect of the proposed agreement. The model predicts fairly dramatic increases in the volume of bilateral trade between the United States and Switzerland, with US exports to Switzerland increasing by 32 percent and Swiss exports to the United States increasing by approximately 12 percent. One reason for the dramatic increase in US exports is that Swiss imports from other countries may decline, once US firms enjoy a preferential tariff structure. This effect, known as trade diversion, seems quite strong in Switzerland's case.[15] Swiss tariffs on agriculture are high, and the United States would become a preferred supplier alongside the European Union. The overall welfare effects of the agreement are estimated to be small for both economies, and positive for Switzerland.[16]

The unilateral benchmark results indicate somewhat why the welfare outcomes are what they are. The United States is already a very open economy, and hence, has little to gain in efficiency from further liberalization. In fact, it loses in welfare terms from unilateral reform, due to shifts in

---

14. An alternative assumption, consistent with the same results, is that unemployment rates for labor and capital remain the same before and after full adjustment.

15. Swiss trade diversion is also reflected in the significant drop in Swiss tariff revenues, shown in the third section of table 8.4, and in the adverse terms-of-trade shift (discussed below).

16. The welfare effects presented in table 8.4 are measured as the equivalent variation (EV) in income. This is essentially the change in household income that equals the proposed change, at constant consumer prices.

Table 8.4 CGE changes in key variables, Swiss-US FTA

	United States			Switzerland		
	Initial value (millions of dollars)	Free trade area	Unilateral benchmark	Initial value (millions of dollars)	Free trade area	Unilateral benchmark
		(percent change or millions of dollars)			(percent change or millions of dollars)	
Total import value	1,289,855	0.1	2.9	97,559	1.9	3.1
From partner	14,909	12.3	2.1	10,981	32.4	5.5
From rest of world	1,274,946	-0.1	2.9	86,578	-2.0	2.8
Total export value	881,759	0.6	4.4	107,007	1.0	1.9
To partner	10,811	32.0	5.7	14,683	12.2	3.5
To rest of world	870,948	0.2	4.4	92,324	-0.8	1.6
Tariff revenue	19,946	-192	-19,946	2,445	-821	-2,445
From partner	157	-157	-157	324	-324	-324
From rest of world	19,789	-35	-19,789	2,120	-496	-2,120
Welfare as percent of GDP		0.0	-0.1		0.0	0.1
Total welfare effects (equivalent variation)	—	-94	-11,510	—	106	186
Allocative efficiency	—	-145	1,716	—	-30	33
Terms of trade	—	51	-13,226	—	135	154

Source: Initial data from the GTAP6 database (Dimaranan and McDougall 2005). Estimates from simulation results.

terms of trade, though by only a small fraction of GDP.[17] Recall also that the GTAP model results do not incorporate returns to scale, or competitive or dynamic effects—and all of these are important, especially for the services sector. Finally, since the Swiss market is relatively small, there are few opportunities to counter adverse terms-of-trade shifts with increased market access. For Switzerland, the gains from unilateral liberalization are larger, reflecting higher protection levels in a few key markets and much smaller adverse terms-of-trade effects.

It should be emphasized that alternative modeling techniques suggest much larger GDP gains from expanded Swiss-US trade than the gains calculated by our static CGE analysis using the GTAP framework. Based on table 8.4, Swiss-US bilateral trade might increase by $5.3 billion in the wake of a Swiss-US FTA.[18] Research reported elsewhere (Bradford et al. 2005), using a variety of alternative techniques, suggests that annual GDP gains to each partner would amount to about 20 percent of the expanded trade, or about $1.1 billion annually.[19] These gains reflect the adoption of improved production methods in response to competitive pressures, the exit of less efficient firms, scale and network economies, reduced markup margins, more intense use of imported inputs, and greater variety in the menu of available goods and services. For the United States, as a percentage of GDP, the annual gains calculated by the static GTAP model are very small, but for Switzerland, they represent about 0.5 percent in GDP.

The welfare effects of the Swiss-US FTA on third countries are presented in more detail in table 8.5. Most other economies suffer very small welfare losses because of the FTA, though China incurs the largest adverse effects. Preference dilution—the phenomenon whereby existing FTA partners lose the benefits of preferential access to the Swiss or US market when Switzerland enters into free trade with the United States—does not seem to be significant for either NAFTA or EFTA members, though the European Union sees a slight effect. As a proportion of regional GDP, all welfare effects on nonmembers are very minor. Under unilateral reform, by contrast, nonmembers generally benefit.

The CGE model predicts that Switzerland would gain twice as much in GDP terms if the United States unilaterally abolished its barriers with all

---

17. This result for US unilateral trade liberalization is commonly found in CGE models that use the GTAP framework. It emphasizes the importance of concerted, reciprocal trade liberalization for a large economy, such as the United States, to avoid adverse terms-of-trade effects. For a smaller economy, such as Switzerland, reciprocal trade liberalization is not so essential to avoid an adverse movement in terms of trade.

18. In addition, the United States would slightly expand its imports from the rest of the world, but Switzerland would slightly contract its imports.

19. This rough rule of thumb finds strong support in the econometric literature, but of course counterexamples can be cited in which GDP gains are not related in a simple fashion to trade expansion. On the other hand, GDP gains could be much larger than the figures cited in the text if two-way trade doubled as the gravity model calculations suggest.

Table 8.5 CGE changes in net welfare by region, Swiss–US FTA

Country	Initial GDP (billions of dollars)	Free trade area (millions of dollars)			Unilateral benchmark — United States (millions of dollars)			Unilateral benchmark — Switzerland (millions of dollars)		
		Total	Allocative efficiency	Terms of trade	Total	Allocative efficiency	Terms of trade	Total	Allocative efficiency	Terms of trade
Australia	350.4	9	5	4	224	1	223	9	0	9
Brazil	490.9	18	10	8	389	107	283	102	13	89
Central America	102.2	–3	–1	–2	757	320	437	–6	0	–6
Chile	65.0	1	1	0	58	1	57	1	–1	2
China	1,061.6	–21	8	–29	3,060	795	2,266	51	–18	68
Eastern Europe	817.2	9	19	–9	493	22	471	144	–8	152
European Union	7,781.7	–16	204	–220	4,925	253	4,672	171	11	161
Hong Kong	165.3	7	3	4	–4	–63	59	–27	–3	–24
Japan	4,027.3	90	17	73	2,019	352	1,666	47	9	37
Morocco	32.9	–1	0	–1	21	7	14	82	6	75
New Zealand	49.8	–4	1	–5	73	0	74	5	–1	6
Rest of EFTA	198.6	5	3	1	143	–10	153	7	0	7
Rest of South America	693.0	22	12	10	545	118	427	10	0	10
SACU	10.0	–1	0	–1	28	2	26	0	0	0
South Korea	408.6	–3	2	–6	848	55	793	4	–6	10
Switzerland	242.5	106	–30	135	204	–5	208	207	1,146	–939
Taiwan	275.9	–10	1	–11	623	4	619	1	–2	3
Rest of world	1,939.7	–2	28	–31	1,566	100	1,466	174	77	98

(table continues next page)

239

Table 8.5 CGE changes in net welfare by region, Swiss-US FTA *(continued)*

Country	Initial GDP (billions of dollars)	Free trade area			Unilateral benchmark					
					United States			Switzerland		
		Total	Allocative efficiency	Terms of trade	Total	Allocative efficiency	Terms of trade	Total	Allocative efficiency	Terms of trade
		(millions of dollars)			(millions of dollars)			(millions of dollars)		
Indonesia	140.6	-6	0	-6	323	-69	392	11	-2	13
Malaysia	86.9	-5	4	-9	150	-52	203	4	-3	7
Philippines	67.4	-4	-3	-2	246	68	178	4	3	0
Singapore	84.8	1	2	-1	8	-22	30	-6	-2	-3
Thailand	111.7	-8	0	-8	280	-48	328	4	-1	5
Vietnam	31.2	-4	0	-4	178	92	86	12	4	8
All ASEAN	522.6	-26			1,186			28		
Canada	703.8	54	12	42	-844	37	-881	29	4	25
Mexico	599.3	0	-15	15	-1,175	-101	-1,074	28	-3	31
United States	9,987.0	-94	-145	51	-11,510	1,716	-13,226	186	33	154
All NAFTA	11,290.1	-40			-13,529			244		
All world	30,525.3	138			3,630			1,254		

EFTA = European Free Trade Association
SACU = Southern African Customs Union

Source: Initial data from the GTAP6 database (Dimaranan and McDougall 2005). Estimates from simulation results.

countries instead of just entering an FTA with Switzerland. This result presumably reflects the spur to global growth that would result from unilateral US trade reform. While unilateral reform is not in the cards, if a Swiss-US FTA is implemented, the calculation suggests that Switzerland can be relaxed about further US liberalization in the Doha Round or other trade contexts.

Table 8.6 contains details on the change in the pattern of overall trade by region. The effects of the Swiss-US FTA on nonmember exports to the United States are very small. For Switzerland, however, the effects are more significant and consistently negative, especially for Australia, New Zealand, China, and the members of the Association of Southeast Asian Nations (ASEAN).

CGE models also allow us to predict which sectors are most likely to be affected by the proposed agreement. The results of the analysis appear in tables 8.7 and 8.8. Table 8.7 presents the estimated changes in bilateral and total exports by economic sector. The simulations predict some very large gains in US exports of agricultural products, including grains, oil seeds, animal products, dairy, and other manufactures. Dairy in particular could see extremely large gains, but from a very small base of only $1.8 million in 2001. These results reflect very high protection levels for Switzerland in 2001 in the GTAP6 database: 34 percent for grains, 21 percent for oil seeds, 101 percent for animal products, and 108 percent for dairy. Other manufactures—excluding motor vehicles, machinery and electronic equipment—could see export gains of 73 percent.[20] From the perspective of overall US trade, only the Swiss tariff changes in raw animal products, dairy products, and other manufactures are large enough to have a significant impact on US bilateral exports.

For Switzerland, the bilateral export gains are much smaller, but still very significant in dairy, textiles, metal products, and some agricultural products. Reflecting the comparatively large role that the United States plays in Switzerland's bilateral trade profile, these translate into significant overall trade expansion in the areas of raw animal products, dairy products, and certain manufactures.

The predicted changes in bilateral trade in services are positive but relatively small, at 10 percent for US exports to Switzerland and 13 percent for Swiss exports to the United States.[21] Moreover, total US exports of services are in fact predicted to decline, indicating that the increase in US exports to Switzerland represents a diversion. There are three model-related

---

20. Based on the data in appendix E, we have assumed that the Swiss tariff barrier for this category is 11 percent. This is well below the implausibly high figure in the GTAP6 database, namely 155 percent.

21. These estimates are very conservative. Using a similar gravity model approach for bilateral services trade as the model presented earlier in the chapter for merchandise trade, Ceglowski (2005) estimates that trade in services among partners to a regional trade agreement is 38 percent higher than among other nonmember trading partners. Moreover, she also finds a 0.6 to 0.7 correlation coefficient between increased trade in services and trade in goods. Based on our two estimates for increased merchandise trade (100 percent from the gravity model and 20 percent from the CGE model) the upper and lower estimates for trade creation in services could range from 14 to 70 percent.

Table 8.6 CGE changes in the regional pattern of exports, Swiss-US FTA

Country/region/ group	Initial value (billions of dollars)			Free trade area (percent change)			Unilateral benchmark (percent change)			
							United States		Switzerland	
	Total	To the United States	To Switzerland	Total	To the United States	To Switzerland	Total	To the United States	Total	To Switzerland
Australia	72.3	8.6	0.4	0.0	0.0	-6.1	0.3	4.7	0.0	2.2
Brazil	67.8	16.0	0.5	-0.1	-0.1	-3.6	0.3	4.4	0.0	88.3
Central America	34.1	13.4	0.3	0.0	0.0	-5.7	1.7	11.6	0.0	-0.7
Chile	21.7	4.0	0.1	0.0	0.0	-3.4	0.2	2.3	0.0	6.2
China	379.6	108.4	1.5	0.0	-0.1	-3.7	1.2	9.8	0.0	22.3
Eastern Europe	340.8	24.3	5.8	0.0	-0.1	-0.7	0.2	1.1	0.1	13.3
European Union	2,477.9	287.1	62.6	0.0	-0.1	-1.8	0.3	3.2	0.0	0.0
Hong Kong	98.2	20.4	0.9	0.0	0.0	-4.6	0.6	7.5	0.0	2.7
Japan	448.8	123.9	2.0	-0.1	-0.3	-0.7	0.4	4.3	0.0	5.8
Morocco	11.2	1.1	0.1	0.0	0.0	-4.0	0.3	1.9	0.3	300.2
New Zealand	18.1	2.8	0.1	0.0	-0.1	-20.9	0.4	5.9	0.0	33.6
Rest of EFTA	66.4	7.8	0.4	0.0	0.0	-3.3	0.0	0.3	0.0	-4.5
Rest of South America	119.7	33.5	1.3	0.0	0.0	-1.9	0.4	2.7	0.0	0.9

SACU	6.2	0.5	0.0	0.0	0.0	-7.9	0.9	24.4	0.0	-6.6
South Korea	175.4	37.2	0.6	0.0	-0.1	-0.7	0.6	6.3	0.0	3.1
Switzerland	107.0	14.7	—	1.0	12.2	—	0.3	2.1	1.9	0.0
Taiwan	135.7	36.1	0.5	0.0	-0.1	-0.6	0.6	5.2	0.0	0.7
Rest of world	507.5	99.8	3.5	0.0	0.0	-4.9	0.5	2.7	0.0	2.9
Indonesia	68.0	11.4	0.2	0.0	-0.1	-1.3	1.0	13.2	0.0	6.9
Malaysia	124.4	24.0	0.3	0.0	-0.1	-2.2	0.4	3.0	0.0	1.6
Philippines	37.9	11.5	0.1	0.0	-0.1	-4.2	0.1	5.4	0.0	-1.9
Singapore	110.4	17.8	0.5	0.0	-0.1	-7.8	0.2	1.0	0.0	5.1
Thailand	79.4	17.2	0.5	0.0	-0.1	-2.9	0.3	6.3	0.0	4.8
Vietnam	15.3	1.4	0.1	0.0	0.0	-1.5	0.2	8.3	0.0	-1.5
All ASEAN	435.3	83.4	1.7	0.0	-0.1	-4.0	0.4	5.1	0.0	3.7
Canada	265.3	198.2	0.6	0.0	0.0	-3.5	-0.9	-2.2	0.0	4.1
Mexico	164.3	129.5	0.5	0.0	0.0	-2.6	-0.5	-1.8	0.0	22.3
United States	881.8	—	10.8	0.6	—	32.0	4.4	—	0.0	5.4
All NAFTA	1,311.4	327.8	11.9	0.4	0.0	28.9	2.7	-2.0	0.0	6.0
All world	6,835.1	1,250.9	94.1	0.1	0.1	1.9	0.9	2.8	0.1	3.1

EFTA = European Free Trade Association
SACU = Southern African Customs Union

Source: Initial data from the GTAP6 database (Dimaranan and McDougall 2005). Estimates from simulation results.

Table 8.7 CGE changes in the sectoral pattern of exports, Swiss-US FTA

	United States					Switzerland				
	Initial value (millions of dollars)		Free trade area (percent change)		Total: Unilateral benchmark (percent change)	Initial value (millions of dollars)		Free trade area (percent change)		Total: Unilateral benchmark (percent change)
Sector	Total	To Switzerland	Total	To Switzerland		Total	To the United States	Total	To the United States	
Grains	9,638	8	0.1	401.4	1.5	64	0	6.3	7.0	72.9
Oil seeds	5,698	11	0.2	115.1	1.3	9	0	4.8	5.1	27.7
Plant-based fibers	2,209	4	−0.1	0.4	5.4	50	0	1.4	5.4	9.0
Other crops	8,062	57	0.1	21.4	2.1	205	7	3.8	33.9	30.8
Raw animal products	12,287	32	7.6	2,880.1	2.0	118	8	24.6	30.8	111.2
Wool	9	0	−0.3	−1.3	13.5	3	0	2.5	21.3	19.6
Forestry	1,254	3	0.0	2.8	1.2	129	0	0.3	13.6	1.3
Coal, oil, and gas	4,246	2	−0.1	10.3	2.9	57	0	0.2	1.8	4.4
Dairy products	802	2	26.5	11,799.7	2.5	361	35	41.3	349.8	31.1
Other food products	19,615	123	0.8	105.1	1.2	1,888	102	2.4	29.6	13.7

Textiles and clothing	19,337	65	0.5	60.7	8.8	2,180	172	6.1	82.7	-0.1
Wood products	8,212	17	0.3	12.0	1.7	823	27	0.0	4.3	-1.0
Paper products	20,031	88	0.4	26.6	0.9	2,001	78	-0.4	1.0	-1.5
Chemicals	117,946	1,451	0.3	3.6	1.5	24,126	2,797	0.4	11.4	-1.8
Ferrous metals	6,932	36	0.3	8.2	0.9	994	36	-0.2	9.5	-1.6
Nonferrous metals	11,379	223	0.3	1.1	2.7	5,626	465	-0.4	3.3	-1.7
Metal products	14,857	52	0.4	16.6	1.3	2,823	276	1.6	22.6	-1.9
Motor vehicles	108,533	597	0.3	3.9	1.4	2,068	336	0.1	3.2	-1.7
Electronic equipment	110,550	514	0.4	1.5	2.9	2,901	408	-1.0	-0.4	-2.7
Machinery and equipment	165,096	1,241	0.5	3.8	2.5	30,230	3,939	0.3	8.1	-2.3
Other manufactures	15,588	2,029	9.8	73.1	3.6	4,739	659	1.8	10.8	1.4
Nontraded services	4,083	16	0.4	0.9	1.8	2,715	20	-0.8	-1.1	-1.7
Traded services	215,394	4,240	-0.1	10.2	11.2	22,898	5,316	2.1	13.1	12.2

Source: Initial data from the GTAP6 database (Dimaranan and McDougall 2005). Estimates from simulation results.

Table 8.8 CGE changes in the sectoral pattern of production, Swiss-US FTA (percent change in volume)

Sector	United States			Switzerland		
	Initial value (millions of dollars)	Free trade area (percent change)	Unilateral benchmark (percent change)	Initial value (millions of dollars)	Free trade area (percent change)	Unilateral benchmark (percent change)
Grains	27,807	0.2	0.4	259	-0.8	-28.1
Oil seeds	12,589	0.1	0.4	36	-1.2	-7.1
Plant-based fibers	7,202	0.0	-1.1	70	1.4	9.3
Other crops	58,248	0.6	-0.2	1,028	-6.4	-19.0
Raw animal products	249,552	0.0	-0.2	7,362	1.6	-7.6
Wool	121	0.4	-0.5	3	2.9	19.8
Forestry	17,760	0.1	-0.1	678	-0.1	-1.2
Coal, oil and gas	112,617	0.1	0.2	1,237	-0.1	-0.3
Dairy products	83,610	0.3	-1.3	3,516	2.9	-2.1
Other food products	499,685	0.1	-0.2	10,526	0.0	-0.4
Textiles and clothing	267,866	0.2	-9.0	3,765	3.6	-1.4
Wood products	225,048	0.1	0.1	1,565	-0.5	-2.9
Paper products	388,380	0.1	0.0	10,208	-0.4	-0.8
Chemicals	980,688	0.1	-0.7	38,495	-0.1	-2.0
Ferrous metals	141,164	0.2	-0.3	7,262	0.0	-1.8
Nonferrous metals	109,351	0.2	-0.1	8,966	-0.5	-2.1
Metal products	286,796	0.1	-0.4	5,467	0.8	-1.9
Motor vehicles	654,361	0.1	-0.2	15,920	0.5	-0.4
Electronic equipment	347,619	0.2	1.4	5,775	-0.7	-2.1
Machinery and equipment	779,360	0.2	0.1	36,836	0.0	-2.5
Other manufactures	63,740	2.5	0.3	7,813	-1.8	-6.5
Nontraded services	2,476,501	0.0	-0.1	51,699	0.5	0.3
Traded services	9,981,558	-0.1	0.2	208,258	0.0	1.4

Source: Initial data from the GTAP6 database (Dimaranan and McDougall 2005). Estimates from simulation results.

explanations for these small and counterintuitive changes. The first is that the trade flow barriers estimated by Dee, Hanslow, and Phamduc (2003) are relatively low, about 5 percent on an ad valorem–equivalent basis. The second is that certain types of barriers, such as taxes on interest, dividends, and sales, are not region-specific in the GTAP model. The third and perhaps most important possibility is that barriers to trade in services limit trade flows to a greater extent than is modeled in the GTAP framework. Trade barriers in services may hinder firms from investing in foreign market (GATS mode 3); reducing them could spur FDI in the affected service sectors and beneficially enhance competitive pressures. The GTAP model does not capture such positive productivity effects. Hence, the applied general equilibrium analysis reported here very likely understates the potential for expanded bilateral services trade under a Swiss-US FTA.

Table 8.8 contains the estimated changes in output by sector. These figures are useful for understanding the extent of structural adjustment that the agreement might require. In the United States, the only sector affected by the proposed FTA, beyond a marginal extent, is the "other manufactures" sector, which enjoys an expansion of 2.5 percent. This finding suggests that US adjustments in response to the Swiss-US FTA would be negligible.

In Switzerland, the adjustment burdens are likely to be more substantial, with significant output declines predicted in manufacturing and crops. However, output gains are estimated in dairy, textiles, and apparel. Overall, while Swiss adjustments are much greater than those predicted for the United States, the burden seems to be manageable—especially when the bilateral FTA is compared with the unilateral benchmark, for which the required adjustments are substantial (table 8.8).

A final issue of concern is how the benefits of the proposed FTA are likely to be spread across different members of society. The GTAP framework deals with this issue in the Ricardian tradition, by estimating changes in the rewards to the primary factors (capital, labor, and land) used in the production process. The estimated percentage changes in real factor rewards are presented in table 8.9. In the United States, all effects are relatively minor. In Switzerland, important changes are predicted—in particular, a decline in the returns to land and natural resources, suggesting that agricultural households are likely to come under pressure from increased US agricultural exports, although again by a much smaller amount than would occur under unilateral reform.

Since the United States has recently signed several new FTAs and is considering others, it is important to consider how their presence affects our outcomes. As noted above, we consider a scenario in which the proposed Swiss-US agreement is implemented simultaneously with other current and prospective US FTAs that conceivably might enter into force by 2006, with the United States as the FTA hub (Chile, Australia, Singapore, Morocco agreed; CAFTA, SACU, and Thailand prospective). The results are presented in tables 8.10 through 8.14.

Table 8.9 CGE changes in returns to factors of production, Swiss-US FTA (percent change at constant prices)

Factor of production	United States		Switzerland	
	Free trade area	Unilateral benchmark	Free trade area	Unilateral benchmark
Land	0.6	0.2	−9.7	−40.9
Unskilled labor	−0.3	−0.1	0.1	1.8
Skilled labor	−0.3	0.0	0.1	2.0
Capital	−0.3	−0.1	0.8	2.4
Natural resources	0.2	0.7	−2.1	−7.6

Table 8.10 shows that the presence of the other FTA partners does not substantially alter the predicted changes in bilateral trade between the United States and Switzerland. However, there are substantial increases in total US trade, reflecting the broader array of trading opportunities that arise under the hub formation. Similarly, while the overall welfare effect is only slightly reduced for Switzerland, the benefits from multiple FTAs are much greater for the United States. Even so, they are still very small as a fraction of US GDP, reflecting both low initial US barriers to trade and the relatively small economic size of its current and prospective FTA partners.

Table 8.10 shows estimated regional welfare effects. Under the multiple FTA scenario, the effects on nonpartner countries are magnified, especially for NAFTA partners and EU members. However, the negative effects on nonmembers remain at small proportions to their GDP levels.

The regional trading pattern estimates in table 8.11 indicate that, when the Swiss-US FTA is considered in conjunction with other FTAs, the volume of bilateral trade between other US partners and Switzerland is significantly reduced. This happens because the hub-and-spoke structure does not eliminate barriers between Switzerland and the other US partners.

While estimated changes in the sectoral pattern of trade (tables 8.12 and 8.13) are not significantly different from those already discussed (tables 8.7 and 8.8), there are some differences in the volume of total US trade, especially in animal products, dairy, food, and textiles. However, tables 8.12 and 8.13 indicate that a large fraction of the projected trade changes are redirection, and production changes remain relatively small.

Summing Up

The quantitative results from the gravity and CGE models presented in this chapter offer two useful views of the economic prospects of a Swiss-US

Table 8.10 CGE changes for key variables, all US FTAs

Key variable	United States	Switzerland	Chile	Australia	Singapore	Morocco	CAFTA	SACU	Thailand
Import value (percent)	0.8	1.8	2.8	1.6	1.4	9.4	11.3	7.4	3.1
From partner(s)	38.6	31.7	36.8	17.9	1.9	143.6	53.3	48.7	53.2
From rest of world	-1.3	-2.1	-4.7	-2.1	1.3	0.1	-1.9	3.9	-2.6
Export value (percent)	1.7	1.0	1.5	0.7	2.3	-3.5	7.7	-1.6	1.1
To partner(s)	27.3	12.1	9.7	14.5	9.2	12.6	41.4	65.1	22.0
To rest of world	-0.4	-0.8	-0.4	-1.1	0.9	-5.3	-14.0	-7.9	-4.6
Tariff revenue (millions of dollars)	-2,596	-819	-241	-421	0	-153	-922	-20	-658
From partner(s)	-2,246	-324	-189	-333	0	-85	-844	-25	-444
From rest of world	-350	-494	-52	-88	0	-68	-77	6	-214
Welfare (percent of GDP)	0.0	0.0	0.2	0.0	-0.3	0.8	1.8	1.6	0.6
Total welfare effects (equivalent variation, millions of dollars)	1,137	53	141	132	-219	261	1,820	156	651
Allocative efficiency	6	-40	37	-24	-206	138	806	66	-154
Terms of trade	1,131	93	104	156	-13	123	1,013	90	805

Table 8.11 CGE changes in the regional pattern of exports, all US FTAs

Country/region	Initial value (billions of dollars)			Free trade area (percent change)		
	Total	To the United States	To Switzerland	Total	To the United States	To Switzerland
Australia	72.3	8.6	0.4	0.7	14.5	-7.3
Brazil	67.8	16.0	0.5	0.0	-0.4	-3.3
Central America	34.1	13.4	0.3	7.7	41.4	-20.0
Chile	21.7	4.0	0.1	1.5	9.7	-5.6
China	379.6	108.4	1.5	-0.2	-1.0	-3.3
Eastern Europe	340.8	24.3	5.8	0.0	-0.4	-0.8
European Union	2,477.9	287.1	62.6	0.0	-0.3	-1.8
Hong Kong	98.2	20.4	0.9	-0.1	-1.5	-4.3
Japan	448.8	123.9	2.0	0.0	0.1	-0.5
Morocco	11.2	1.1	0.1	-3.5	12.6	-9.7
New Zealand	18.1	2.8	0.1	-0.1	-0.7	-20.6
Rest of EFTA	66.4	7.8	0.4	0.0	0.0	-3.4
Rest of South America	119.7	33.5	1.3	-0.1	-0.6	-1.5
SACU	6.2	0.5	0.0	-1.6	65.1	-10.4
South Korea	175.4	37.2	0.6	-0.1	-0.5	-0.5

Switzerland	107.0	14.7	—	1.0	12.1	—
Taiwan	135.7	36.1	0.5	-0.1	-0.4	-0.4
Rest of world	507.5	99.8	3.5	-0.1	-1.1	-4.7
Indonesia	68.0	11.4	0.2	-0.1	-2.2	-1.0
Malaysia	124.4	24.0	0.3	0.0	-0.4	-2.3
Philippines	37.9	11.5	0.1	0.0	-1.1	-3.5
Singapore	110.4	17.8	0.5	2.3	9.2	-6.5
Thailand	79.4	17.2	0.5	1.1	22.0	-8.3
Vietnam	15.3	1.4	0.1	0.0	-1.1	-1.3
All ASEAN	435.3	83.4	1.7	0.8	5.9	-5.1
Canada	265.3	198.2	0.6	-0.1	-0.1	-3.3
Mexico	164.3	129.5	0.5	0.0	-0.1	-2.2
United States	881.8	—	10.8	1.7	—	31.3
All NAFTA	1,311.4	327.8	11.9	1.1	-0.1	28.3
All world	6,835.1	1,250.9	94.1	0.3	0.8	1.8

EFTA = European Free Trade Association
SACU = Southern African Customs Union

Source: Initial data from the GTAP6 database (Dimaranan and McDougall 2005). Estimates from simulation results.

Table 8.12 CGE changes in the sectoral pattern of exports, all US FTAs

| | United States | | | | | Switzerland | | | | |
| | Initial value (millions of dollars) | | Free trade area (percent change) | | Total: Unilateral benchmark (percent change) | Initial value (millions of dollars) | | Free trade area (percent change) | | Total: Unilateral benchmark (percent change) |
Sector	Total	To Switzerland	Total	To Switzerland		Total	To the United States	Total	To the United States	
Grains	9,638	8	3.0	391.5	1.5	64	0	6.3	8.4	72.9
Oil seeds	5,698	11	0.8	112.5	1.3	9	0	4.8	4.6	27.7
Plant-based fibers	2,209	4	1.0	-1.2	5.4	50	0	1.1	6.2	9.0
Other crops	8,062	57	1.0	20.3	2.1	205	7	3.8	34.0	30.8
Raw animal products	12,287	32	8.5	2,869.1	2.0	118	8	24.4	28.6	111.2
Wool	9	0	-1.5	-3.9	13.5	3	0	2.4	18.0	19.6
Forestry	1,254	3	-0.1	2.4	1.2	129	0	0.3	14.0	1.3
Coal, oil, and gas	4,246	2	1.3	9.1	2.9	57	0	0.9	2.3	4.4
Dairy products	802	2	42.1	11,723.2	2.5	361	35	40.2	339.6	31.1
Other food products	19,615	123	3.7	104.3	1.2	1,888	102	2.2	28.6	13.7
Textiles and clothing	19,337	65	20.4	60.9	8.8	2,180	172	4.8	69.4	-0.1
Wood products	8,212	17	2.2	11.3	1.7	823	27	0.0	4.6	-1.0
Paper products	20,031	88	1.5	25.7	0.9	2,001	78	-0.5	1.3	-1.5
Chemicals	117,946	1,451	1.6	3.0	1.5	24,126	2,797	0.4	11.5	-1.8
Ferrous metals	6,932	36	0.4	7.4	0.9	994	36	-0.2	9.8	-1.6
Nonferrous metals	11,379	223	0.7	0.0	2.7	5,626	465	-0.6	3.4	-1.7
Metal products	14,857	52	1.6	15.5	1.3	2,823	276	1.6	23.0	-1.9
Motor vehicles	108,533	597	1.1	3.1	1.4	2,068	336	0.0	3.4	-1.7
Electronic equipment	110,550	514	0.2	0.5	2.9	2,901	408	-1.0	-0.3	-2.7
Machinery and equipment	165,096	1,241	1.2	2.7	2.5	30,230	3,939	0.2	8.3	-2.3
Other manufactures	15,588	2,029	11.8	72.3	3.6	4,739	659	1.8	10.9	1.4
Nontraded services	4,083	16	-0.1	0.2	1.8	2,715	20	-0.9	-0.8	-1.7
Traded services	215,394	4,240	0.2	9.9	11.2	22,898	5,316	2.3	12.9	12.2

Source: Initial data from the GTAP6 database (Dimaranan and McDougall 2005). Estimates from simulation results.

Table 8.13   CGE changes in the sectoral pattern of production, all US FTAs (percent change at constant prices)

Sector	United States	Switzerland	Chile	Australia	Singapore	Morocco	CAFTA	SACU	Thailand
Grains	1.0	-0.7	0.9	-0.9	0.7	-4.3	-8.4	-8.8	-1.4
Oil seeds	0.2	-1.1	0.7	0.1	0.1	-3.0	-3.7	-5.6	-5.2
Plant-based fibers	0.3	1.3	0.8	0.2	0.3	-0.6	6.5	30.5	6.0
Other crops	-0.1	1.7	1.6	0.0	0.5	-1.2	-3.5	-5.3	0.7
Raw animal products	0.6	-6.4	0.8	1.6	1.5	0.6	-0.9	-4.7	-0.7
Wool	-0.8	2.7	1.1	-1.3	1.3	-0.2	3.8	-2.6	11.6
Forestry	0.1	-0.1	0.6	-0.2	0.9	10.4	-5.0	-4.7	-4.3
Coal, oil, and gas	0.0	0.0	0.3	-0.4	4.7	-15.2	-14.0	-8.6	-1.6
Dairy products	0.4	2.8	2.8	-0.3	3.7	-5.1	-4.5	-10.6	-2.3
Other food products	0.2	-0.1	0.8	0.5	1.7	-0.4	-2.9	-3.0	-0.3
Textiles and clothing	0.3	2.8	1.4	0.6	29.7	-0.1	40.2	42.7	19.1
Wood products	0.1	-0.4	1.5	-0.8	4.1	-1.0	-13.2	-5.4	-8.1
Paper products	0.1	-0.3	-0.5	-0.4	2.9	-4.5	-7.4	-6.9	-2.8
Chemicals	0.2	0.0	0.9	-0.6	4.4	-2.4	-7.3	-3.9	-2.5
Ferrous metals	0.1	0.0	0.7	-0.8	3.4	-1.4	-14.6	-3.7	-3.3
Nonferrous metals	0.1	-0.6	2.1	-1.7	3.9	-4.5	-21.4	8.4	-4.4
Metal products	0.1	0.7	0.8	-0.5	3.3	-0.7	-11.7	0.5	-5.2
Motor vehicles	0.1	0.4	0.7	-0.6	4.1	1.6	-6.7	-3.5	-0.9
Electronic equipment	-0.1	-0.7	-4.6	-0.7	1.9	-4.9	-23.7	0.6	-4.8
Machinery and equipment	0.2	0.0	0.4	-1.2	5.1	-1.3	-21.0	2.4	-3.2
Other manufactures	2.8	-1.7	0.7	-0.6	3.2	-2.8	-12.6	-11.4	-4.6
Nontraded services	0.0	0.4	1.6	0.3	-0.5	10.6	4.4	13.1	2.5
Traded services	-0.1	0.1	-1.3	0.0	-1.7	-0.4	-1.4	1.3	-1.6

CAFTA = Central American Free Trade Agreement
SACU = Southern African Customs Union

Table 8.14 CGE changes in returns to factors of production, all US FTAs (percent change at constant prices)

Country	Land	Unskilled labor	Skilled labor	Capital	Natural resources
United States	2.0	−0.2	−0.2	−0.2	0.1
Switzerland	−9.6	0.1	0.1	0.8	−1.9
Chile	0.5	−0.1	−0.1	0.4	−1.8
Australia	3.4	−5.5	−8.3	1.3	0.3
Singapore	−5.3	−5.4	−9.4	12.0	−20.2
Morocco	−10.7	2.1	0.5	6.9	−18.9
CAFTA	0.1	−4.1	−4.7	−2.6	3.7
SACU	−2.4	−2.8	−6.2	2.5	−3.8
Thailand	−10.0	−3.6	−6.8	13.6	−24.4

CAFTA = Central American Free Trade Agreement
SACU = Southern African Customs Union

FTA, though importantly, the estimates from the two models concur that an FTA between Switzerland and the United States would significantly expand bilateral two-way trade between the two countries. The gravity model estimates gains of about 100 percent for total trade while the GTAP projects more modest gains of between 32 percent (US exports to Switzerland) and 12 percent (Swiss exports to the United States), averaging out to an increase of about 20 percent in bilateral two-way trade. Both models suggest that much of the expansion in bilateral trade might be focused in agriculture, as the two countries currently maintain significant protection for domestic producers of dairy, grain, livestock, and other farm products, owing to the political strength of the agriculture lobbies in both countries.

The general equilibrium estimates of the GTAP model provide additional insights into the impact of a Swiss-US FTA. Although they find little improvement in overall economic welfare,[22] they point to particular sectors of both economies that would benefit from the expansion of bilateral exports. These include the dairy, grain, oilseed, and other manufacturing sectors in the United States, and dairy, raw animal products, and select manufacturing sectors in Switzerland. As for the limited overall economic gains found by the CGE model, in important respects, this outcome likely reflects deficiencies in modeling the services sector. By contrast, sector-specific studies suggest strong positive effects from liberalizing services trade (Copenhagen Economics 2005).

---

22. It deserves mention that the GTAP protection data for manufactured goods almost exclusively refers to tariffs, even though nontariff barriers (NTBs) are often important. If the Swiss-US FTA can make a dent in these NTBs, the calculated welfare benefits will be larger.

Spillover effects arising from trade diversion under the hypothesized Swiss-US FTA would adversely impact third countries, especially China, EU members, and NAFTA partners of the United States. These effects are generally modest in magnitude, however, and in the case of the European Union and NAFTA, they largely reflect leveling of the playing field for Swiss and US exporters owing to the dilution of preferences enjoyed by competing Canadian and Mexican exporters in the US market, and EU exporters in the Swiss market.

The essential point of the models is that a Swiss-US FTA would very likely benefit both parties. However, the spillover effects are not without their political consequences. It is thus worth examining what the consequences might be for Switzerland, as a landlocked country surrounded by members of the European Union. This is taken up in the next chapter.

9

Swiss Relations with the European Union

Switzerland is a landlocked nation surrounded by four European Union members, including three of its largest economies: Germany, France, and Italy. Given this geographical reality, the European Union currently plays a preponderant role in Swiss trade flows and policy. For the same reason, Swiss-EU trade relations will continue to occupy a central place in Bern's thinking, even if a Swiss-US free trade agreement (FTA) becomes a reality.

This chapter considers the implications of a Swiss-US FTA for Bern's relationship with the European Union. Bern-Brussels trade relations have a long and peculiar history that is essential background for understanding the likely impact of a Swiss-US FTA. Hence, this chapter begins with a brief discussion of the main postwar steps in Swiss-EU trade ties. To explore the possible consequences of a Swiss-US FTA, we stress the political economy logic that guided the relationship. The final section considers specific problems and speculates on their outcome.

In short, we argue that a Swiss-US FTA will not cause major difficulties in Swiss-EU trade relations. Three central reasons support this stance. First, through 50 years of bilateral negotiations, the European Union has already obtained almost all of the market access it wants from Switzerland. Major barriers remain only in farm trade, but here the lack of reciprocal market access is firmly supported by the "body politic" in both Bern and Brussels. Second, except in agriculture, Swiss most favored nation (MFN) tariffs are low, so the margin of preference extended to US firms will be modest. Third, the Swiss market is a relative minor concern to EU exporters, so the modest erosion of EU preferential access implied by a Swiss-US FTA is unlikely to cause a severe backlash in Brussels.

Historical Perspective

Even today, World War II continues to shape intra-European trade relations. Its massive death and destruction, following on the heels of devastation from World War I, radically altered attitudes in Europe. All Europeans agreed that economic integration was critical to avoiding another war, but opinions differed on whether it would be enough. The Six,[1] led by France and Germany, believed that Europe's former enemies needed political as well as economic integration. Their citizens, having lived through such spectacular governmental failures, thought it was a good idea to bind their national sovereignty in supranational organizations, such as the European Coal and Steel Community (1950) and the European Economic Community (EEC, 1958). For the Swiss, the lessons of the war were exactly the opposite. Absolute national sovereignty and strict noninvolvement, they believed, were exactly what saved Switzerland from wreckage in the two world wars.

First Reaction: EFTA and the EEC

When the Six rebuffed the United Kingdom's attempt, in the late 1950s, to set up a pan-European free trade area that would include the EEC, Britain proposed creating the European Free Trade Association (EFTA), and Switzerland became a founding member in 1960.

For the next 40 years, Swiss relations with the EEC/European Union were dominated by a string of similar reactions to events decided in Brussels. The 1960s saw rapid intra-EEC and intra-EFTA trade liberalization. Discriminatory integration by the two blocs had a dramatic effect on trade patterns. The EEC's share of trade with itself rose from 30 to 50 percent,[2] while the share of EEC imports from other European nations stagnated or fell. This discrimination meant lost profit opportunities for exporters in both groups, but since the EEC market was more than twice the size of EFTA's, and growing faster, the EEC was far more attractive to exporting firms. This generated new political economy forces within the EFTA nations, forces that pushed for EEC membership.

The United Kingdom was the first domino to fall. Despite the United Kingdom's leading role in creating EFTA, its government reacted to new trade pressures by applying for EEC membership in 1961. Three more dominos fell

---

1. The European Six, original members of the European Economic Community, are Germany, France, Italy, Netherlands, Belgium, and Luxembourg.

2. See Baldwin and Wyplosz (2004). Chapter 5 gives details, while chapter 1 provides a broader historical perspective.

immediately.[3] If the United Kingdom were to jump to the EEC customs union, exporters in the remaining EFTA nations would face discrimination in even more markets. In reaction, Ireland, Denmark and Norway—nations that had found it politically optimal to avoid EEC membership in 1958—also applied in 1961. But Switzerland, which wished to maintain its political neutrality in the escalating Cold War, decided to stay with EFTA.[4]

Second Reaction: Swiss-EU FTA

When the EEC finally enlarged in 1973, many more dominos fell. The impending UK accession, which would heighten discriminatory effects facing Swiss exporters, created further political economy forces. Exporters in Switzerland and the other remaining EFTA nations pushed their governments to sign bilateral FTAs with the EEC in 1973.

This second Swiss reaction set the pattern that governs Swiss-EU relations today. In retrospect, we can discern three salient points. Any EU initiative that threatens important new discrimination for Swiss exporters elicits a Swiss reaction, but Bern follows and Brussels leads. The Swiss reaction addresses the new economic realities in a way that minimizes political integration. Finally, agriculture is excluded by mutual agreement. Neither the EU members nor the Swiss have ever shown as great an interest in freer trade in food products as the United States has. Instead, both sides are happy to forgo reciprocal market access in exchange for a free hand on farm policy.

As part of this reactive pattern, Switzerland has been in a relationship that might be called a "virtual FTA union" with the European Union for the last 40 years. Each time the European Union signs a new free trade deal with a third nation, Switzerland follows suit. Again, the domino logic prevails. The 1991 EU-Poland trade deal would have given German firms an edge over their Swiss rivals in the Polish market; this impending discrimination generated new political economy forces in Switzerland that pushed Bern into signing its own FTA with Poland under EFTA auspices.

Switzerland's list of actual and planned FTAs—negotiated under the EFTA umbrella with its partners, Norway, Iceland, and Liechtenstein—is similar to the European Union's list. Like the European Union, EFTA partners have negotiated agreements with Bulgaria, Chile, Croatia, Israel, Jordan, Macedonia, Mexico, Morocco, the Palestinian Authority, Romania, Singapore, Tunisia, and Turkey.[5] Unlike the European Union, however,

---

3. See Baldwin (1994, 1995, 2005b) for details on the "domino theory of regionalism."

4. See Nell (1994) for a more extensive review of Swiss-EU trade relations.

5. An FTA with Lebanon has been signed, but has not entered into force.

EFTA has already concluded an FTA with Singapore, which is in force, and has recently completed negotiations with South Korea. EFTA is also negotiating with Canada and Thailand, and exploratory talks are under way with Japan. None of these countries are EU partners yet.

The Swiss-US FTA would be exceptional as the first Swiss FTA separate from its EFTA partners. In the past, apart from its bilateral FTAs with the European Union and the Faroe Islands, Switzerland has negotiated FTA pacts as part of the EFTA group.

Third Reaction: The EEA and Bilateral Accords

Switzerland's reactive pattern toward FTAs was tested when the European Union decided to radically deepen its goods and factor market integration with its Single European Act of 1986. To redress the impending discrimination, Switzerland joined the other EFTA nations in negotiating the European Economic Area (EEA) agreement. This arrangement extended the Single Market to the EFTA nations; as usual, political integration was minimized and agriculture largely excluded.

The EEA negotiations were long and difficult, since the depth of the economic integration was unprecedented in the world of commercial diplomacy. When talks were launched, nonagricultural tariffs and quotas had been gone for two decades. The negotiations concerned the free movement of capital and labor, as well as behind-the-border trade measures that were previously viewed as purely national concerns. Given the diffuse and ever-changing nature of behind-the-border barriers, extending the Single Market to EFTA would require surveillance and enforcement mechanisms akin to the European Commission and the EU Court of Justice.

The lessons from the EEA talks for the EFTA nations were crystal clear. Truly deep economic integration was almost impossible without some form of political integration. The real options facing the EFTA nations were either to accept hegemonic authority from Brussels on Single Market matters—retaining the ultimate ability to say "no" on particular issues, but only at the cost of jeopardizing the whole relationship—or to join the European Union.

This realization, in conjunction with the end of the Cold War in the early 1990s, convinced the Swiss government that joining the European Union was the best way to redress the impending discrimination of the Single Market. Indeed, by the end of EEA talks, all of the EFTA nations except Iceland and Liechtenstein came to the same conclusion.[6]

However, despite the efforts of Swiss political leaders, Swiss voters rejected the EEA agreement in a referendum held in December 1992. Brus-

---

6. Iceland's dependence on fishing and Liechtenstein's on private banking both reduced the impact of being outside the EU circle and increased the cost of joining, given the European Union's questionable Common Fishery Policy and its negative attitude towards bank secrecy.

sels took this vote as a rejection of membership, and Swiss accession talks never started. In essence, Swiss citizens did not share their government's conclusions that truly deep economic integration required political integration, or that the best form of political integration was membership.

The adverse 1992 referendum has dominated Swiss-EU relations ever since. Bern has struggled to redress the Single Market's discriminatory effects by negotiating a string of bilateral agreements with the European Union. As always, these have minimized political integration and included only limited concessions on agriculture. The modest opening of Swiss-EU food trade was driven by the outcome of the WTO's Uruguay Round.

From Reactive to Proactive

Switzerland's reactive stance is not unusual. Small nations around the world tend to depend heavily on a single dominant trade partner, and accordingly, their trade policies are typically shaped by that relationship.

Historically, this political economy reality has led to hub-and-spoke bilateralism. In North America and Europe, one sees many bilateral FTAs between economically small nations and the dominant economy (the United States or the European Union). An Asian hub-and-spoke system also seems to be emerging, but it appears to have two hubs, China and Japan (Baldwin 2003, 2005a).

In recent years, however, some of the "spokes" have shifted from reactive to proactive trade policies. Mexico, which is even more dependent on the US market than Switzerland is on the EU market, provides the classic example of this "anti-spoke" strategy (Baldwin 2005a). It has signed an impressive list of FTAs in recent years, two of which—with the European Union and Japan—stand out in sharp contrast to standard practice. By signing these FTAs, Mexico broke free of the traditional hub-and-spoke pattern, whereby the commercial policies of small spoke economy are narrowly focused on the dominant hub economy. Having FTAs with the world's three largest economies means that Mexico now probably has the best market access in the world from the standpoint of tariff barriers confronting its exports. Of course, trade barriers are only one component of locational competitiveness, but Mexico has used its trade policy to maximize this component. Singapore has followed a similar strategy.

The Swiss-US FTA is the most important but not the only plank in the new proactive Swiss FTA strategy. Through EFTA, Switzerland has already concluded an FTA with Singapore that is in force. Negotiations have recently been concluded with South Korea and are also under way, at different stages, with Canada and Thailand. Finally, exploratory talks are taking place with Japan.

In considering the EU reaction to a Swiss-US FTA, it is useful to examine the US view of Mexico's anti-spoke strategy. The United States has not reacted negatively to Mexican initiatives, for four main reasons. First, given that market access is power in an FTA negotiation, the uneven market sizes meant that the United States obtained almost everything it wanted in direct market access through the North American Free Trade Agreement (NAFTA). Second, Japan and the European Union are relatively minor players in the Mexican market. Third, while the Mexican market is important, it is not a priority for most US exporters. Fourth, since Mexican MFN tariffs are now modest, US preference margins in the Mexican market were correspondingly limited in the post-NAFTA era. What all these considerations mean is that the erosion of US preferences arising from Mexico's new FTAs has caused little concern to US exporters.

Would the European Union Object to a Swiss-US FTA?

The Swiss-US FTA can be viewed as part of a strategy akin to what Mexico has pursued. A trade deal with the United States would reduce Swiss dependence on EU policy, while simultaneously improving Swiss market access to the world's largest economy. There are, however, two important factors that might make a Swiss anti-spoke strategy more of a problem for the European Union than the Mexican strategy is for the United States.

First, the European Union is a customs union with a single external tariff, while NAFTA creates a free trade area in which each partner can set its own tariffs on third-country imports. If Switzerland ever joined the European Union, it would have to withdraw from the Swiss-US FTA, unless a US-EU FTA was negotiated in the meantime, which seems remote at this point. This could pose a problem for a future Swiss government and the European Union; after all, the Swiss application to join the European Union is frozen, but it has not been withdrawn.

Second, a Swiss-US FTA would create substantial preferences in agricultural goods. Swiss MFN tariffs for manufacturing are already very low, so the Swiss-US FTA would imply very little preference erosion for EU industrial firms selling into Switzerland. The story is quite different in food trade. Swiss MFN barriers on agriculture are some of the highest in the world. If the Swiss-US FTA lowered these barriers substantially, US food exporters might take a sizeable share of the Swiss market at the expense of third-nation exporters, including EU exporters.

This development could prove to be a problem for the European Union; however, it is unlikely to become a major issue. Unlike US agribusiness, the EU farm sector does not have a tradition of aggressively pushing for better market access. To a large extent, this commercial policy stance follows from the Common Agricultural Policy (CAP), which entails domestic price floors for most major export commodities; in turn, this means that improved foreign market access only indirectly benefits EU farmers. Better export access mainly shows up in lower export subsidies, and thus, lower EU budgetary costs. Given the indirect nature of this link, EU farm organizations have never invested heavily in lobbying for improved foreign market access. Indeed, the European Union has shown a willingness, even an eagerness, to exclude agriculture from the dozens of FTAs that it has concluded with third countries.

These features, combined with the fact that the Swiss market is a minor outlet for EU farm exporters, suggests that preferential access for US farmers would not elicit a major reaction from Brussels. As in US-Mexican relations, lopsided market size has allowed the European Union to obtain almost all of the market access in Switzerland that it wanted. Swiss-EU agricultural trade barriers remain high to this day, but largely because the European Union is content with that arrangement.

Indirect Effects on Political Forces

Swiss trade policy is driven mainly by the struggle between protrade and antitrade forces inside Switzerland. The size and political power of protrade and antitrade groups are, however, affected by Swiss trade policy. In light of the "juggernaut theory of trade liberalization" (Baldwin 1994; Baldwin and Wypolsz 2004), it is worth considering the indirect impact of a Swiss-US FTA on the political forces that will guide future Swiss liberalization with the European Union and more broadly.

Again, the Mexican example provides useful insight. Up until the late 1980s and early 1990s, Mexico followed a classic import-substitution policy: Tariffs were extreme, and not until 1986 could President Miguel de la Madrid lead a reluctant Mexico into the General Agreement on Tariffs and Trade (GATT). NAFTA, launched by President Carlos Salinas in 1992, changed all of this.[7] Once NAFTA was implemented in 1994, Mexico had zero tariffs on three-quarters of its imports. Moreover, because the United States and Canada have very low MFN tariffs, from Mexico's perspective, NAFTA was not much different than unilateral free trade with the world.

In textbook fashion, NAFTA's liberalization caused massive restructuring in Mexico. By the late 1990s, almost all Mexican firms that would be harmed by MFN free trade had already been driven out by bilateral free trade. The US-Mexico bilateral arrangement—the heart of NAFTA—changed the array of protrade and antitrade forces inside Mexico to substantially lower the political cost to the Mexican government of further liberalization. The Mexican government might have followed Adam Smith's counsel to pursue unilateral free trade, but Mexico devised what it considered to be a superior strategy: It improved market access for its own firms by signing

---

7. For a detailed account of NAFTA, see Hufbauer and Schott (2005).

FTAs with every important country. Simplifying to make the point, NAFTA started a juggernaut rolling across the Mexican political scene, crushing most internal opposition to further liberalization.

The Swiss-US FTA may have a similar effect in Switzerland. The main opposition to further MFN liberalization is the Swiss farm sector. If a Swiss-US FTA brings about substantial cuts in Swiss farm protection, the result will be a restructuring that ultimately shifts the balance of power towards the protrade camp. This political economy shift is likely to make the future liberalization of Swiss-EU farm trade much easier than otherwise. Although this scenario involves a good deal of abstract reasoning, it does provide an argument that a Swiss-US FTA will ultimately improve EU access to the Swiss market.

10

Conclusions

This report has identified both benefits and obstacles to a Swiss-US free trade agreement (FTA). Our central message is that an FTA can be highly worthwhile for both parties, but requires a strong commitment to surmount entrenched interests. The size of potential benefits is directly related to the capacity of each government to liberalize trade and investment more than either has done before. Policy officials need to not only make path-breaking concessions at the negotiating table, but also build persuasive coalitions for liberalization at home.[1]

The US trade promotion authority (TPA) expires in June 2007. Without that authority, it will be almost impossible for the United States to negotiate and ratify a free trade pact with Switzerland. For the United States, as for Switzerland and most other countries, the major trade event over the next 18 months is completing the World Trade Organization (WTO) Doha Development Round. In practical terms, that means the Swiss-US FTA must be agreed by late 2006, so that it can be brought to Congress either shortly before, or as a companion to, the Doha Round package. The contentious debate over ratification of the Central American–Dominican Republic Free Trade Agreement (CAFTA-DR) will not be repeated with Switzerland, as none of the labor or environmental issues that featured so prominently will be present, but some congressmen and senators may oppose it because of difficult commercial issues.

On the Swiss side, two aspects will attract considerable political notice and very likely spark a referendum. One of those is the liberalization of

---

1. We use the term "concession" in the time-honored sense of mercantilism. In this sense, nearly all trade and investment concessions benefit the country that makes them.

agriculture, even if phased in over the working life of today's farmers. The other is the precedent of a stand-alone agreement with the United States, outside of the framework of the European Free Trade Association (EFTA), and as a counterpart to Switzerland's strong economic ties to the European Union. Swiss leaders will need to persuade the population that the benefits of an FTA with the United States, especially the spur to investment and growth, justify a departure from traditional ways of managing a prosperous but lethargic economy.

Strong Links, Similar Values, Large Benefits

The United States is Switzerland's most important economic partner after the European Union. On a number of political economy criteria (summarized in chapter 1), Switzerland ranks at or near the top of partners that the United States is considering for new FTA pacts. To be sure, on national security grounds, Switzerland ranks low in the US queue, like most non-Muslim countries. However, as the US-Chile and US-Singapore FTAs as well as CAFTA-DR attest, national security is not the only touchstone for launching or concluding US FTAs. Commercial relations between Switzerland and the United States rest firmly on large investment holdings, substantial two-way flows of business services, and significant bilateral merchandise trade.[2] As leading advocates of market capitalism, Switzerland and the United States are well situated to conclude an FTA that breaks new ground in dismantling barriers.

Calculations based on gravity and computable general equilibrium (CGE) models, reported in chapter 8, suggest that a Swiss-US FTA could augment bilateral merchandise trade flows by between 20 percent (CGE model) and 100 percent (gravity model). The CGE model calculates a very modest increase in two-way services trade of about 12 percent, but this figure probably reflects limitations in modeling services trade and estimating the height of barriers. Gravity models of foreign direct investment (FDI), surveyed in chapter 7, suggest that a free trade area might increase the stock of FDI in Switzerland by some 40 percent, giving a strong push to Swiss technology and trade in services and manufactured goods.

Although the CGE calculates that the projected increase in two-way trade would lead to negligible changes in US and Swiss GDP levels, we are skeptical of this result for Switzerland. The modeling framework does not reflect the benefits of adopting improved technology in the wake of more intense competition, the exit of less-efficient firms, and greater scale and network economies. Based on alternative methodologies, also summarized in chapter 8, the annual GDP gains to each partner from expanded trade could

---

2. Two-way FDI and portfolio investment levels, as well as two-way merchandise trade flows, are well above the norm predicted by gravity models of trade and investment.

be on the order of $1.1 billion. For Switzerland, this amounts to a permanent gain of about 0.5 percent of GDP. The abovementioned expansion of inward FDI stock, perhaps by 40 percent, would add significantly to this figure.

Other benefits, hard to model but no less important, could flow from a forward-looking Swiss-US FTA. The pact might push agricultural reform both in the European Union and the United States. And it might influence, in a positive way, the multilateral agenda for liberalizing trade in services, government procurement, and other areas.

Answering the Skeptics

If launched, undertaking an FTA will require reasoned responses to skeptics. In chapters 1 and 9, we addressed three systemic concerns, first, that a bilateral FTA might impede progress on the WTO Doha Round. In our view, this argument invokes a false dichotomy. Swiss-US FTA negotiations should not drain the resources of the US trade representative's office. A Swiss-US FTA should fully comply with Article 24 of the General Agreement on Tariffs and Trade (GATT), which requires that states eliminate barriers on substantially all the merchandise trade between the partners. To be sure, we have recommended 20-year phaseouts for barriers on sensitive agricultural products, twice as long as the agreed norm in the WTO's 1994 Understanding on the Interpretation of Article 24. In light of the practice already established in multiple FTAs, we believe a fair review would conclude that the standards of Article 24 are met if these long phaseouts are accompanied by our WTO-plus recommendations in other areas.

Nonetheless, we recommend that Switzerland and the United States invite the director general of the WTO to appoint an independent group of experts to critique the agreement for its consistency with the text and spirit of Article 24. This independent review would be additional to the customary Article 24 reviews by government representatives, which in virtually all cases—including past FTAs entered into by the United States and EFTA—have led to inconclusive findings.[3] The independent review should not only critique the new FTA, but also suggest appropriate remedies, or even compensation to other WTO members, to the extent that the agreement falls short.

In some areas, the Swiss-US FTA could set a benchmark for WTO agreements in the Doha Round and subsequent multilateral agreements, and go beyond the minimal requirements of Article 24. Topics for pathbreaking provisions include eliminating barriers to services trade, including movement of skilled personnel; new rules on geographical indications (GIs) and government procurement; and very liberal rules of origin.

---

3. See Sutherland et al. (2004) for an acid critique of the banal nature of past Article 24 reviews.

A second systemic concern is that a Swiss-US FTA would simply add to the "spaghetti bowl" of preferential trade agreements, numbering some 300 concluded and proposed (Sutherland et al. 2004), that critics claim are eroding the multilateral trading system. If the GATT/WTO system could have achieved liberalization equivalent to that of the "strong" bilateral and regional agreements, the FTA process would be rightly deplored. But the postwar history of trade negotiations does not suggest that equivalent liberalization was remotely possible. A worthwhile Swiss-US FTA will go far beyond the achievements of the Doha Round, and could in fact set a model for diminishing the "spaghetti bowl" problem through liberal rules of origin. Moreover, most of the trade diversion resulting from a Swiss-US FTA can be categorized as preference dilution, since the new agreement would create a more level playing field between existing partners (EU and NAFTA members) and the new partner (the United States or Switzerland).[4]

A third systemic concern, which seems to be fading from the public debate anyway, concerns the formation of "hub-and-spoke" systems and supraregional trading blocs with political as well as economic dimensions. Obviously a Swiss-US FTA would do nothing to consolidate supraregional blocs in Europe or the Western Hemisphere; quite the opposite. By the same token, however, as spelled out in chapter 9, a Swiss-US FTA has the character of a "reverse-hub-and-spoke" agreement, alleviating the commercial disadvantages that confront a small "spoke" country (in this case, Switzerland).

Managing Agriculture

Agriculture is by far the toughest area, both from the standpoint of negotiations and adjustment. Chapters 2 and 3 showed that difficult issues spring not only from the extremely high tariffs and strict tariff-rate quotas (TRQs), but also from certain sanitary and phytosanitary (SPS) measures as well as different ideas about the protection of GIs. The combined result of various barriers is that agricultural trade between the United States and Switzerland remains well below potential.

The gravity and CGE models suggest that completely eliminating agricultural barriers would more than double two-way trade, increasing each partner's exports by more than a billion dollars annually. In previous negotiations, through EFTA or on its own, Switzerland has liberalized agricultural trade to a very limited extent, using a "positive list" approach. This

---

4. A more general observation can be made: Since many FTAs are already in existence, each new FTA that has a major country as one partner is likely to level the playing field in a way that adds to global economic efficiency. As a major country's network of FTAs expands, the list of "outsiders" grows shorter and shorter, as does the prospect of harmful trade diversion when an additional country is added to the FTA roster.

would not be an acceptable modus operandi for a Swiss-US FTA. However, as chapter 2 points out, prior US FTAs have always allowed for long phaseouts, a very limited number of exceptions through TRQs, and special safeguards on the path to eventually eliminating agricultural barriers. The US-Morocco FTA has small TRQs and no phaseout periods for at least four product categories. The same is true for CAFTA-DR for sugar imports by the United States.

SPS standards are closely related to agricultural trade. While ostensibly designed to ensure animal and human health, at times, SPS measures can amount to nontariff barriers. Some issues are best left to the WTO, but others can be addressed in the Swiss-US FTA. Chapter 3 recommends that the United States and Switzerland incorporate the best elements of their respective SPS agreements with Australia and the European Union into the Swiss-US FTA. They should also create a standing group of senior government officials to promote the convergence of SPS standards and, where possible, resolve current and future disagreements.

Chapter 3 also examines how the United States and Switzerland use GIs to protect certain sectors through "branding." Like the United States, Switzerland applies a strong regime of intellectual property protection, but Swiss authorities believe that the current US system does not adequately protect holders of GI rights. A forward-looking agreement should endorse "state of the art protection"—to borrow Ambassador Zoellick's expression—or all forms of intellectual property, including GIs. The United States should certify appropriate Swiss agricultural goods as "distinctive products," and support Switzerland's position in WTO talks.

Finally, and critically important to enlist domestic support, the Swiss-US FTA should contain special safeguard provisions for agriculture, accompanied by meaningful adjustment programs for adversely affected workers, firms, and communities. Robust assistance will be necessary to manage the transition from extreme protection to freer trade, especially in beef, pork, dairy products, cereals, oilseeds, and sugar.

Expanding Trade in Manufactures

More than 95 percent of merchandise trade between the United States and Switzerland involves manufactured products. While the vast majority of manufactures trade enters free or pays only nuisance tariffs, the remaining high tariffs catalogued in chapter 4 still restrict trade in a number of products. Moreover, eliminating even nuisance tariffs can spark commerce, as industrial firms can then rationalize production and invest in new facilities with no fear of trade barriers.

The gravity model reported in chapter 8 suggests that a Swiss-US FTA could more than double two-way manufactures trade, while the CGE model suggests an expansion of about 20 percent. Market access negotiations for manufactured products should be smooth, and most tariffs should be eliminated immediately. Longer phaseouts will be necessary for the most sensitive products. The Swiss-US FTA could further contribute to seamless global production by adopting liberal rules of origin (especially with respect to cumulation and certification) by giving greater scope for mutual recognition of standards and permitting more self-assessment.

Services: The Future of International Trade

Both the United States and Switzerland recognize the crucial role of services as a source of sustained competitiveness and export expansion. Barriers remain, but both countries have affirmed their intention to further liberalize their service sectors. Chapter 5 documents the barriers that affect financial services, network industries, the audiovisual sector, and professional personnel. In its FTAs with Singapore and Australia, the United States negotiated WTO-plus provisions that the Swiss-US FTA could readily adopt. But the Swiss agreement should go further and set a higher standard: In particular, it should extend unconditional most favored nation (MFN) rights with respect to services, advance the process of mutual recognition of educational and professional credentials, and extend national treatment to responsible insurance firms based in each country.

Government Procurement

Opening government procurement in Switzerland and the United States would make public spending more efficient and set a useful precedent for WTO negotiations. The WTO Government Procurement Agreement (GPA), signed by both countries, does not cover all federal procurement in either nation. Moreover, Switzerland reserved its application of the GPA to US firms in important sectors, arguing that the United States had not given equivalent access to Swiss firms. The Swiss-US FTA is a new opportunity for reciprocal extension of GPA benefits to firms in both countries. Both countries should extend their federal procurement coverage, offering the best terms negotiated in prior FTAs and enhancing access for research and development as well as transportation and utility services.

Further, the FTA should include initiatives to open more US states to procurement from Swiss firms to the same extent that Swiss cantons are already open to US firms, as explained in chapter 6. The United States should seek to cover two or three "holdout" states, in addition to states that have previously agreed to GPA or FTA procurement provisions.[5]

---

5. As an aside, the CGE model reported in chapter 8 does not attempt to reflect barriers on government procurement. Meaningful liberalization of these highly protected purchases could make a significant addition to the calculated trade and welfare gains.

Investment

Investment is the bedrock of Swiss-US commercial relations, and the synergy between direct investment and trade is now widely recognized. Most of the literature endorses the idea that addressing the remaining frictions in investment relations could foster Swiss-US two-way trade.

On every investment question of global importance, Swiss and US policies are closely aligned. Still, a Swiss-US FTA would improve the investment environment. Both governments need to further liberalize sectors dominated by public monopolies, relax impediments to foreign ownership in selected sectors, allow easier access to temporary employees, and review conditions for licensing professional personnel. The FTA should proclaim the rights of private investors with respect to national treatment, and ensure appropriate compensation in the event of public taking of private property. It should also establish arbitration procedures for resolving disputes between private investors and host states, including an appellate body to ensure the consistent application of legal principles.

Swiss-EU Relations

Our penultimate chapter explored the implications of a Swiss-US FTA on Swiss-EU economic relations. Brussels will surely take notice of a US agreement with Switzerland—the first US FTA with a European country—but there are reasons to believe that the pact would not damage relations between Bern and Brussels. From a purely commercial point of view, apart from agriculture, EU producers have already obtained almost unfettered access to the Swiss market. Brussels has historically respected the Swiss tradition of operating on a different and somewhat independent commercial track. Very likely, as chapter 9 suggests, the European Union will come to view the Swiss-US FTA in the same benign light that the United States views the EU-Mexico FTA.

Wrapping Up

Our bottom line is that a Swiss-US FTA makes very good sense, if negotiated as an agreement that pushes the frontier of liberalization. The agreement can point both the United States and Europe in a different, less distorting direction for agriculture, preserving the scenic and cultural values of rural life without burdening consumers with high prices and world markets with subsidized output. The agreement can quickly reach the goal of tariff-free trade in manufactured goods, coupled with liberal rules of origin and significant progress on aligning technical standards and conformity assessment systems. The WTO General Agreement on Trade in Services (GATS) is practically an empty vessel: While the principles are strong and solid, they apply to very little trade. By contrast, the Swiss-US FTA can extend the principles quite widely, going as far as strict national treatment for foreign investors, and mutual recognition of professional degrees and certificates.

The economic payoff from these and other terms will be significant: a sharp expansion of bilateral trade, more choice and lower prices for household consumers and industrial users, and an influx of direct investment, especially in Switzerland. If the Swiss-US FTA becomes a touchstone for future trade and investment agreements, the political and economic payoff will be even larger, not only as a trade agreement between two countries, but as a model for others to follow.

APPENDICES

Appendix A

Phaseout Schedules for Agricultural Barriers in US Free Trade Agreements

This appendix describes phaseouts for 15 selected categories of agricultural products and includes a summary table of concessions on selected products across different free trade agreements (FTAs) (see table A.1). The products considered are beef; corn and corn products; cotton; dairy products; distilled spirits; fruits, vegetables, and nuts; certain grains; processed foods; peanuts; poultry; soybeans; sugar; tobacco; wheat; and wine. The information in this Appendix has been obtained entirely from official sources in the US Government that actively participate in bilateral negotiations on agriculture, mainly the United States Department of Agriculture (USDA) Foreign Agricultural Service and the United States Trade Representative (USTR).[1] We also relied on documents published by official agencies of partner countries, as well as the actual texts of the agreements.[2]

---

1. The specific US sources are NAFTA Agricultural Fact Sheets (USDA-FAS), US-Australia Free Trade Agreement: Commodity Fact Sheets (USDA-FAS), US-Central America-Dominican Republic Free Trade Agreement: Overall Agriculture Fact Sheet (USDA-FAS), US-Chile Free Trade Agreement: Commodity Fact Sheets (USDA-FAS), and US-Morocco Free Trade Agreement Agriculture Provisions (USTR). All sources are listed under references. Other sources consulted include: The Australia-US Free Trade Agreement: Advancing Australian Agricultural Exports (Australian Department of Foreign Affairs and Trade), Principales Logros y Resultados (Department of Foreign Trade of Costa Rica), and Tratado de Libre Comercio Chile-Estados Unidos (Foreign Affairs Ministry of Chile).

2. The information in this appendix is designed to give readers a better sense of the distance between the actual achievements of US trade negotiations and the pure free trade ideal. Care was taken to highlight products that tend to fall short of the ideal on both sides. The appendix, however, does not fully and systematically discuss US phaseout schedules. Readers interested in the details should consult the texts of the respective FTAs.

Table A.1 Maximum FTA phaseout terms for selected agricultural products

Product	NAFTA: United States–Mexico	United States–Australia	United States–Chile	United States–Morocco	CAFTA-DR
Beef	Mexico: IMM United States: IMM Except Mexico: Beef offal	Australia: IMM United States: TRQ→18y WTO TRQ and preferential TRQ SSG >> 18y (United States)	Chile: TRQ→4y United States: TRQ→4y	Morocco: TRQ >> 18y United States: TRQ→15y	CAFTA-6: Tariff→15y United States: TRQ→15y Except Dominican Republic: TRQs→15y
Poultry	Mexico: TRQ→10y United States: IMM	Australia: Zero United States: Tariff→4y	Chile: TRQ→10y United States: TRQ→10y SSG (Chile)	Morocco: TRQ→25y United States: Tariff→10y SSG (Morocco)	CAFTA-6: TRQ→20y United States: Zero SSG (CAFTA-6)
Turkey	Mexico: TRQ→10y United States: IMM	Australia: Zero United States: Tariff→4y	Chile: TRQ→10y United States: TRQ→10y SSG (United States, Chile)	Morocco: TRQ→19y United States: Tariff→10y SSG (Morocco)	CAFTA-6: Tariff→10y United States: Zero
Pork	Mexico: TRQ→10y United States: IMM SSG (Mexico)	Australia: Zero United States: IMM	Chile: IMM United States: IMM	Morocco: IMM	CAFTA-6: TRQ→15y United States: Zero SSG (CAFTA-6)

	Mexico / United States	Australia / United States	Chile / United States	Morocco / United States	CAFTA-6 / United States
Corn	Mexico: TRQ→15y United States: IMM	Australia: Zero United States: IMM	Chile: Tariff→4y United States: IMM	Morocco: Tariff→5y United States: IMM	CAFTA-6: TRQs >> 15y United States: Zero SSG (CAFTA-6)
Soybeans, flour, and meal	Mexico: Tariff→10y United States: IMM	Australia: IMM United States: IMM	Chile: IMM United States: IMM	Morocco: Tariff→5y United States: IMM	CAFTA-6: IMM United States: Zero
Soybean oil	Mexico: Tariff→10y United States: Tariff→4y	Australia: IMM United States: Tariff→10y	Chile: Tariff→12y United States: Tariff→12y	Morocco: Tariff→10y United States: Tariff→10y	CAFTA-6: Tariff→15y United States: Zero SSG (CAFTA-6)
Wheat	Mexico: Tariff→10y United States: Tariff→10y	Australia: Zero United States: IMM	Chile: IMM United States: IMM Except Chile: Price band→12y Wheat flour, tariff→12y SSG (Chile)	Morocco: TRQ >> 15y United States: IMM	CAFTA-6: Zero United States: Zero Except CAFTA-6: Wheat flour, tariff→12y
Rice	Mexico: Tariff→10y United States: Tariff→10y	Australia: Zero United States: IMM Except United States: Parboiled rice, tariff→4y	Chile: Tariff→12y United States: IMM SSG (Chile)	Morocco: Tariff→10y United States: IMM	CAFTA-6: TRQ→18–20y United States: Zero SSG (CAFTA-6)
Other grains	Mexico: TRQ→10y United States: IMM	Australia: Zero United States: IMM	Chile: Tariff→12y United States: IMM	Morocco: Tariff→15y United States: IMM	CAFTA-6: Tariff→15y United States: Zero

(table continues next page)

Table A.1 Maximum FTA phaseout terms for selected agricultural products (*continued*)

Product	NAFTA: United States–Mexico	United States–Australia	United States–Chile	United States–Morocco	CAFTA-DR
Nuts	Mexico: IMM United States: IMM	Australia: Zero United States: Tariff→4y	Chile: IMM United States: Tariff→4y	Morocco: Tariff→5y United States: Tariff→10y Except Morocco: TRQ almonds (15y) SSG (Morocco)	CAFTA-6: Tariff→10y United States: Zero
Peanuts and peanut butter	Mexico: Zero United States: TRQ→15y	Australia: IMM United States: TRQ→18y	Chile: Tariff→8y United States: Tariff→12y	Morocco: Tariff→10y United States: TRQ→15y	CAFTA-6: IMM United States: TRQ→15y Except Guatemala and Nicaragua: Tariff→5–10y SSG (United States)
Raw cotton	Mexico: Tariff→10y United States: TRQ→10y	Australia: Zero United States: TRQ→18y	Chile: IMM United States: Tariff→12y	Morocco: IMM United States: TRQ→15y	CAFTA-6: IMM United States: Tariff→15y
Milk products and creams	Mexico: TRQ→10y United States: TRQ→10y	Australia: IMM United States: TRQ >> 18y, same T	Chile: Tariff→8y United States: TRQ→12y	Morocco: Tariff→15y United States: TRQ→15y	CAFTA-6: TRQ→20y United States: TRQ→20y SSG (all parties)
Cheese	Mexico: Tariff→10y United States: TRQ→10y	Australia: IMM United States: TRQ >> 18y, same T	Chile: Tariff→4y United States: TRQ→12y	Morocco: Tariff→10y United States: TRQ→15y	CAFTA-6: TRQ→20y United States: TRQ→20y SSG (all parties)

	Mexico	Australia	Chile	Morocco	CAFTA-6
Butter	Mexico: n.a. United States: n.a.	Australia: IMM United States: TRQ >> 18y, same T	Chile: Tariff→ 4y United States: TRQ→ 12y	Morocco: Tariff→ 8y United States: TRQ→ 15y	CAFTA-6: TRQ→ 20y United States: TRQ→ 20y SSG (all parties)
Fruits	Mexico: Tariff→ 10y United States: TRQ→ 10y Except Mexico: TRQ apples SSG (United States, Mexico)	Australia: Zero United States: Tariff→ 18y SSG (United States)	Chile: IMM United States: Tariff→ 12y SSG (United States)	Morocco: Tariff→ 10y United States: Tariff→ 18y Except Morocco: TRQ apples SSG (United States)	CAFTA-6: Tariff→ 15y United States: Zero
Fruit juices	Mexico: TRQ→ 15y United States: TRQ→ 15y	Australia: IMM United States: Tariff→ 18y SSG (United States)	Chile: IMM United States: Tariff→ 12y SSG (United States)	Morocco: Tariff→ 10y United States: Tariff→ 15y SSG (United States)	CAFTA-6: Tariff→ 15y United States: Zero
Vegetables	Mexico: Tariff→ 10y United States: TRQ→ 10y Except Mexico: TRQ potatoes SSG (United States, Mexico)	Australia: Zero United States: Tariff→ 18y Except United States: TRQ avocados (18y) SSG (United States)	Chile: Tariff→ 8y United States: Tariff→ 12y Except United States: TRQ avocados, artichokes (12y) SSG (United States)	Morocco: Tariff→ 15y United States: Tariff→ 18y Except United States: TRQ onions, garlic, tomato products (paste, puree, sauces) (15y) SSG (United States, Morocco)	CAFTA-6: Tariff→ 15y United States: Zero Except Costa Rica: TRQ >> 20y on onions and potatoes

(table continues next page)

Table A.1 Maximum FTA phaseout terms for selected agricultural products *(continued)*

Product	NAFTA: United States–Mexico	United States–Australia	United States–Chile	United States–Morocco	CAFTA-DR
Sugar and sugar products	Mexico: TRQ→15y United States: TRQ→15y	Australia: IMM United States: No change	Chile: Tariff→12y United States: TRQ→12y	Morocco: Tariff→18y United States: TRQ→15y	CAFTA-6: TRQ→15y United States: TRQ >> 15y
Tobacco	Mexico: Tariff→10y United States: Tariff→10y	Australia: Zero United States: TRQ→18y	Chile: IMM United States: TRQ→12y	Morocco: Tariff→10y United States: TRQ→15y	CAFTA-6: Tariff→15y United States: TRQ→15y
Distilled spirits and beer	Mexico: Tariff→8y United States: Tariff→10y	Australia: IMM United States: Tariff→18y	Chile: Tariff→2y United States: Tariff→12y	Morocco: Tariff→15y United States: Tariff→15y	CAFTA-6: Tariff→15y United States: Zero
Wine	Mexico: Tariff→10y United States: Tariff→10y	Australia: IMM United States: Tariff→11y	Chile: Tariff→12y United States: Tariff→12y	Morocco: Tariff→10y United States: Tariff→11y	CAFTA-6: Tariff→10y United States: Zero

n.a. = not available

TRQ→18y: Tariff-rate quotas (TRQs) will be eliminated in 18 years (numbers vary).

Tariff→8y: Tariffs to be phased out in 8 years (numbers vary).

Same T: In-quota tariff will remain at pre-FTA rate.

IMM: Immediate duty-free treatment.

Zero: Zero duty before FTA.

SSG: Country retains right to invoke special safeguards.

TRQ, SSG, tariffs >> 18y : TRQ (or special safeguards or tariffs) will outlive 18-year phaseout period (numbers vary).

Except: Product exception to the phaseout.

Sources: Tariff schedules in US bilateral FTAs: USTR (2003b, 2004a, 2004c, 2004f); information on NAFTA (United States–Mexico): USDA (1998).

Beef

North American Free Trade Agreement (NAFTA), US-Mexico. The United States and Mexico immediately eliminated tariffs on beef cattle; fresh, chilled, and frozen beef; and veal. The only exception is Mexico's import tariff on beef edible offal, which was phased out over a 10-year period (see section on cattle in USDA 1998).

NAFTA, US-Canada. Canadian beef became exempt from quantity restrictions under the US Meat Import Act. US beef was exempted from Canada's quantitative import restrictions (see section on cattle in USDA 1998).

US-Australia. All Australian tariffs on beef imported from the United States will be immediately eliminated. The United States will establish preferential tariff-rate quotas (TRQs) for Australian beef. Out-of-quota tariffs will be phased out over 18 years. Beef imported within the TRQ will enter the United States duty free. A volume-based safeguard will be applied during the transition period; this will be converted to a price-based safeguard after the transition period (see section on beef in USDA 2004b).

US-Chile. Chile established TRQs on US fresh and frozen beef and other meat products, to be eliminated in the fourth year of the agreement. The United States granted reciprocal treatment to Chilean beef products. Each government agreed to immediately recognize the other's grading system. Chilean beef is prohibited from accessing the US beef market because the USDA has not recognized Chile's meat inspection system. A technical group has been formed to eliminate barriers related to inspection procedures (see section on beef in USDA 2003b).

US-Morocco. Morocco will establish two preferential TRQs for US beef. For high-quality beef (prime or choice), the in-quota tariff will be eliminated over 5 years, the over-quota tariff in 18 years. For standard quality beef, the in-quota tariff will be eliminated over 5 years, while the over-quota tariffs will remain unless Morocco negotiates reductions with other partners. The United States will establish zero-duty preferential TRQs for beef imports from Morocco. The over-quota tariff will be phased out over 15 years.

Beef and beef product and poultry and poultry product imports must be accompanied by an export certificate to be allowed entry into Morocco. Morocco's veterinary services, in cooperation with the USDA's Food Safety and Inspection Service, will work together in good faith to define the content of the certificates that will accompany US beef and poultry imports (USTR 2004d).

Central American–Dominican Republic Free Trade Agreement (CAFTA-DR). Tariffs applied by CAFTA-DR countries on US prime and choice cuts of beef are immediately eliminated, except by the Dominican Republic, which establishes a 15-year TRQ. For all other beef products, most CAFTA-DR partners will phase out tariffs within 15 years. El Salvador, Guatemala, and the Dominican Republic will establish 15-year TRQs. The United States establishes preferential TRQs for beef products originating in CAFTA-DR countries. Over-quota tariffs will be eliminated in 15 years. These preferential TRQs, however, will only kick in after the existing US Section 22 TRQs provided for these countries are filled. CAFTA-DR partners are working toward recognizing US meat inspection and certification systems (USDA 2005b).

Corn and Corn Products

NAFTA, US-Mexico. The United States immediately eliminated its tariff on corn imports from Mexico. Mexico established a preferential TRQ for corn imports from the United States. The TRQ will be in effect for 15 years, and tariff cuts will be back-loaded. Under the agreement, however, to bolster its livestock industry, Mexico liberalized corn imports much faster than NAFTA required (section on corn in USDA 2005b).

US-Australia. Australia does not have tariffs on imported corn, and the United States will immediately eliminate its duties on Australian corn.[3]

US-Chile. Both countries immediately eliminate tariffs that are not already zero (USDA 2003b).

US-Morocco. Upon the agreement's entry into force, Morocco will reduce its tariffs on US corn and corn products by 50 percent, eliminating the remaining tariffs on these products over five years. The United States will eliminate its tariffs on corn and corn products immediately (USTR 2004d).

CAFTA-DR. Under the Caribbean Basin Initiative (CBI), US imports of grains from CAFTA-DR countries enjoyed duty-free access already. El Salvador, Honduras, and Nicaragua established preferential TRQs on yellow corn,[4] the over-quota tariffs of which are phased out over 15 years. Guatemala established a 10-year phaseout. Costa Rica and the Dominican Republic immediately eliminated tariffs.

---

3. Australia agreed to work with the United States in WTO agriculture negotiations to develop disciplines that eliminate restrictions on the right to export. Australia has state trading organizations (STOs) with sole authority to export grains, and these STOs are the object of US negotiating efforts. For more information, see section on grains at USDA (2004b).

4. In the United States, white corn is considered a food-grade corn, while yellow corn is primarily used for animal feed. The distinction is rather arbitrary, and price differentials partly explain their different usages.

El Salvador, Guatemala, Honduras, and Nicaragua will not reduce their out-of-quota tariffs for white corn, though some liberalization will occur through duty-free in-quota TRQs, which grow 2 percent per annum in perpetuity. In Costa Rica, white corn tariffs will be gradually eliminated over 15 years.[5] The Dominican Republic will immediately eliminate its tariffs on US white corn (USDA 2005b).

Raw Cotton

AFTA, US-Mexico.   Mexico's tariffs on cotton were phased out over either 5 or 10 years. Existing US quotas on Mexican cotton were replaced by NAFTA TRQs, which are phased out over a 10-year transition period. Cotton products are subject to NAFTA rules of origin (section on cotton in USDA 1998).

US-Australia.   Australia continues its duty-free tariff treatment for cotton. The United States will establish a preferential TRQ for Australian cotton, which is phased out in equal annual steps over 18 years (section on cotton in USDA 2003b).

US-Chile.   US import tariffs on Chilean cotton are phased out over 12 years, while Chile's import tariff is immediately eliminated. Chile does not produce or export cotton (section on cotton in USDA 2003b).

US-Morocco.   Morocco will immediately eliminate its tariffs on US cotton. The United States will establish a preferential TRQ for Moroccan cotton. The over-quota tariff will be phased out over 15 years (USTR 2004d).

CAFTA-DR.   CAFTA-DR partners will eliminate all duties on US raw cotton immediately. The US import duty on raw cotton from all six countries will be phased out over 15 years. The agreement establishes rules of origin that strongly favor US cotton and synthetic fabrics.[6]

---

5. Nearly 0.9 million acres of white food-grade corn were grown in the United States in 2002, while yellow corn acreage ranged between 1.2 million and 1.5 million acres. White corn producers have benefited in the past from preferential access under bilateral FTAs. For example, in recent years, the demand for white corn has increased in Mexico.

6. Limited amounts of apparel and textiles that are in short supply in the US market may contain third-country fabrics, whether they are made from cotton, synthetic, or natural fibers. For more information, see USDA (2005b).

Dairy

NAFTA, US-Mexico. The United States established a NAFTA TRQ on imports of milk powder from Mexico. The over-quota tariff was phased out over 10 years. The US NAFTA TRQ on cheese, also phased out over 10 years, covered all cheese items previously subject to US Section 22 quotas.

Mexico applied a NAFTA TRQ on milk powder and cheese. The over-quota tariffs were phased out over 10 years. Tariffs on US exports of fresh cheese and other cheeses to Mexico will be eliminated over a 10-year transition period (see sections on cheese and milk powder in USDA 1998).

US-Australia. Australia locks in its previous duty-free tariff treatment for all US dairy products. The United States will provide Australia with two types of TRQ access for dairy items. First, the Australian country-specific dairy TRQs agreed by the United States in the Uruguay Round will immediately receive duty-free treatment for in-quota shipments to the US market. Second, Australia will have additional access through the creation of preferential TRQs. Preferential in-quota volumes will be duty free, growing at an average of 5 percent per annum in perpetuity. For many dairy products, out-of-quota tariffs will remain at base year rates. Tariffs on dairy items not included in TRQs will be phased out over 18 years in most cases. The TRQ system will apply to American cheese, cheddar, European-type cheese, Goya cheese, Swiss cheese, other cheese (not specifically provided for), nonfat dry milk, other milk powders, condensed and evaporated milk, butter and butterfat, creams and ice cream, and other dairy products (see section on dairy in USDA 2004b).

US-Chile. Chile will phase out its tariffs on cheeses, butter and butterfat, whey products, and yogurts over 4 years, while tariffs on liquid, condensed, and evaporated milk and cream will be eliminated over 8 years. The United States created preferential TRQs for Chilean dairy products, which are eliminated after 12 years. Products covered by the TRQ system include cheeses, butter and butterfat, milk powders, condensed and evaporated milk, and other dairy products, including some chocolates and food preparations.[7]

US-Morocco. Morocco will immediately eliminate its tariffs on US pizza cheese and whey products. Tariffs on other US cheeses will be eliminated in 5 or 10 years, depending on the product; tariffs on US butter will be eliminated in eight years; and tariffs on US milk powders will be eliminated in

---

7. The Food and Drug Administration (FDA) will continue to test and approve imports from Chile. Chile also recognizes the authority of the FDA to approve US food processing plants that are eligible for export to Chile. For more information, see section on dairy at USDA (2003b).

12 or 15 years. The United States will create preferential TRQs for creams and ice cream, cheese, milk powders, butter, and other dairy products. Over-quota tariffs will be phased out over 15 years (see USTR 2004d).

CAFTA-DR. The FTA commits all parties to duty-free access for dairy products after 20 years. The FTA establishes reciprocal duty-free TRQs. Most tariffs on over-quota dairy imports are phased out over a 20-year transition period, though for a few products the time period is 10 to 15 years.[8] The United States will apply TRQs to all partner countries on cheese, ice cream, fluid fresh milk and cream, sour cream, and other dairy products. The US TRQ on butter will affect Costa Rica, El Salvador, and Honduras, while the US TRQ on milk powder targets only Costa Rica. CAFTA countries will establish preferential TRQs on US milk, milk powder, butter, cream, cheese, ice cream, and other dairy. Safeguard duties will also be phased out within 20 years. All parties may apply quantity-based agricultural safeguards during the transition period (USDA 2005b).

Distilled Spirits

NAFTA, US-Mexico. Most US tariffs on Mexican distilled spirits that were not already duty free were eliminated immediately (e.g., brandy). The major exception was the tariff on rum, which was phased out over 10 years. US tariffs on beer were phased out over 8 years. Mexico immediately eliminated the tariff on US bourbon whiskey, while its tariff on US rum was eliminated 4 years later. Mexican tariffs on beer were phased out over 8 years (see section on alcoholic beverages in USDA 1998).

US-Australia. Australia will immediately eliminate tariffs on distilled spirits. Duty-free entry is locked in for distilled spirits that already enter duty-free. All distilled spirits except rum already enjoyed duty-free access into the United States. US tariffs on two rum tariff lines (2208.4020 and 4060) will be removed in 18 years (see section on processed foods and beverages in USDA 2004b).

US-Chile. Chile will fully eliminate tariffs on most distilled spirits in 2 years. All distilled spirits except rum already enjoyed duty-free access into the United States. US tariffs on two rum tariff lines (2208.4020 and 4060) will be removed in 12 years. In addition, both countries agree to recognize bourbon whiskey, Tennessee whiskey, *pisco chileno, pajarete,* and *vino*

---

8. Guatemalan tariffs on over-quota imports of "other dairy products" will be eliminated in 10 years. Similarly, the Dominican Republic will eliminate over-quota TRQs on butter over 10 years.

asoleado as distinctive products that can only be produced in Tennessee or Chile respectively (see section on wine in USDA 2003b).

US-Morocco.   Morocco will immediately eliminate its tariffs on all distilled spirits. All distilled spirits except rum already enjoyed duty-free access into the United States. US tariffs on two rum tariff lines (2208.4020 and 4060) will be removed in 15 years (USTR 2004d).

CAFTA-DR.   All distilled spirits, with no exceptions, will receive duty-free access into the United States. The CBI access condition into the US market will not change for some ethyl alcohol products, for example HTS 2207.1060; Central American countries will face TRQs on these products (essentially ethanol). Costa Rica and El Salvador obtained larger TRQs; however, only the US TRQ for El Salvador will expand after 15 years.

CAFTA-DR countries will immediately eliminate tariffs on gin and whiskey.[9] Tariffs on certain US liquors (tariff lines 2208.70) will be phased out over 10 years in the Dominican Republic and over 5 years in El Salvador, Guatemala, and Nicaragua. Costa Rica and Honduras granted immediate duty-free access for imports of those products. All CAFTA-DR countries will phase out tariffs on US rum over 12 to 15 years,[10] except for El Salvador, which will phase out tariffs over 10 years (USDA 2005b).

Fruits, Vegetables, and Nuts

NAFTA, US-Mexico.   Mexico phased out tariffs on most US fruit products over 4 years, but applied a 10-year NAFTA TRQ on apples.[11] Mexico also had a 10-year phaseout for peaches, nectarines, and grapes. The United States eliminated tariffs on fruits immediately, with the exception of citrus products and melons, which were subject to a 10-year NAFTA TRQ.

Under NAFTA, the United States established 10-year TRQs on many vegetable products—15 years for asparagus and broccoli—and reserved the right to apply special agricultural safeguards on imports of certain horticultural products. Mexico matched the US tariff line changes and phaseouts for imports of vegetable products from the United States, and consequently, eliminated tariffs on most vegetables over 10 years. For potatoes, however, Mexican treatment of US imports differs from this rule, as Mexico applied a 10-year NAFTA TRQ.

---

9. The Dominican Republic will phase out its tariffs on gin over 10 years, and Costa Rica will phase out tariffs on whiskey over five years.

10. The transition period will last 12 years for Costa Rica and Guatemala, and 15 years for the Dominican Republic, Honduras, and Nicaragua.

11. Mexico may apply special agricultural safeguards on imports of US apples.

Both countries immediately eliminated their import tariffs on raisins, prunes, and fresh and dried nuts. The United States may apply agricultural safeguards on imports of onions, tomatoes, eggplants, chili peppers, squash, and watermelons. Mexico, in turn, applies this special safeguard on apples and potato products (USDA 1998).

US-Australia. Australia locked in already existing duty-free tariff treatment for all US exports of fruits, vegetables, and nuts. The United States will eliminate its tariffs for Australian fruits over 4 years. US tariffs on watermelons, cantaloupes, boysenberries, papayas, mangoes, cherries, prunes, and other figs will be eliminated in 10 years. Tariffs on Australian canned dates, canned watermelon, canned pears, canned apricots, canned peaches and nectarines, and grapefruit will be phased out over 18 years.

US tariffs on most Australian vegetables are eliminated over 4 years. Tariffs on Australian leeks, cauliflower, Brussels sprouts, globe artichokes, celery, spinach, pumpkins, okra, and potatoes will be eliminated over 10 years. US tariffs on asparagus, preserved tomatoes, packed artichokes, Agaricus mushrooms, dried onions, garlic, and certain sweet corn products will be phased out in 18 years.

The United States immediately eliminates tariffs on nuts, and has also established an 18-year preferential TRQ for avocados. The United States maintains phytosanitary restrictions on imports of many Australian fruits, such as avocados and tropical fruit. The United States may impose special agricultural safeguard measures on certain fruits and horticultural products, such as onions, garlic, canned fruits, and tomato products (USDA 2004b).

US-Chile. Chile immediately eliminated tariffs on all products contained in chapter 8 (fruits and nuts). Many US fruit tariffs are phased out according to schedules ranging from immediate elimination to 12 years. Tariffs on limes, grapes, pears, kiwis, plums, and raspberries are immediately dropped; tariffs on oranges and mandarins will be phased out over 4 years; and tariffs on lemons, grapefruit, and frozen berries are reduced and then eliminated over 8 years. The tariff phaseout will be completed in 12 years for canned pears, canned apricots, canned nectarines, and canned fruit mixtures. The United States may apply special agricultural safeguards on frozen cherry products, canned pears, canned apricots, canned nectarines, and canned fruit mixtures.

The phaseout period for most tariffs on fresh and processed vegetables in both countries varies by product, from immediate elimination to elimination after 8 years. Exceptions on the US side are dried tomatoes, garlic, onions, mushrooms, sweet corn, Brussels sprouts, leeks, broccoli, carrots, artichokes, spinach, and fresh tomatoes. Chile will eliminate most tariffs on vegetables immediately, except for tariffs on spinach, sweet corn, certain leguminous vegetables, and peas, which will be eliminated over 8 years.

The United States may apply special agricultural safeguards on avocados, asparagus, tomato products, garlic, spinach, and broccoli. US tariffs on nuts will be phased out either immediately or in 4 years for almonds and hazelnuts. Chile will eliminate its tariff on US nuts immediately. Technical discussions regarding Chile's phytosanitary standards that limit trade are ongoing (USDA 2003b).

US-Morocco. Morocco will eliminate most tariffs on US fruits within 5 years. Moroccan tariffs on US raisins will be phased out over 8 years. Additionally, Morocco will phase out tariffs on US dates, avocados, dried apricots, dried prunes and plums, and dried cherries and peaches over 10 years. Morocco will create a 10-year preferential TRQ for US apples. US tariffs on most Moroccan fruit products will be phased out within 5 years. US tariffs on Moroccan avocados, boysenberries, papayas, cherries, dried prunes, and plums will be phased out over 10 years. Seasonal tariffs on grapefruits will be phased out over 15 years. The United States will eliminate tariffs on canned pears, canned apricots, and canned peaches and nectarines in 18 years.

Morocco will eliminate tariffs on most US vegetables immediately. Moroccan tariffs on US certain onions, some peas, sweet corn, and sliced potatoes will be phased out over 5 years. Tariffs on US potatoes, seeds of certain peas, dried and broad beans, and lentils will be phased out over 10 years. Most US tariffs on Moroccan vegetables will be phased out within 5 years. Tariffs on fresh asparagus will be eliminated over 8 years. The United States will apply 10-year phaseouts for its tariffs on Moroccan leeks, broccoli, celery, spinach, Brussels sprouts, Agaricus mushrooms, preserved olives, preserved oranges, Jerusalem artichokes, and Chinese water chestnuts. The US will create 15-year preferential TRQs for Moroccan dried onions, dried garlic, tomato sauces, and other processed tomato products. Quotas will be lifted at the end of the 15-year period. The US will eliminate tariffs on canned asparagus over 18 years.

US tariffs on walnuts and certain mixes of nuts and dried fruits will be phased out in 5 and 10 years respectively. All other Moroccan nut products will receive duty-free treatment. Morocco will eliminate tariffs on most US nuts over 5 years, and will create a 15-year preferential TRQ for US almonds. Tariffs on US almonds not subject to TRQs will be phased out in 15 years (USTR 2004d).

The United States has recourse to special agricultural safeguards on imports of certain canned fruits, vegetables such as dried onions and garlic, preserved tomatoes, canned asparagus, canned pears, canned apricots, and other products. Morocco may apply agricultural safeguards on chickpeas and lentils, prunes, and almonds. A side letter to the agreement excludes nonbitter almonds, designated by Moroccan HS subheadings 0802.11.0091, 0802.11.0099, 0802.12.0091, and 0802.12.0099, from the list of products subject to special safeguards.

CAFTA-DR. Prior to the agreement, imports of all fruits, vegetables, and nuts from CAFTA-DR countries enjoyed duty-free access under the CBI.[12] Over 70 percent of US fruit and nut products will be eligible for immediate duty-free access in the CAFTA-DR market. Tariffs will be phased out over the next 5 to 10 years for another 26 percent of all fruit and nut products. Under this plan, US exporters will gain immediate duty-free access for apples, peaches, pears, grapes, cherries, almonds, walnuts, pistachios, raisins, canned peaches, and canned pears. CAFTA tariffs on US oranges will be phased out within 5 to 15 years. Costa Rica will eliminate its tariffs on kiwis over 5 years.

Most Central American and Dominican Republic tariffs on mushrooms and sweet corn were immediately eliminated. All CAFTA-DR countries will eliminate tariffs on US fresh and canned tomatoes and tomato pastes, frozen vegetables, lettuce, cauliflower, broccoli, and canned asparagus over periods of up to 15 years (USDA 2005b).

Other Grains

NAFTA, US-Mexico. Both countries immediately eliminated tariffs on grain sorghum. The United States also eliminated its tariffs on barley and malt immediately, but Mexico imposed a NAFTA TRQ with a 10-year phaseout on these two products. Both countries agreed to 10-year phaseouts on rice tariffs (USDA 1998).

US-Australia. Australia does not have any tariffs on imports of wheat, rice, barley, sorghum, or rye oats.[13] The United States will immediately eliminate its duties on barley, corn, and sorghum. Oats already enjoyed duty-free access in the US market. US tariffs on parboiled rice will be phased out over 5 years, while all other varieties of rice will receive immediate duty-free treatment (see section on grains in USDA 2004b).

US-Chile. Both countries immediately eliminated tariffs on barley, barley malt, and sorghum. Chilean tariffs on rice fall to zero in equal increments over 12 years. Chile can apply special agricultural (price-based) safeguards on US rice until tariffs are eliminated. The United States imme-

---

12. Certain US sanitary and phytosanitary (SPS) measures, however, prevented Central American countries from fully benefiting from these preferences.

13. Australia agreed to work with the United States in the WTO agriculture negotiations to develop disciplines that eliminate restrictions on the right to export. Australia has state trading organizations (STOs) with sole authority to export rice and grains, and these STOs are the object of US negotiating efforts.

diately eliminated tariffs on rice. Oats already enjoyed duty-free access in the US market (see section on grains in USDA 2004b).

US-Morocco. Morocco will immediately eliminate its tariffs on sorghum and oats. Morocco's tariffs for barley will be phased out in 5 or 15 years, depending on the final use. Morocco's tariffs on rice will be phased out in either 5 years or 10 years, depending on the specific product. US tariffs on sorghum, barley, and rice will be eliminated immediately. Oats already enjoyed duty-free access in the US market (USTR 2004d).

CAFTA-DR. US imports of these other grains from CAFTA-DR countries already enjoy duty-free access. All CAFTA-DR countries immediately eliminate gain tariffs on US barley, oats, and rye. Costa Rica retains tariffs on sorghum over the transition period. Each US CAFTA-DR partner will establish zero-duty TRQs for several varieties of US rice. Out-of-quota tariffs will be eliminated during a transition period of 18 to 20 years. During this transition period, special agricultural (volume-based) safeguards are available to CAFTA-DR countries (USDA 2005b).

Other Processed Foods

NAFTA, US-Mexico. US tariffs on some processed fruits and juices imported from Mexico are being phased out over 10 years. Mexico lowered its duty to match the US rate and is phasing-out from there. The United States and Mexico are applying 15-year NAFTA TRQ tariffs on frozen concentrated orange juice, as well as special agricultural (price-based) safeguards. Strict rules of origin apply to NAFTA fresh citrus fruit (USDA 1998).

US-Australia. Australia locks in immediate duty-free tariff treatment for all US processed foods and beverages (e.g., chocolate bars, pet foods, breakfast cereals, soups and broths, fruit juices, and pasta). US tariffs are immediately eliminated for many other processed food products, including soups and pet foods. US tariffs on certain breakfast cereals and pasta are eliminated over 4 years. US import tariffs on chocolate bars are phased out over 10 years in equal annual cuts. With the exception of lime juice, which received immediate duty-free treatment, the United States will eliminate its tariffs on most other citrus fruit juices in 4 years (grapefruit) or 18 years (orange and lemon). The United States has recourse to special agricultural safeguards on imports of grape and orange juice from Australia (see section on processed foods and beverages at USDA 2004b).

US-Chile. Initial duty-free quotas are established for some Chilean chocolates and food preparations, and the quotas are eliminated after 12 years. Pet foods, breakfast cereals, soups and broths, and pasta gain preferential access as tariffs fall to zero immediately in both countries. With the exception of lime juice, which will receive immediate duty-free treatment, the United States will eliminate its tariffs on all other citrus fruit juices (orange, lemon, and grapefruit) in 10 or 12 years. Chile will grant immediate duty-free treatment for US citrus juices. On instant coffee and other coffee extracts and concentrates, the United States will eliminate its tariffs immediately, while Chile will do so over 12 years. The United States has recourse to special agricultural safeguards on imports of grape and orange juice from Chile (USDA 2003b).

US-Morocco. Morocco will phase out its tariffs on processed foods over periods ranging from immediate elimination to up to 15 years, depending on the product. Morocco will phase out its tariffs on breakfast cereals, pet food, and certain food preparations in 8 years. Moroccan tariffs on soups and broths and nearly all US fruit juices will be phased out over 10 years.[14] A "preference clause" will apply to Moroccan imports of certain US pasta products. Morocco will establish TRQs that will grow at the annual rate of 2 percent per annum in perpetuity after year 10 (USTR 2004d).

The United States will immediately eliminate its tariffs on food preparations, pet food, pasta, and soups and broths. Tariffs on certain breakfast cereal products will be phased out over 10 years. US tariffs on most Moroccan citric juices, with the exception of lime juice, which is immediately duty-free, will be eliminated over 15 years. The United States has recourse to special agricultural safeguards on imports of certain fruit juices (e.g., orange juice) from Morocco.

CAFTA-DR. Prior to the agreement, US imports of processed foods from CAFTA-DR countries already enjoyed duty-free access under the CBI. El Salvador and Guatemala will immediately eliminate tariffs on US dog and cat food, while the other Central American countries will eliminate duties over 5 to 15 years. Tariffs on US soups will be eliminated immediately in Costa Rica and Honduras, over 5 years in the other three Central American countries, and over 15 years in the Dominican Republic. US exporters will obtain immediate duty-free access on frozen concentrated grapefruit juice in all six countries, and on frozen concentrated orange juice in all Central American countries (see section on processed foods at USDA 2005b).

Peanuts and Peanut Products

NAFTA, US-Mexico. Mexican imports of US peanuts were already duty-free before NAFTA. The United States established a NAFTA TRQ, which is phased out over a 15-year transition period. Roasting or blanching of

---

14. The only exceptions are tariffs on certain US apple and pineapple juices that will be eliminated over 5 years.

non-NAFTA peanuts does not confer origin. 100-percent Mexican-grown peanuts must be used to make products that qualify for NAFTA preferential tariffs (see section on peanuts at USDA (1998).

US-Australia. Australia immediately eliminated tariffs on groundnuts and groundnut butter (HS 1202.01, 1202.02, 2008.11, and 2008.19). The United States will establish preferential FTA TRQs for Australian peanuts and peanut butter. Over-quota rates will be reduced to zero in equal annual steps over 18 years (see section on oilseeds at USDA 2004b).

US-Chile. The United States will grant Chilean peanut exports duty-free access by year 12. Meanwhile, tariffs will be phased out in equal annual cuts. Chile immediately eliminated its tariffs on US peanut butter, and will eliminate its tariffs on US peanuts over 8 years.

US-Morocco. Morocco will phase out tariffs on peanuts and peanut butter over 10 years. Tariffs on peanut oil and flour will be phased out immediately. The United States will establish a preferential TRQ for peanuts and peanut butter from Morocco. Over-quota tariffs will be phased out over 15 years (USTR 2004d).

CAFTA-DR. Tariffs on US peanuts and peanut butter are immediately eliminated in most countries except Guatemala and Nicaragua (5 to 10 years). The United States will establish a preferential TRQ for peanuts and peanut butter for CAFTA countries that will be phased out over a 15-year period. The United States may apply special agricultural safeguards during the transition period (USDA 2005b).

Poultry and Other Meats

NAFTA, US-Mexico. Most of these products already entered the United States duty free; with NAFTA, The United States immediately eliminated its remaining tariffs on pork, poultry, and eggs (see section on poultry at USDA 1998).

Mexico established a 10-year NAFTA TRQ on certain pork products, poultry, and eggs. For Mexico's TRQ on pork products, the in-quota tariff was phased out over 10 years. Additionally, Mexico implemented a combination of tariffs with a 10-year phaseout and special agricultural safeguards for slaughter swine, pork, and hams. Turkey products received the same treatment as poultry products in both countries.

US-Australia. Australia locked in its duty-free tariff treatment for US pork, poultry, lamb, and mutton, and immediately eliminated tariffs on certain processed meats. US tariffs on goat, poultry, sausages, and preserved meats will be phased out over a 4-year period. The United States immediately eliminated its tariff on lamb, mutton, and all other pork (see section on meats at USDA 2004b).

US-Chile. Both countries established preferential TRQs on poultry, which will be completely liberalized over 10 years. Chile immediately eliminated tariffs on pork and processed pork products. Chile has recourse to special agricultural (price-based) safeguards if import prices of US eggs and turkey drop below certain thresholds. The United States may apply price-based safeguards on imports of turkey from Chile. Chile determined that the US meat inspection system is equivalent to its own. The US tariff on processed pork products will be immediately eliminated. Chilean exporters will gain access to the United States upon approval of Chile's meat inspection system.

US-Morocco. Morocco will create four preferential TRQs for US exports of chicken leg quarters and wings, whole chickens and turkeys, frozen chicken thigh meat, and other frozen poultry meat. The over-quota tariffs will be phased out in 10 to 25 years, using a nonlinear formula. For all other products, Moroccan tariffs will be eliminated in 5 to 10 years, except for tariffs on mechanically deboned chicken and chicken nuggets, strips, and patties, which will be eliminated immediately. Morocco has recourse to special agricultural (quantity-based) safeguards for poultry and turkey products. For chicken leg quarters and wings, Morocco and the United States will evaluate the need for a post-transition safeguard.

The United States will eliminate its tariffs on Moroccan frozen whole chickens and fresh or chilled cuts over 5 years, while US tariffs on frozen chicken cuts will be eliminated over 10 years (USTR 2004d).

US exports of beef and poultry must be accompanied by an export certificate for entry into Morocco. Morocco's veterinary services, in cooperation with the USDA's Food Safety and Inspection Service, will work together in good faith to define the content of export certificates that will accompany US beef and poultry.

CAFTA-DR. Prior to the agreement, US imports of poultry and pork from CAFTA-DR countries already enjoyed duty-free access under the CBI. Tariffs on US poultry products, such as mechanically deboned meat as well as wings and breast meat, will be eliminated immediately or within 5 years by all CAFTA-DR countries. Each CAFTA-DR country will establish preferential TRQs on US chicken legs that expand annually as duties are eliminated in 17 to 20 years. Central American and Dominican tariffs on pork will be eliminated over 15 years. Certain pork products will be subject to duty-free in-quota TRQs that will expire over 15 years. During the transition period, CAFTA-DR countries will have recourse to special agricultural safeguards for these products.

Each CAFTA-DR country is working toward recognizing the US meat inspection and certification systems to facilitate US exports (USDA 2005b).

Soybeans, Soybean Meal, and Soybean Oils

NAFTA, US-Mexico. Mexican exports of soybeans and soybean meal already enjoyed, or were immediately conferred, duty-free access to the United States. US tariffs on Mexican crude and refined soybean oil were eliminated over a 4-year phaseout period. Mexico eliminated its tariffs on US soybeans, soybean meal, and crude and refined soybean oil over a 10-year period (see section on soybeans and products at USDA 1998).

US-Australia. Australia immediately eliminated its tariffs for all oilseeds and products. Australia gained preferential access as US tariffs fell immediately to zero for soybeans, soybean flour, soybean meal, and cottonseed. US tariffs on Australian crude and refined soybean oil will be eliminated in 10 years, while tariffs on crude and refined peanut oil will be removed over 18 years (see section on oilseeds at USDA 2004b).

US-Chile. Both countries immediately eliminate tariffs on soybean and soybean meal. US seeds for sowing were granted immediate duty-free access by Chile. Chile continues to enjoy free access to the US market for these products. US tariffs on crude and refined soybean oil will be removed in 12 years, while tariffs on peanut oils will be eliminated in 10 or 12 years. Chilean tariffs on soybean and peanut oils will be phased out on a back-loaded schedule over 12 years (see section on soybeans and meal at USDA 2003b).

US-Morocco. Morocco will eliminate tariffs on soybeans, other oilseeds, and soybean meal over the next 5 years. Tariffs on other oilseeds items will be phased out over 10 years. The United States will immediately eliminate tariffs on soybeans, most other oilseeds, and soybean meal. US tariffs on soybean oil will be phased out over 10 years (USTR 2004d).

CAFTA-DR. Prior to the agreement, US imports of soybean, soybean meal, soybean oil, and other vegetable oil from CAFTA-DR countries already enjoyed duty-free access under the CBI. CAFTA-DR countries will immediately eliminate their tariffs on US soybean and soybean meal. However, Costa Rican tariffs on soybean meal will be eliminated over 15 years. US crude soybean oils gain preferential access since CAFTA-DR tariffs are immediately eliminated in all countries, except Costa Rica and Honduras, which employ 12- to 15-year phaseouts. All CAFTA-DR countries will phase out tariffs on US refined soybean oil over 12 or 15 years, though all except Nicaragua reserve the right to apply special agricultural safeguards on it (USDA 2005b).

Sugar

NAFTA, US-Mexico. The United States and Mexico established NAFTA TRQs on sugar, though at the end of year 15, there is supposed to be free trade in sugar between them. The United States and Mexico will each allow duty-free access to imports of the following sugars: raw sugar that will be refined in the importing country, then exported again to the original country; and sugar that has been refined from raw sugar produced in and exported from the other country. However, since NAFTA was ratified, the United States and Mexico have been involved in continuous disputes over sugar and high fructose corn syrup (HFCS) (see section on sugar at USDA 1998).

Mexican tariffs on sugar-containing products were phased out over 10 years. The United States established a NAFTA TRQ on sugar-containing products, which was phased out over a 10-year transition period.

US-Australia. Many sugar and sugar-containing products already entered Australia duty free. Australia immediately eliminated its tariffs for all other sugar and sugar-containing products. US duties on sugar are maintained indefinitely. Australia's sugar access to the United States remains unchanged, at 87,402 tons per annum, and Australia maintains its single desk arrangements for marketing sugar exports to the world. In the wake of the FTA, it implemented a new buy-out program for Australian sugar farmers, who were bitterly disappointed by the US refusal to liberalize its sugar market.

US-Chile. Chilean duties on sugar and sugar-containing products will be eliminated by year 12, but most tariff cuts will occur after year 5. US imports of sugar and sugar containing products are limited by a TRQ that will be phased out over 12 years.

US-Morocco. Morocco will phase-out its sugar tariffs in 5, 10, and 18 years. The United States will establish a TRQ for Moroccan sugar and sugar-containing products. Over-quota tariffs will be phased out in year 15. Unless it is a net exporter of sugar to the world, Morocco cannot export sugar to the United States (USTR 2004d).

CAFTA-DR. The United States will establish TRQs for each Central American country and the Dominican Republic. The total duty-free in-quota volume of all these TRQs is established at 109,000 metric tons (mt) for US imports of Central American and Dominican Republic sugar and sugar-containing products. This quantity will gradually increase over a 15-year period to 153,140 mt. After year 15, the preferential TRQ will increase by 2,000 mt annually in perpetuity. The agreement also includes provisions that ensure that only net exporting countries benefit from the increased access under the FTA. Thus, the quantity allowed under each country's TRQ is the lesser of the amount of each country's net trade surplus in sugar, or the specific amounts set out in each country's TRQ. The agreement also includes a mechanism that allows the United States, at its option, to compensate CAFTA exporters in place of imports of sugar. US over-quota tariffs on sugar will not change under CAFTA. At over 100 percent, the US over-quota tariff is prohibitive; it is one of the highest tariffs in the US tariff schedule (see section on tobacco in USDA 2005b).

Tobacco

NAFTA, US-Mexico. The United States and Mexico eliminated tariffs on tobacco products over 10 years (see section on tobacco at USDA 1998).

US-Australia. The United States established preferential TRQs for Australian tobacco products. Over-quota tariffs will be phased out over 18 years. Tobacco products already enjoyed duty-free treatment in Australia.

US-Chile. The United States established preferential TRQs for Chilean tobacco products. Over-quota tariffs will be phased out over 12 years. Chile will immediately eliminate its tariffs on all imports of tobacco from the United States.

US-Morocco. The United States established preferential TRQs for Moroccan tobacco products. Over-quota tariffs will be phased out over 15 years. Morocco will phase out its tariffs on most tobacco products over 10 years. The exceptions are unprocessed tobacco products (HS 2401), which will face transition periods of 5 years (USTR 2004d).

CAFTA-DR. The United States established preferential TRQs for tobacco products originating in CAFTA-DR countries. Over-quota tariffs will be phased out over 15 years. US tobacco imports from Central America and Dominican Republic that already enjoyed duty-free access under the CBI will continue to receive such treatment. CAFTA-DR countries will eliminate tariffs on US tobacco products over 15 years (USDA 2005b).

Wheat

NAFTA, US-Mexico. The United States phased out its tariff on durum wheat imports from Mexico over 10 years. For nondurum wheat from Mexico, the US tariff was eliminated on January 1, 1998. Mexican tariffs on US wheat exports were eliminated over a 10-year transition period (see section on wheat at USDA 1998).

US-Australia. Australia does not have tariffs on imported wheat. It does have a state trading organization (STO) with the sole authority to export wheat. Australia has agreed to work with the United States in WTO agriculture negotiations to develop disciplines that eliminate restrictions on the right of other firms to export wheat. The United States will immediately eliminate its duties on wheat (see section on grains at USDA 2004b).

US-Chile. Both countries immediately eliminate tariffs on durum wheat. Chile committed to eliminate its price band mechanism on nondurum wheat and wheat flour, as it relates to the United States, over a 12-year transition period. Chile has recourse to special agricultural safeguards during the transition period (see section on grains in USDA 2003b).

US-Morocco. Morocco will create preferential TRQs for durum and common wheat. For durum wheat, Morocco's over-quota tariff will remain in place unless Morocco negotiates a reduction with another partner (e.g., the European Union). The in-quota tariff will be eliminated in 10 years. For common (red) wheat, TRQ in-quota quantities are based on Morocco's domestic production of common wheat.[15] The over-quota tariff will remain in place unless Morocco negotiates a reduction with another trading partner (USTR 2004d).

CAFTA-DR. Prior to the agreement, US wheat imports from CAFTA-DR countries already enjoyed duty-free access under the CBI. With the exception of Costa Rica, which will eliminate its tariffs on US wheat immediately, all CAFTA-DR countries already allowed duty-free access for most US wheat products. Tariffs on US wheat flour will be phased out over 12 years in the five Central American countries, and over 15 years in the Dominican Republic (USDA 2005b).

Wine

NAFTA, US-Mexico. US tariffs on most grape wines imported from Mexico were phased out over 10 years. Mexican tariffs on grape wine were eliminated over 10 years, on wine coolers over 6 years, and on most grape brandies over 10 years (see section on alcoholic beverages in USDA 1998).

US-Australia. Australia locks in immediate duty-free tariff treatment for all US wine. US tariffs for wine are phased out over 11 years using a formula similar to that used in the US-Chile FTA (see section on processed food and beverages at USDA 2004b).

---

15. The formula determining the in-quota volume is highly complex. For more information, see USTR (2004d).

US-Chile. Following a graduated schedule, tariffs in both countries will be eliminated in year 12 (see section on wine at USDA 2003b).

US-Morocco. Morocco will eliminate its tariffs on wine over a period of 10 years. The United States will eliminate its wine tariffs using a harmonization formula, under which they will be progressively reduced over 10 years until all US wine tariffs are duty-free in year 11 (USTR 2004d).

CAFTA-DR. Prior to the agreement, the United States already granted duty-free treatment to wine imports from CAFTA-DR countries under the CBI. These countries will eliminate tariffs on US wine over 5 years (USDA 2005b). CAFTA does not increase access to the US market for ethanol exports from CAFTA-DR countries (USDA 2005c).

Appendix B

Sanitary and Phytosanitary Measures in US and Swiss Trade Agreements

Sanitary and Phytosanitary Measures in US Trade Agreements

This section reviews US negotiating experience on sanitary and phytosanitary (SPS) measures. The agreements considered are NAFTA, US-Australia FTA, US-Chile FTA, US-Morocco FTA, CAFTA-DR; the US-EU Veterinary Agreement; and selected memoranda of understanding including SPS provisions.

North American Free Trade Agreement (NAFTA)

The NAFTA SPS agreement disciplines the development, adoption, and enforcement of SPS measures.[1] These disciplines are designed to prevent using SPS measures to disguise trade restrictions, while safeguarding each country's right to take SPS measures to protect human, animal, or plant life or health.

NAFTA encourages using relevant international standards to develop SPS measures. At the same time, it confirms the right of each country to establish the level of SPS protection that it considers appropriate, as long as the SPS measures meet three tests: They are based on scientific principles

---

1. The section on NAFTA draws extensively on information available on the USDA Foreign Agricultural Service (FAS) Web site at www.fas.usda.gov. The specific source consulted is *NAFTA Agricultural Fact Sheet: Sanitary/Phytosanitary.*

and a risk assessment; they are applied only to the extent necessary for a country's chosen level of protection; and they do not result in unfair discrimination or disguised trade restrictions.

Against the background of these principles, the NAFTA parties agreed to work toward equivalent SPS measures. Each NAFTA country committed to accept the SPS measures of another NAFTA country as equivalent to its own, provided that the exporting country demonstrated that its measures met the importing country's chosen level of protection. NAFTA requires public notice prior to adopting or modifying any SPS measure that may affect trade in North America.

NAFTA establishes standards for risk assessment, including evaluating the likelihood of entry, establishment, or spread of pests and diseases. Risk assessment methods should reflect techniques developed by international or North American standards organizations.

The section on regional conditions establishes rules for designating pest-free or disease-free areas and areas of low-pest or low-disease prevalence. An exporting country, for example, must provide objective evidence that its goods originate in a pest-free or low-pest prevalence area.

An SPS Committee was established to facilitate the enhancement of food safety and sanitary conditions, promote the harmonization and equivalence of SPS measures, facilitate technical cooperation and consultations, and consult on disputes involving SPS measures.

US-Australia FTA

SPS issues were a central part of negotiations between the United States and Australia. Though both countries apply strict SPS protection, Australia's approach to quarantine is considered conservative, and before the negotiations, US stakeholders argued that Australia's SPS measures unjustifiably limited US access. The Australian government welcomed consultations within the context of the negotiation as an opportunity to placate US critics (Parliament of Australia Senate 2004, 146).

During the negotiation, an ad hoc group was established, and the first meeting was held in August 2002. High-priority issues for the United States included market access for pork, California table grapes, Florida citrus, stonefruit, and poultry meat. Australia identified access for feeder cattle, honeybees, Riverland citrus, cherries, and a variety of tropical fruits as its priority issues.

The final text of the US-Australia FTA reaffirms the parties' commitment to World Trade Organization (WTO) rules and to science-based decision making on matters affecting quarantine and food safety. The dispute mechanism under chapter 21 of the FTA specifically does not apply to chapter 7 (SPS provisions); rather, the WTO SPS agreement will be applied should a dispute arise between the parties.

The US-Australia FTA also establishes a framework to discuss specific products, consisting of an SPS Committee and a standing technical working group on animal and plant health measures. Such a working group is not found in any other US bilateral FTA.[2]

The SPS Committee is a forum for discussing general matters and enhancing the understanding of SPS regulatory processes. An official of the Australian Department of Agriculture Forestry and Fisheries, Virginia Greville, stated in her testimony to the Australian Senate,

> the idea of the overarching SPS Committee is very much cooperation, increasing understanding and providing each with the opportunity to explain to each other how [each understands and applies the WTO agreement] so that misunderstandings do not occur and accusations do not fly backwards and forwards about bad citizenship under the WTO and SPS agreements. (Parliament of Australia Senate 2004, 153)

The working group will focus on technical and scientific aspects of quarantine matters relating to trade in specific animal and plant products. According to an Animal Plant and Health Inspection Service (APHIS) technical trade report, the working group "would provide a forum for the parties to engage at the earliest appropriate time in each other's regulatory processes on such issues [technical and scientific aspects] and to cooperate in developing science based measures that facilitate trade between them." (US APHIS 2004, 3)

Even though the working group and the SPS Committee are not decision making bodies, their establishment generated controversy in Australia. Much of the debate reflected a fear of unknown consequences and anxiety over the interpretation of key provisions. The agreement mandates the SPS Committee to "review progress on and, as appropriate, resolve through mutual consent, sanitary and phytosanitary measures." Annex 7-A specifically mentions "resolving specific bilateral animal and plant health matters" and "whenever possible, achieving consensus on scientific issues" as objectives of the working group (USTR 2004a). No other US bilateral FTA contains such explicit language on the purpose of the SPS Committee. The US-Chile FTA uses the weaker expression "shall provide a forum for" rather than "mandating" the SPS Committee to resolve and review progress on outstanding SPS measures (USTR 2003b). Australian government officials highlighted that these are nonetheless consultative bodies to discuss technical and scientific interest. The Australian chief negotiator, Stephen Deady, said "there is nothing in the establishment of these committees that will impact on the integrity of the Import Risk Analysis processes in Australia" (Parliament of Australia Senate 2004, 149).

---

2. Other US bilateral FTAs, such as US-Chile, contemplate the possibility of establishing working groups, but these are not established in the agreement.

Nevertheless, the Federation of Australian Scientific and Technological Societies objected that the working group and SPS Committee "may undermine the fundamental role that proper scientific analysis must have in a sound quarantine system" (Parliament of Australia Senate 2004b, 9).[3] Referring to the demands of US exporters, the Australian Senate Select Committee pointed out that "there has been some comment that the bilateral committees may have the potential to be *de facto* dispute settlement regimes" (Parliament of Australia Senate 2004, 5.23). Some critics noted that, even if the working group and SPS Committee did not become dispute settlement mechanisms, they would nonetheless allow the United States to put pressure on Australian quarantine decisions, watering down Australia's reputation for a strong SPS regime. Still, the Senate's Select Committee concluded that "Australia's processes *may be* robust enough to withstand such pressure should it arise" (Parliament of Australia Senate 2004, 154).

In a side letter to the agreement, the United States and Australia agreed to work cooperatively in the World Organization for Animal Health (OIE), Codex, and other forums to secure science-based standards and guidelines that address risks to food safety and animal health from bovine spongiform encephalopathy (BSE).

US-Chile FTA

According to APHIS, the successful negotiation and ratification of the US-Chile FTA made it a road map for subsequent SPS discussions "in the Western Hemisphere and elsewhere" (US APHIS 2004, 6).

Before negotiations, stakeholders in both countries had expressed concerns about elements of the other party's SPS regime. For example, the United States prohibited importation of meats from Chile, while Chile limited market access for some US fruit and meat products.

As in the US-Australia FTA, an ad hoc special working group was established during negotiations to address outstanding SPS issues. Although these SPS discussions were not part of formal negotiations, they went as far as possible in finding technical solutions before Congressional ratification. Some of these involved modifying SPS import measures in each party, which improved market access conditions for horticultural, meat, and dairy products of both countries. According to the Dirección General de Relaciones Económicas Internacionales (Direcon 2003), the principal achievements of the working group were the following:

■ The partners reached an equivalence agreement on meat-cut classification systems for bovine meats.

---

3. The Federation of Australian Scientific and Technological Societies (FASTS) was established in 1985. The Federation consists of societies representing the interests of Australian scientists and technologists.

- Chile recognized the US inspection system for bovine, pork, and sheep meat. The United States established a work plan to recognize the Chilean inspection system for those same products. A bilateral work plan was established to exchange recognition of inspection systems for poultry meats as well.

- The United States began work to recognize Chile as a classical swine fever free country.

- The Chilean Secretaría de Agricultura granted the US Food and Drug Administration (FDA) authority to inspect, on behalf of Chile, US producing plants that export dairy products to Chile.

- Chile authorized the importation of Californian pit-containing fruits, and advanced regulatory reforms to allow access to California citric products and cherries as well as Florida grapefruits.

- The United States agreed to speed up regulatory changes to allow imports of Chilean clementines.

- Both countries pledged to work to harmonize measures regulating tomato importation.

The US-Chile FTA reaffirms the parties' commitment to WTO rules and to science-based decision making on matters affecting human, animal, and plant safety. The WTO SPS agreement and dispute settlement mechanism will be applied should a dispute arise between the parties on SPS matters.

Chapter 6 also establishes an SPS Committee, charged with overseeing the implementation of the WTO SPS agreement between the parties and providing a forum for technical discussions on applying SPS measures in each country. The SPS Committee will "review progress on addressing sanitary and phytosanitary matters" that may arise between the parties and "enhance mutual understanding and consultation on SPS regulatory processes" (USTR 2003b). The Committee may establish ad hoc working groups, but, unlike the US-Australia FTA, the agreement itself does not establish a standing working group.

Since the entry into force of the US-Chile FTA in January 2004, the SPS Committee has dealt with outstanding SPS issues. It established two ad hoc working groups, one on grapes and another on meats. In July 2004, APHIS declared Chile to be a "free of classical swine fever" country (US APHIS 2004, 7). The US Food Safety and Inspection Service (FSIS) conducted two in loco audits to certify the Chilean red-meat inspection system. In December 2004, the USDA allowed importation of Chilean clementines and tangerines into the United States. In May 2005, the USDA published proposed rules and regulations that include Chile in the list of countries eligible to export meat and meat products to the United States. These recognize the Chilean inspection system as equivalent to the Federal Meat Inspection

Act and its implementing rules. The proposed amendment will eliminate the current prohibition on importing Chilean meat products of cattle, sheep, swine, goats, horses, mules, or other equines (US FSIS 2005). Still pending are regulatory changes that will facilitate bilateral tomato and poultry trade, as well as the importation of Chilean grapes into the United States.

Central American–Dominican Republic Free Trade Agreement (CAFTA-DR)

Central American products already enjoyed duty-free access through the Caribbean Basin Initiative (CBI), and therefore the need to address non-tariff barriers (NTBs), including SPS barriers, was a priority for these countries. Central American countries considered that certain US SPS measures had prevented them from obtaining the full benefit of CBI preferences. For example, fruit flies in Central America have prevented the export of fruits and vegetables to the United States without costly treatment. Many US exporters had likewise complained about the application of SPS measures in CAFTA-DR countries, pointing to lengthy, complex, and in some cases, arbitrary processes of SPS approval: costly local testing requirements, temporary bans on exports of beef and poultry products, and the use of sanitary certificates as an import licensing device for meat and dairy products.[4]

The CAFTA-DR negotiation differed from those of the US-Chile FTA and the US-Australia FTA, in that the Central American partners had a relatively poor SPS infrastructure. Several official and independent studies assessing the phytosanitary capacity of Central American nations identified deficiencies in the number of employees and laboratories for inspection services, as well as in the awareness of SPS requirements in partner country.[5] Since SPS infrastructure deficiencies limited CAFTA-DR countries' ability to gain market access, the United States pledged technical assistance from US sanitary and agriculture agencies. According to the United States trade representative (USTR 2005b), "the objective [of SPS negotiations] was to leverage the impetus of active trade negotiations to seek difficult changes to the Central American countries' SPS regimes."

---

4. See sections on Costa Rica, El Salvador, Guatemala, Honduras, Nicaragua, and Dominican Republic in USTR (2005b).

5. Official studies were conducted by the FTAA Tripartite Committee. The studies are published as a series titled "National Trade Capacity Building Strategies" and can be accessed at www.ftaa-alca.org. The USTR also conducted evaluations of trade capacity needs. These reports are available at its Web site at www.ustr.gov. Researchers at the Bush School conducted an evaluation at request of the US Department of Agriculture. The publication is titled "CAFTA: Sanitary and Phytosanitary Evaluation" and is available at http://bush.tamu.edu.

A parallel working group on SPS measures was established during Central American Free Trade Agreement (CAFTA) negotiations to exchange views on outstanding SPS issues and improve market access for all parties.[6] The USTR reported several achievements:

- The United States obtained a commitment from the Central American nations to resolve specific measures affecting US exports to those countries.

- Central American countries pledged to move towards recognizing import eligibility for all producing plants inspected under the US safety and inspection system, in particular for meat, dairy, and poultry products.

- The United States committed to resolve delays in food inspection procedures for meat and poultry products from Central America.

- The United States presented a schedule to resolve sanitary issues that affect the export of poultry, dairy products, tomatoes, and peppers from Honduras.

- Nicaragua received help solving SPS problems for exports of cheese, papaya, *pitahaya*, peppers, and tomatoes.

- Costa Rica obtained guaranteed access of ornamental plants over 18 inches in height, more flexible sanitary treatment for some of its flower exports, and recognition of its poultry inspection system (USTR 2004e).

CAFTA-DR reaffirms rights and obligations under the WTO SPS agreement. No country will have recourse to the dispute settlement under CAFTA-DR for any matter arising under chapter 6 (SPS measures).

Article 3 of chapter 6 of the agreement also establishes an SPS Committee that will continue the work of the ad hoc working group. The SPS Committee is a forum for technical discussions on applying SPS measures in each country, reviews progress on outstanding SPS issues, and provides an avenue for consultation on SPS regulatory processes. It is instructed to help each party implement the SPS agreement, assisting them to protect human, animal, or plant life or health.[7]

Uniquely, CAFTA-DR's SPS Committee is required to facilitate a party's response to a written request for information from another party

---

6. The Dominican Republic did not participate in this group because it negotiated separately with the United States.

7. SPS Committees under US-Chile FTA and US-Australia FTA include objectives geared to "enhance each party's implementation" of the SPS agreement. The language is stronger in the case of CAFTA, reflecting the greater need of support in Central America. Also, the SPS Committees under US-Chile FTA and US-Australia FTA are not instructed to "assist parties to protect," but rather just to "protect" human, animal, or plant life or health (USTR 2003b, 2004a).

with minimal delay. Other provisions for the committee are nearly identical to those in the US-Chile FTA, except that CAFTA-DR committee decisions will be taken by consensus, a consequence of having seven rather than two parties to the FTA. Also, unlike the US-Chile FTA, Annex 6.3 of CAFTA lists the agencies of each party that will participate in the committee.

US-Morocco FTA

SPS issues did not play a significant role in negotiations between the United States and Morocco. The agreement does not include a chapter on SPS measures, and treats the subject in three short articles. The provisions are general in nature, including a reaffirmation of existing rights and obligations under the WTO SPS agreement and the absence of recourse to dispute settlement under the US-Morocco FTA for SPS issues.

The parties "affirm their desire" to provide a forum for addressing SPS, but the agreement does not establish an SPS Committee. According to the APHIS Trade Support Team, given the lack of SPS issues and the relatively small volume of bilateral agricultural trade, "the US strategy was to reaffirm the commitments under the WTO SPS agreement" (US APHIS 2004, 8). Still, in side letters between Moroccan and US officials, Morocco pledged to accept US export certificates issued by the USDA FSIS for beef and poultry products.

In the negotiations, Morocco attempted to obtain commitments on technical assistance and market access, but the United States was not responsive. According to APHIS, "By initially expecting too much and then failing to scale back expectations to more realistic parameters, Morocco may have lost some genuine opportunities for receiving US technical assistance" (US APHIS 2004, 8).[8] On market access, Morocco expected APHIS approval of some plant products for entry in the United States. The United States refused to circumvent normal procedural channels, and deemed the request as "not appropriate for FTA negotiations." Perhaps as a consolation, a subcommittee for discussion of SPS matters was established in a side letter, but even here, the United States agreed reluctantly. Given the lack of substantive issues on both sides, the forum will convene only on an as-needed basis.

US-EU Veterinary Agreement

Early efforts to tackle outstanding SPS matters preceded the US-EU Veterinary Agreement: In November 1992, the US-European Community Agree-

---

8. Morocco had sought a US commitment to upgrade Morocco's entire plant and animal health infrastructure. US authorities pointed out that Morocco failed to prioritize their needs, demonstrate how that assistance would facilitate trade, or explain how that assistance could be coordinated with technical cooperation from the European Union (US APHIS 2004, 8).

ment on Meat Inspection Standards touched upon some of the issues that the Veterinary Agreement revisited. Through the 1992 agreement, the parties agreed to recognize the equivalence of regulatory requirements regarding trade in fresh bovine and swine meat, consider approving plants certified by the other party's responsible authority, and initiate discussions as soon as possible on other problems in the veterinary field.

The US-EU Veterinary Agreement entered into force in August 1999. Under the agreement, the parties reaffirmed their WTO obligations. The scope of the 1999 agreement was limited to sanitary measures applied to live animals and animal products listed in Annex I. For these products, the agreement includes provisions for equivalency determination on health requirements, consultations, exchange of information, notification of disease developments, scientific exchange, and verification and audit.

Article 6 of the Veterinary Agreement recognizes the principle of regionalization. Specifically, for trade purposes, the importing party recognizes the health status of regions as determined by the exporting party.[9] However, this provision applies only to the animal and aquaculture diseases specified in Annex III. BSE is not listed there.[10]

Annex V sets forth the status of consultations and lists the live animals and animal product areas, sectors, or parts of sectors for recognizing the equivalency of a party's sanitary measures and applicable trade conditions.

The Veterinary Agreement also establishes a joint management committee. At least once a year, the committee reviews activities under the agreement and recommends changes to the annexes. Parties agree to establish technical working groups to identify and address technical and scientific issues arising from the agreement.

At a meeting in October 2003, the joint management committee issued a recommendation concerning the determination of equivalence for gelatin and collagen for human consumption, and as a result, the United States and European Union agreed to incorporate these new equivalences into Annex V.

The European Union and the United States have also used other channels to deal with outstanding SPS issues. In 2002, the resumption of exports of Spanish clementines to the United States, and the resumption of US poultry exports to the European Union, were resolved within the context

---

9. The EU Commission (2004a) argues "the United States has failed repeatedly to apply the regionalization provisions of the Veterinary Agreement."

10. The list of diseases for which regional designation is recognized includes foot and mouth disease, swine vesicular disease, peste de petits ruminants, contagious caprine pleuropneumonia, sheep and goat pox, African swine fever, enterovirus encephalomyelitis, Newcastle disease, pseudorabies/Aujeszky's disease, vesicular stomatitis, rinderpest, contagious bovine pleuropneumonia, bluetongue, African horse sickness, classical swine fever, fowl plague (avian influenza), and Venezuelan equine encephalomyelitis.

of the Positive Economic Agenda Initiative. Yet the European Union still lists 10 US SPS measures as NTBs.[11]

SPS Matters in Memoranda of Understanding (MoUs)

To date, the United States has signed six MoUs that include SPS provisions with Argentina,[12] China, Colombia, Peru, Russia, and Uruguay.[13] Except for the Argentinean MoU, they establish bilateral consultative committees on agriculture as a forum for resolving trade issues and cooperating in a number of areas, including food safety, animal and plant health, and biotechnology.

Article IV of the US-China MoU, signed before China's accession to the WTO, calls for science-based SPS requirements administered in a nondiscriminatory manner. The MoU also calls for continuous scientific and technical consultations concerning scientifically unjustified SPS restrictions. In 2004, Chinese and US authorities exchanged letters of intent that pledged to "further enhance" their technical exchanges and long-term cooperation in the fields of food safety and animal and plant health. The letters establish a consultative mechanism to "demonstrate their strong commitment to work cooperatively to address outstanding bilateral SPS issues in accordance with each country's domestic rules and regulations" (USDA 2005d).

The MoUs with Peru, Colombia, and Uruguay do not reaffirm WTO commitments, but they do establish consultative committees on agriculture (CCAs). Former Secretary of Agriculture Ann Veneman stated that these "set the stage for improved communication and coordination in a number of areas including food safety, research and sanitary and phytosanitary issues" (USDA 2003c).

---

11. These are plants in growing media, bovine animals and products, pathogen-free areas, hardy nursery stock, goats/risk of scrapie, noncomminglement, uncooked meat products, inspection of egg production, Columbia-Meat/on-site inspection, meat and meat products (European Commission, 2005). More information is at http://mkaccdb.eu.int/sps/index.html.

12. The MoU between the United States and Argentina was signed within the framework of the Uruguay Round of Multilateral Trade Negotiations and is significantly different from other MoUs.

13. In all cases, the timing of the MoUs was linked to broader trade issues. Signatures on MoUs with Colombia and Peru (April 2003 and October 2002) correspond to the launching of FTA negotiations with the United States. Uruguay has repeatedly made public its desire to engage in FTA negotiations with the United States, but other commitments, notably its membership in Mercosur, have limited US interest. Following President Jorge Batlle's February 2002 visit to the White House, however, the United States and Uruguay established a Joint Commission on Trade and Investment. The Commission has pursued a work plan, while the MoU on agriculture dates from April 2003 and a bilateral investment treaty was concluded in September 2004. US MoUs with China and Russia date from periods when neither country was a WTO member (October 1992 and September 2003), but both were engaged in WTO accession.

SPS Measures in Swiss Trade Agreements

This section describes the Swiss negotiating experience in sanitary and phytosanitary issues. The section reviews SPS provisions in several Swiss bilateral agreements such as the Swiss-EU Agreement on Trade in Agricultural Products and the bilateral FTAs through the European Free Trade Association (EFTA).

SPS Issues in the Swiss-EU Agreement on Trade in Agricultural Products

The Swiss-EU Agreement on Trade in Agricultural Products, which entered into force in June 2002, aims to facilitate trade in farm products by eliminating tariffs and NTBs. The agreement addresses SPS issues in Annex 4 on plant health, Annex 5 on feed, Annex 6 on seeds, and Annex 11 on animal health.[14] Except for Annex 5, which is still under negotiation, all of these annexes go to great lengths to establish the equivalence of EU and Swiss SPS regulations. According to the Switzerland Integration Office (2005b), "The agreement will reduce or eliminate altogether a number of technical barriers in the veterinary bracket (dairy hygiene, epizootic diseases) and in relation to pesticides, animal feeds, seeds, biological products and rules for the sale of wines, generally on the basis of arrangements which arise out of the mutual recognition of the equivalence of each other's legislation." We focus our discussion on Annexes 4 and 11.

Annex 4: Plant Health

Annex 4 recognizes the equivalence of protection levels resulting from domestic legislation on the introduction and propagation of harmful organisms. The equivalence, however, applies only to those plants and plant products listed in Appendix 1 of the agreement. For these products, the parties recognize the "plant passports," issued by responsible organizations in each country, that attest conformity with those pieces of domestic legislation deemed equivalent under the agreement, and fulfill documentary requirements for movement of plants and plant products. The annex also limits border checks: Plant health sampling may not exceed certain percentages of consignments of plants and plant products.[15]

---

14. Additionally, Annexes 5, 6, 9, and 10 recognize legislative equivalence and eliminate border conformity checks for certain animal feed, seeds, organic products, and fruits and vegetables. However, these annexes deal more directly with standards rather than SPS measures.

15. The agreement establishes a maximum sampling limit at 10 percent of consignments. Moreover, the percentage will be set on a product-by-product basis according to plant-health risk as determined by the Agricultural Committee, based on proposals from the Working Group on Plant Health.

Annex 4 requires countries to inform other parties of any proposal to adopt new plant-health measures regarding plants and plant products listed in the agreement. Countries can apply derogations for regions within or the entire territories of other parties, so long as they indicate their reasons. Derogations may be applied immediately, but parties must engage in consultations with a view to finding appropriate solutions.

Finally, Annex 4 establishes a working group on plant health that considers all matters that may arise in connection with the annex and its implementation. The working group may submit proposals to update Appendices to the Agricultural Committee.

Annex 11: Veterinary Annex

Also known as the Veterinary Agreement, it regulates trade in live animals and animal products, such as semen, embryos, foods of animal origin, and animal waste. It also establishes that Swiss animal disease control legislation is identical in substance to, and achieves the same objectives as, the corresponding EU legislation; consequently, it grants Switzerland similar trading conditions with the European Union as EU member states enjoy.

The agreement does not stipulate border checking of products or animals, but it allows border inspection of accompanying documents to ensure compliance with animal protection legislation. Still, simplifying border checks will not entail eliminating product inspections; they will just be done away from the border. According to the Swiss Federal Veterinary Office, "unavoidably, to maintain the health of the animal population at its current high level, more checks will have to be conducted within the country (as practiced in EU member states)" (Jemmi and Herholz 2003, 16).

Regarding live animals, semen, and embryos, the parties recognize that certain products and animals of each party are free of specific diseases. Switzerland obtained guarantees on the status of pigs (Aujeszky's disease), cattle (brucellosis, tuberculosis, and IBR/IPV), sheep and goats (brucellosis), and poultry and hatching eggs ("not vaccinating" against ND). Since June 2003, Switzerland has requested the extension of guarantees to include other diseases that are not found in Switzerland; however, "the European Union categorically refuses any extension of guarantees" (Jemmi and Herholz 2003, 15). The Veterinary Agreement prevents countries from placing embargoes on imports of animals without a good reason. Outbreaks of disease are, however, a good reason.

Concerning foods of animal origin, the European Union recognized Swiss legislation only on milk and dairy products as equivalent to its corresponding legislation. Easing restrictions on exports for other food products of animal origin will require harmonizing the Swiss Ordinance on Foodstuffs with the corresponding EU legislation. In late 2003, the Swiss Federal Veterinary Office stated that it began efforts to tackle these pending issues, and it was preparing a proposal for discussion in the agreement's joint committee.

The joint committee oversees the application and functioning of the bilateral Swiss-EU agreements, as well as the Veterinary Agreement. To date, three working groups have been established: the Animal Health Working Group, which deals with issues regarding the certificates used in cross-border trade; the Working Group for Animal Movement, which handles matters related to simplifying border checks; and the Bovine Spongiform Encephalopathy (BSE) Working Group, which analyzing alternatives so as to lift the ban on imports of Swiss cattle. In the BSE Working Group, a draft text was drawn up proposing the adoption of EU regulations. At the end of 2003, the EU Council of Agricultural Ministers recognized the equivalence of Swiss regulations regarding BSE, allowing exports of Swiss cows to the European Union to resume.

SPS Issues and Recent Swiss/Bilateral FTAs with EFTA

Recent bilateral FTAs negotiated by EFTA include, for the most part, rather weak approaches to tackling SPS matters. This may reflect the absence of outstanding SPS issues, and the small volumes of bilateral agricultural trade. Also, agricultural liberalization has not been a major concern for Switzerland in bilateral FTAs, as evidenced by the low wedge between applied preferential and most favored nation (MFN) tariff rates.

Many recent EFTA FTAs include commitments to apply SPS regulations in a nondiscriminatory fashion and prevent implementing new measures that may have the effect of "unduly obstructing trade." The EFTA-Jordan, EFTA-Macedonia, EFTA-Morocco, EFTA–Palestine Authority, and EFTA-Romania FTAs limit their treatment of SPS matter to these provisions. The EFTA-Croatia, EFTA-Lebanon, and EFTA-Singapore FTAs include an additional provision that reaffirms obligations under the WTO SPS Agreement. The EFTA-Mexico and EFTA-Tunisia FTAs only reaffirm rights and obligations under the WTO SPS Agreement.

The FTA agreement between EFTA and Chile goes beyond the other agreements, as the parties pledge to strengthen cooperation in SPS measures, with a view toward increasing the mutual understanding of their respective systems. Expert consultations may be convened at the request of a party. Finally, the agreement calls to develop bilateral arrangements between respective regulatory agencies for better implementation of the SPS provisions under the agreement.

Appendix C

Geographical Indication Provisions in US and Swiss Trade Agreements

GI Provisions in Selected US FTAs

This section describes the treatment of geographical indications in previous US negotiating experiences. Agreements considered include FTAs such as US-Australia FTA, CAFTA-DR , US-Chile FTA, as well as other pacts.

US-Australia FTA

According to Article 17.2 of the agreement, entitled "Trademarks, including geographical indications," each party will allow GIs to be eligible for protection as trademarks.[1] Article 17.2 also allows parties to refuse an application for protection or recognition of a GI if it is likely to be confused with a mark (trademark) that is the subject of a good-faith pending application or registration, or if it is likely to be confused with a preexisting mark (trademark), the rights to which have been acquired through use in good faith in the territory of the party (USTR 2004a).

If a GI is refused, the parties will provide the applicant with a written communication of the reasons for the refusal, and allow the applicant the opportunity to respond. Interested parties must also be able to oppose registration or seek cancellation after registration.

---

1. The US Free Trade Agreement Implementation Act 2004, passed by the Australian Parliament, amends the Australian Wine and Brandy Corporation Act 1980, but does not amend the Trade Marks Act 1995. The Australian Wine and Brandy Corporation Act 1980 (AWBC) protects the names of Australian grape-growing regions. For more information, see Freehills (2004).

US-Chile FTA

The US-Chile FTA also treats GIs as trademarks. To qualify for this treatment, GIs must satisfy the same conditions that apply in the US-Australia FTA. Chile specifically recognizes bourbon whiskey and Tennessee whiskey as distinctive products of the state of Tennessee. Accordingly, Chile will not permit the sale of any product labeled as such, unless it has been manufactured in the United States in accordance with the US laws and regulations governing its manufacture.

Similarly, the United States recognizes *pisco chileno, pajarete,* and *vino asoleado,* which are authorized in Chile to be produced only in Chile, as distinctive products of Chile. Accordingly, the United States will not permit the sale of any product under those labels unless it has been manufactured in Chile in accordance with the laws and regulations governing its manufacture.

The US-Chile FTA applies the principle of "first in time, first in right" to trademarks and GIs. This means that the first to file for a trademark is granted the first right to use that name, phrase, or geographical place-name (USTR 2003b).

Central American–Dominican Republic Free Trade Agreement (CAFTA-DR)

CAFTA uses a similar definition for GIs that the US-Australia and US-Chile FTAs use. However, it expands on procedures regarding them: Each party will provide the legal means to identify and protect GIs, and will provide the means for persons of another party to apply to protect or petition to recognize them. Countries commit to limit formalities on the application procedure and to publicize GI petitions. Each party will ensure that similarities between a GI and a preexisting trademark constitute grounds for refusing protection or recognition. The US-Morocco FTA has similar language.

Article 3.12 of Chapter 3, National Treatment of Market Access for Goods, recognizes Bourbon Whiskey and Tennessee Whiskey as distinctive products of the United States, and grants the Joint Committee competence to recommend recognition under article 3.12 to other products (USTR 2004f).

US–European Community Distilled Spirits and Spirit Drink Agreement

This agreement was based on an exchange of letters between the United States and the European Union in March 1994. This agreement provides for the mutual recognition of distilled spirits.

The United States agreed to restrict the use of the product designations: "Scotch whisky," "Irish whiskey"/"Irish whisky," "Cognac," "Armagnac," "Calvados," and "Brandy de Jerez" to distilled spirits/spirit drinks products of the Member States of the European Community, produced in compliance with Council Regulations. These products shall continue to be subject to all of the labeling requirements of the United States.

Likewise, the European Community restricted the use of the product designations: "Tennessee whisky"/"Tennessee whiskey," "Bourbon whisky"/"Bourbon whiskey," and "Bourbon" as a designation for Bourbon whisk(e)y to distilled spirits/spirit drinks products of the United States produced in compliance with US laws and regulations. These whiskies shall continue to be subject to all of the labeling requirements of the European Union.

GI Provisions in Selected Swiss FTAs

This sections describes the Swiss negotiating experience on GIs. Agreements reviewed include EFTA bilateral FTAs and Swiss-EU bilateral agreement.

European Free Trade Association (EFTA)–Israel

Signed in September 1992, Article 1 of Annex V, on definitions and scope of protection, states that intellectual property protection includes protection of GIs. Article 3 of that same annex, on additional substantive standards, affirms that "the Parties shall ensure in their national laws at least adequate and effective legal means to protect geographical indications, including appellations of origin, with regard to all products, at least to the extent that their use is misleading the public" (EFTA 1992). The EFTA-Romania FTA, signed in December 1992, includes similar text.

EFTA-Bulgaria

Signed in March 1993, the agreement's original provisions on intellectual property rights were revised by decision of the Joint Meeting of the EFTA-Bulgaria Committee No. 7 of 1997. Article 1 of Annex X, on the definition and scope of protection, states that intellectual property protection comprises protection of GIs, including appellations of origin. Article 3 of Annex X, on additional substantive standards, states that parties to the agreement "shall ensure in their national laws at least adequate and effective means to protect geographical indications, including appellations of origin, with regard to all products and services" (EFTA 1993). Other agreements with similar text include EFTA-Croatia (2001), EFTA-Jordan (2001), EFTA-Macedonia (2000), EFTA-Morocco (1997), and EFTA-Turkey (1991).

EFTA-Mexico

Signed in November 2000, its provisions under Article 1, on definitions and scope of protection, are similar to those of EFTA-Bulgaria, Article 3 of Annex XXI, on additional substantive standards. However, the EFTA-Mexico language differs from EFTA-Bulgaria in stating that "a Party shall, *ex officio*, if its legislation so permits, or at the request of an interested party, refuse or invalidate the registration of a trademark which contains or consists of a geographical indication with respect to services not originating in or connected to the territory indicated, if use of the indication in the trademark for such services in that Party is of such a nature so as to mislead the public as to the true place of origin" (EFTA 2000).

Swiss-EU Agreement on Agricultural Products

The agreement on trade in agricultural products between Switzerland and the European Union was signed in June 1999, and entered into force in June 2002. According to the Joint Declaration on the protection of GIs and designations of origin of agricultural products and foodstuffs (appendix D), parties allow the incorporation of provisions to mutually uphold protected denominations of origin (PDOs) and protected geographical indicators (PGIs).

In July 2003, Switzerland and the European Union established a working group on the protection of GIs. Work on mutual protection provisions awaits the full application of Article 17 (simplified procedure) of Regulation (EEC) No. 2081/92. Meanwhile, the European Union proposed to set up a working group to explore the mutual protection of PDOs and PGIs; the consideration of all related matters; and the exchange of the information required to implement this protection. Also, two other working groups were formed for wines and distilled spirits (Switzerland Integration Office 2005b).

EFTA-Singapore

Signed in June 2003, Article 1 of Annex XII, on definition and scope of protection, goes beyond previous agreements to clarify that "appellations of origin are understood to be one form of geographical indications." (EFTA 2002a). Paragraph 1 of Article 5 in Annex XXI, on the issue of GIs, affirms the same principles as does Article 3 of Annex X of EFTA-Bulgaria; however, paragraph 2 further states that "the Parties may provide different legal means in accordance to the TRIPS Agreement to prevent the misleading use of geographical indications in relation to services than that provided for the protection of geographical indications for products and shall be deemed to be in full compliance with the obligations under paragraph 1" (EFTA 2002a).

EFTA-Chile

Signed in June 2003, this agreement uses the same definition of intellectual property rights as do previous agreements, such as EFTA-Bulgaria. However, Article 6 of Annex XII, on GIs, reaffirms the parties' commitment to ensuring protection in accordance with Articles 22, 23, and 24 of the Agreement on Trade-Related Aspects of Intellectual Property Rights (TRIPS). The EFTA-Tunisia FTA, signed in December of 2004, includes similar provisions (EFTA 2003).

EFTA-Lebanon

Signed in June 2004, this agreement uses similar language on intellectual property rights as do previous agreements, such as EFTA-Bulgaria. However, Article 6 of Annex XII, on GIs, also affirms that "Lebanon shall make every effort to protect geographical indications with regard to all services" (EFTA 2004).

Appendix D

Preferential Trade Agreements and Foreign Direct Investment: Selected Literature

The connection between trade and foreign direct investment (FDI) has been widely studied in the last two decades.[1] Blomström and Lipsey (1987) examine the relation between US and Swedish FDI and trade, while Blomström and Kokko (1997) and Dunning (1997, 2000) have published articles with a comparative perspective. Brainard (1997) has offered methodological contributions.[2] Recent empirical studies by Hejazi and Safarian (1999) and Graham and Wada (2000) find complementary relationships between exports and the stock of outward FDI.[3]

Within this general topic, the relationship between preferential trade agreements (PTAs, an umbrella term that includes FTAs), trade volumes, and FDI has attracted attention in policy circles. Theoretical analysis has been inconclusive, because arguments can be advanced for both positive and negative relations between trade and FDI. In principle, the impact of trade liberalization on FDI depends crucially on whether FDI is a substitute or complement to trade. We report the results of selected gravity models here. The numerical coefficients are summarized in table D.1.

Many studies find a positive relation between PTAs and the inward stock of FDI, for both PTA partners and third countries. Perhaps the most skeptical comment comes from the US International Trade Commission

---

1. Earlier studies exist, but they were not based on gravity models.

2. For example, Brainard contends that it makes more sense to examine foreign production by multinational enterprises rather than FDI.

3. Dunning (1993) and Hejazi and Safarian (1999, 2001) review the empirical literature.

Table D.1 Relationship between PTAs, FDI, and exports

PTAs and FDI: Studies covering all countries

Adams et al. (2003)
Dependent variable: LN (inward FDI stock$_{ijt}$)
Selected independent variables

	ASEAN	APEC	EFTA	European Union	NAFTA
MRTA$_{ij}$[a]	5.77	−1.11	0.05	−0.69	n.a.
3wave$_{ij}$[b]	−9.65	0.71***	30.77*	0.05	−10.11**
MRTA$_{ij*}$[a]	−0.02	0.04	1.15	0.37	−2.60
3wave$_{ij*}$[b]	4.05	0.68***	−41.56***	3.18**	4.9***

Levy-Yeyati, Stein, and Daude (2003)
Dependent variable: LN (inward FDI stock$_{ijt}$ + 1)
Selected independent variables

LN (EM$_{it}$)[c]	0.10***
LN (EM$_{jt}$)[d]	−0.05***
Same FTA$_{ijt}$[e]	0.24***

Jaumotte (2004)
Dependent variable: LN (inward FDI Stock$_{ijt}$)
Selected independent variable

LN (REGY)[f]	0.40**

Hallward-Driemeier (2003)
Dependent variable: FDI inflows$_{ijt}$
Selected independent variables

NAFTA dummy:	256.31**

PTAs and FDI: Studies covering NAFTA partners

Buckley et al. (2000)
Dependent variable: LN (inward Canadian FDI stock from UK, France, and US)
Selected independent variables

	United Kingdom	France	United States
LN (USGDP*FTAdummy)	0.01**	0.04**	0.01**

Globerman and Shapiro (1999)
Dependent variable: FDI stock in Canada
Selected independent variables

	Inward			Outward		
	Manufac-turing	Services	Energy	Manufac-turing	Services	Energy
FTA/ NAFTA dummy	−16.4	−380.6***	−204.7	1676.8***	860.6***	709.50**

(table continues next page)

Table D.1 Relationship between PTAs, FDI, and exports *(continued)*

Hejazi and Safarian (2002)
    Dependent variable: LN (inward Canadian FDI stock$_{jt}$)
    Selected independent variables

NAFTA dummy: −0.17*
    Dependent variable: LN (outward FDI stock from Canada$_{jt}$)
    Selected independent variables

NAFTA dummy: 0.34**

Exports and FDI: Complements, not substitutes
Graham and Wada (2000)
    Dependent variable: LN (outward US FDI stock$_{ijt}$)
    Selected independent variables

	Low income	High income
LN (imports$_{ijt}$)	0.79*	−0.39**
LN (exports$_{ijt}$)	1.3*	1.59**

Hejazi and Safarian (1999)[g]
    Dependent variable: LN (Canadian imports$_{ijt}$)
    Selected independent variable

LN (inward Canadian FDI stock$_{ijt}$)   0.02

    Dependent variable: LN (exports$_{ijt}$)
    Selected independent variables

LN (outward Canadian FDI stock$_{ijt}$)   0.07***

*** = significance at 1% level; ** = significance at 5% level; * = significance at 10% level.

a. MRTA captures merchandise trade provisions of a PTA, takes the value of the member liberalization index (MLI) if both countries i and j belong to the same PTA; MRTAij* means that country J* does not belong to the PTA.
b. 3wave captures "new age" provisions of a PTA, takes the value of nonmerchandise MLI if both countries i and j belong to the same PTA and 0 otherwise. 3waveij* means that country J* does not belong to the PTA.
c. EMit is the logarithm of joint GDP of all countries to which the host has tariff-free access due to common membership in an FTA (includes the host's own GDP as well).
d. EMjt is the logarithm of joint GDP of the source country, plus all countries that are FTA partners of source country.
e. Same FTA is a dummy that takes a value of 1 when the source and the host countries belong to the same free trade area.
f. REGY denotes market size extended to include regional market size for all countries belonging to a regional trade agreement.
g. Hejazi and Safarian (1999) also model the relationship at sectoral level for 14 sectors of the Canadian economy.

Sources: Adams et al. (2003), Levy-Yeyati, Stein, and Daude (2003), Jaumotte (2004), Hallward-Driemeier (2003), Globerman and Shapiro (1999), Hejazi and Safarian (2002), Graham and Wada (2000), Hejazi and Safarian (1999).

(USITC 2005a, 6-2), which concludes, "The investment provisions of the covered FTAs are not expected to yield large changes in total foreign direct investment between the United States and its FTA partners."[4]

Studies Covering All Countries

Using a dataset that reflects the experience of 20 FDI source countries (OECD members) investing in 60 host countries from 1982 through 1999, Levy-Yeyati, Stein, and Daude (2003) find that, when countries join an FTA, the bilateral FDI stock between the members increases by about 24 percent on average. The size of the "extended market" of the host country—that is, adding up the GDP figures for the FTA partners—has a positive effect on the bilateral FDI stock attracted from the source country. The elasticity of the bilateral FDI stock regarding the size of the "extended market" of the host country is about 0.1.

Adams et al. (2003) examine a sample of 116 countries from 1988 to 1997. They create dummies to capture separately the effect of "traditional market access" provisions and "third wave provisions" (investment, government procurement, services, etc.). They also create dummies to separate the effect of inward FDI stock from PTA partners and third countries (see table D.1). They find that market access provisions are not statistically significant, but that third-wave provisions are, for FDI stocks from both within the PTA and outside the area. The third-wave provisions of the North American Free Trade Agreement (NAFTA) are correlated with a 10 percent decrease in intraregional FDI, but an almost 5 percent increase in inward FDI stock from external countries. Third-wave provisions in the European Union are associated with a 3 percent increase in inward FDI stock from external countries; the effect of the Southern Cone Common Market (Mercosur) is much larger, a 32 percent increase. However, the European Free Trade Association (EFTA) is associated with a 41 percent decrease in inward FDI stock from external countries, perhaps because non-EFTA investors chose the European Union rather than EFTA.

Jaumotte (2004) reports on a sample of 71 developing countries from 1980 to 1999, mostly South-South integration initiatives. She finds that a 1.0 percent increase in the regional market size—again, adding together the markets of both partners—is correlated with a 0.4 percent increase in the stock of FDI for each party to the agreement. The result reflects a more general finding about FDI, namely, that it favors large markets as measured by GDP (see, e.g., Graham and Wada 2000).

---

4. The USITC (2005a, 6-2) also concludes that "in specific sectors, however, the covered FTAs may generate new outbound U.S. investment."

Studies Covering NAFTA Partners

Globerman and Shapiro (1999) evaluate Canadian FDI from 1950 to 1995, using annual data for FDI stock (book value) disaggregated by sector. They find that the Canada–United States Free Trade Agreement (CUSFTA)/ NAFTA dummy variable is correlated with greater Canadian outward direct investment in all sectors. The authors also conclude that the CUSFTA/ NAFTA was not associated with net foreign investment in Canada, although they highlight a trade-induced increase in manufacturing FDI.[5]

Hejazi and Safarian (2002, 20) indicate that "NAFTA has resulted in reduced Canadian inward FDI and increased Canadian outward FDI, both to the United States and especially beyond." They find that the NAFTA dummy variable is correlated with a 17 percent decrease in inward FDI stock to Canada, and an almost 34 percent increase in Canadian outward FDI stock.

By contrast, Buckley et al. (2005) find that "the introduction of the free trade agreements between Canada and the USA increased the responsiveness of US investors to growth in the Canadian economy by a factor of two." In a 2000 working paper, the same authors find that an increase in a compound variable that measures both the size of the US GDP and the existence (or not) of an FTA between Canada and the United States is correlated with larger non-NAFTA partner FDI stocks placed in Canada: A 1 percent increase in the compound variable is associated with a 0.04 percent increase in the French FDI stock placed in Canada, and a 0.01 percent increase in the US stock.

Hallward-Driemeier (2003) examines the relationship between bilateral investment treaties (BITS) and FDI flows. Her dataset covers bilateral outflows from 20 OECD countries to 31 developing countries from 1980 to 2000. She finds a nonsignificant negative correlation between BITS and flows.[6] Interestingly, however, she also finds that NAFTA did increase FDI flows to Mexico, as the NAFTA dummy is correlated with an increase in the level of FDI flows from OECD countries into Mexico.

Exports and FDI: Complements, Not Substitutes

Finally, it is worth reporting the analysis by Graham and Wada (2000) of the connection between US exports and US FDI stocks placed in host countries

---

5. The authors, however, do not conclude that CUSFTA/NAFTA caused a net outflow of capital, since "the direct investment data for Canada indicate that (in the post-1989 period) Canadian outward direct investment increased especially for destinations other than the United States." Among other forces, they point to integration in the European Union as a "pull–factor." (Globerman and Shapiro 1999, 19).

6. Adams et al. (2003) reach the same conclusion in their analysis of the relationship between BITS and FDI.

with different income levels. Among other host countries, they examine the experience of some 19 high-income countries from 1983 to 1996. They find that US FDI and US exports complement one another: On average, a 1 percent increase in the US outward FDI stock is associated with a 0.6 percent increase in US manufactured exports to the host country.

Hejazi and Safarian (1999) also confirm the complementary relationship between exports and FDI for Canada. They find that a 1.0 percent increase in the Canadian outward FDI stock is correlated with a 0.7 percent increase in Canadian exports, and that higher levels of inward FDI stock increase imports into Canada, but that the size of the import associations is only one-third the size of the export association.[7]

---

7. The study also analyzes the relationship at the sectoral level. The authors find that the relationship between exports and the outward FDI stock is positive for nine sectors and negative for four sectors.

Appendix E

Technical Aspects of the Gravity and CGE Models

Gravity Model

Dataset Construction

As mentioned in chapter 8, the gravity model analysis underlying this study is based on a dataset constructed by joining elements of two large datasets developed by other researchers. The first of these is the extensive gravity model dataset developed by Andrew Rose (2004), which covers aggregate bilateral merchandise trade between 178 countries from 1948 to 1999 (with gaps and excluding Taiwan and some centrally planned economies), compiled from the International Monetary Fund (IMF 2005b). The bilateral trade figures in the Rose dataset are averages of f.o.b export and c.i.f import data in US dollars, deflated by the US consumer price index.

The Rose dataset also includes "core" and regional trading arrangement (RTA) explanatory variables, discussed in chapter 8 and identified in tables 8.1 and 8.2.[1] The core explanatory variables are drawn from several standard sources, including the Central Intelligence Agency (2005), the IMF (2004), Penn World Tables (CIC 2005), and the World Bank (2005b).

To give the Rose gravity model and dataset somewhat greater analytical depth, the Rose dataset was concorded with bilateral merchandise trade data at the 1-digit SITC level, taken from the highly disaggregated bilateral trade dataset compiled by Feenstra et al. (2005). This dataset covers bilateral trade data from 1962 to 2000, organized by 4-digit SITC (revi-

---

1. The Swiss-US trade integration and openness variables were compiled for the present study and added to the dataset by the authors.

sion 2) categories. In contrast to the Rose trade data, world trade flows in the Feenstra-Lipsey dataset are drawn from United Nations (UN) data sources and are based primarily on reporter-country import data, supplemented as possible where import data gaps occur by reporter-country export data. The Feenstra-Lipsey dataset covers a somewhat smaller number of trading countries than the Rose dataset does, especially from 1984 to 2000, when the dataset contains bilateral trade for only 72 countries, though this still accounts for 98 percent of world exports from 1996 to 2000.

For the present study, the Feenstra-Lipsey world trade data were aggregated to the 1-digit SITC level by country pairs and deflated by the US consumer price index (1983 = 100). After transforming these real trade flows to natural-log terms, they were finally integrated with the Rose data using a concordance between the UN (Feenstra-Lipsey) and IMF (Rose) country codes. In the process, account was taken of all reported adjustments to the UN trade data by Feenstra et al. (2005), except the estimated redistribution of value added in trade between China and Hong Kong, separately reported in Feenstra et al. (2005). Lost in the process, however, were disaggregated trade flows for the former Soviet bloc countries, some less developed countries, and Taiwan, for which no UN (Feenstra-Lipsey) or IMF (Rose) country codes were available. The separate UN country codes for former West Germany and present-day Germany were merged in the Feenstra-Lipsey dataset before integrating the two datasets, thus preserving pre-1991 observations on West Germany's bilateral disaggregated trade, including with Switzerland. Table E.1 describes the regression variables included in the combined Feenstra-Lipsey and Rose dataset.

Estimating Techniques

As might be expected, estimating gravity models using cross-sectional time-series data presents some complex and difficult problems in econometric methodology (Egger 2002, Hsiao 2003). Essentially, ordinary least squares (OLS) regression is unsatisfactory because it does not admit possible unobserved effects related to combinations of commodities and pairs of trading countries in the dataset. As a consequence, the analysis reported in chapter 8 uses a random-effects variant of the gravity model, with generalized least squares (GLS) as the estimating technique. For a discussion of the application of the GLS technique to a random-effects regression model, see Hsiao (2003). An important assumption of the random-effects approach, embodied in the estimation results reported in chapter 8, is that the unobservable random-effects variable is uncorrelated with the observed explanatory variables included in the regression equation.

Reservations about Contrary Results

Adams et al. (2003), colleagues at the Australia Productivity Commission (APC), report negative RTA coefficients using an analytic framework in the

Table E.1 Gravity model regression variables, 1962–69

Regression variable	Description
Dependent variable	Log value of bilateral trade by 1-digit SITC, real US dollars
Distance	Log of distance
GDP	Log of product of real GDPs
GDP per capita	Log of product of real GDPs per capita
Common language	Common language dummy
Common border	Land border dummy
Landlocked	Number of countries landlocked (0/1/2)
Island	Number of island countries (0/1/2)
Land area	Log of product of land areas
Common colonizer	Dummy for common colonizer, post-1945
Colony	Dummy for country pairs currently in colonial relationship
Ever a colony	Dummy for country pairs ever in colonial relationship
Common country	Dummy for same nation/perennial colonies
Currency union	Strict currency union dummy
GSP	GSP dummy
RTAs	RTA dummy covering 10 regional trading arrangements
Swiss-US trade	Dummy for Swiss-US trade
US openness	Dummy for US trade with all partners
Swiss openness	Dummy for Swiss trade with all partners

Note: Dependent variable based on bilateral trade flows drawn from Feenstra–Lipsey dataset. Swiss-US trade and openness variables constructed by the authors. All other variables drawn directly from Rose 2004 dataset. RTA variable covers the Association of Southeast Asian Nations (ASEAN), European Union (EU), US-Israel FTA, NAFTA (North American Free Trade Agreement), Caribbean Community (Caricom), Agreement on Trade and Commercial Relations between the Government of Australia and the Government of Papua New Guinea (PATCRA), Australia–New Zealand Closer Economic Relations Trade Agreement (ANZCERTA), Central American Common Market (CACM), South Pacific Regional Trade and Economic Cooperation Agreement (SPARTECA), and Southern Cone Common Market (Mercosur).

Sources: Rose (2004), Feenstra et al. (2005), and authors' calculations.

spirit of the gravity model and a database that ends in 1997. These authors claim to find net trade diversion for 12 out of 16 recent preferential trade agreements (PTAs). The 12 PTAs for which the authors claim net trade diversion (see their table 4.3) are the ASEAN Free Trade Area (AFTA), the European Free Trade Association (EFTA), the European Community/European Union, the Southern Cone Common Market (Mercosur), the North American Free Trade Agreement (NAFTA), the Australia–New Zealand Closer Economic Relations agreement, EU-Switzerland, Chile-Colombia, Australia-Papua New Guinea, Chile-Mercosur, EU-Egypt, and EU-Poland. The 4 PTAs for which the authors claim net trade creation are the Andean Pact, the Latin American Free Trade Association (LAFTA)/ Latin American Integration Association (LAIA), US-Israel, and the South Pacific Regional Trade and Economic Cooperation Agreement (SPARTECA).

For several reasons, we do not subscribe to the APC findings. To begin with, their technique for measuring net trade diversion is poorly explained and justified in the paper. The APC authors add up their three RTA coefficients in a different manner—and often get a different sign—from the methodological predecessor paper authored by Soloaga and Winters (2001). The text description of the variables does not match up with the tables. Nowhere in the APC paper is there a simple table showing the amount of trade created between RTA members and diverted from nonmembers; we believe such a table might cast considerable doubt on the estimated coefficients. Instead of deleting zero-trade observations from the database as is customary, the authors represent them in a curious manner in the regression analysis that could bias the estimated coefficients. The "dynamic" gravity model used by the APC authors—adding a time dimension to annual observations—is not, to us, a persuasive alternative to the customary before-RTA and after-RTA analysis.

Computable General Equilibrium (CGE) Model

As mentioned in chapter 8, our CGE model is the Global Trade Analysis Project (GTAP) framework, a publicly available and widely adopted model. Multiregion and multisector, it assumes perfect competition and constant returns to scale. Bilateral trade is handled via the Armington assumption, which treats goods from alternative sources as imperfect substitutes. Import demand functions are separated by agent (sometimes called the Salter specification).[2] Production conditions are modeled using "nested" constant elasticity of substitution (CES) functions,[3] and intermediate goods are used in fixed proportions.[4] Representative household demand takes into account changes in demand structures as incomes rise.[5] These and other aspects of

---

2. In other words, the aggregate household, government, investor, and each firm all make their own individual choices about how much of each intermediate input to source domestically, and how much to import.

3. The CES function treats primary factors of production (capital, skilled and unskilled labor, natural resources, and land) as imperfect substitutes in the production process, with a single elasticity describing substitutability between all factor pairs. Intermediate inputs are used in fixed proportion to output.

4. For any given proportional change in output, intermediate input will grow by the same proportion. The input-output (IO) coefficients are obtained from the IO tables routinely produced by statistical agencies in most economies, and constructed for the few regions where the data in unavailable.

5. Changes in demand structure are modeled by so-called "non-homothetic" demand functions.

the GTAP model are fully documented in Hertel (1997) and the GTAP Web site (www.gtap.org). Recent surveys of the application of CGE models to regional trade negotiations include Scollay and Gilbert (2000), Scollay and Gilbert (2001), Gilbert and Wahl (2002), Robinson and Thierfelder (2002), and Lloyd and MacLaren (2004).

Base Data

The base data for the simulations are drawn from the GTAP6 database (final release), the most complete dataset available. It represents the world economy as it was in 2001. The database contains input-output representations of individual economies, obtained from national statistical agencies, international trade and income data from the UN Comtrade database, and the World Bank, respectively. The GTAP6 database improves significantly on GTAP5 by incorporating new protection data from the AMAD and MACMAPS databases. The latter feature bilateral tariffs, so RTAs in place in 2001 are fully integrated. Full database documentation can be found in Dimaranan and McDougall (2005).

Aggregation Strategy

While the GTAP6 database features 87 regions and 57 sectors, it must be aggregated for reasons of computational efficiency. The aggregation strategy we have chosen is given in table E.2. We ranked the total exports of the United States and Switzerland and the bilateral exports of the two countries, then used this ranking, along with "natural" sectoral groupings, to aggregate the data. A similar approach was followed for regional aggregation, where care was also taken to include current US partners within NAFTA, and also new and prospective FTA partners—Chile, Australia, Singapore, Morocco, Central American Free Trade Agreement (CAFTA) members, Southern African Customs Union (SACU) members, and Thailand.

Data Adjustments

While agricultural protection data in GTAP6 is excellent, services protection data is limited. Dee, Hanslow, and Phamduc (2003) have published their estimates of barriers to services trade at the aggregate level. In this study, we split services into traded and nontraded categories, following the classification adopted by Dee, Hanslow, and Phamduc (2003) and using the estimates of services barriers from that study. These barriers are implemented using several instruments: import tax equivalents, export tax

Table E.2 Aggregation scheme for GTAP6 database

Sectoral aggregation	Regional aggregation
Grains	Australia
Oil seeds	New Zealand
Plant-based fibers	China
Other crops	Hong Kong
Raw animal products	Japan
Wool	South Korea
Forestry	Taiwan
Coal, oil, and gas	Indonesia
Dairy products	Malaysia
Other food products	Philippines
Textiles and wearing apparel	Singapore
Wood products	Thailand
Paper products	Vietnam
Chemicals	Canada
Ferrous metals	United States
Nonferrous metals	Mexico
Metal products	Brazil
Motor vehicles	Chile
Electronic equipment	Rest of South America
Machinery and equipment	Central America
Other manufactures	European Union
Nontraded services	Switzerland
Traded services	Rest of EFTA
	Eastern Europe
	Morocco
	SACU
	Rest of world

equivalents, taxes on output, and taxes on domestic capital. The various tax rates were imposed on the GTAP6 dataset prior to the major simulation using the ALTERTAX procedure. This procedure fixes the current account balance and uses parameters such that all key shares in the model remain constant when the new taxes are imposed, while ensuring that the database remains consistent.

An important data adjustment regarding the Swiss ad valorem equivalent (AVE) tariff on imports of other manufactures requires mention. "Other manufactures" is a GTAP6 basket category that includes all manufactures except motor vehicles, machinery, and electronic equipment. GTAP6 records the Swiss AVE tariff on this category as 155 percent, an implausible figure that is not supported by the detailed tariff information presented in chapter 4. Based on the UNCTAD data summarized in table E.3, we have assumed that the Swiss tariff barrier for this category is 11 percent,

Table E.3 High Swiss tariffs on selected US manufactured exports (4-digit level headings facing average applied tariffs exceeding 5 percent)

Heading (HS-4)	Tariff item	Average Swiss tariff[a] (2001)	Swiss tariff lines > 5%	US exports 2004 (millions of dollars) Switzerland
7318	Screws, bolts, nuts, hooks, and similar articles, of iron or steel	75.2	30	15
8526	Radar, radio navigational aid, and remote control apparatus	48.6	1	12
2403	Tobacco and substitute manufactures; extracts and essences	29.1	7	13
8708	Parts and accessories motor vehicles of various purposes	28.0	33	13
4911	Printed matter, nesoi, including printed pictures and photographs	24.1	4	24
8529	Parts for television, radio and radar apparatus	22.6	2	18
8524	Records, tapes and other recorded media	20.1	2	21
3917	Tubes, pipes and hoses, and fittings, of plastics	18.4	9	13
3304	Beauty or make-up and skin care preparations	17.1	5	36
8504	Electrical transformers and power supplies for adp machines	15.8	13	22
8483	Transmission, gears, clutches, and other auto parts	15.7	13	10
8501	Electric motors and generators (excluding generating sets)	14.2	15	10
8409	Parts for spark-ignition or internal combustion piston engines	12.3	10	191
8481	Taps, cocks, valves, and similar appliances for pipes	12.2	7	31
7307	Tube or pipe fittings of iron or steel	8.5	9	41
3824	Binders for foundry molds or cores	6.5	10	71
8413	Pumps for liquids, liquid elevators, and parts	6.4	1	13
8421	Filtering or purifying machinery and apparatus and parts	5.3	5	12
	Subtotal for high tariff HS-4 manufactured exports	21.1[b]	176	565
	Total HS-4 manufactured exports over $10 million	6.1[c]	205	8,306

a. Values reported correspond to averages of ad valorem equivalents for non *ad valorem* tariffs. All entries in the Swiss tariff schedule are non ad valorem.
b. Simple average of all observations in that column.
c. Simple average of tariffs for US HS-4 exports to Switzerland exceeding $10 million. By comparison, in 2004, the simple average Swiss MFN tariff for nonagricultural products (WTO definition) was 2.3 percent.

Sources: UNCTAD (2005).

although even that figure might be exaggerated.[6] The figure of 11 percent is calculated by giving two-thirds weight to the simple average Swiss tariff (6.1 percent) on all US HS-4 manufacture categories where US exports are over $10 million, and one-third weight to the Swiss average tariff (21.1 percent) on those HS-4 manufactured exports where the Swiss tariff exceeds 5 percent.

---

6. Detailed comparisons of UNCTAD and WTO AVE tariff figures for Switzerland (for example, as reported in the notes to chapter appendix table 4A.2) suggest that UNCTAD figures are often too high. The problem in evaluating Swiss tariffs arises because many duties are specific, and different methodologies are used to compute their ad valorem equivalents.

References

Acqnet (US government source for acquisition information). 2005. Subpart 25.4—Trade Agreements. Available at www.arnet.gov (accessed on November 15, 2005).

Adams, R., P. Dee, J. Gali, and G. McGuire. 2003. *The Trade and Investment Effects of Preferential Trading Arrangements—Old and New Evidence.* Productivity Commission Staff Working Paper (May). Canberra: Australian Government Productivity Commission.

AFIRE (Association of Foreign Investors in Real Estate). 2004. Barriers to Foreign Investment in US REITs Removed. *AFIRE Newsletter* (November/December). Available at www. afire.org (accessed on November 5, 2005).

Australia Department of Foreign Affairs and Trade. 2005. The Australia–United States Free Trade Agreement: Advancing Australian Agricultural Exports. Available at www.dfat. gov.au (accessed on November 5, 2005).

Baldwin, Richard E. 1994. *Towards an Integrated Europe.* London: Centre for Economic Policy Research.

Baldwin, Richard E. 1995. A Domino Theory of Regionalism. In *Expanding European Regionalism: The EU's New Members,* ed. R. Baldwin, P. Haaparanta, and J. Kiander. Cambridge: Cambridge University Press.

Baldwin, Richard E. 2003. *The Spoke Trap: Hub and Spoke Regionalism in East Asia.* KIEP Discussion Paper Number 04-02 (December). Seoul: Korea Institute for International Economic Policy.

Baldwin, Richard E. 2005a. Asian Regionalism: Promises and Pitfalls. In *East Asian Economic Regionalism: Feasibilities and Challenges,* ed. Choong Yang Ahn, Richard E. Baldwin, and Inkyo Cheong. New York: Springer.

Baldwin, Richard E. 2005b. Stepping Stones or Building Blocs? Regional and Multilateral Integration. In *Regional Economic Integration in a Global Framework,* ed. J. McKay, M. O. Armengol, and G. Pineau. Frankfurt: European Central Bank.

Baldwin, Richard E., and Charles Wyplosz. 2004. *The Economics of European Integration.* London: McGraw-Hill.

Bernier, Ivan. 2004. The Recent Free Trade Agreements of the United States as Illustration of Their New Strategy Regarding the Audiovisual Sector. Available at www. mediatrademonitor.org (accessed on November 5, 2005).

Blomström, Magnus, and Ari Kokko. 1997. *Regional Integration and Foreign Direct Investment.* NBER Working Paper 6019. Cambridge, MA: National Bureau of Economic Research.

Blomström, Magnus, and Robert E. Lipsey. 1987. Transnational Corporations in U.S. and Swedish Trade. *CTC Reporter*, no. 24 (Autumn): 51–54.

Bradford, Scott C., Paul L. E. Grieco, and Gary C. Hufbauer. 2005. The Payoff to America from Global Integration. In *The United States and the World Economy: Foreign Economic Policy for the Next Administration*, ed. C. Fred Bergsten. Washington: Institute for International Economics.

Brainard, Lael S. 1997. An Empirical Assessment of the Proximity-Concentration Trade-Off Between Multinational Sales and Trade. *American Economic Review* 87, no. 4: 520–44.

Buckley, Peter J., Jeremy Clegg, Nicoals Forsans, and Kevin T. Reilly. 2000. *Assessing NAFTA's Impact on the Strategies of Multinational Firms in Canada: A First Econometric Investigation.* Working Paper (April). Leeds: Leeds University Business School.

Buckley, Peter J., Jeremy Clegg, Nicoals Forsans, and Kevin T. Reilly. 2005. A Simple and Flexible Dynamic Approach to Foreign Direct Investment Growth: The Canada-United States Relationship in the Context of Free Trade. Available at http://ideas.repec.org/e/pre23.html (accessed on November 5, 2005).

CBO (Congressional Budget Office). 2005. *Policies that Distort World Agricultural Trade: Prevalence and Magnitude.* Washington: Congress of the United States Congressional Budget Office.

Ceglowski, Janet. 2005 (forthcoming). Does Gravity Matter in a Services Economy? *Review of World Economics (Weltwirtschaftliches Archiv).*

CIA (Central Intelligence Agency). 2005. CIA—The World Factbook. Available at www.cia.gov (accessed on November 7, 2005).

CIC (Center for International Comparisons). 2005. Penn World Tables. Available at http://pwt.econ.upenn.edu/ (accessed on November 7, 2005).

Choi, Inbom, and Jeffrey J. Schott. 2001. *Free Trade between Korea and the United States.* Washington: Institute for International Economics.

Confoederatio Helvetica (Federal Authorities of the Swiss Confederation). 1997. Ordonnance du DFE sur l'Agriculture Biologique. Available at www.admin.ch (accessed on November 6, 2005).

Confoederatio Helvetica (Federal Authorities of the Swiss Confederation). 2001. Ordonnance du 28 Février 2001 sur la Protection des Végétaux (OPV). Available at www.admin.ch (accessed on November 6, 2005).

Confoederatio Helvetica (Federal Authorities of the Swiss Confederation). 2003. Loi Fédérale sur l'Agriculture. Available at www.admin.ch (accessed on November 6, 2005).

Confoederatio Helvetica (Federal Authorities of the Swiss Confederation). 2005a. Ordonnance sur l'Allégement Douanier Selon l'Emploi. Available at www.admin.ch (accessed on November 6, 2005).

Confoederatio Helvetica (Federal Authorities of the Swiss Confederation). 2005b. Le Conseil Fédéral Veut Assouplir le Monopole des Lettres. Available at www.admin.ch (accessed on November 6, 2005).

Copenhagen Economics. 2005. *Economic Assessment of Barriers to the Internal Market for Services.* Available at www.copenhageneconomics.com (accessed on November 5, 2005).

Curzon, Gerard. 1965. *Multilateral Commercial Diplomacy: GATT and Its Impact on National Commercial Policies and Techniques.* London: Michael Joseph Limited.

Dee, Philippa, K. Hanslow, and T. Phamduc. 2003. Measuring the Cost of Barriers to Trade in Services. In *Trade in Services in the Asia-Pacific Region*, ed. Takatoshi Ito and Anne O. Krueger. Chicago, IL: University of Chicago Press.

DeRosa, Dean, and John Gilbert. 2005. The Economic Impacts of Multilateral and Regional Trade Agreements in Quantitative Economic Models: An *Ex Post* Evaluation. Draft paper prepared for the Institute for International Economics, Washington (June).

Dimaranan, Betina, and Robert A. McDougall, eds. 2005 (forthcoming). Global Trade, Assistance, and Protection: The GTAP6 Database. Center for Global Trade Analysis. West Lafayette: Purdue University.

Direcon (Dirección General de Relaciones Económicas Internacionales). 2003. Tratado de Libre Comerico Chile-Estados Unidos (US-Chile Free Trade Agreement) Santiago: Government of Chile. Available at www.sice.oas.org (accessed on February 9, 2006).

Dunning, John H. 1993. *Multinational Enterprises and the Global Economy*. Wokingham, England: Addison-Wesley Publishing Company.

Dunning, John H. 1997. The European Internal Market Programmed and Inbound Foreign Direct Investment. *Journal of Common Market Studies* 35, no. 2 (June): 189–223.

Dunning, John H., ed. 2000. *Regions, Globalization, and the Knowledge-Based Economy*. Oxford: Oxford University Press.

EFTA (European Free Trade Association). 1992. *Agreement Between the EFTA States and Israel*. Geneva: EFTA Secretariat. Available at http://secretariat.efta.int.

EFTA (European Free Trade Association). 1993. *Agreement Between the EFTA States and the Republic of Bulgaria*. Geneva: EFTA Secretariat. Available at http://secretariat.efta.int.

EFTA (European Free Trade Association). 2000. *Agreement Between the EFTA States and Mexico*. Geneva: EFTA Secretariat. Available at http://secretariat.efta.int.

EFTA (European Free Trade Association). 2002a. *Agreement Between the EFTA States and Singapore*. Geneva: EFTA Secretariat. Available at http://secretariat.efta.int.

EFTA (European Free Trade Association). 2002b. *Introduction to the Agreement Between the EFTA States and Mexico*. Geneva: EFTA Secretariat. Available at http://secretariat.efta.int.

EFTA (European Free Trade Association). 2003. *Free Trade Agreement Between the EFTA States and the Republic of Chile*. Geneva: EFTA Secretariat. Available at http://secretariat.efta.int.

EFTA (European Free Trade Association). 2004. *Free Trade Agreement Between the EFTA States and the Republic of Lebanon*. Geneva: EFTA Secretariat. Available at http://secretariat.efta.int.

EFTA (European Free Trade Association). 2005. Algeria-EFTA Discuss Future Trade Relations. November 9, 2005. Geneva: EFTA Secretariat. Available at http://secretariat.efta.int (accessed on November 30, 2005).

EIU (Economist Intelligence Unit). 2005a. *Country Profile: Switzerland*. London.

EIU (Economist Intelligence Unit). 2005b. *Country Profile: United States*. London.

Egger, Peter. 2002. An Econometric View on the Estimation of Gravity Models and the Calculation of Trade Potentials. *World Economy* 25, no. 2 (February): 297–312.

Embassy of Switzerland. 2005. Economy, Finance, and Commerce. Washington. Available at Switzerland's Federal Department of Foreign Affairs' Web site at www.eda.admin.ch (accessed on November 7, 2005).

European Commission. 2002. Agreement Between the European Community and Swiss Confederation Agreement on Trade in Agricultural Products. Available at the European Union's portal site at http://europa.eu.int (accessed on November 5, 2005).

European Commission. 2004a. *Report on US Barriers to Trade and Investment* (December). Brussels.

European Commission. 2004b. *User's Handbook to the Rules of Preferential Origin Used in Trade between the European Community and Other European Countries*. Brussels.

European Commission. 2005. Market Access Database: Sanitary and Phytosanitary Export Database. Available at http://mkaccdb.eu.int.

FAS (Foreign Agricultural Service). 2005. US Trade Internet System. Washington: US Department of Agriculture. Available at www.fas.usda.gov/ustrade (accessed in December 2005).

Feenstra, Robert C., Robert E. Lipsey, Haiyan Deng, Alyson C. Ma, and Hengyong Mo. 2005. *World Trade Flows: 1962–2000*. NBER Working Paper 11040. Cambridge, MA: National Bureau of Economic Research.

Findlay, C., and T. Warren, eds. 2000. *Impediments to Trade in Services: Measurement and Policy Implications*. New York: Routledge.

Findlay, C., and T. Warren. 2005. Measures in Restrictions on Trade in Services Database. Available at the Australian Government Productivity Commission's Web site at www.pc.gov.au (accessed on November 15, 2005).

Frankel, Jeffrey A. 1997. *Regional Trading Blocs in the World Economic System*. Washington: Institute for International Economics.

Freehills. 2004. Brief Overview of the FTA—Trade Marks and Geographical Indications. Available at www.freehills.com.au (accessed on November 7, 2005).

Freeman, Gary P., Luis F. B. Plascencia, and Mark Setzler. 2003. The Decline of Barriers to Immigrant Economic and Political Rights in the American States: 1977–2001. *International Migration Review* 37, no. 1 (spring): 5–23.

GATS (General Agreement on Trade in Services). 2002. Request from the European Commission and Its Member States to the United States. Available at www.gatswatch.org (accessed on November 5, 2005).

Gilbert, J., and T. Wahl. 2002. Applied General Equilibrium Assessments of Trade Liberalisation in China. *World Economy* 25, no. 5: 697–731.

Globerman, Steven, and Daniel Shapiro. 1999. The Impact of Government Policies on Foreign Direct Investment: The Canadian Experience. *Journal of Business Studies* 30, no. 3 (September): 513–32.

Graham, Edward M., and Paul R. Krugman. 1995. *Foreign Direct Investment in the United States.* Washington: Institute for International Economics.

Graham, Edward M., and Erika Wada. 2000. Appendix B: Is Foreign Direct Investment a Complement to Trade? In *Fighting the Wrong Enemy: Antiglobal Activists and Multinational Enterprises,* by Edward Graham. Washington: Institute for International Economics.

Graham, John D. 2003. The Perils of the Precautionary Principle: Lessons from the American and European Experience. Paper presented at regulatory forum at the Heritage Foundation, Washington (October).

Greenaway, David, and Chris Milner. 2002. Regionalism and Gravity. *Scottish Journal of Political Economy* 49, no. 5: 574–85.

Hallward-Driemeier, Mary. 2003. *Do Bilateral Investment Treaties Attract Foreign Direct Investment? Only a Bit—And They Could Bite.* World Bank Policy Research Working Paper 3121. Washington: World Bank.

Hejazi, Walid, and Edward A. Safarian. 1999. Modelling Links between Canadian Trade and Foreign Direct Investment. *Micro: Micro-Economic Policy Analysis Branch Bulletin* 7, no. 3: 4.

Hejazi, Walid, and Edward A. Safarian. 2001. Canada and Foreign Direct Investment: A Study of Determinants. University of Toronto Centre for Public Management, Toronto. Photocopy.

Hejazi, Walid, and Edward A. Safarian. 2002. Explaining Canada's Changing FDI Patterns. Paper presented at the 37th annual meeting of the Canadian Economics Association, Carleton University, Ottawa (September).

Hertel, Thomas, ed. 1997. *Global Trade Analysis: Modeling and Applications.* New York: Cambridge University Press.

Hewitt Associates. 2002. *Bilateral Agreement with the EU on Free Movement of Persons (Switzerland).* Available at http://was4.hewitt.com (accessed on November 30, 2005).

Hsiao, Cheng. 2003. *Analysis of Panel Data.* Cambridge: Cambridge University Press.

Hufbauer, Gary C., and F. M. Adler. 1968. *Overseas Manufacturing Investment and the Balance of Payments.* US Treasury Department Tax Policy Research Study no. 1. Washington: US Government Printing Office.

Hufbauer, Gary C., and Jeffrey J. Schott. 2005. *NAFTA Revisited: Achievements and Challenges.* Washington: Institute for International Economics.

Hufbauer, Gary C., and Yee Wong. 2005. Prospects for Regional Free Trade in Asia. Paper presented at the RAND-China Reform Forum Conference, RAND Corporation, Santa Monica.

ICSID (International Centre for Settlement of Investment Disputes). 2005. ICSID Cases. Available at the World Bank's Web site at www.worldbank.org/icsid/cases/cases.htm (accessed on November 7, 2005).

IMF (International Monetary Fund). 2005b. *Direction of Trade Statistics* (May). Washington.

Jaumotte, Florence. 2004. Foreign *Direct Investment and Regional Trade Agreements: The Market Size Effect Revisited.* IMF Working Paper 206. Washington: International Monetary Fund.

Jemmi, T., and Cornelia Herholz. 2003. Bilateral Veterinary Agreement between Switzerland and the EU. *FVO Magazine* 4–5: 11–14.

Josling, Tim, and Dale Hathaway. 2004. *This Far and No Farther? Nudging Agricultural Reform Forward.* Policy Brief Number PB 04-1. Washington: Institute for International Economics.

Josling, Tim, Donna Roberts, and David Orden. 2004. *Food Regulation and Trade: Toward a Safe and Open Global System.* Washington: Institute for International Economics.

Levy-Yeyati, E., Ernesto Stein, and Christian Daude. 2003. *Regional Integration and the Location of FDI.* IDB Research Department Working Paper 492. Washington: Inter-American Development Bank.

Linnemann, Hans. 1966. *An Econometric Study of International Trade Flows.* Amsterdam: North Holland.

Lloyd, P. J., and D. MacLaren. 2004. Gains and Losses from Regional Trading Agreements: A Survey. *Economic Record* 80, no. 251: 445–97.

Mann, Catherine. 2006. *Accelerating the Globalization of the America: Information Technology.* Washington: Institute for International Economics (forthcoming).

Meltzer, Eleanor K. 2002. What You Need to Know about Geographical Indications and Trademarks. *Virginia Lawyer* (June/July).

Ministerio de Comercio Exterior de Costa Rica (Comex). 2004. *Tratado de Libre Comercio entre Centroamérica y los Estados Unidos: Logros y Resultados* (number 8, January). San Jose, Costa Rica.

NAFTA Free Trade Commission. 2005. Note of Interpretation. Available at www.webapps.dfait-maeci-gc.ca (accessed in March 2005).

Nell, Philippe G. 1994. Les Déterminants de l'Évolution de la Politique d'Intégration Européenne de la Suisse: 1948–1994. *Revue d'Allemagne* (July–September).

OECD (Organization for Economic Cooperation and Development). 2002. *OECD Economic Surveys: Switzerland 2001–2002.* Paris.

OECD (Organization for Economic Cooperation and Development). 2003. *Agricultural Policies in OECD Countries—Monitoring and Evaluation.* Paris.

OECD (Organization for Economic Cooperation and Development). 2004a. *OECD Economic Surveys: Switzerland 2003–2004.* Paris.

OECD (Organization for Economic Cooperation and Development). 2004b. *Economic Surveys: United States 2003–2004.* Paris.

OECD (Organization for Economic Cooperation and Development). 2004c. *Trends and Recent Developments in Foreign Direct Investment (June).* Paris.

OECD (Organization for Economic Cooperation and Development). 2004d. *United States: Report on Competition Law and Institutions.* Paris.

OECD (Organization for Economic Cooperation and Development). 2004e. Agricultural Policy Indicators: Producer and Consumer Support Estimates. Paris.

OECD (Organization for Economic Cooperation and Development). 2005. *Economic Outlook 77.* Paris.

Owen, Claire. 2005. Report: Fact Finding Mission to Switzerland. Institute for International Economics, Washington. Photocopy (June).

Panagariya, A. 2000. Preferential Trade Liberalization: The Traditional Theory and New Developments. *Journal of Economic Literature* 38, no. 2: 287–331.

Parliament of Australia Senate. 2004a. Final Report of Select Committee on the Free Trade Agreement between Australia and the United States of America. Available at www.aph.gov.au (accessed on November 5, 2005).

Parliament of Australia Senate. 2004b. Submission of the Federation of Australian Scientific and Technological Societies (FASTS) to the Inquiry into the free trade agreement between Australia and the United States of America. Available at www.aph.gov.au (accessed on November 5, 2005).

PWC (PricewaterhouseCoopers). 1999. *Corporate Taxes 1999–2000: Worldwide Summaries.* Hoboken: John Wiley & Sons.

Reddaway, William B. 1967. *Effects of UK Direct Investment Overseas: An Interim Report.* London: Cambridge University Press.

Robinson, S., and K. Thierfelder. 2002. Trade Liberalisation and Regional Integration: The Search for Large Numbers. *Australian Journal of Agricultural and Resource Economics* 46, no. 4: 585–604.

Rosales, Osvaldo V. 2003. *TLCs de Chile con Estados Unidos y la Union Europea*. Available at the Chilean Foreign Affairs Ministry Web site at www.direcon.cl (accessed on November 6, 2005).

Rose, Andrew K. 2000. One Money, One Market: The Effect of Common Currencies on Trade. *Economic Policy* 15, no. 30: 7–46.

Rose, Andrew K. 2004. Do We Really Know that the WTO Increases Trade? *American Economic Review* 94, no. 1: 98–114.

Salazar-Xirinachs, Jose M., and Jaime Granados. 2004. The US-Central America Free Trade Agreement: Opportunities and Challenges. In *Free Trade Agreements: US Strategies and Priorities*, ed. Jeffrey J. Schott. Washington: Institute for International Economics.

Schott, Jeffrey J. 2004a. Reviving the Doha Round. Paper for the Institute for International Economics. Washington (May). Available at www.iie.com (accessed on February 9, 2006).

Schott, Jeffrey J. 2004b. Free Trade Agreements: Boon or Bane of the World Trading System? In *Free Trade Agreements: US Strategies and Priorities*, ed. Jeffrey J. Schott. Washington: Institute for International Economics.

Scollay, Robert, and John Gilbert. 2000. Measuring the Gains from APEC Trade Liberalisation: An Overview of CGE Assessments. *World Economy* 23, no. 2: 175–93.

Scollay, Robert, and John Gilbert. 2001. *New Regional Trading Arrangements in the Asia Pacific?* Washington: Institute for International Economics.

Singapore Customs. 2003. Rules of Origin for the Export of Textile and Garment Products to United States under the United States-Singapore FTA Agreement (USSFTA). Available at www.customs.gov.sg (accessed on November 6, 2005).

Singapore Ministry of Trade and Industry. 2003. Information Paper on the US-Singapore Free Trade Agreement (USSFTA), May 16. Available at www.mti.gov.sg (accessed on November 6, 2005).

Soloaga, I., and L. A. Winters. 2001. Regionalism in the Nineties: What Effect on Trade? *North American Journal of Economics and Finance* 12, no. 1: 1–29.

Sutherland, Peter, Jagdish Bhagwati, Kwesi Botchwey, Niall FitzGerald, Koichi Hamada, John H. Jackson, Celso Lafer, and Thierry de Montbrial. 2004. *The Future of the WTO: Addressing Institutional Challenges in the New Millennium*. Geneva: World Trade Organization.

Swiss-American Chamber of Commerce. 2002. Chamber Suggests to Include Switzerland in US-EFTA Mutual Recognition Agreement. Available at www.amcham.ch (accessed on November 6, 2005).

Swiss-American Chamber of Commerce. 2005. *Yearbook 2004–2005*. Zurich.

Swiss Federal Customs Administration. 2005. Tares. Available at www.tares.ch (accessed in December 2005).

Swiss Federal Department of Foreign Affairs. 2003. Memorandum of understanding between the Food and Drug Administration Department of Health and Human Services of the United States of America and SWISSMEDIC of the Swiss Confederation regarding the exchange of information about pharmaceutical products for human and animal use and medical devices. Available at www.eda.admin.ch (accessed on November 5, 2005).

Swiss Federal Institute of Intellectual Property. 2005. Geographical Indications. Available at www.ige.ch (accessed on November 6, 2005).

Swiss Federal Office for Agriculture. 2005. Evolution Future de la Politique Agricole. *Politique Agricole 2011*. Bern.

Swiss Federal Office of Public Health. 2003. *The Precautionary Principle in Switzerland and Internationally*. Bern.

Swiss National Bank. 2004. *Development of Direct Investment in 2003*. Zurich.

Swiss National Bank. 2005a. *Bulletin Mensuel de Statistiques Economiques*. Zurich.

Swiss National Bank. 2005b. Statistical Data (Overview). Available at www.snb.ch (accessed on November 7, 2005).

Switzerland Integration Office. 2005a. Bilateral Agreements I: Switzerland and the European Union of 1999, Explanatory Documents. Available at www.europa.admin.ch (accessed on June 8, 2005).

Switzerland Integration Office. 2005b. Bilateral Agreements I: Switzerland–European Union of 1999, Fact Sheets. Available at www.europa.admin.ch (accessed on November 7, 2005).

Switzerland Integration Office. 2005c. Bilateral Agreements I: Explanatory Documents, Agriculture. Available at www.europa.admin.ch (accessed on November 7, 2005).

Switzerland Integration Office. 2005d. Fact Sheets: Bilateral Agreements II, Processed Agricultural Products. Available at www.europa.admin.ch (accessed on November 7, 2005).

Switzerland Ministry of Economy (Staatssekretariat für Wirtschaft). 2004. *Report on Foreign Economic Policy*. Bern.

Switzerland Ministry of Economy (Staatssekretariat für Wirtschaft). 2005. Agreements of Mutual Recognition. Bern. Available at www.seco.admin.ch (accessed on November 6, 2005).

UNCTAD (United Nations Conference on Trade and Development). 2004a. *The Generalised System of Preferences*. New York: United Nations.

UNCTAD (United Nations Conference on Trade and Development). 2004b. *World Investment Report 2004: The Shift Towards Services*. New York: United Nations.

UNCTAD (United Nations Conference on Trade and Development). 2005. Trade Analysis and Information System. Geneva.

US APHIS (Animal and Plant Health Inspection Service). 2004. *Special Focus: SPS Issues and Free Trade Agreements*. Washington: US Department of Agriculture.

US BEA (Bureau of Economic Analysis). 2004a. *Survey of Current Business* (July). Washington.

US BEA (Bureau of Economic Analysis). 2004b. *Survey of Current Business* (September). Washington.

US BEA (Bureau of Economic Analysis). 2005a. US Direct Investment Abroad: Balance of Payments and Direct Investment Position Data. Washington. Available at www.bea.gov (accessed on November 6, 2005).

US BEA (Bureau of Economic Analysis). 2005b. US International Transactions Accounts Data. Washington. Available at www.bea.gov (accessed on November 6, 2005).

US BLS (Bureau of Labor Statistics). 2005. Employer Costs for Employee Compensation. Washington. Available at www.data.bls.gov (accessed on November 6, 2005).

US Chamber of Commerce. 2004. Precautionary Principle. Washington. Available at www.uschamber.com (accessed on November 6, 2005).

USDA (US Department of Agriculture). 1998. NAFTA Agriculture Fact Sheets: Commodities and Other Topics. Washington. Available at www.fas.usda.gov (accessed on November 8, 2005).

USDA (US Department of Agriculture). 2003a. The United States and Chile Free Trade Agreement. Washington. Available at www.fas.usda.gov (accessed on November 6, 2005).

USDA (US Department of Agriculture). 2003b. US-Chile Free Trade Agreement: Commodity Fact Sheets. Washington. Available at www.fas.usda.gov (accessed on October 30, 2005).

USDA (US Department of Agriculture). 2003c. Press Release: United States and Colombia Establish Consultative Committee on Agriculture. Washington. Available at www.fas.usda.gov (accessed on October 30, 2005).

USDA (US Department of Agriculture). 2004a. NAFTA Agriculture Fact Sheet: Sanitary/Phytosanitary. Washington. Available at www.fas.usda.gov (accessed on November 6, 2005).

USDA (US Department of Agriculture). 2004b. NAFTA Agriculture Fact Sheet: Special Agricultural Safeguard Provision. Washington. Available at www.fas.usda.gov (accessed on November 6, 2005).

USDA (US Department of Agriculture). 2004c. United States and Australia Free Trade Agreement. Washington. Available at www.fas.usda.gov (accessed on November 6, 2005).

USDA (US Department of Agriculture). 2004d. US-Australia Free Trade Agreement: Commodity Fact Sheets. Washington. Available at www.fas.usda.gov (accessed on October 30, 2005).

USDA (US Department of Agriculture). 2004e. United States and Morocco Free Trade Agreement. Washington. Available at www.fas.usda.gov (accessed on November 6, 2005).

USDA (US Department of Agriculture). 2004f. *EU-25 Trade Policy Monitoring: EU-Switzerland Agricultural Trade Relations 2004.* Washington. Available at www.fas.usda.gov (accessed in December 2005).

USDA (US Department of Agriculture). 2005a. United States–Canada Consultative Committee on Agriculture (CCA), November 19, 2004. Washington. Available at www.fas.usda.gov.

USDA (US Department of Agriculture). 2005b. United States–Central America–Dominican Republic Free Trade Agreement: Overall Agriculture Fact Sheet. Washington. Available at www.fas.usda.gov (accessed on October 30, 2005).

USDA (US Department of Agriculture). 2005c. United States–Central American–Dominican Republic Free Trade Agreement: Ethanol Provisions in the CAFTA-DR. Washington. Available at www.fas.usda.gov (accessed on November 6, 2005).

USDA (US Department of Agriculture). 2005d. Memorandum Of Understanding between the Government of the People's Republic Of China and the Government of the United States of America Concerning Market Access. Washington. Available at www.fas.usda.gov.

USDA (US Department of Agriculture). 2005e. Global Traceability and Labeling Requirements for Agricultural Biotechnology-Derived Products: Impacts and Implications for the United States. Washington. Available at http://w3.usda.gov (accessed on November 6, 2005).

US Department of Commerce. 2003. *Country Commercial Guide: Switzerland.* Washington.

US Department of Commerce. 2005. Trade Statistics Express. Washington. Available at http://tse.export.gov (accessed in December 2005).

US Department of State. 2004a. United States–Morocco Free Trade Agreement. Washington. Available at www.moroccousafta.com (accessed on November 6, 2005).

US Department of State. 2004b. Trade Accord Opens Huge Opportunities for Moroccan Business in the US. Washington. Available at http://usinfo.state.gov (accessed on November 6, 2005).

US Department of State. 2005. 2005 Investment Climate Statement—Switzerland. Washington. Available at www.state.gov (accessed on November 6, 2005).

US Department of the Treasury. 2005. Treasury International Capital System: Cross-Border Portfolio Holdings of Securities—TIC Annual and Benchmark Surveys. Washington. Available at www.ustreas.gov (accessed on November 7, 2005).

US FDA (Food and Drug Administration). 2002. The Bioterrorism Act of 2002. Washington. Available at www.fda.gov (accessed on November 6, 2005).

US FSIS (Food Safety and Inspection Service). 2005. Proposed Rules: Addition of Chile to the List of Countries Eligible To Export Meat and Meat Products to the United States. *Federal Register* 70, no. 89 (May 10).

US IRS (Internal Revenue Service). 1998. Convention between the United States of America and the Swiss Confederation for the Avoidance of Double Taxation with Respect to Taxes on Income. Washington. Available at www.irs.gov (accessed on November 7, 2005).

USITC (US International Trade Commission). 2003. *US-Singapore Free Trade Agreement: Potential Economywide and Selected Sectoral Effects.* Washington.

USITC (US International Trade Commission). 2004a. *The Economic Effects of Significant US Import Restraints.* Washington.

USITC (US International Trade Commission). 2004b. *US-Australia Free Trade Agreement: Potential Economywide and Selected Sectoral Effects.* Washington.

USITC (US International Trade Commission). 2004c. *United States–Central America–Dominican Republic Free Trade Agreement: Potential Economywide and Selected Sectoral Effects.* Washington.

USITC (US International Trade Commission). 2005a. *The Impact of Trade Agreements Implemented Under Trade Promotion Authority.* Washington.

USITC (US International Trade Commission). 2005b. Tariff Information Center: Official Harmonized Tariff Schedule of the United States Annotated. Washington. Available at www.usitc.gov (accessed on November 6, 2005).

USITC (US International Trade Commission). 2005c. USITC Tariff Database Tables. Washington. Available at http://reportweb.usitc.gov (accessed on November 6, 2005).

USITC (US International Trade Commission). 2005d. Interactive Tariff and Trade Dataweb. Washington. Available at http://dataweb.usitc.gov (accessed on November 6, 2005).

US Patent and Trademark Office. 2005. Geographical Indications. Washington. Available at www.uspto.gov (accessed on November 6, 2005).

US Supreme Court. 2000. Crosby et al. v. National Foreign Trade Council. US Supreme Court, no. 99-474. Washington.

USTR (US Trade Representative). 2002a. Free Trade with Singapore: America's First Free Trade Agreement in Asia. Washington. Available at www.ustr.gov (accessed on November 6, 2005).

USTR (US Trade Representative). 2002b. Free Trade with Chile: Summary of the U.S.-Chile Free Trade Agreement. Washington. Available at www.ustr.gov.

USTR (US Trade Representative). 2003a. Singapore FTA: Text of the Agreement. Washington. Available at www.ustr.gov (accessed on November 6, 2005).

USTR (US Trade Representative). 2003b. Chile FTA: Final Text. Washington. Available at www.ustr.gov (accessed on July 15, 2005).

USTR (US Trade Representative). 2003c. Free Trade in Services: Opening Dynamic New Markets. Washington. Available at www.ustr.gov (accessed on November 6, 2005).

USTR (US Trade Representative). 2003d. National Trade Estimate Report on Foreign Trade Barriers. Washington. Available at www.ustr.gov (accessed on November 6, 2005).

USTR (US Trade Representative). 2003e. The US-Singapore Free Trade Agreement (FTA): Report of the Industry Sector Advisory Committee on Services for Trade Policy Matters (ISAC 13). Washington. Available at www.ustr.gov (accessed on November 6, 2005).

USTR (US Trade Representative). 2004a. Final Text of the U.S.-Australia Free Trade Agreement. Washington. Available at www.ustr.gov (accessed on November 6, 2005).

USTR (US Trade Representative). 2004b. The US-Australia Free Trade Agreement (FTA): Report of the Industry Sector Advisory Committee on Services for Trade Policy Matters (ISAC 13). Washington. Available at www.ustr.gov (accessed on November 6, 2005).

USTR (US Trade Representative). 2004c. Final Text of the Morocco Free Trade Agreement. Washington. Available at www.ustr.gov (accessed on November 6, 2005).

USTR (US Trade Representative). 2004d. U.S.-Morocco Free Trade Agreement Agriculture Provisions. Washington. Available at www.ustr.gov (accessed on November 8, 2005).

USTR (US Trade Representative). 2004e. The 2004 National Trade Estimate Report on Foreign Trade Barriers. Sections on Costa Rica, El Salvador, Honduras, Guatemala, and Nicaragua. Washington. Available at www.ustr.gov.

USTR (US Trade Representative). 2004f. CAFTA-DR Final Text. Washington. Available at www.ustr.gov.

USTR (US Trade Representative). 2005a. Free Trade in Services: Opening Dynamic New Markets, Supporting Good Jobs. Washington. Available at www.ustr.gov (accessed on November 6, 2005).

USTR (US Trade Representative). 2005b. The 2005 National Trade Estimate Report on Foreign Trade Barriers. Washington. Available at www.ustr.gov (accessed on November 6, 2005).

USTR (US Trade Representative). 2005c. *Switzerland.* Washington. Available at www.ustr.gov (accessed on November 6, 2005).

Vega-Cánovas, Gustavo, and Gilbert R. Winham. 2002. The Role of NAFTA Dispute Settlement in the Management of Canadian, Mexican and US Trade and Investment Relations. *Ohio Northern University Law Review* 28, no. 3: 651–706.

Woolgar, Tony. 2004. Submission from the Textile, Clothing and Footwear Union of Australia (TCFUA) to the Senate Select Committee on the Free Trade Agreement between Australia and the United States of America. Available at www.aph.gov.au (accessed on November 6, 2005).

World Bank. 2005a. Nigeria, Switzerland Hail Return of Stolen Funds, Say Safe Havens No Longer Exist. Press Review for September 28, 2005. Washington. Available at www.worldbank.org (accessed on September 28, 2005).

World Bank. 2005b. *World Development Indicators.* Washington. Available at www.worldbank.org (accessed on November 7, 2005).

WTO (World Trade Organization). 1995a. *Committee on Anti-dumping Practices—Notification of Laws and Regulations under Article 18.5 of the Agreement—Switzerland.* Report number G/ADP/N/1/CHE/1. Geneva.

WTO (World Trade Organization). 1995b. *Committee on Subsidies and Countervailing Measures—Notification of Laws and Regulations under Article 32.6 of the Agreement—Switzerland.* Report number G/SCM/N/1/CHE/1. Geneva.

WTO (World Trade Organization). 1996. *Trade Policy Review: Switzerland* (April). Geneva.

WTO (World Trade Organization). 2000a. *United States—Definitive Safeguard Measures on Imports of Wheat Gluten from the European Communities.* 2000 WL 1911912. Geneva.

WTO (World Trade Organization). 2000b. WTO Negotiations on Agriculture: Proposal by Switzerland. Report Number: G/AG/NG/W/94. Geneva.

WTO (World Trade Organization). 2001a. *Trade Policy Review: United States* (September). Geneva.

WTO (World Trade Organization). 2001b. *Committee on Agriculture—Addenda to Table MA:1 Notifications.* General Council Decision WT/L/284. Report Number G/AG/N/USA/2/Add.3. Geneva.

WTO (World Trade Organization). 2002a. Request for the Establishment of a Panel by Switzerland on US Definitive Safeguard Measures on Imports of Certain Steel Products. Geneva. Available at www.wto.org (accessed on July 15, 2005).

WTO (World Trade Organization). 2002b. *Committee on Sanitary and Phytosanitary Measures—Submission by Switzerland on United States Restrictions on the Import of Meat and Meat Products.* Report Number G/SPS/GEN/321 (June). Geneva.

WTO (World Trade Organization). 2002c. *Committee on Agriculture—Notification—United States: Special Safeguard.* Report number G/AG/N/USA/41. Geneva.

WTO (World Trade Organization). 2002d. *United States—Definitive Safeguard Measures on Imports of Circular Welded Carbon Quality Line Pipe from Korea.* 2002 WL 228478. Geneva.

WTO (World Trade Organization). 2002e. *United States–Sub-Central Government Entities which Procure in Accordance with the Provisions of this Agreement* (October 16). WT/Let/431. Geneva. Available at www.wto.org (accessed on November 30, 2005).

WTO (World Trade Organization). 2003a. *Domestic Review Mechanisms Related to Transparency in Government Procurement.* Report Number WT/WGTGP/W/39 (February). Geneva.

WTO (World Trade Organization). 2003b. Notes Generales et Derogations aux Dispositions de l'Article III. Geneva. Available at www.wto.org (accessed on November 15, 2005).

WTO (World Trade Organization). 2003c. *United States—Definitive Safeguard Measures on Imports of Certain Steel Products.* 2003 WL 22630278. Geneva.

WTO (World Trade Organization). 2004a. *Committee on Sanitary and Phytosanitary Measures—Specific Trade Concerns: Revision to Note from the Secretariat.* Report Number G/SPS/GEN/204/Rev.4. Geneva.

WTO (World Trade Organization). 2004b. *Trade Policy Review: Switzerland and Liechtenstein* (November). Geneva.

WTO (World Trade Organization). 2004c. *Trade Policy Review: United States* (January). Geneva.

WTO (World Trade Organization). 2005a. *Semi-Annual Report under Article 16.4: United States.* Geneva.

WTO (World Trade Organization). 2005b. *Committee on Sanitary and Phytosanitary Measures—Specific Trade Concerns: Revision to Note from the Secretariat.* Report Number G/SPS/GEN204R5. Geneva.

WTO (World Trade Organization). 2005c. Statistics on Antidumping. Geneva. Available at www.wto.org (accessed on November 6, 2005).

WTO (World Trade Organization). 2005d. *United States Notification to WTO Committee on Anti-Dumping Practices.* Report number G/ADP/N/126/USA (March). Geneva.

WTO (World Trade Organization). 2005e. Regional Trade Agreements. Geneva. Available at www.wto.org (accessed on November 7, 2005).

Index

antidumping (AD) and countervailing
duties (CVD), 35, 44, 107–108, 107n,
108n
Appellation d'origine contrôle (AOC),
95–96
Argentina, 308, 308n
art, works of
Swiss exports to US, 124t
US exports to Switzerland, 135t
ASME. *See* American Society of Mechanical Engineers
ATPDEA. *See* Andean Trade Promotion
and Drug Eradication Act
Australia. *See also* US-Australia Free Trade
Agreement
bilateral trade, tariffs with US, 113–14
corruption index for, 20t
environmental standards, 22t
labor standards, 24t
MFN tariff rates, 18t
position on yarn-forward rule, 119, 119n
"right to export" negotiations, 282n
state trading organizations, 289n
trade with US, 16t, 17t
two-way FDI with US, 14t
Australian Wine and Brandy Corporation
Act, 313n
AVE tariffs. *See* ad valorem equivalent
tariffs

BAA. *See* United States, Buy America Act
Bahrain
corruption index for, 20t
environmental standards, 22t
labor standards, 24t
MFN tariff rates, 18t
trade with US, 16t, 17t
two-way FDI with US, 14t
Bangladesh
corruption index for, 21t
environmental standards, 23t
labor standards, 25t
MFN tariff rates, 19t
trade with US, 16t, 17t
two-way FDI with US, 15t
banking services. *See also* financial services
foreign restriction index for, 154–55,
155t
in Switzerland, 165–66
US impediments to foreign participation in, 156
US-Singapore FTA provisions related
to, 175
Batlle, Jorge, 308n

beer, distilled spirits
tariff/TRQ phaseout terms under US
FTAs, 280t
biotechnology products, 86, 86n
labeling requirements, 89–90
boilers, machinery, and mechanical
appliances
Swiss exports to US, 128t–29t
US exports to Switzerland, 137t–38t
Bolivia
corruption index for, 20t
environmental standards, 23t
labor standards, 25t
MFN tariff rates, 18t
trade with US, 16t, 17t
two-way FDI with US, 15t
bovine spongiform encephalopthy (BSE),
84n, 85, 91, 92
concern about the risk of, 87–88, 87n
Bush administration
economic diplomacy and potential FTA
partners, 7
business and professional services. *See also*
banking services; financial services
accounting and auditing services,
163–64
Swiss barriers to, 171–72
architecture and engineering services,
172
audiovisual services
Swiss barriers to, 170–71
US FTA provisions related to, 173–74
cultural services, 177
education services, 153t
engineering, 164
insurance services
barriers to, 156–57, 166
US FTA provisions related to, 174,
175–76
US-Swiss trade data, 153t
legal services, 163, 172
restrictiveness index for, 161, 162t
securities services, 157–58, 176
Swiss barriers to, 171–72
US barriers to, 157–58, 161–64
US exports, imports of, 161
US FTA provisions related to, 175,
176–77, 177n
US-Swiss trade, 153t

CAFTA, CAFTA-DR. *See* Central
America–Dominican Republic
Free Trade Agreement
Calvo doctrine, 213

Iceland, 111, 260*n*
IFA. *See* Switzerland, Investment Fund
  Act
Indication géographique protégée (IGP),
  95–96. *See also* geographical indication
Indonesia
  corruption index for, 20*t*
  environmental standards, 23*t*
  labor standards, 25*t*
  MFN tariff rates, 18*t*
  trade with US, 16*t*, 17*t*
  two-way FDI with US, 14*t*
industrial products. *See* manufactured
  products
infant formulas, 32
Integrated Acquisition Environment (IAE)
  initiative, 193
integrated sourcing initiative (ISI), 119
International Plant Protection Convention
  (IPPS), 85
international standards, regulations,
  108–110
Investment Company Act of 1940, 158
IPPS. *See* International Plant Protection
  Convention
ISI. *See* integrated sourcing initiative
Israel
  average US tariffs, 31*t*
  corruption index for, 20*t*
  environmental standards, 22*t*
  labor standards, 24*t*
  MFN tariff rates, 18*t*
  trade with US, 16*t*, 17*t*
  two-way FDI with US, 14*t*

jewelry
  pearls, precious metals, and stones
    US-Swiss trade, 129*t*–30*t*, 138*t*
  tariff/TRQ phaseouts for, 146*t*, 148*t*
Jordan
  average US tariffs, 31*t*
  corruption index for, 20*t*
  environmental standards, 22*t*
  labor standards, 24*t*
  MFN tariff rates, 18*t*
  trade with US, 16*t*, 17*t*
  two-way FDI with US, 14*t*

labeling requirements
  for organic products, 90–91
  recommendations for reaching agree-
    ment on, 92
  US, Swiss equivalent standards, 89–91,
    89*n*

labor standards
  country comparisons, 24*t*–25*t*
  index, indicators for, 10–11
  methodology for labor indicators,
    25*t*–26*t*
LCart. *See* Switzerland, Federal Act on
  Cartels and Other Restraints of
  Competition
less developed countries (LDC)
  average US tariffs, 31*t*
  Swiss preferential tariffs, 56*t*
Liechtenstein, 106, 111, 260*n*
Luxembourg, 203

machinery, electrical apparatus, parts
  Swiss exports to US, 127*t*–28*t*
  US exports to Switzerland, 137*t*
Malaysia
  corruption index for, 20*t*
  environmental standards, 23*t*
  labor standards, 25*t*
  MFN tariff rates, 18*t*
  trade with US, 16*t*, 17*t*
  two-way FDI with US, 14*t*
manufactured products. *See also under
  names of specific products*
  ad valorem tariffs, above, 106, 141*t*–43*t*
  gravity, CGE model estimates for
    Swiss-US FTA, 269–70
  mutual recognition of product stan-
    dards, 110–12
  recommendations for Swiss-US FTA,
    121–23
  and rules of origin, 116–18
  safeguard measures for, 106–107
  tariff/TRQ phaseouts under US-Singa-
    pore FTA, 146*t*–47*t*
  tariffs
    high Swiss tariffs on US exports, 331*t*
    high US tariffs on Swiss exports,
      144*t*–45*t*
    US, Swiss MFN tariff rates, 11
    US, Swiss tariffs, TRQs, 102–106
  US safeguard measures for, 106–107
  and use of trade-weighted tariffs, 104,
    104*n*, 105*t*
  US-Swiss bilateral trade, 101–102, 102*t*,
    103*t*
meat inspection standards
  meatpacking facilities, 87
  negotiations under US-EU Veterinary
    Agreement, 307
  under US-Chile FTA, 303

meats, meat products
beef
export certificates for, 293
Swiss agricultural protection of, 63
Swiss consumer prices for, 76t
Swiss imports from US, 64, 64n
tariff/TRQ phaseout terms under US
FTAs, 276t, 281–82, 284–85
US, Swiss PSEs for, 37t
US TRQs on, 32, 71t
dried meat
phasing out Swiss-EU agricultural
barriers, 58
pork
tariff/TRQ phaseout terms under US
FTAs, 276t
US PSE for pigmeat, 37t
Swiss restrictions on US imports, 87
tariff/TRQ phaseout terms under US
FTAs, 292–94
veal
US, Swiss PSEs for, 37t
merchandise trade
US trade with FTA partners, potential
partners, 8, 16t
Mexico
average US tariffs, 31t
corruption index for, 20t
environmental standards, 22t
free trade agreements, 196, 261
US view of, 261–62
labor standards, 24t
MFN tariff rates, 18t
trade with US, 16t, 17t
two-way FDI with US, 8, 14t
mineral water, 30
MNE. See multinational enterprises
Morocco. See also US-Morocco Free Trade
Agreement
corruption index for, 20t
environmental standards, 22t
labor standards, 24t
MFN tariff rates, 18t
trade with US, 16t, 17t
two-way FDI with US, 14t
most-favored nation (MFN) tariffs, 18t–19t
applied to Swiss agricultural products,
73t
applied to US agricultural products,
67t–68t
country comparisons of rates, rankings,
18t–19t
preferential rates, 30–31, 31n, 31t
rates for US FTA partners, 9, 18t–19t

Swiss rates, 11, 41t
US rates, 11, 30–31, 30n, 31t
for US trading partners, 9, 18t–19t
motor vehicles
tariff/TRQ phaseouts for, 146t, 148t
top US exports to Switzerland, 136t–37t,
139t–40t
multinational enterprises (MNE), 206, 207t
mutual recognition agreements (MRA),
111–12

natural gas, 168
Nestlé, 206, 207t
Netherlands, 203
network industries. See under electricity;
natural gas; postal services; telecommunications
New Zealand
corruption index for, 20t
environmental standards, 23t
labor standards, 25t
MFN tariff rates, 18t
trade with US, 16t, 17t
two-way FDI with US, 14t
Nigeria
return of Abacha's money to, 218n
nontariff barriers. See sanitary and phytosanitary measures
NOP. See US Department of Agriculture,
National Organic Program
North American Free Trade Agreement
(NAFTA)
agricultural products with safeguards,
49, 49n, 50
Chapter 11 dispute settlement mechanism, 213, 214, 214n
impact on FDI stock value, 323
impact on Mexico's strategy, government, 263
SPS Committee, 300
SPS measures, principles, 82, 299–300
tariff/TRQ phaseout schedules, terms
for agricultural products, 44–50,
276t–80t
for corn, 282
for cotton, 283
for dairy products, 284
for distilled spirits, wine, 285, 297
for fruit products, 286–87, 286n
for grains, 289
with Mexico, 285, 295, 296, 297
for nuts, 287
for peanuts, peanut products, 291–92
for potatoes, 286

preferential trade agreements (PTAs)
(*cont.*)
  relationship with trade, FDI, 319,
    320*t*–21*t*, 322–24
prise en charge system, 44, 44*n*
processed foods
  tariff/TRQ phaseout terms under US
    FTAs, 290–91
producer support estimates (PSE), 36
  for agricultural products, 37*t*, 45, 46*t*
  Swiss, US, OECD, 46*t*
protected denominations of origin (PDO),
  316
protected geographical indications (PGI),
  316
PTA. *See* preferential trade agreements

Qatar
  corruption index for, 20*t*
  environmental standards, 23*t*
  labor standards, 25*t*
  MFN tariff rates, 18*t*
  trade with US, 16*t*, 17*t*
  two-way FDI with US, 14*t*

retail, wholesale trade, 152
Rose, Andrew, 225*n*, 325
  dataset for gravity model, 227, 228*n*, 325
royalties, license fees
  US-Swiss trade, 152*t*, 153*t*
rules of origin
  and build-up, build-down methods,
    118, 118*n*
  certification methods, 118
  cumulation issue, 117–18
  diagonal cumulation, 121, 122
  full cumulation, 121
  for manufactured goods, 116–18
  for remanufactures, 118
  substantial transformation, 118, 123
  in Swiss FTAs, 120–21
  trade deflection, 117*n*
  in US FTAs, 118–20
  yarn-forward rule, 119–20, 119*n*

safeguard measures. *See also* tariff rate
    quotas
  price based vs. volume based, 34*n*
  Swiss, 44–45
  US exclusion of FTA partners from, 34,
    34*n*
  for US manufactured goods, 106–107
  for US steel, 107

Salinas de Gortari, Carlos, 263
Sanitary and Phytosanitary (SPS) Com-
    mittee
  under NAFTA, 300
  under US-Australia FTA, 301
  under US-Chile FTA, 303
sanitary and phytosanitary (SPS) mea-
    sures, issues
  animal diseases with regional designa-
    tion of agreement, 307, 307*n*
  under CAFTA-DR, 304–306
  committees, ad hoc and working
    groups for, 83, 83*n*, 84
  dispute settlement mechanism, 82
  in EFTA, 85
  food safety, 88
  foods of animal origin, 310
  impact on trade, 81–82, 269
  under NAFTA, 299–300
  objectives of, 81
  plant health, 309–10
  in Swiss FTA negotiations, 309–11
  in US memorandums of understanding,
    308
  in US trade agreements, 82–84
  US vs. Swiss approach to, 86–88
  under US-Australia FTA, 300–302
  under US-Chile FTA, 302–304
  under US-EU Veterinary Agreement,
    306–308
  under US-Morocco FTA, 306
  working group for animal health, 91
Sarbanes-Oxley Act, 158, 158*n*
  impact on Swiss auditing firms, 164
services trade. *See also* business and pro-
    fessional services
  model estimates of, 241, 241*n*, 247
  sectors, 11–12
  Swiss barriers to, 164
  US barriers to
    financial services, 154–58
    professional services, 161–64
    in telecommunications, 160–61
  US exports, imports, 17*t*
  US trade with FTA partners, potential
    partners, 8–9, 17*t*
  US-Swiss trade data, 152*t*
    by industry, 153*t*
Singapore. *See also* US-Singapore Free
    Trade Agreement
  corruption index for, 10, 20*t*
  environmental standards, 22*t*
  labor standards, 24*t*

Other Publications from the Institute for International Economics

* = out of print

POLICY ANALYSES IN INTERNATIONAL ECONOMICS Series

International Debt: Systemic Risk and Policy
Response*   William R. Cline
1984   ISBN 0-88132-015-3
Trade Protection in the United States: 31 Case
Studies*   Gary Clyde Hufbauer, Diane E. Berliner,
and Kimberly Ann Elliott
1986   ISBN 0-88132-040-4
Toward Renewed Economic Growth in Latin
America* Bela Balassa, Gerardo M. Bueno, Pedro-
Pablo Kuczynski, and Mario Henrique Simonsen
1986   ISBN 0-88132-045-5
Capital Flight and Third World Debt*
Donald R. Lessard and John Williamson, editors
1987   ISBN 0-88132-053-6
The Canada-United States Free Trade Agreement:
The Global Impact*
Jeffrey J. Schott and Murray G. Smith, editors
1988   ISBN 0-88132-073-0
World Agricultural Trade: Building a Consensus*
William M. Miner and Dale E. Hathaway, editors
1988   ISBN 0-88132-071-3
Japan in the World Economy*
Bela Balassa and Marcus Noland
1988   ISBN 0-88132-041-2
America in the World Economy: A Strategy for
the 1990s*   C. Fred Bergsten
1988   ISBN 0-88132-089-7
Managing the Dollar: From the Plaza to the
Louvre*   Yoichi Funabashi
1988, 2d. ed. 1989   ISBN 0-88132-097-8
United States External Adjustment and the World
Economy*   William R. Cline
May 1989   ISBN 0-88132-048-X
Free Trade Areas and U.S. Trade Policy*
Jeffrey J. Schott, editor
May *1989*   ISBN 0-88132-094-3
Dollar Politics: Exchange Rate Policymaking in
the United States*
I. M. Destler and C. Randall Henning
September 1989   ISBN 0-88132-079-X
Latin American Adjustment: How Much Has
Happened?*   John Williamson, editor
April 1990   ISBN 0-88132-125-7
The Future of World Trade in Textiles and
Apparel*   William R. Cline
1987, 2d ed. June *1999*   ISBN 0-88132-110-9
Completing the Uruguay Round: A Results-
Oriented Approach to the GATT Trade
Negotiations*   Jeffrey J. Schott, editor
September 1990   ISBN 0-88132-130-3
Economic Sanctions Reconsidered (2 volumes)
Economic Sanctions Reconsidered:
Supplemental Case Histories
Gary Clyde Hufbauer, Jeffrey J. Schott, and
Kimberly Ann Elliott
1985, 2d ed. Dec. 1990   ISBN cloth 0-88132-115-X
                          ISBN paper 0-88132-105-2

Economic Sanctions Reconsidered: History and
Current Policy   Gary Clyde Hufbauer,
Jeffrey J. Schott, and Kimberly Ann Elliott
December 1990   ISBN cloth 0-88132-140-0
                          ISBN paper 0-88132-136-2
Pacific Basin Developing Countries: Prospects for
Economic Sanctions Reconsidered: History
and Current Policy   Gary Clyde Hufbauer,
Jeffrey J. Schott, and Kimberly Ann Elliott
December 1990   ISBN cloth 0-88132-140-0
                          ISBN paper 0-88132-136-2
Pacific Basin Developing Countries: Prospects
for the Future*   Marcus Noland
January 1991   ISBN cloth 0-88132-141-9
                          ISBN paper 0-88132-081-1
Currency Convertibility in Eastern Europe*
John Williamson, editor
October 1991   ISBN 0-88132-128-1
International Adjustment and Financing: The
Lessons of 1985-1991*   C. Fred Bergsten, editor
January 1992   ISBN 0-88132-112-5
North American Free Trade: Issues and
Recommendations*
Gary Clyde Hufbauer and Jeffrey J. Schott
April 1992   ISBN 0-88132-120-6
Narrowing the U.S. Current Account Deficit*
Alan J. Lenz/ *June 1992*   ISBN 0-88132-103-6
The Economics of Global Warming
William R. Cline/ *June 1992*   ISBN 0-88132-132-X
US Taxation of International Income: Blueprint
for Reform*   Gary Clyde Hufbauer,
assisted by Joanna M. van Rooij
October 1992   ISBN 0-88132-134-6
Who's Bashing Whom? Trade Conflict in High-
Technology Industries   Laura D'Andrea Tyson
November 1992   ISBN 0-88132-106-0
Korea in the World Economy*   Il SaKong
January 1993   ISBN 0-88132-183-4
Pacific Dynamism and the International
Economic System*
C. Fred Bergsten and Marcus Noland, editors
May 1993   ISBN 0-88132-196-6
Economic Consequences of Soviet Disintegration*
John Williamson, editor
May 1993   ISBN 0-88132-190-7
Reconcilable Differences? United States-Japan
Economic Conflict*
C. Fred Bergsten and Marcus Noland
June 1993   ISBN 0-88132-129-X
Does Foreign Exchange Intervention Work?
Kathryn M. Dominguez and Jeffrey A. Frankel
September 1993   ISBN 0-88132-104-4
Sizing Up U.S. Export Disincentives*
J. David Richardson
September 1993   ISBN 0-88132-107-9

Trade and Income Distribution   William R. Cline
November 1997   ISBN 0-88132-216-4
Global Competition Policy
Edward M. Graham and J. David Richardson
December 1997   ISBN 0-88132-166-4
Unfinished Business: Telecommunications
after the Uruguay Round
Gary Clyde Hufbauer and Erika Wada
December 1997   ISBN 0-88132-257-1
Financial Services Liberalization in the WTO
Wendy Dobson and Pierre Jacquet
June 1998   ISBN 0-88132-254-7
Restoring Japan's Economic Growth
Adam S. Posen
September 1998   ISBN 0-88132-262-8
Measuring the Costs of Protection in China
Zhang Shuguang, Zhang Yansheng, and Wan
Zhongxin
November 1998   ISBN 0-88132-247-4
Foreign Direct Investment and Development:
The New Policy Agenda for Developing
Countries and Economies in Transition
Theodore H. Moran
December 1998   ISBN 0-88132-258-X
Behind the Open Door: Foreign Enterprises
in the Chinese Marketplace
Daniel H. Rosen
January 1999   ISBN 0-88132-263-6
Toward A New International Financial
Architecture: A Practical Post-Asia Agenda
Barry Eichengreen
February 1999   ISBN 0-88132-270-9
Is the U.S. Trade Deficit Sustainable?
Catherine L. Mann
September 1999   ISBN 0-88132-265-2
Safeguarding Prosperity in a Global Financial
System: The Future International Financial
Architecture, Independent Task Force Report
Sponsored by the Council on Foreign Relations
Morris Goldstein, Project Director
October 1999   ISBN 0-88132-287-3
Avoiding the Apocalypse: The Future of the
Two Koreas   Marcus Noland
June 2000   ISBN 0-88132-278-4
Assessing Financial Vulnerability: An Early
Warning System for Emerging Markets
Morris Goldstein, Graciela Kaminsky, and
Carmen Reinhart
June 2000   ISBN 0-88132-237-7
Global Electronic Commerce: A Policy Primer
Catherine L. Mann, Sue E. Eckert, and Sarah
Cleeland Knight
July 2000   ISBN 0-88132-274-1
The WTO after Seattle   Jeffrey J. Schott, editor
July 2000   ISBN 0-88132-290-3

Intellectual Property Rights in the Global
Economy   Keith E. Maskus
August 2000   ISBN 0-88132-282-2
The Political Economy of the Asian Financial
Crisis   Stephan Haggard
August 2000   ISBN 0-88132-283-0
Transforming Foreign Aid: United States
Assistance in the 21st Century   Carol Lancaster
August 2000   ISBN 0-88132-291-1
Fighting the Wrong Enemy: Antiglobal Activists
and Multinational Enterprises Edward M. Graham
September 2000   ISBN 0-88132-272-5
Globalization and the Perceptions of American
Workers
Kenneth F. Scheve and Matthew J. Slaughter
March 2001   ISBN 0-88132-295-4
World Capital Markets: Challenge to the G-10
Wendy Dobson and Gary Clyde Hufbauer,
assisted by Hyun Koo Cho
May 2001   ISBN 0-88132-301-2
Prospects for Free Trade in the Americas
Jeffrey J. Schott/*August 2001* ISBN 0-88132-275-X
Toward a North American Community:
Lessons from the Old World for the New
Robert A. Pastor/*August 2001* ISBN 0-88132-328-4
Measuring the Costs of Protection in Europe:
European Commercial Policy in the 2000s
Patrick A. Messerlin
September 2001   ISBN 0-88132-273-3
Job Loss from Imports: Measuring the Costs
Lori G. Kletzer
September 2001   ISBN 0-88132-296-2
No More Bashing: Building a New Japan–United
States Economic Relationship   C. Fred Bergsten,
Takatoshi Ito, and Marcus Noland
October 2001   ISBN 0-88132-286-5
Why Global Commitment Really Matters!
Howard Lewis III and J. David Richardson
October 2001   ISBN 0-88132-298-9
Leadership Selection in the Major Multilaterals
Miles Kahler
November 2001   ISBN 0-88132-335-7
The International Financial Architecture:
What's New? What's Missing?   Peter Kenen
November 2001   ISBN 0-88132-297-0
Delivering on Debt Relief: From IMF Gold
to a New Aid Architecture
John Williamson and Nancy Birdsall,
with Brian Deese
April 2002   ISBN 0-88132-331-4
Imagine There's No Country: Poverty,
Inequality, and Growth in the Era
of Globalization   Surjit S. Bhalla
September 2002   ISBN 0-88132-348-9

DISTRIBUTORS OUTSIDE THE UNITED STATES

Australia, New Zealand,
and Papua New Guinea
D. A. Information Services
648 Whitehorse Road
Mitcham, Victoria 3132, Australia
Tel: 61-3-9210-7777
Fax: 61-3-9210-7788
Email: service@dadirect.com.au
www.dadirect.com.au

India, Bangladesh, Nepal, and Sri Lanka
Viva Books Private Limited
Mr. Vinod Vasishtha
4737/23 Ansari Road
Daryaganj, New Delhi 110002
India
Tel: 91-11-4224-2200
Fax: 91-11-4224-2240
Email: viva@vivagroupindia.net
www.vivagroupindia.com

Mexico, Central America, South America,
and Puerto Rico
US PubRep, Inc.
311 Dean Drive
Rockville, MD 20851
Tel: 301-838-9276
Fax: 301-838-9278
Email: c.falk@ieee.org
www.uspubrep.com

Southeast Asia (*Brunei, Burma, Cambodia,*
Indonesia, Malaysia, the Philippines,
***Singapore, Taiwan, Thailand, and Vietnam*)**
APAC Publishers Services PTE Ltd.
70 Bendemeer Road #05-03
Hiap Huat House
Singapore 333940
Tel: 65-6844-7333
Fax: 65-6747-8916
Email: service@apacmedia.com.sg

Canada
Renouf Bookstore
5369 Canotek Road, Unit 1
Ottawa, Ontario KIJ 9J3, Canada
Tel: 613-745-2665
Fax: 613-745-7660
www.renoufbooks.com

Japan
United Publishers Services Ltd.
1-32-5, Higashi-shinagawa
Shinagawa-ku, Tokyo 140-0002
Japan
Tel: 81-3-5479-7251
Fax: 81-3-5479-7307
Email: purchasing@ups.co.jp
For trade accounts only. Individuals will find
IIE books in leading Tokyo bookstores.

Middle East
MERIC
2 Bahgat Ali Street, El Masry Towers
Tower D, Apt. 24
Zamalek, Cairo
Egypt
Tel. 20-2-7633824
Fax: 20-2-7369355
Email: mahmoud_fouda@mericonline.com
www.mericonline.com

United Kingdom, Europe
(*including Russia and Turkey*), Africa,
and Israel
The Eurospan Group
c/o Turpin Distribution
Pegasus Drive
Stratton Business Park
Biggleswade, Bedfordshire
SG18 8TQ
United Kingdom
Tel: 44 (0) 1767-604972
Fax: 44 (0) 1767-601640
Email: eurospan@turpin-distribution.com
www.eurospangroup.com/bookstore

Visit our Web site at:
www.iie.com
E-mail orders to:
IIE mail@PressWarehouse.com

GPSR Authorized Representative: Easy Access System Europe, Mustamäe tee
50, 10621 Tallinn, Estonia, gpsr.requests@easproject.com

www.ingramcontent.com/pod-product-compliance
Lightning Source LLC
Chambersburg PA
CBHW072045020426
42334CB00017B/1391